ANGLO-SCOTTISH RELATIONS
FROM 1603 TO 1900

PROCEEDINGS OF THE BRITISH ACADEMY • 127

ANGLO-SCOTTISH RELATIONS FROM 1603 TO 1900

Edited by
T. C. SMOUT

Published for THE BRITISH ACADEMY
by OXFORD UNIVERSITY PRESS

Oxford University Press, Great Clarendon Street, Oxford OX2 6DP

Oxford New York
Auckland Bangkok Bogotá Buenos Aires Cape Town Chennai
Dar es Salaam Delhi Hong Kong Istanbul Karachi Kolkata
Kuala Lumpur Madrid Melbourne Mexico City Mumbai Nairobi
São Paulo Shanghai Singapore Taipei Tokyo Toronto

Oxford is a registered trade mark of Oxford University Press
in the UK and certain other countries

Published in the United States
by Oxford University Press Inc., New York

British Library Cataloguing in Publication Data
Data available

ISBN 0–19–726330–5   978–0–19–726330–3

Typeset in Times
by J&L Composition, Filey, North Yorkshire
Printed in Great Britain
on acid-free paper by
Creative Print and Design (Wales)
Ebbw Vale

Contents

List of Figures

Notes on Contributors

Rosemary Ashton, FBA is Quain Professor of English Language and Literature at University College London. She is the author of two books on Anglo-German literary and cultural relations in the nineteenth century, and of critical biographies of S. T. Coleridge, George Eliot, G. H. Lewes, and, in 2002, of Thomas and Jane Carlyle.

Keith Brown, FRSE is Professor of Scottish History at the University of St Andrews and Director of the Scottish Parliament Project also based at St Andrews. Among his most recent publications is *Noble Society in Scotland: Wealth, Family and Culture From Reformation to Revolution* (2000). He is editor with R. J. Tanner of *Parliament and Politics in Scotland, 1235–1560* (2004), and with A. J. Mann of *Parliament and Politics in Scotland, 1567–1707* (2005).

Tom Devine, FRSE, FBA is Glucksman Research Professor of Irish and Scottish Studies at the University of Aberdeen and Director of the AHRB Centre for Irish and Scottish Studies (Aberdeen, Queen's University, Belfast, and Trinity College, Dublin). His most recent major publications are *Scotland's Empire 1700–1815* (2003) and, with C. H. Lee and G. C. Peden (eds), *The Transformation of Scotland* (2005).

John Ford is a Fellow and the Senior Tutor of Gonville and Caius College, Cambridge. The first of a series of three books he is writing about Stair's Institutions of the Law of Scotland is nearing completion.

Bob Harris is Professor of British History at the University of Dundee. His most recent book, *Politics and the Nation: Britain in the Mid-Eighteenth Century*, was published by Oxford University Press in 2002. He has edited a volume of essays on *Scotland in the Age of the French Revolution*, which is scheduled to appear in 2005. He is currently working on a book on the same topic.

Iain Hutchison is Reader in History at the University of Stirling. He is the author of *A Political History of Scotland, 1832–1924* (1986) and *Scottish Politics in the Twentieth Century* (2000).

Clare Jackson is Lecturer and Director of Studies in History at Trinity Hall, Cambridge. She is the author of *Restoration Scotland, 1660–1690: Royalist Politics, Religion and Ideas* (2003), as well as a number of articles on the history of ideas in early modern Scotland.

Colin Kidd, FRSE is Professor of Modern History at the University of Glasgow. His publications include *Subverting Scotland's Past: Scottish Whig Historians and the Creation of an Anglo-British Identity, 1689–c.1830* (1993) and *British Identities before Nationalism: Ethnicity and Nationhood in the Atlantic World 1600–1800* (1999).

Paul Langford, FBA is Rector of Lincoln College and Professor of History at the University of Oxford. He was the first Chairman and Chief Executive of the Arts and Humanities Research Board. His numerous publications include *A Polite and Commercial People, 1727–83* (1989) and *Englishness Identified: Manners and Character, 1650–1850* (2000).

John Morrill, FBA is Professor of British and Irish History at the University of Cambridge and a past Vice-President of the British Academy. His many books include *The Nature of the English Revolution* (1994), *Revolt in the Provinces: the English People and the Tragedies of War 1634–1648* (1999), and (with Brendan Bradshaw) *The British Problem 1534–1707*.

Christopher Smout, FBA, FRSE is Emeritus Professor of Scottish History at the University of St Andrews and Historiographer Royal in Scotland. He is author of *A History of the Scottish People, 1560–1830* (1969) and *A Century of the Scottish People, 1830–1950* (1986), and he has edited for the British Academy and the Royal Society of Edinburgh a previous collection of essays from an earlier joint symposium, *Victorian Values* (1992).

Christopher Whatley, FRSE is Professor of Scottish History at the University of Dundee. Recent publications include *Scottish Society: Beyond Jacobitism, Towards Industrialisation* (2000) and *Bought and Sold for English Gold? Explaining the Union of 1707* (2001). He is currently working on a new book, *The Scots and the Union*, to be published by Edinburgh University Press in 2006.

Jenny Wormald is Fellow and Tutor in Modern History at St Hilda's College, Oxford. Her original research, on the greater and lesser aristocracy of late medieval and early modern Scotland, led to her book *Lords and Men in Scotland: Bonds of Manrent, 1442–1603* (1985). She then moved into the field of 'British' history with her current work on James VI and I, on whom she has published a number of articles and about whom she is currently writing a book.

Acknowledgements

The editor would like to thank the staff of the British Academy for the exemplary efficiency with which they organised both the lecture in March and the Symposium in September 2003. He is also grateful to Professor David Cannadine, his fellow member on the organising committee, and especially to Margaret Richards, who made the editorial process so much easier with her unrivalled secretarial skills.

Chris Smout

1

Introduction

T. C. SMOUT

ON 24 MARCH 1603, QUEEN ELIZABETH I OF ENGLAND DIED, naming James VI
of Scotland as her successor. Thus began the Union of the Crowns of the two
kingdoms, developing just over one hundred years later into the Union of
Parliaments, and enduring to the present day, in altered, devolutionary form,
as the basis of the British state. The fourth centenary of so momentous an
event seemed a good time to take another look at Anglo-Scottish relations in
the long run, and the British Academy and the Royal Society of Edinburgh
came together to organise a triple commemoration. The first part was a
lecture given in the Academy's rooms in London on 24 March 2003 by Jenny
Wormald describing the drama and tension of the accession, and the history of
the Union of the Crowns in the lifetime of James. Then, on 17–18 September,
this was followed by a symposium on the broad theme of 'Anglo-Scottish
relations 1603–1914' and, on 6–7 November, by a further symposium in the
Royal Society of Edinburgh's premises in Scotland carrying the same theme
forward to the present day and attempting to peer a little into the future. The
first two occasions were the sole province of historians, albeit inclusive of
historians of law and literature as well as of politics, economics, ideas and
culture. The third was a wider interdisciplinary occasion, with political scientists, historians and sociologists all involved, and with its eye much on contemporary affairs. This volume brings together Dr Wormald's lecture and the
papers given at the September meeting, while a second volume has been
prepared dealing with more recent times.

The papers presented here are of great range. Following Jenny Wormald's
introduction, Keith Brown and John Morrill gave us an overview of the first
six decades of the Union of the Crowns, Clare Jackson a picture of the uses
to which judicial torture was put after 1660 and Chris Whatley a summary of
the straits in which Scotland found itself in the opening years of the eighteenth
century. John Ford looked at the problems which union posed to maritime
lawyers of both nations, Paul Langford took us into the dark reception that

Proceedings of the British Academy, **127**, 1–12. © The British Academy 2005.

the Scots received in eighteenth-century England, and Colin Kidd was concerned with the way Enlightenment Scotland viewed the British unions. Three papers then studied the Union of 1707 at work—facilitating the ambitions of Scottish élites in India, from Tom Devine; as the frame for radical co-operation in the age of the Friends of the People and later, from Bob Harris; and as the background for the sojourn of Thomas and Jane Carlyle in London, from Rosemary Ashton. Finally, Iain Hutchison surveyed Anglo-Scottish relations on the political scene in the nineteenth century. The meeting was a rewarding mixture of the general and the particular which it would be pretentious to attempt fully to summarise. This is one person's gleanings and reflections from an extremely lively symposium and the preceding lecture.

In what follows, the editor owes a special debt to the discussants of the various papers, but also owes them an apology for not at all being able to do justice to the scope and detail of their observations.

The first point is perhaps too obvious. There was nothing natural or inevitable, nothing determined by geography, in Anglo-Scottish relations leading to a political union of the island of Great Britain. European history has many islands and peninsulas that are home to disparate states, though several were indeed temporarily joined in union: Spain and Portugal, Norway and Sweden, Northern Ireland and the Republic of Ireland. The force of a great neighbour might indeed overwhelm a lesser pinned against the sea, as England did Wales, but just as often ambition failed, as Edward I's ambition then failed in Scotland. Even if once united, the lesser power might wrest itself free again, as Portugal did from Spain and Norway from Sweden. For unions between distinct and established medieval kingdoms of some reputation, like England and Scotland, to last for four hundred years, is a rare thing in European history.

Secondly, the particular circumstances of the Union of 1603 were less favourable, and therefore the making and short-term success of the union also less inevitable, than they generally seem in retrospect. The point was well made by Jenny Wormald and the other early speakers and discussants. True, dynastic union had been anticipated as a possibility since the marriage of James IV and Margaret Tudor in 1503, when Henry VII famously remarked that 'the greater would draw the less'. It had been widely expected to happen and fervently hoped for by the Stuarts in the last four decades of the sixteenth century. Yet, as Roger Mason pointed out in discussion, it was nearly derailed with the deposition of Mary, Queen of Scots in 1567 and the subsequent Civil War, and in particular with her execution in 1587 when the Scottish nobility pleaded with James VI at a convention and parliament to invade England to avenge his mother's death. Then there was the considerable matter of Henry VIII's will, which declared that no foreigner should inherit the throne of England, and which had to be set aside on Elizabeth's death.

Once the new king had arrived in England, he was regarded with deep suspicion as much on account of his policy of European peace as for any matter of domestic or ecclesiastical policy. James VI, moreover, arrived with a conscious British agenda which Scots intellectuals in particular were broadly prepared to endorse, none more enthusiastically than David Hume of Godscroft, whose vision of a bicameral parliament at York and a supreme council of the realm composed equally of English and Scots, was a degree removed from the absolutist tendencies of James.[1] The English, however, with a highly developed sense of their own antique distinctive national identity, were not in the least keen on the novelty of a British state incorporating obvious aliens. Nor were they prepared for more than the very minimum sharing of their valuable privileges with the poverty-stricken Scots, and royal attempts to bring about a more comprehensive union of both realms were simply made impossible by the opposition of the London parliament. The Union of the Crowns itself survived partly because James lived so long after inheriting the throne, so that his ways became familiar, and his courtiers and ministers had time to put down their own network of vested interests. James also survived because the old Tudors, so raddled with disease, left no plausible alternative inheritors around whom disaffected Englishmen could rally. Once set up for a quarter of a century, mere survival ensured that the Union of the Crowns had a good chance of continuing for a while thereafter.

By 1638, however, as John Morrill emphasised, Anglo-Scottish relations had again sunk to a low ebb, the English considering that an intrusive Scottish élite had gained too much from the opportunities at court since 1603, the Scots on the contrary believing that their voice had been lost in affairs of state. However, in the tumultuous decades that followed, it was always the Scots who wished for a more realistic union in which their voice could be heard in the south, and the English who by 1649 were prepared to offer the Scots a break, a return to the situation before 1603, when the Stuarts ruled in Scotland but not in England. It was only after the Scots defiantly crowned Charles II at Scone as king of Britain and Ireland, that Cromwell felt it necessary to enforce the union of 1654 as a way of eliminating a royalist threat from the North. In 1660, both sides were very content to revert to the settlement of 1603.

At the time of its first centenary, however, there was almost universal belief in both kingdoms that the existing Union of the Crowns had become a disaster. The English held the view that the Scottish parliament was an ungovernable mess of faction and party that could hardly be trusted in the

---

[1] P. J. McGinnis and A. H. Williamson (eds), *The British Union: a Critical Edition and Translation of David Hume of Godscroft's De Unione Insulae Britannicae* (Aldershot, 2002); B. Galloway, *The Union of England and Scotland, 1603–1608* (Edinburgh, 1986).

long run with the vital security of the northern English border. All they had
got from the Stuarts was a duff line of kings, forever pushing monarchical
privilege at the expense of the liberties of the subject. They had executed one
and deposed another, but the line continued as pretenders to threaten the
security of England. For their part, the Scots believed more strongly than
ever that the loss of independence without a closer say in foreign policy and
major affairs of state had reduced them to the position of a mere satellite,
and furthermore completely ruined their chance to maintain any sustainable
economic growth, a view for which, in Chris Whatley's opinion, there was
much to be said. The union appeared to very diverse contemporaries at the
start of the eighteenth century as 'the only surce and spring of our misfortunes', and Scotland, as 'totally neglected, like a farm managed by servants'.[2]
In the event, the English reversed another half-century of opposition to
closer union (since 1660) by insisting that Scotland joined in a Union of
Parliaments in 1707, as the only way to counteract the threat of a Jacobite
regime in the north allied to the French. The Scots, to say the least, were
divided and ambivalent, but not drawn in to the Treaty by threats and bribes
alone. The debate in the Scottish parliament was passionate, and the negotiations protracted and real.[3] Above all, nothing could have been done without
placating the presbyterians by confirming their sway as the established church
north of the Border.

For all its ultimate longevity, parliamentary union did little in the short
run for Anglo-Scottish relations. The security problem was not really settled
until after 1745, and economic dividends for Scotland from union only
appeared about the same time. The image of 'Sauny', the itchy, lousy, sneaky
Scot, as Paul Langford showed, remained a stock figure for English cartoon-
ists as late as the 1790s. John Robertson commented in discussion, however,
that the turning point in the way the Scots were viewed in London probably
came ten years earlier in the American War, when the Scots generally stayed
loyal and did not seek political advantage, which the Irish 'conspicuously and
irritatingly did'. He also noted that it was in the 1780s that interest in the
Union of 1707 as a possible model for a further union with Ireland can be
seen to grow, as indicated by the re-issue in 1786 of Defoe's *History of the
Union*, with De Lolme's remarkable preface, surveying the history of Anglo-
Scottish and Anglo-Irish relations up to that point and concluding that,
'Upon the whole, an incorporate Union of Great Britain and Ireland may be

---

[2] The quotations are from Sir John Clerk of Penicuik (National Archives of Scotland, Clerk of
Penicuik MSS 3122) and Andrew Fletcher of Saltoun (*Political Works*, 1749, p. 276).
[3] The most recent discussion is C. A. Whatley, *Bought and Sold for English Gold? Explaining the
Union of 1707*, 2nd edn (East Linton, 2001).

pronounced a most desirable object to both Kingdoms; yet it is certainly not without its difficulties.'[4]

The Union of 1603, however, was still regarded as a seventeenth-century disaster for Scotland by Scots of the eighteenth century, who, then, in Colin Kidd's words, 'thought more about unions than they did about identity'. In the eyes of the *literati* of the Enlightenment, as for their predecessors, it had brought nothing but misery on the country, though its disadvantages were now seen differently. For William Robertson and John Millar, its worst effect had been to make the king near-absolute and the nobility, removed from royal oversight, overmighty and oppressive to the commons. In this view, the Cromwellian union could be considered distinctly superior even to that of 1707 in its original form, as the latter had left too many noble and particular privileges intact, at least prior to the abolition of feudal jurisdictions in 1747. There were other Scots (Jacobites) for whom 1654 and 1707 were anything but ideal models, but the pretenders themselves thought solely and unappealingly in terms of a return to 1603. Prince Charles Edward was prepared to revoke 1707, but still to march on London. No more than his predecessor in 1651 was he ready to contemplate merely being a Stuart king of Scotland, and, indeed, in his dotage he insisted on being addressed as king of England. It proved not to be an ideology with enough appeal.

In the course of the eighteenth century, there emerged in Scotland a mood of positive accommodation to the parliamentary union, running some decades ahead of a similar mood of accommodation in England, if the latter can be placed in the 1780s as suggested. In a way it had been foreshadowed by the dissatisfaction Scots had intermittently shown in the seventeenth century towards the incompleteness of 1603, and some of it had been prefigured and long incubated by necessity, as John Ford showed in his study of the law of the sea. Much more, however, was created by immediate opportunity, as Tom Devine showed in his meticulous identification of the penetration of the British Empire by the younger sons of the Scottish landed class. It was a mood of accommodation where the Scots realised how a genuinely conjoined Britain solved certain of their long-term structural difficulties in operating successfully at home and abroad, and the English realised that it was, after all, better to have Scots inside their tent than outside. England had wealth and force. Scotland had an educated élite ambitious for success in commerce and arms. Now came the first and most enduring popular usages of the prefix 'British': significantly, the British Empire and the British Army. Even early in the seventeenth century Scots in royal service in Europe had written

<hr/>

[4] *The History of the Union between England and Scotland* (edn London, 1786), containing J. L. de Lolme, 'An essaying containing a few strictures on the Union of Scotland with England, and on the present situation of Ireland', pp. 1–95, quotation on p. 91.

of themselves as British,[5] but now Scots thought of themselves in the context of any material or intellectual ambition that led them furth of their country, as British. Being generally Protestant and becoming anti-French no doubt helped, as Linda Colley has insisted,[6] but shared élite ambition was in itself quite sufficient reason for Scots at least to glory, like George III himself, in the name of Briton.

The consequence was a new atmosphere where it gradually became natural, as Bob Harris emphasised, for the Scottish radicals of the period 1790–1820 to maintain close links with London and to speak of the strength of one British movement for liberty, even to contemplate a new, democratic union replacing the 'corrupt' settlement of 1707. Similarly it became natural for Thomas Carlyle to refer to Robert Burns 'not only as a true British poet, but as one of the most considerable British men of the eighteenth century', meaning by that, of course, that he compared well with any English poet of the age.[7]

'Britain' was now to many Scots on many occasions the name of the theatre where Englishmen and Scots acted out, independently or together, their roles on life's stage. Of course, it did not replace 'Scotland' in their consciousness, but it formed the outer ring of a concentric loyalty. At this point Scottish people internalised the notion of Britain, as the English never did and never have. For the English the usual name both for their state and for the theatre of their lives was and still is England: the empire might be British but the homeland was England, as it had been from Saxon times.[8] As A. N. Wilson said in a recent radio interview, Britain is only a term the English use for their country when they remember to be polite to the Scots. The residual irritations that the Scots had concerning their neighbours in the nineteenth century usually revolved (just as in the revolutionary decades of the seventeenth century) round England not being British enough. That is to say, the Scots did not concede that English laws and customs were the appropriate norms for the whole island of Great Britain, at least not without proper negotiation and discussion.

Yet there were now actually quite clear limits to this English sense of hegemony over the north of the island. In the nineteenth century, England

[5] S. Murdoch, 'James VI and the formation of a Scottish-British military identity', in S. Murdoch and A. Mackillop (eds), *Fighting for Identity: Scottish Military Experience c.1550–1900* (Leiden, 2002).

[6] L. Colley, *Britons: Forging the Nation, 1707–1837* (London, 1992).

[7] E. L. Miller (ed.), *Carlyle's Essay on Burns* (Detroit, 1896), p. 22. The essay was originally published as a review of J. G. Lockhart's *Life of Robert Burns*, in the *Edinburgh Review*, No. 96 (1828).

[8] J. C. D. Clark, 'Protestantism, nationalism and national identity, 1660–1832', *Historical Journal* 43 (2000), pp. 249–76.

and Scotland did not merge. As Iain Hutchison wisely put it, they meshed. No one supposed that the extraordinary couple who lived in Cheyne Walk, Chelsea, were or should pretend to be English: Thomas Carlyle exercised a huge influence on English thought, but he and Jane were ostentatiously Scots. No one seriously supposed, even as the presbyterian church in Victorian Scotland was wrenching itself apart, that the right solution to the tormented ecclesiastical politics of Scotland was to embrace an Anglican episcopalian-ism that would celebrate Christmas and be relaxed about the Sabbath. No one considered it wise at Westminster, once the Scottish MPs had decided that the peculiarities of Scottish parliamentary affairs demanded a specialised unit of government, determinedly to oppose the creation of a Scottish Office. If the previous three centuries had taught the English anything, it was that if the Scots wished to be peculiar they were certainly best left to be so.

It was this flexibility that made the union not only workable at that time but unshakeable, even in the century of the rise of European and Irish nationalism. The symposium did not consider in detail what Graeme Morton has elsewhere called 'unionist nationalism';[9] it is worth a digression to explain it from example. John Kerr, writing in the 1880s, was a presbyterian writing on Scottishness and Britishness—not an original thinker of his age, but a typical one. He traced back 'the nationality that has continued from that time to this' to the medieval Anglo-Scottish Wars of Independence and 'the spirit formed by Wallace'. Both England and Scotland had gained from the struggle, he said, because it 'prepared the way for an equal and honorable union' and 'made the British Empire richer by all the contributions of literature and social character which a separate history has enabled Scotland to give'. Such a sense of nationality had moreover hindered centralisation, so dangerous to liberty and progress, but not weakened the United Kingdom by any divided allegiance. The British were a great people rendered stronger by 'the friendly play of the electric currents that have their origin in a diversity that is held in friendship'. But, he went on, Knox and the Covenanters were no less part of the essential Scottish nationality than the heritage of Wallace. He concluded:

> We shall do more for the British Empire as Scotsmen than as mongrel Englishmen, and more for Christianity as good Presbyterians than if, from indifference or affectation, we let slip the stimulating motives that come from such ancestry.[10]

It was easy for a convinced presbyterian in the nineteenth century, as in the seventeenth, to feel that the English were a touch more in need of God's mercy than the Scots.

---

[9] G. Morton, *Unionist-nationalism: Governing Urban Scotland, 1830–1850* (East Linton, 1999).
[10] J. Kerr, *Scottish Nationality and Other Papers* (Edinburgh, 1887), pp. 2–6, 18.

That Kerr and others like him could express their nationalism in such unionist terms was due to the nature of the settlement in 1707, which gave the Treaty of Union an unexpected flexibility and lasting power. This was not the product of some far-sighted statesmanship, but of an ability to negotiate a compromise in order to achieve immediate political aims. England and the Crown, though threatening force and offering sweet bribes, also saw the points at which the Scots would not yield for all the threats and gold on offer, which concerned the church and the civil law. In particular, few European monarchs a hundred years earlier could seriously have entertained institutionalising religious differences by having two established churches in the same state. James VI certainly aimed at a measure of religious uniformity in his Kingdoms. To do otherwise not only went against the practical political theory of *cuius regio cuius religio*, but its relativism was positively blasphemous. A century later, it was still a novel idea, but after the shedding of so much blood over religious differences, one that might be entertained. It was the alternative that was now unthinkable. To have tried in 1707 to reimpose episcopalianism on Scotland would have given joy to Jacobites, have formally abrogated the settlement of 1690 and, most horrifyingly, have opened the door to a renewal of Covenanting resistance. Clare Jackson well described the confrontation between state terror and popular terror of that period, but, as John Young observed at the seminar, the full depth of the trauma and division in Restoration Scotland needs more scholarly appreciation.[11] So the politicians of 1707 took a new constitutional road, albeit the only one open to them. In the event, not only two established churches but two systems of civil law and two types of provision for poor law and education, survived the miscalled Incorporating Union.

In the first half of the nineteenth century, Scottish intellectuals often expressed misgivings about the forthcoming demise of an identifiable Scotland.[12] Sir John Sinclair alluded in 1804 to the need to assert Scottish identity before 'Scotland becomes completely confounded in England'.[13] Sir Walter Scott in 1826 talked of the ministers at Westminster 'gradually destroying what remains of nationality and making the country *tabula rasa* for doctrines of bold innovation'. He feared a chaotic democracy would be the consequence. 'If you *unscotch* us', he wrote to an English correspondent,

---

[11] But see also C. Jackson, *Restoration Scotland, 1660–1690: Royalist Politics, Religion and Ideas* (Woodbridge, 2003).

[12] I am indebted to Tom Devine for emphasising this point and for drawing my attention to the three following quoted passages.

[13] *Observations on the Propriety of Preserving the . . . Customs of the Ancient Inhabitants of Scotland* (Edinburgh, 1804), quoted in P. Womack, *Improvement and Romance: Constructing the Myth of the Highlands* (London, 1989), p. 145.

'you will find us damned mischievous Englishmen.'[14] Henry Cockburn in
1852 described the early years of the nineteenth century as 'the last purely
Scotch age that Scotland was destined to see, when still the whole country
had not begun to be absorbed in the ocean of London'. Edinburgh in mid-
century had, he believed, still been able to retain to a certain degree its independent tastes, ideas and pursuits; 'But now that London is at our door, how
precarious is our hold of them, and how many have we lost.'[15] No doubt the
speed of contemporary social and economic change, apparently driving
England and Scotland in the same cultural direction, fed these jeremiads. So
perhaps did the inheritance of the Scottish Enlightenment, devising through
history and philosophy ambitious universal rules for the guidance of humanity. Scotland would transcend a barbarous national past. 'A certain attenuated
cosmopolitanism had in good measure taken [the] place of the old, insular
home feeling. Literature was, as it were, without any local environment . . .'
was how Carlyle perceptively, if dismissively, put it.[16]

Yet those prophecies were to be largely falsified. In the nineteenth century
the Scots reinvented the 'old, insular home feeling' with a vengeance, adopt-
ing the kilt, the haggis and the bagpipe as national (as opposed to merely
Highland) symbols, celebrating hearth and home from Walter Scott to the
Kailyard novels, and glamorising the romance of the Highlands through the
paintings of Horatio McCulloch and Thomas Faed (ably assisted by that
urbane Englishman, Edwin Landseer). They recovered a distinct history to be
proud of, bloody but redeemed by Wallace, Knox, and other heroes, and they
re-emphasised it by constructing national museums and art galleries like any
independent European country. This could all be done without threatening
the British state because, as Kerr's approach to union so clearly demonstrated, the treaty of 1707 was seen not as incorporating into one but as
embracing the difference in two. Difference up to a point, that is, because
even in Great Britain both the native Highland Gaels and the immigrant Irish
Gaels might with reason have thought that Anglo-Saxon Protestantism
smothered more than it embraced, and excluded more than it included.

Colin Kidd has elsewhere shown how novel theories of race came to be
entertained in nineteenth-century Britain by thinkers of many persuasions,
and how in Scotland this came to split the 'imagined community' into those
identified as Celts (roughly the Highlanders) and those identified as Saxons
(roughly the Lowlanders, plus the inhabitants of Orkney and Shetland).[17]

---

[14] J. G. Lockhart, *Memoirs of the Life of Sir Walter Scott* (edn 1900), IV, pp. 474, 483.
[15] H. Cockburn, *Life of Lord Jeffrey* (1852: edn 1872), pp. 150–4, quoted in P. H. Scott, 'The last
purely Scotch age', in D. Gifford (ed.), *The History of Scottish Literature*, III (Aberdeen, 1988), p. 15.
[16] *Essay on Burns*, p. 53.
[17] C. Kidd, 'Race, Empire and the limits of nineteenth-century Scottish nationhood', *Historical
Journal* 46 (2003), pp. 873–92.

The former were seen as being racially the same as the Irish, the latter as the English. Generally, the Saxons were seen as intrinsically superior to the Celts, so Lowlanders and English were lined up as better than and different to the Highlanders and Irish. The persistence of this mode of ethnic or racial identification did not preclude the adoption of tartan, bagpipes and other Highland symbols as national ones, but perhaps we should not expect consistency in the realm of image-building. As much as anything these were military symbols, and certainly the denigration of the Highlanders never extended to the Highland regiments, of which all Scots were inordinately proud.

So Scotland, despite its divisions, retained a positive distinction from England. Yet the impression of a determinedly peculiar Victorian Scotland is not wholly true. For all sorts of reasons, forms of Anglicisation did make Scottish life less distinctive, as Cockburn and others sensed. Some had to do with adapting to the needs of a modern imperial-industrial state, like alterations to the traditional curriculum of the Scottish universities. Others had to do with technology—an island with railways, penny post, telegraph, and telephone was bound to be more integrated than one without. Others again had to do with the growth of state power. Apart from setting the terms of external political and commercial relations, taxation and, ultimately, imposing some forms of military service in some places through the press-gang, the state as such had relatively little to do in the first century after 1707. In the nineteenth century it gathered to itself many new powers, ranging from public health and factory legislation to the protection of wild birds and the regulation of alcohol consumption. Because Scotland had a distinctive system of law, the growth of the state prompted (after a campaign) the foundation of a Scottish Office to oversee the administrative process and to help to guide the legislative process as it applied to Scotland, which ensured a measure of continual distinctiveness. And there was in exchange a certain amount of Scotticisation of England, seen in banking legislation, in publicly funded universal primary education and, in the twentieth century, in forestry policy. The state became more unitary as it became more prominent, and although it is correct to speak of meshing rather than merging, Iain Hutchison's own paper demonstrated how comfortable Englishmen were representing Scottish parliamentary seats in large numbers in the late nineteenth century, as they certainly would not be today and would not have been earlier when Islay and Dundas held sway over patronage and approved only fellow Scotsmen as their political clients. Perhaps, as proposed by Keith Robbins in discussion, Gladstone was the prototype by inclination, birth and upbringing, for a new truly British politician, just as Victoria, with her sojourns at Balmoral, was the prototype for a new British monarch.[18]

---

[18] See also K. Robbins, *Nineteenth-Century Britain: Integration and Diversity* (Oxford, 1988).

Yet it is important not to forget, as both Ian McBride and Keith Robbins reminded us, that in the nineteenth century the Anglo-Scottish union was no longer the sole or dominant constituent national relationship. The formation of a United Kingdom of Great Britain and Ireland in theory threatened to relegate Scotland to third place in the 'three kingdoms', perhaps to make it as unimportant and indistinct as eighteenth-century Wales had been within 'England and Wales': this may have added to the concerns of Scots about their future distinctiveness at the time of the Irish union.

That this did not happen is surely connected with the same notions of fundamental racial difference as those which split Scotland into Celtic Highlanders and Saxon Lowlanders. By the nineteenth century, Anglo-Scottish union had begun to appear as a relatively comfortable union between partners—the vicious cartoons of the eighteenth-century London press had been replaced by a comparatively affectionate Punch stereotype of Scots as dour and parsimonious. Depictions of the Irish remained very different, still as ragged, simian, threatening, savage. Neither the English nor the Lowland Scots were ever really comfortable with the Irish, nor did they ever lose the feeling that Ireland was a colony, not a partner. 'The Irish problem' is still the way modern Britons are taught to regard their relationship with the Irish from Victorian times onwards, obliterating from collective memory what the United Kingdom actually was for 120 years. There were in fact similarities in the Scottish union and the Irish union, not least in the large role played by the Irish in the British armed forces and in the colonial civil service, but at root the Union of 1801 remained no more than a solution to the security problem of 1798.

An indication of the degree to which the Irish remained other, 'not one of us', came tragically in the Great Famine. Had a million people been threatened by death from hunger in Lancashire or Clydeside in 1846, it is unthinkable that the remainder of the British would not have abandoned every ideological prejudice and expended every resource of money and effort to save them. Some historians have too generously excused the metropolitan power on the grounds of the unprecedented nature of the famine, its scale and the logistical problems involved. As Joel Mokyr has observed, a nation that fought the Crimean War could certainly more effectively have relieved the Great Famine had it chosen to do so.[19]

No doubt the problem was exacerbated by the majority of the Irish determinedly remaining Catholic, if we accept Linda Colley's formulation of British identity in the late eighteenth and early nineteenth century as specifically Protestant. But by Victorian times, when Cardinal Newman was accepted as

[19] J. Mokyr, *Why Ireland Starved: a Quantitative and Analytical History of the Irish Economy, 1800–1850* (London, 1983), p. 292.

unquestionably a true Englishman, it was the assumed racial inferiority of Celts that did the real damage. Charles Trevelyan, permanent secretary at the Treasury who had a dominating influence on famine relief from 1846, combined a doctrinaire belief in *laissez-faire* with an open belief in the racial inferiority of the Celts, the Highlanders differing from the Irish only in that the former were no longer 'turbulent or blood-thirsty'.[20] The Irish ultimately developed a form of nationalism more akin to the European model than to the Scottish unionist nationalism exemplified by Kerr, but they did so at least partly in response to their rejection by Great Britain. Otherwise the Union of 1801 might have lasted: it takes two to make a divorce.

As Keith Robbins also remarked, the meaning of 'Anglo-Scottish relations' changes over time. In the sixteenth century and even in the seventeenth century, it encapsulates inter-nation relationships, so that one can speak of Anglo-Scottish relations in the same way as Anglo-French or Anglo-Italian relations. After 1707, and especially after 1800 when the processes of assimilation increase and the state itself is British, Anglo-Scottish relations become less inter-nation and increasingly inter-person, ultimately made up of an infinite multitude of encounters. Nevertheless, most 'English lives' and 'Scottish lives' continued to exist quite separately without much interpenetration until long after the end of the eighteenth century. As the nineteenth century wore on, English tourism in Scotland brought a growing volume of superficial contacts, and Scottish economic migration into England a growing volume of more profound ones. In many cultural, political, and sociological senses the English encountered the Scots in a more peripheral sense than the Scots encountered the English, except perhaps abroad in the British Empire where the relative weights of the two (and of the Irish) were more equal. The Scots, outnumbered by the English by about 5:1 in 1707 and by 10:1 in 1901, had more to worry about, most to gain and most to lose by the way the relationship worked.

It became clear from the symposium that the Scots indeed worried and worry a lot about Anglo-Scottish relations, but the English worried and worry about them hardly at all, except at times of exceptional crisis, as in 1638–54, 1703–7, 1745–7 and perhaps much later in the 1970s after oil had been discovered. The union survived to 1900 and beyond as a *modus vivendi* between two very unequal partners, eventually a cultural and political norm that by then it seemed eccentric to question. However, within union, Scotland remained distinctively and consciously Scottish and England distinctively and almost unthinkingly English. The continued existence of Great Britain would in the twentieth century come again both to be questioned and to be actively worked for, but that is the territory of the following volume.

[20] T. M. Devine, *The Great Highland Famine* (Edinburgh, 1988), p. 126.

2

O Brave New World? The Union of England and Scotland in 1603

JENNY WORMALD

O wonder!
How many goodly creatures are there here!
How beauteous mankind is! O brave new world
That has such people in it.
(Miranda, *The Tempest*, V. i)[1]

WELL, PERHAPS, IN SHAKESPEARE'S ENCHANTED ISLE OF 1611. What about the real isles, united in 1603 under the monarchy of James VI and I, these isles which James wanted to call Great Britain? Were they the brave new world? Sadly, it seems not. Miranda's 'goodly creatures' translated into creatures who, with the exception of the king himself, were timorous, resentful, distrustful about the union of England and Scotland. ''Tis new to thee' was Prospero's response to Miranda, said perhaps wearily, perhaps sarcastically. If so, the response far better reflected the reaction to the real new world of 1603 than Miranda's ringing joy. Perhaps this should not surprise us. None of the many unions of early modern Europe elicited that ecstasy. Yet 24 March 2003 witnessed the celebration of the fourth centenary of the union of England and Scotland, one of the few which has survived. So although it was an event surrounded by gloom and doom rather than happiness and enthusiasm, there may have been the glimmerings of a brave new world in Jacobean Britain, which may explain that survival.

It began between two and three in the morning of 24 March 1603, when Elizabeth at last died. For her English subjects, the King of Scots, and his Scottish subjects, she had hung on to life for far too long. Now, with great speed, James VI was proclaimed King of England; and on that day the proclamation, already drafted by Cecil and shown to James, was printed and

---

[1] William Shakespeare, *The Tempest*, ed. Stephen Orgel (Oxford, 1987), pp. 197–8.

Proceedings of the British Academy, **127**, 13–35. © The British Academy 2005.

issued in the name of the lords spiritual and temporal, the Privy Council, the mayor, aldermen and citizens of London and other worthies.[2] It was a proclamation which heralded the English view of the brave new world. It announced his lineal descent, which gave him his right to the throne; he was the heir of Henry VII through his elder daughter Margaret, the sister of Henry VIII. Naturally there was no reference to previous acts of succession nor to Henry VIII's will, which prevented an alien from inheriting the English throne. Nor was there any mention of his mother Mary, Queen of Scots, nor of his father Henry, Lord Darnley, with his junior claim as the descendant of Margaret Tudor and her second husband Archibald, Earl of Angus— 'Anguisshe', as she called him. Strictly speaking, there was no need to mention James's Scottish descent, for it was as King of England, not Britain, that he was proclaimed.

However, there was one very odd feature of the proclamation. It referred to Henry VII's wife Elizabeth of York and the marriage which had brought to an end the 'bloody and Civil Warres . . . to the joy unspeakable of this Kingdome'. That marriage had no relevance to James's claim. So why was it included? The Tudor myth, of bringing dynastic stability to the war-torn land of the later fifteenth century, was just that: myth. It is hard to think of a more dynastically disastrous dynasty. Henry VIII's meandering and messy matrimonial career, his Acts of Succession, and the reigns of a child who died young, a woman who tried but tragically failed to have children, and a woman who would not try at all, produced doubts about the succession from the mid-1520s; and the English lived out the second half of the century in mounting fear about the future which, on Elizabeth's death, might see foreign invasion from Spain, even France, or—ultimate irony—civil war sparked off by internal claimants to the throne. So the proclamation, setting out the best hope of a peaceful succession, gave a final nod to the Tudor myth, by restating the theme of the late fifteenth-century union of Lancaster and York.

But surely the only reason for mentioning that union was to take the theme through to the new and much greater Union of 1603. James himself would certainly pick up on it, with his coin proclaiming *Henricus rosas regna Jacobus.* And Henry VII had apparently forecast the possibility that the marriage of his daughter Margaret to James IV of Scotland might in time draw the lesser kingdom, Scotland, to the greater, England.[3] But the proclamation was wholly uninterested in this. It was ruthlessly silent about James's Anglo-Scottish ancestry. The marriage of Henry VII and Elizabeth of York was

[2] J. F. Larkin and P. L. Hughes (eds), *Stuart Royal Proclamations* (Oxford, 1973), I, pp. 1–4.
[3] I. H. Stewart, *The Scottish Coinage* (London, 1955), p. 102; Francis Bacon, *The History of the Reign of King Henry the Seventh*, ed. R. Lockyer (London, 1971), p. 206.

highlighted, that of Margaret Tudor to James IV, which was the key to 1603, ignored. The proclamation was not about the union. It was exclusively about England—England in 1485, England in 1603.

So the King of England was proclaimed. Unfortunately he was in Scotland; and Sir Robert Carey was madly galloping north. He paused only to change horses and to proclaim the king at Morpeth and Alnwick: these were the times when he intentionally got off his horse. Other times were less intentional: when he arrived in Edinburgh on the evening of 26 March—a very considerable feat—he tottered into the king's presence in Holyrood, still 'bebloodied with great falles and bruses'.[4] James reacted with punctiliousness, withdrawing to mourn for Elizabeth's death, and with tact, spending the next few days in conference with his nobility about the future government of his Scottish kingdom; he did, however, take time on 27 March to write to Robert Cecil, confirming him and the other English councillors in office, and adding in his own hand a postscript: 'How happy I think myself by the conquest of so faithful and so wise a counsellor I reserve it to be expressed out of my own mouth unto you.'[5] It was not, therefore, until 31 March that he was solemnly proclaimed as King of Scotland, England, France and Ireland, at the market cross of Edinburgh, to the great joy and grief of his Scottish subjects; unlike the English proclamation, the Scottish one did recognise union. And on 5 April he began his journey south. There had been no challenge. The Union of the Crowns was now reality.

It was a stunning event, not least because it was a Scot who would now rule England, the kingdom which had, over the previous three centuries, made so many efforts to annex Scotland. It was also wholly abnormal. The very fact that the new King of England was almost 400 miles away from his capital meant that Englishmen had to pour north to greet the ultimate source of patronage, even going up to Scotland, which the Scots found inconvenient and which was perhaps a little unnecessary as the king would be coming south. Still, getting in quickly to fix one's interest with the new king was of crucial importance; as that marvellous correspondent John Chamberlain said, in a letter of 30 March 1603, 'There is much posting that way, and many run thether of theyre owne errand, as yf it were nothing els but first come first served, or that preferment were a goale to be got by footmanship.'[6] Cecil, trapped in London, but desperate to ensure Cecilian pre-eminence in the new reign, was heavily dependent on his brother Thomas, Lord Burghley for information and contact. Burghley was in York by 27 March, sending his son

[4] J. Nichols, *The Progresses, Processions and Magnificent Festivities of King James the First . . .* (London, 1828), I, p. 56.

[5] Historical Manuscripts Commission, *Salisbury MSS* (London, 1883–1976), XV, pp. 9–10.

[6] N. E. McClure (ed.), *The Letters of John Chamberlain* (Philadephia, 1939), I, p. 189.

Edward on to Scotland; from York, he wrote enthusiastically to Cecil that 'the contentment of the people is unspeakable, seeing all things proceed so quietly, whereas they expected in the interim their houses should have been spoiled and sacked'; the only sour note was struck by a disgruntled Scotswoman, heard to say that she would have preferred the king to be received less peaceably, presumably in the hope that there might then be attainted lands for the picking. Burghley gave Cecil the credit for the peace and contentment. On 4 April, he could report the even more welcome news that the king 'said he heard you were but a little man, but he would shortly load your shoulders with business'. Meanwhile there was all the hurly-burly of preparing for the king's journey—where he would stay *en route* to London, whether Elizabeth's officers or James's Scottish ones would arrange provisioning, whether Burghley would be bankrupted by putting him up in York and at Burghley House; Cecil, said Burghley, would have to do the honours at Theobalds.[7] On 1 April the Scot Sir James Elphinstone wrote to Cecil with a very pressing problem. What could the Scots do about money, when there was no recognised exchange rate with England; would they be cheated when they crossed the border?[8] The first two proclamations by the new king epitomise all the abnormality. The first, on 5 April, said that all those who were in office on Elizabeth's death should continue so until he gave further direction, and that much as His Majesty appreciated the 'earnest and longing desire' of his subjects to enjoy the sight of him, he would prefer it if their flood north was somewhat dammed. The second, on 8 April, laid down an Anglo-Scottish exchange rate.[9]

This then was the 'brave new world' of the Union of 1603. As jubilant Scots *literati* like William Alexander, William Drummond of Hawthornden and later Archbishop Spottiswoode pointed out, it had been foretold by Scotland's greatest prophet, the thirteenth-century Thomas the Rhymer, and announced to no less a person than Solomon himself by a sort of amalgam of the Sibyl of Cumae and the Queen of Sheba, when chatting to him about the future emperor Constantine and 'the Sixte King of the name of Steward of Scotland'; and in 1603 'The Whole prophecie of Scotland, England and some part of France and Denmark, prophesied bee mervuellous Merling . . . Thomas Rymour . . . Sibbilla' and others was published by Robert Waldegrave, king's printer in Edinburgh.[10] Brave and heady stuff! Not quite the reality. Reality was some relief, and a great deal of confusion, scramble and uncer-

---

[7] HMC, *Salisbury*, XV, pp. 10–11, 18, 28, 31–2, 33.

[8] HMC, *Salisbury*, XV, pp. 26–8.

[9] *Stuart Proclamations*, I, pp. 4–6, 7.

[10] In D. Laing (ed.), *Collection of Ancient Scottish Prophecies in Alliterative Verse: Reprinted from Waldegrave's edition MDCIII*, Bannatyne Club, 44 (Edinburgh, 1833).

tainty. That might have been only temporary, arising from the exceptional nature of James's accession to the English throne. But there was a much more fundamental problem: neither England nor, as it transpired, Scotland really wanted union.

Yet there was enormous potential in the Union of the Crowns. Protector Somerset in the 1540s, William Cecil and the Scottish Protestants in the 1560s, had recognised the huge advantages in England and Scotland drawing closer together. So the union looked like a triumph. Two Protestant nations had come together, immediately creating a stronger bulwark against that nightmare which had for so long troubled Elizabethan dreams, invasion by the great Catholic powers; and the male King James might be expected to fulfil the role of the militant Calvinist prince, defending the embattled Protestants of Europe, as his predecessor, the female Queen Elizabeth, had so signally failed to do. So now the British Isles—Britain, as James VI and I perceived them—could have an impact on the affairs of Europe which would go far beyond the final two decades of Elizabeth's reign, which had witnessed the half-hearted intervention in the Netherlands, and then fifteen years of slog and stalemate in the ongoing war with Spain, after the one high point, the glorious defeat of the Armada. It was a vision never forgotten by James's English subjects, one which would come back to haunt him in the last years of his reign. But in 1603 it was not as simple as that.

To begin with, what was wanted in 1603, certainly by Cecil and his associates and, indeed, the new king, was not war but peace: an end to the war in Ireland, and, even more important, to the war with Spain. In 1603 and 1604, both were achieved. Peace with Spain was a huge diplomatic triumph and an economic necessity. It was also, unfortunately for King James, monumentally unpopular. It did not help that there was even a union twist here; as he said, as King of Scots he had not been at war with Spain, and why should he be as King of England? It was emphatically not a line that went down well with militantly Protestant and anti-Spanish Englishmen. Nor did the king help himself by trying to do something for his Catholic subjects. Infinitely less rabidly anti-Catholic than Elizabeth, he genuinely hoped to reduce the intolerable burden under which they had laboured in the last two decades of her reign, the savage recusancy fines. He substantially reduced these fines in 1603. But the Exchequer became understandably restive about the loss of revenue, particularly under a much more expensive monarchy. So the answer was to get Spain to pay them, as part of the peace treaty. Spain, however, preferred to spend its money on handouts to Protestant politicians. Thus James lost out twice over. Nothing was achieved for the Catholics, but making the attempt further tarnished his reputation as the hoped for Protestant prince.

Within a year of union, therefore, England seemed to have slipped from being a proud and warlike nation into one involved in humiliating peace. It was not a brave new world; for English Protestants, it was a profoundly feeble one. So men began to invent a brave new world in the past. The dismal decade of the 1590s, Elizabeth's own dismal reputation, were now forgotten. William Camden in his *Annales*, written between 1608 and 1615, and Fulke Greville in his *Dedication to Sir Philip Sidney*, probably completed in 1612, depicted her as the heroic Protestant princess.[11] Yet Greville, who made the comparison between the heroic Elizabeth and the singularly unheroic James clear enough, knew perfectly well what the truth had been; he had been a friend of Sidney and a member of that circle who, in the 1580s, had desperately sought to bring English succour to the threatened Protestants of the Netherlands, and had been infuriated and frustrated by their endlessly pusillanimous queen.

Thus after 1603, perception and reality pulled apart. In actual fact, Britain—or the British kingdoms—became a much bigger player on the European stage than Elizabeth's England could ever have been, because instead of a childless queen there was now a king with a family; dynastic diplomacy became possible. No longer, therefore, was English foreign policy mainly reactive. But one can hardly say that patriotic English hearts swelled with pride at the new opportunities on offer. For the English never really did appreciate that, with the end of the Hundred Years War in 1453, England had lost her position as one of the major kingdoms of Europe, and become instead the greater of these two offshore kingdoms, England and Scotland. By the turn of the sixteenth century, they had found a means of concealing from themselves their new and reduced status, an excessive pride in being English and a growing xenophobia, already a matter for comment by foreign observers. In Elizabeth's reign, that pride would be greatly heightened when it became channelled into the concept of the elect Protestant nation. That inculcated in at least some English Protestants—the Leicester and Sidney group, and later Essex—the passionate desire to fulfil the workings of Providence by fighting for the Protestants of Europe. More generally, it inculcated in English Protestants the profound sense of being themselves embattled. It is a very curious fact that from the beginning of her reign Elizabeth and her governments spent their time in deep fear of Spanish invasion or of a Catholic League of France and Spain united against England, without, it seems, any awareness that both Spain and France had far more immediate and pressing problems to deal with. The second, the League, existed only in their fevered imaginings. The first, the invasion, materialised thirty years late, in 1588, when Philip II was finally provoked into taking action against

---

[11] William Camden, *The Historie of the Most Renowned and Victorious Princesse Elizabeth, Late Queene of England*, trans. Robert Norton (London, 1630): for example, II, p. 86; J. Gouws (ed.), *The Prose Works of Fulke Greville, Lord Brooke* (Oxford, 1986), for example, ch. 15.

England because of Elizabeth's half-hearted intervention in the Netherlands. But Elizabethan perceptions made it difficult in the extreme for the English to adapt to a monarch with a totally different approach to his kingdom's place in Europe.

Scotland also had an exaggerated sense of her own importance, but one born out of victory rather than defeat. What she could easily forget was that very few people had actually thought her worth conquering. What she could remember was that those who did—Romans, Danes, English—had all failed in the attempt. Moreover, she was significantly out of line with the major kingdoms of late medieval and early modern Europe, in that she never actually tried to conquer anyone else. The Scots had a high reputation for military prowess, but it was almost always, apart from the occasional Anglo-Scottish battle, displayed in foreign armies, notably the French. But once the active threat from England was over, by the end of the fourteenth century, she could develop her own sense of identity by being very consciously European, involving herself in the affairs of Europe through diplomacy rather than war. Scotland had no list of mighty warrior kings, such as Edward I, Edward III, Henry V, Henry VIII, to whom she could look back with pride; she had only one, the genuine success story of them all, Robert Bruce, and naturally much was made of Bruce. But what James VI had inherited from his Stuart ancestors, most notably James IV and the even more effective James V, was a lofty vision of the diplomatic importance of the King of Scots and his ability to have an impact on other European countries. Thus the foreign policy of the king of Protestant Scotland included a new level of friendship with England—the Amity, begun in 1584. But that policy was not restricted exclusively to the Amity, as the English expected; to her abiding fury, Elizabeth was never able to dominate, let alone determine, James's dealings with foreign powers, for James, unlike his mother, never made his claim to the English throne the cornerstone of his foreign policy. So despite howls from Elizabeth and, of course, the reformed kirk, diplomatic and trading links with France went on; and, even worse, diplomatic and trading links with Spain were opened up. For the Scots before 1603 Philip II was never the sinister and threatening figure he was to the English. And although, as in England, the Reformation produced in Scotland a new definition of identity, it was focused on an elect nation covenanted with God, the nation where one of the purest kirks under heaven could be found, rather than a nation whose religious destiny came increasingly to be identified with combat with Catholic Spain.

That is the background to the failure of early seventeenth-century Britain to become 'great' in anything other than the purely geographic sense: greater rather than lesser Britain, Brittany. In 1603, when the military tradition of the English and the diplomatic one of the Scots came together, it was a hopeless mix. In 1604, peace with Spain violently changed the direction of English foreign policy. The fact that James's handling of foreign policy thereafter—that very Scottish way—did indeed raise Britain's profile in Europe very naturally impressed English Protestants not at all, when Anglo-Spanish diplomacy became its focal point. Nor did it impress the Scots. Even if his approach was still that of a Scottish king, he was visibly pursuing English foreign policy, and the Scots could only demand that they should be kept informed and given copies of treaties. But the king, that most ecumenically minded of monarchs, confidently continued his belief in himself as one of the big figures in European diplomacy, and naturally therefore dealt with the top; and the top for him was Spain. It was an approach reinforced by the remarkably close friendship he developed with the Spanish ambassador Gondomar, who arrived in England in 1613. For with some shrewdness, Philip III sent to England a noted scholar and bibliophile, bound to appeal to the scholar king, just as in 1629 Philip IV would include Rubens on the embassy sent to negotiate peace with Charles I, the lover of art.

Gondomar's relationship with the king was viewed with very deep suspicion. This was not the continuation of the brave world of Elizabeth's reign, or rather, that mythical Elizabethan world invented in James's reign. It could only be a humiliating one, so long as a king of England was seen to be run by a Spanish ambassador. And it all came horribly to a head after 1618, when the Bohemians rebelled against their Habsburg ruler, Archduke Ferdinand, and then offered the crown to James's son-in-law, the Calvinist Frederick, Elector Palatine. The inevitable happened. In 1620 Frederick was defeated by Ferdinand, now Holy Roman Emperor, and lost not only Bohemia but his Palatinate to the vengeful Habsburgs. Now surely the moment had arrived when at last there would be a brave new world, where Protestant good would triumph over Catholic evil. Now surely the northern king, James, the Lion of Scotland, would show that he was the Lion of the North, who would overthrow the ungodly, the Lion foretold as the king of the north in the books of Isaiah, Jeremiah and Daniel, and heralded by Merlin—as recorded, or invented, by that medieval bestseller, Geoffrey of Monmouth—and in the sixteenth century by Paracelsus. With passionate optimism, one Thomas Gee wrote in his commonplace book in 1623 a garbled version of the Merlin prophecy which made the identification with James utterly clear: 'A prince out of the North shall come, Crowned babe, his brest uppon, A lyon Rampant, and Sir J. S. is cleped he . . .'[12]—that is, the king crowned as an infant, his symbol the lion rampant, called James Stuart—and of course of English descent. It was a hopeless vision. James's only connection with lions

---

[12] Folger Shakespeare Library, Folger MS V.b.303, p. 232.

was to extend the Lion Tower in the Tower of London, and build an exercise yard with high platforms for spectators to watch these regal beasts in safety. But he was no Lion of the North. He was the self-styled *Rex Pacificus*, with his motto *beati pacifici*; and he regarded Frederick as a dangerous fool. Once again, the king completely let the side down.

At home and abroad, *Rex Pacificus* was the object of violent Protestant criticism and contempt. Twice over he failed, as defender of the true religion and as kinsman to his son-in-law Frederick, now whingeing bitterly in his exile in the Hague, and his daughter Elizabeth. Yet despite the opprobrium, he and Gondomar pressed on undaunted with their solution to the European crisis. Anglo-Spanish friendship should be invoked to encourage the Spanish Habsburgs to persuade the Austrian Habsburgs to restore Frederick to at least part of the Palatinate, and thereby avert war; and that friendship should be sealed by the marriage of his son Charles to the Spanish Infanta Maria, a match long intended by a king who wanted to use his dynastic clout to give Britain a balancing role in Europe by linking it to both Protestants and Catholics. Possibly James and Gondomar were over-optimistic. But the king did survive the hostility of his English parliament of 1621, that parliament, like all others of the period, stuffed with Protestant xenophobic gentry, their heads filled with Elizabethan myth and hatred of Spain. The delays over the completion of the marriage treaty and its ultimate failure lay far more in the shift of power in Spain: the death of Philip III in 1621, the rise of Olivares, who hated Gondomar, and who was much less inclined to a diplomatic solution. So Charles and Buckingham made their mad dash to Spain in 1623 in an attempt to end the stalemate.[13] Charles was following Scottish tradition, for two of his Scottish ancestors had done just that; both James V and James VI went abroad to claim their brides, in the first case Madeleine, daughter of Francis I, in the second Anna of Denmark. Like Charles, they had a long and enjoyable holiday. Unlike Charles, they were not there as suppliants. Charles was strung along, as the negotiating stakes were increasingly raised; and eventually he had to admit defeat. So he and Buckingham came home to patriotic Protestant roars of joy and roars for war. James's policy was in ruins, and in 1624 Charles, Buckingham, and a bellicose parliament got their

---

[13] On the negotiations leading to Charles's visit to Spain and analysis of what happened while he was there, see the very lively and closely researched new account by Glyn Redworth, *The Prince and the Infanta: the Cultural Politics of the Spanish Match* (Yale, 2003). For a rather different interpretation, B. P. Pursell, 'James I, Gondomar and the Dissolution of the Parliament of 1621', *History* 85 (2000), and 'The end of the Spanish match', *Historical Journal* 45 (2002), pp. 699–726.

way. England declared war on Spain.[14] The brave Elizabethan world which, since 1603, had ensured that the world of the Union of the Crowns could not be brave, triumphed.

It was a disaster. James prophetically warned his son that parliament would demand war, but would not pay for it; and so it transpired. England embarked on four inglorious years of war, only to find that she was utterly incapable of meeting the demands of modern warfare. Buckingham achieved the rare feat of embroiling England in fighting with both these longstanding enemies, Spain and France, at the same time, when he added war in defence of the French Huguenots to war with Spain. The Scots, true to their own tradition, went off to gain military experience in the armies of Gustavus Adolphus, the real fulfilment of the prophecies of the Lion of the North. And in 1629 Charles made peace. Both the Elizabethan and the Jacobean dreams were over. Elizabethan England, the great enemy of Spain, was a thing of the past. Jacobean Britain, almost but not quite a major European power and the preserver of peace in Europe, had failed. We should not write off the Jacobean vision, however. 'How beauteous mankind is', said Shakespeare's Miranda. For James, beauteous mankind was a mankind which sought peace and religious accommodation. Had he achieved his vision, there would have been peace; and thousands of Europeans slaughtered in the long and brutal Thirty Years War would not have died. Ironically England, the kingdom that resisted the Jacobean vision and wanted war, got off very lightly because its involvement was so short-lived. Thereafter, the British kingdoms withdrew into almost unbroken isolation. It would be another sixty years before another king, William of Orange, set out, though in very different ways, to recreate James's desire to put Britain firmly in the centre of the international stage, and in doing so turned its eyes to the future of world power and empire. Like James, he too was a foreigner.

So however much potential there was in theory, there was in practice no brave new British world in European terms. In domestic terms, it was even worse. Indeed, if it took almost a century before the international potential was realised, it could be said that we are still waiting for the domestic one. For this was more than a matter of conflicting traditions. In 1603, the brutal fact was that the Scots and the English disliked one another intensely; forty years of the veneer of friendship imposed by a common cause in religion—itself a veneer, given the profound differences between the two churches—was certainly not enough to offset three centuries of hostility, and if anything the union increased rather than diminished that hostility. Passions may not run

---

[14] This is marvellously evoked by Thomas Cogswell, *The Blessed Revolution: English Politics and the Coming of War, 1621–1624* (Cambridge, 1989), which is also essential reading for the events of these years.

quite so high in the twenty-first century, though the decision in 1984 to end that series of annual football matches which showed a distressing tendency to recreate the atmosphere of past Anglo-Scottish battles, does rather indicate that the diplomatic 'amity' of the late sixteenth century and the Union of 1603 have not yet put down deep roots. Indeed, if anything, 2003 has redrawn the battle-lines of 1603. With the honourable exception of the British Academy, it was in Scotland that James was remembered, the Royal Society of Edinburgh leading the way, while concentration in England was on the last monarch of the independent kingdom of England, Elizabeth. *The Times* of 24 March 2003 made amazing reading: according to a poll about knowledge of the queen, Elizabeth introduced to England curry, gin and corgis, and 49 per cent did not know that James I was a Scot. Its leading article patriotically extolled Elizabeth, contrasting her with 'an imported monarchy' which would, after 1603, plunge England into confusion.[15]

If that was the situation in 2003, one can hardly expect mutual enthusiasm in 1603. Of course some efforts were made. One was the special purchase of oatcakes by the Earl of Rutland for a visit by Lord Burghley to Belvoir in February 1608; this was followed up by Gervase Markham, whose *English Housewife* of 1615 and 1623 devoted a chapter to 'the excellency of oats', 'the crown of the housewife's garland'. So the lowly Scottish oatcake was now a favoured food, fit even for a nobleman's table. Another example comes from a farmhouse near Ripley Castle in Nidderdale, where James stayed in 1603 on his journey south. Recently the owner of the farmhouse removed limewash over his mantelpiece—and found a painting of the arms of England and Scotland. Presumably the loyal farmer of 1603 was not only summoned to produce provisions for the king and his entourage but felt moved to put up this memento of the king's visit.[16]

The Rutland family were good at this kind of thing, with their oatcakes and their frieze of thistles and roses from a single stem in the long gallery of Haddon Hall. But that is far less remarkable than the splendid Yorkshire farmer. He lived, after all, only some twenty-five miles from York, whose memory of raiding Scots was so long-lasting that legend has it that it is still legal for any citizen of York who encounters a Scotsman within or outwith the walls after sunset to shoot him—provided he has his bow and arrow with him. The Rutlands, by contrast, bring us into the world of those who might

---

[15] *The Times*, 24 March 2003.
[16] I am deeply indebted to Dr Joan Thirsk for this information, and for the following references: Historical Manuscripts Commission, *Rutland MSS* (London, 1890–1905), IV, p. 460 and Gervase Markham, *The English Housewife, 1615, 1623*, ed. M. R. Best (London, 1994), ch. 8, and also for a copy of the letter from the archivist at Ripley Castle confirming that James VI and I stayed there in April 1603.

be expected to pay at least lip-service to the new union, and many, of course, did. Scottish and English poets lauded the coming together of two mighty nations, former enemies, now joined by God's providence and King James. Alexander Craig, catching the theme of the greater security offered by the union, hailed James as the 'father and a famous prince' who 'Keepes Britaine whole, least it be overthrowne'. Samuel Daniel urged England to:

> Shake hands with Union, O thou mighty State!
> Now thou art all Great Britain and no more;
> No Scot, no English now, nor no debate . . .
> Being subjects all to one Imperial Prince.[17]

What a wonderful piece of wishful thinking, as was the British imperial imagery of the great arches designed by Ben Jonson for James's ceremonial entry into London in March 1604. But lip-service it was, and no more than that. Jonson himself almost destroyed his dazzling career as the Horace and Virgil to James's Augustus before it had begun, by being one of the authors of *Eastward Ho*, with its overtly anti-Scottish jokes. And a much more powerful force than Jonson and his fellow poets stepped in to put an end to any hope of Britishness. What impact did the arches of 1604 really have when in that year James held his first parliament and was told firmly by the House of Commons that 'Great Britain' was a wholly unacceptable term?

I have pursued the theme of Anglo-Scottish hostility at length elsewhere, and will only briefly summarise here. At every level—the streets and theatres of London, the horse-races at Croydon, the court itself—the English and the Scots simply quarrelled with one another, verbally and physically, when they met. Writers and pamphleteers—Anthony Weldon, Francis Osborne, Bishop Goodman—poured out anti-Scottish vitriol. The redoubtable Lady Anne Clifford recorded in her diary her first meeting with the king in 1603 when she was thirteen, a meeting at which the king was gracious, but 'when we were all lousy by sitting in the chamber of Sir Thomas Erskine'; apparently fleas as well as Scots now assailed the English court.[18] The instances of this kind of thing are almost innumerable. And it is in that atmosphere that the king's other major policy in the first years of his reign must be set: his stated desire for a 'perfect' union, famously summed up in his call for *unus rex, unus grex, una lex*, and symbolised in his demand for the new title King of Great

---

[17] D. Laing (ed.), *The Poetical Works of Alexander Craig of Rosecraig* (Hunterian Club, 1873), p. 25; Nichols, *Progresses*, I, p. 121.
[18] Anthony Weldon, *The Court and Character of King James*, and Francis Osborne, *Traditional Memoyres of the Raigne of King James the First*, in Walter Scott (ed.), *The Secret History of the Court of King James* (Edinburgh, 1811), I, pp. 1–298, II, pp. 1–20; Godfrey Goodman, *The Court of King James*, ed. J. S. Brewer (London, 1839); *The Diary of Lady Anne Clifford*, ed. V. Sackville-West (London, 1923), p. 6.

Britain.[19] It was as unpopular as his peace with Spain. Between 1604 and 1607 it was the major issue in parliament; it produced intense disquiet outside parliament; and in the end the king failed to get his way. For his English subjects, the Scots were an alien nation, not subjects of the King of England; the loss of the name of England would be a matter of profound dishonour, and also confusion; foreigners would no longer know who the English were. Thus argued the Commons of 1604; and it was these attitudes which would prevail. And so the optimistic Scots of 1603 were, by 1607, very worried indeed, afraid that Scotland would be reduced to the provincial status of Ireland; and attitudes to union were further soured.[20]

Thus there was as little likelihood of a brave new world at home as there was in Britain's place abroad. Rather, the situation was dire, much more dire than I used to think. In modifying my views, I would now focus much less in terms of English xenophobia and in particular English dislike of the Scots, important though they were, much more on what the English lost by the union. England was, after all, already the centre of a multiple monarchy, with its satellite and reluctant kingdom of Ireland and the principality of Wales. Now it was asked to downgrade itself to become the equal partner of a smaller and poorer kingdom. Moreover, the inhabitants of that kingdom immediately showed a distinct reluctance to stay there. It would be another 160 years before Samuel Johnson produced his dictum that 'the noblest prospect which a Scotchman ever sees, is the high road that leads him to England!' and a further 150 before James Barrie claimed that 'there are few more impressive sights in the world than a Scotsman on the make'.[21] In 1603, England was abruptly awakened to Scotsmen on the make—hordes of them—pouring down that 'noblest prospect', the high road to England. For them, it was not impressive. It was terrifying. They spoke with unfamiliar and unacceptable accents. So of course did the king, as Francis Bacon pointed out. But that just had to be accepted, even if unfortunate, and Bacon was being purely descriptive. There was far more bite in Sir Thomas Howard's account in 1611 of James teaching Latin to his favourite, Robert Carr: 'I

[19] C. R. McIlwain (ed.), *The Political Works of James I* (repr. New York, 1965), p. 292: speech to the English parliament, 31 March 1607. *Stuart Proclamations*, I, pp. 94–8, 20 October 1604; asserting the title of King of Great Britain by proclamation when it had been rejected in parliament appeared as an act of arbitrary kingship which naturally worried his English subjects, as did his imposition of a British flag, the Union Jack, again by proclamation, on 12 April 1616: *ibid*, pp. 135–6.
[20] PRO SP14/7/59; *Register of the Privy Council of Scotland*, eds J. H. Burton and others (Edinburgh, 1877–), VII, p. 536. See the excellent study by B. Galloway, *The Union of England and Scotland, 1603–1608* (Edinburgh, 1986).
[21] Boswell's *Life of Johnson*, ed. G. B. Hill, revised L. F. Powell (London, 1934–50), I, p. 425; J. M. Barrie, *What Every Woman Knows* (London, 1925), p. 55.

think', said Howard sourly, 'some one should teach him English too; for as he is a Scottish lad, he hath much need of better language.'[22] The sheer sound of Scottish voices was a constant reminder that the Scots were self-confident, arrogant, demanding, high-handed and in some cases wildly extravagant. They enjoyed what the English regarded as a disproportionate amount of the king's patronage. They tried to muscle in on English jobs, at court and in government, in the church and the universities. When there was already an English employment problem, Scotsmen on the make were truly appalling.

But it was not only the unwelcome presence of the Scots that caused fear and outrage, the sense of a difficult but still ordered world now horribly disrupted. There was genuine concern, for example, that the closer union sought by the king could not be achieved because of the difference between the two churches, differences now played up in the interests of undermining union, where at the beginning of Elizabeth's reign they had been played down in the interests of encouraging Anglo-Scottish friendship. There was even concern expressed, somewhat remarkably, for the king's safety. English courtiers, English MPs, found offensive and outrageous the boldness and familiarity with which the Scots treated their king, the numbers crowding into his presence; they thought it dangerous. Naturally James, long accustomed to it, did not find it in the least dangerous. Indeed, initially he reacted against an English formality which he found excessive. In the future, Charles I, far more at home with English formality than his father had ever been, would agree with the concern of 1604; and his reaction to his over-familiar and blunt-speaking Scottish subjects would indeed be dangerous. But that is another matter.

Moreover, what about the king himself? I was first attracted to this subject because I was keenly aware of a puzzle: historiographically, James VI was a highly effective king, James I was manifestly not. Originally I argued strongly against this schizophrenic approach. But I have been thinking again about the puzzle, if in a different form. For there was a difference between James VI and James I. The Union of 1603 did have a profound impact on his style of kingship. And as he was the leading player in the attempt to make the union work, this is central to the subject.

First, though, an aside, which it is a pity to have to include. Recent scholarship should have ensured that the savage description of James I by the bitter and vengeful household official Anthony Weldon, who invented the vain, shambling, pedantic, cowardly, unwashed buffoon who for so long dominated English historiography, is no longer taken seriously. Sadly, it is back, in

---

[22] Bacon's comment—that James's 'speech is swift and cursory, and in the full dialect of his country'—is quoted in D. H. Willson, *King James VI and I* (London, 1965), p. 166; Howard's stricture, in R. Ashton, *James I by his Contemporaries* (London, 1969), p. 238.

one of the two books on the king published in 2003 to mark the union, that by Alan Stewart, which may be widely read and, worse, believed. Stewart's James is Weldon's cowardly James, the king 'nurtured in fear', who never really wanted to face up to 'the harsh realities of kingship'.[23] Is there any validity in this? James was a coward because he wore great padded breeches, for fear of the assassin's knife; has anyone ever suggested that as the reason for the grotesque circumference of Elizabeth's skirts? James was a coward because he had no taste for martial displays, as Sir John Oglander, otherwise an admirer, recalled. Indeed he disliked war intensely, and was quite open and unrepentant about it. But this was the king who, to the great relief of his Catholic subjects, kept his head amidst the hysteria which surrounded that attempt at wholesale murder by a small group of fanatical terrorists, known as the Gunpowder Plot. This was the king who had seen the assassinations of William of Orange, two kings of France, two Guise brothers, the mightiest aristocrats of Europe, and been the intended victim of both Gunpowder and the Gowrie conspiracy, and who yet refused to have a guard, on the grounds that the love of his people was the best guard for princes. This was the king who, despite spectacular and dangerous falls, never lost his taste for spectacular and dangerous feats of horsemanship. And this cowardly creature was the king who at his own request climbed onto the walls of Berwick on his journey south in 1603, to be very gracious to the soldiers and gunners, and to fire off a cannon himself, apparently very proficiently.[24] James was no coward. What the legend of cowardice tells us is not about King James, but about the English desire for a martial king.

What about reality? Allowing for flattery, the initial accounts by his new English subjects give a very recognisable portrait of the king who was the highly successful James VI, affable, cheerful, witty, relaxed and greeting them with a courteous familiarity. Why then does it become increasingly difficult thereafter to see that figure? For all his undoubted political skills and intelligence, the answer surely lies in the fact that he never really coped with being King of England, just as the English never really coped with their king from Scotland. We can turn English concern on its head and say that what was dangerous for King James was not Scottish familiarity but English flattery. He was in his mid-thirties when he came to England, with long experience of rule, a high and confident sense of his kingship. But this was the king whose sleeve Andrew Melville, leading presbyterian and religious opponent of the king, had famously plucked in the course of one of their furious rows, calling

[23] Alan Stewart, *The Cradle King: A Life of James VI and I* (London, 2003). A far better work written to mark the quatercentenary is Pauline Croft, *King James* (Basingstoke, 2003).
[24] Nichols, *Progresses*, I, pp. 65–6.

him 'God's sillie vassall'.[25] That he could deal with. What he had never encountered, and could not deal with, was the excessive adulation with which Elizabethan courtiers had been carefully trained to treat their monarch. In his sermon of 1605 celebrating the king's delivery from the Gunpowder Plot, William Barlow described him as:

> An universall Scholer, acute in arguing, subtle in distinguishing, Logical in discussing, plentifull in inventing, powerfull in perswading, admirable in discoursing . . . a sound Expositor, a faithfull Christian, and a constant Professor, or affectuall, for Regeneration, an assiduous prayer, a chast husband, of sweet carriage, of humble deportment, of mortified lusts, of sanctified life.[26]

Sir Francis Phelips, writing in 1622 to plead for his brother's release from the Tower for speaking against Spain, opened his letter: 'Most dreade soveraigne. Yf the Thrones of heaven & earth were to be solicited one and the same way, I should have . . . knowne howe to pray to your Majesty', and ended 'ffinally that your felicity in this world may overtake you in the next and make you weare a perpetuall crowne of gods glory and your owne'.[27] No Scottish sermon, no Scottish letter, had ever gone to these lengths. It was no doubt this sort of thing which made a pessimistic Scotsman snarl in 1603 that 'this people will spoil a gud king'.[28] 'Spoil' is not necessarily the right word; but it certainly changed him.

Initially he recognised the trap in which he was floundering, the combination of intense flattery and intense efforts to thwart him. As early as 1604, he told the English parliament that 'in my government bypast in Scotland (where I ruled men not of the best temper) I was heard not only as a king but as a counsellor. Contrary here nothing but curiosity from morning to evening to find fault with my propositions.'[29] In 1607, he protested bitterly that he had been misled over the union project, encouraged to believe that it would be welcome; he was not, in England, allowed clearly to hear dissenting voices, as he had been able to do in Scotland. But who is ever wholly impervious to flattery? And as he became older, he seems increasingly to have listened to the siren voices and begun to lose his sureness of political touch. He certainly lost his sense of humour; pomposity began to creep into his view of himself and his kingship. His *Meditation on . . . the XXVII Chapter of St Matthew*, writ-

[25] David Calderwood, *The True History of the Church of Scotland* (Wodrow Society, Edinburgh, 1842–9), V, p. 440.

[26] William Barlow, *The sermon preached at Paules Crosse, the tenth day of November, being the next Sunday after the discoverie of this late horrible treason* (London, 1606), f.E2v–E3r. I am very grateful to Mr Benjamin Prance for this reference.

[27] Folger MS V.b.303, pp. 239–41.

[28] Arthur Wilson, *The History of Great Britain, being the Life and Reign of King James the First* (London, 1653), p. 3.

[29] SP14/8/93.

ten in 1619, is a deeply distressing work, far removed from the dynamic, pithy earlier writings of this master of prose, and toppling over almost into blasphemy in its comparison of his kingly cares with the sufferings of Christ.[30] He was still formidably active in foreign affairs. But his close association with Gondomar and his tendency to distance himself from his English critics suggests a growing remoteness from the close involvement in domestic politics which had been such a hallmark of James VI and the James I of the first years after 1603.

Yet even in the early years a change was detectable. The king took on an entirely new persona: Jove, the hurler of thunderbolts. Thus he is represented in 1607 in Jonson's masque extolling union, *Hymenaei*; thus he appears again in Shakespeare's union play, *Cymbeline*, written by 1610. Thus, much more menacingly, he was beginning to appear to English MPs. There were the thunderbolts of his proclamation of 1604 when he assumed the title of King of Great Britain denied him by parliament, and that of 1606 whereby he created the union flag. These apparently arbitrary acts were made no better when in 1610 he had the book of his proclamations printed; this was a king who appeared to give too much weight to his own will as expressed through proclamation rather than parliament. Then there was his speech of March 1607 when he twice described himself as *lex loquens*, a concept repeated in May 1610, when once again he seemed to put himself above the law.[31] His ideas were of course traced back to his Scottish kingship, where his two great political tracts on divine-right monarchy, *Basilikon Doron* and *The Trew Law of Free Monarchies*, had been written in 1598–9. But the first was in fact in the advice to princes tradition, written for his son and heir Henry, the second his contribution to the European debate on the source of legitimacy of kingship, begun by the resistance writers of the 1570s with their theories of contractual kingship.[32] The striking fact is that neither disturbed the Scots as they did the English.

This was not the only aspect of his style of rule which became an issue after 1603 where it had not been before. The huntsman and scholar had been as much in evidence in Scotland as they would be in England. But they were

---

[30] *A Meditation upon the 27, 28, 29 Verses of the XXVII Chapter of St Matthew, or A paterne for a Kings inauguration* (London, 1620), printed in J. P. Sommerville (ed.), *King James VI and I: Political Writings* (Cambridge, 1994), pp. 229–49.

[31] McIlwain, *Political Works*, pp. 291, 309.

[32] The texts are printed in McIlwain, *Political Works*, pp. 3–52, 53–70, and Sommerville, *Political Writings*, pp. 1–61, 62–84. These are good and accessible editions, Sommerville's in English. The fullest editions, with their variant texts and extensive notes, remain J. Craigie (ed.), *Basilikon Doron of King James VI* (Scottish Text Society, Edinburgh, 1944–50) and *The Trew Law of Free Monarchies* in J. Craigie and A. Law (eds), *Minor Prose Works of King James VI and I* (Scottish Text Society, Edinburgh, 1982).

never such an object of concern and criticism. Some Scots—Andrew
Melville, David Hume of Godscroft[33]—profoundly disagreed with his ideas,
but in general the Scots did not feel that their government was threatened by
the king's inclination to go off on regular hunting expeditions or to shut himself into his study. The greater weight of government business in England no
doubt had much to do with the concern; much more important was the perception of a remote king, out of touch with his new kingdom. The theme of
the dangers to the state when the ruler abandoned his responsibilities was of
course not confined to Jacobean drama. But it undoubtedly had a topical
resonance in James's reign. It is there in *The Tempest* itself. Prospero lost his
dukedom of Milan to his usurping brother Antonio because he:

> The prime duke, being so reputed
> In dignity, and for the liberal arts
> Without a parallel; those being all my study,
> The government I cast upon my brother . . .
>   (I. ii)[34]

So the political theorist, huntsman and scholar worried the English far
more than the Scots, and this, beneath the initial cloak of civility, produced
strong doubts about his kingship, expressed in dramatic as well as political
criticism. Shakespeare's *Macbeth* of 1606 may have been a compliment to the
royal daemonologist, although if so it was an out-of-date one, given James's
change of heart in 1596–7 about witches. But it has been persuasively argued
that by emphasising James's descent from the non-royal Banquo living at a
time of chaos, and by raising issues about good kingship not only with the
tyrannical Macbeth but also with the apparent hero Malcolm, Shakespeare
was already sounding a warning note to or about James.[35] His *Cymbeline* is a
much more ambivalent discourse on James's kingship than its ending suggests.[36] *The Tempest* has been regarded as a colonial play, but the idea of
union is surely central. Miranda says to Ferdinand 'Yes, for a score of kingdoms you should wrangle, And I would call it fair play' (V. i). Wrangling over
kingdoms? The scholar duke? The masque? Surely these invoked not

[33] P. J. McGinnis and A. H. Williamson (eds), *The British Union: a Critical Edition and
Translation of David Hume of Godscroft's De Unione Insulae Britannicae* (Aldershot, 2002); the
introduction is an excellent discussion of the ideas of James's critics.
[34] *The Tempest*, ed. Orgel, p. 105.
[35] Sally Mapstone, 'Shakespeare and Scottish Kingship: a Case History', in Sally Mapstone and
Juliette Wood (eds), *The Rose and the Thistle: Essays on the Culture of Late Medieval and
Renaissance Scotland* (East Linton, 1998), pp. 158–93.
[36] Leah Marcus, '*Cymbeline* and the unease of topicality', in H. Dubrow and R. Strier (eds), *The
Historical Renaissance: New Essays on Tudor and Stuart Literature and Culture* (Chicago, 1988),
pp. 134–68.

Virginia, but the king, his court at Whitehall and his multiple kingdoms.[37] The King's Men had much to hope for from James, as the company who, under Lawrence Fletcher, had enjoyed great success when he invited them to Scotland before 1603, and who now had, in James and Anna, far more generous patrons than the parsimonious Elizabeth. Yet they were engaged in exploring the issues of Jacobean authority and Jacobean union. We can only guess at audience responses. But it is worth speculating about the response when Miranda turned to the audience and proclaimed 'O brave new world'.

But why was this king of proven ability creating doubts in men's minds so early on, why did this hardheaded Scot give way to English flattery, however tempting? We come back to the union. The king was in an intolerable position. The King of England simply could not bow to English expectations and forget his ancient kingdom. Nor did he want to. He had no alternative, therefore, other than to attempt the impossible and bring the Scots and English together. He failed because he was bound to fail. His vision of an incorporating union was not what he was really trying to bring about, because he was far too shrewd to believe that it could be realised; it was, rather, an initial negotiating position, which enabled him to achieve something, in terms of naturalisation and free trade. But he did want to create an Anglo-Scottish court and an Anglo-Scottish government; and here he had to admit defeat. In the first years of his English reign, one of the leading Scottish politicians, the Earl of Dunbar, was a genuinely Anglo-Scottish figure, moving between Edinburgh and London, but after his death in 1611 the king dealt separately with his governments north and south of the border. Only the Duke of Lennox, as steward of the household, was a prominent Scottish member of his English court.

It is easy to see why his larger vision did not work. In 1603, Cecil clearly thought that he was complimenting his new master when he thanked him for sending Lord Kinloss ahead of him to London; Kinloss was, he said, 'already so good an Englishman'. Lord Keeper Egerton, full of enthusiasm for 'that blessed worke the Union', gave his real feelings away when he endorsed a letter to Francis Bacon which advocated a history of Britain; the endorsement read 'touching the history of England'.[38] There was simply no will for James's British solution. The attitudes of both the king and the English are readily understandable, but they forced a collision course. In fighting for union, James now appeared to put his theory into practice, as he had not done in Scotland; and politicians and common lawyers—Edward Sandys, Nicholas Fuller, Edward Coke and others—began to see in him the tyranny of France

---

[37] *The Tempest*, ed. Orgel, p. 197; Tristan Marshall, '*The Tempest* and the British Imperium in 1611', *Historical Journal* 41 (1998), pp. 375–400.
[38] SP14/1/18, f.38r; Henry E. Huntington Library, Bridgewater and Ellesmere MSS, EL 162, 126.

and Spain. Whatever the extent of the structural problems of English government before 1603, they took on a new dimension under the impact of an
extravagant Scottish king and his Scots in London. There is a sense of unease
and dislocation in James's reign, marvellously encapsulated by one of the
Scottish poets, Robert Aytoun (or Ayton), who accompanied him south:

> The other night from Court returning late
> Tyr'd with attendance, out of love with state
> I mett a boy who ask't if he should goe
> A long to light mee home, I told him noe
> Yet he did urge the darkness of the night
> The foulness of the way requir'd a light
> Its true, good boy, quoth I, yet thou mayst be
> More usefull to some other then to mee.
> I cannot miss my way, but they that take
> The way from whence I came, have neede to make
> A light there guide, for I dare boldly say
> Its ten to one, but they shall lose there way.[39]

'Out of love with state.' But the Scot could still cope, did not need the light.
It was the English who were blundering in the dark.

And so recognition that flattery had misled him, frustration, alienation,
perhaps even an element of despair, first produced a heavy-handed application of theory to practice and then made the king more susceptible to the way
out, indulgence in the soothing balm of flattery. Sadly, this also had an effect
on his Scottish subjects. English endorsement of his idea that kings were lofty
creatures showed up very quickly. For his Scottish parliament, he was no
longer 'our soverane lord', that phrase with a very long tradition; he was now
'his sacred majesty'. His attempt in 1609 to nominate the Lords of the Articles, the committee elected in parliament to deal with the detailed drawing up
of bills, which he suggested would be convenient, was successfully resisted;
James had had a lot of success in the 1590s in managing that outspoken and
difficult body, the Scottish parliament, but this was going too far and only
reflected the beginnings of the loss of his sureness of political touch. That
was only confirmed by his offensive changes in liturgical practice, the Five
Articles of Perth, introduced to bring greater 'congruity' between the
churches of England and Scotland;[40] the Articles were forced through an
unwilling General Assembly in 1618 and, by a new and threatening level of
manipulation, parliament in 1621. Yet he never did alienate his Scottish sub-

---

[39] C. B. Gullans (ed.), *The English and Latin Poems of Sir Robert Ayton* (Scottish Text Society,
Edinburgh, 1963), p. 193.
[40] John Morrill, 'Introduction', in J. Morrill (ed.), *The Scottish National Covenant in its British
Context, 1638–51* (Edinburgh, 1990), p. 8.

jects. He made his continuing interest in Scotland clear, keeping up a constant correspondence with his councillors which demonstrated that, unlike his successor Charles I, he understood the nature of his kingdom and was, for much of the time, still willing to listen; and he had the great good fortune that, apart from Dunbar, those with whom he had worked in the 1590s lived on into the 1620s. These were the men who remembered the king who was James VI, and who were aware, as the reign drew to a close, of what they would lose. There was real pathos in the lament of the Earl of Kellie to the Earl of Mar in November 1623 that 'It maye cume that young folks'—primarily Charles and Buckingham—'shall have their world. I know not if that wilbe fitt for your Lordshipe and me.'[41] After James's death, it would not be fit.

Nevertheless, even in Scotland and certainly in England, union was not a happy experience. It was grim. So why did this fragile union not go the way of so many others and collapse? Why did we celebrate its quatercentenary in 2003?

An obvious answer is that it was very difficult to break because the paucity of Tudor heirs led to the sheer problem of finding different kings for England and Scotland. The only time when there was a chance of ending the union came in 1649, when the Rump Parliament would have allowed Charles II to succeed his father as King of Scotland, while England became a republic.[42] That would certainly have solved the problem of finding two monarchs for England and Scotland. But as neither Charles nor the Scots would accept it, insisting instead that Charles was King of Britain, the idea lapsed, and, ironically, Cromwell imposed a greater degree of union than had been the case hitherto, when he briefly created a single British parliament. By the early eighteenth century, when relations between England and Scotland had worsened to the point where the Scots were certainly contemplating the end of the union, the same problem arose. In 1703, the Scottish parliament passed the Act of Security which said that if Anne died childless, parliament would elect the next king of Scotland, who might not be the same as her successor in England. But as the act insisted on that king being of the royal blood of Scotland and of the Protestant religion, the Catholic Stuarts were cut out, leaving no alternative to James's granddaughter, the Electress Sophia, mother of the future George I, whose succession was already acknowledged by the English Act of Succession. There are to this day various Stuart descendants littering Europe and claiming to be the true heir to the British throne. But that is not a serious consideration.

---

[41] Historical Manuscripts Commission, *Mar and Kellie MSS* (London, 1930), II, p. 183.
[42] This is a point which I owe to John Morrill, who first put it into my surprised head, and convinced me.

Moreover, even in the uncertain period of its initial years, <u>union</u>, however <u>unpopular</u>, was a political reality which had to be accommodated. <u>However they might try to pretend otherwise and force the king to act as ruler of two separate kingdoms, the leading politicians on both sides of the border, the two councils, the parliaments and the churches, could not in fact continue to function as separate entities</u>. Cecil, for example, seeking to maintain under James the political dominance he had enjoyed in Elizabeth's last years, took the obvious step of giving patronage to the Scots. 'Scotsmen on the make' naturally responded with enthusiasm to what was on offer, very quickly learning the excessively flowery English language of patronage and clientage, to the extent that one grateful client, Lord Roxburgh, wrote Cecil a letter so convoluted as to defy understanding.[43] Although Dunbar was not replaced, his very existence in the first eight years of union was a potent reminder, in England and Scotland, of how the world had changed; and it was Dunbar's chaplain George Abbott who succeeded that late Elizabethan hangover Richard Bancroft as Archbishop of Canterbury in 1610. James's Scottish councillors, men like Alexander, Earl of Dunfermline and Thomas, Earl of Melrose, kept up a correspondence not only with the king but with his English councillors. Both councils and both parliaments had to discuss the nature of the union. In 1615, James's English councillors, frantic, as usual, about the state of the king's finances, even tried to capitalise on union when they sought to persuade Lennox to have a Scottish parliament summoned, in the hope that this might encourage James to summon an English one, despite the disaster of the Addled Parliament of 1614. <u>Full diocesan episcopacy was reintroduced to the Scottish church after 1610, and that, along with the Five Articles of Perth, lessened, though did not eradicate, the differences between the two churches</u>, however unpopular and fragile the new arrangements were, as Charles I would fatally discover. None of this made union particularly appealing. What it did do, crucially, was to inculcate the idea of union into men's minds, and begin to establish habits of thought which made it possible to conceive of the British Isles as having some sort of unity.

But above all, the greatest saving grace was that the union was, and remained, so ramshackle. There has never been a fixed and abiding constitutional solution to what the union actually was. Since 1603, Britain has lurched from one constitutional model to another, however ill-defined. The Union of the Crowns of 1603 left huge unanswered questions. The Union of the Parliaments and the creation of James's dreamed-of kingdom of Great Britain in 1707 certainly defies definition; brought into being when the <u>Union of the Crowns was visibly unsustainable</u>, it is neither a federal union, given

43 SP14/8/7, 2 May 1604.

the existence of a single British parliament, nor an incorporating one, given the existence of separate churches and legal and educational systems, which neatly eradicated the fears about James's unifying policy after 1603. Different political pressures in the late twentieth century have brought into being a devolved Scottish parliament and a Welsh assembly—and different voting systems in Westminster, Edinburgh, and Cardiff. No doubt there will be further changes. Pragmatic solutions, as a means of survival, have a lot to be said for them.

In one episode of *This Week*, the Andrew Neil, Diane Abbott and Michael Portillo political chat-show, Diane Abbott claimed that there were an awful lot of Scots in the government—shades of the perceptions of 1603—and that government matters were complicated by their curious Scottish bloodfeuds. I was entranced, because the early modern Scottish bloodfeud and its own particular form of justice were a major theme of my original research—and of course much looked down on, despite its visible advantages as a force for keeping the peace, by early modern English lawyers and politicians. Diane Abbott's comment reminded me that in many ways the English and the Scots still do not really understand one another, and certainly have not become one nation; and the same can be said of the Welsh and the northern Irish. Yet the union survives. For all the difficulties he encountered, the fundamental credit for that surely goes to its original architect, James VI and I, who brought it into being in 1603 and maintained it for almost a quarter of a century, long enough to make it just believable, and even perhaps vaguely acceptable. So when celebrating the fourth centenary of that momentous event, the toast was certainly to King James.

Note. I would like to thank Professor T. C. Smout for all his editorial patience and help, and Dr Sally Mapstone and Dr Margaret Kean for invaluable advice when this paper was being written. I also want to thank my son Luke, himself a historian, for his fortitude in reading and commenting on successive drafts, to my considerable advantage.

3

A Blessed Union? Anglo-Scottish Relations before the Covenant

KEITH BROWN

WHAT ARE WE TO MAKE OF THE REGAL UNION OF 1603 AFTER FOUR HUNDRED YEARS? At a popular level it is probably true to say it is an event that does not greatly excite the public imagination. Nevertheless, in Scotland the four hundredth anniversary opened up political wounds that were surprising and comic in equal measure. The problem for government in 2003, as in 1603, lay in how to represent this happening to the general public. On the BBC website, which to the casual enquirer might be seen as the UK's most accessible official history, we are told that:

> King James compared himself to a beast with one head and two bodies. The monarchs, who stayed in London after the Union of the Crowns, found it difficult to control Scotland, and, eventually, the problem was solved by the Act of Union in 1707.[1]

The interesting point about this text lies in the last phrase, in which the regal union of 1603 is perceived as creating a problem of government, one that was only solved by a later and more complete—a seventeenth-century text would have said 'perfect'—union. Of course, this is the *British* Broadcasting Corporation. Turning to a very different and Scottish organisation that views history as a commercial product within the heritage business, Scotland's tourist industry also has a negative view of the regal union with England. However, unlike the BBC it has no truck with unionist ideology. On its website at http://www.visitscotland.com we are faced with a nationalist interpretation that tells us that after James VI headed south in 1603, 'inevitably Scotland came to be regarded as a political backwater', and that his absence 'created a cultural vacuum at the heart of the nation'. According to Scotland's tourism gurus, primary indicators of this decline into playing second fiddle to

[1] www.bbc.co.uk/history/timelines/scotland/union_crowns.shtml

Proceedings of the British Academy, **127**, 37–55. © The British Academy 2005.

England were the displacement of the Scots language with English and the
crowning of the present monarch as Elizabeth II. To quote this authority
again, Scotland's 'national identity itself even began to be called into question once the Scottish king, symbol and guarantor of Scotland's independence, proved himself to be an absentee monarch'.[2] As is so often the case, here
we find Scotland being marketed as a victim, as a place to visit in spite of all
the bad things done to it by others.

Of course, none of this should matter since the Union of the Crowns
took place a long time ago. That might be correct in England, where 2003
was seen as marking the quatercentenary of the death of Elizabeth I, the end
of the Tudor dynasty, and the closing of an age of English genius. Surely the
'Elizabeth' exhibition at Greenwich was at one level a reflection of English
denial of what happened in 1603? In Scotland, the focus for 2003 was on the
regal union, but the question of what to do to mark its anniversary proved
divisive. In May 2002, the Scottish Nationalist Party warned that the union
must not be celebrated at a time close to the parliamentary elections, and it
continued to hammer away at this theme over the following months.
Demanding that the Queen stay out of politics, the Nationalists suggested
that any official memorialisation of the union prior to the May 2003 elections
would be a flouting of electoral law. However, the First Minister, Jack
McConnell, announced in November 2002 that the regal union would be
celebrated as part of an unfolding package of events. This odd cultural sand-
wich included slices of unionist bread to mark the Union of the Crowns in
2003 and the Union of the Parliaments in 2007, while the meat in the middle
of the delicacy was to be the anniversary of the execution of William Wallace
in 2005. Of course, the SNP was not pleased at this juxtaposition of their
iconic hero with such blatantly unionist celebrations, and 'Union Jack' as the
First Minister was now dubbed, pressed on, delighting the Scottish Tories
with his assertion that 'The events of 1603 led to the best-known royal family
in the world today.' That stunning summation of the significance of the regal
union left Scotland's Old Labour remnant cringing, but the Conservatives
offered a slightly more refined, if predictable, analysis, arguing that 1603 'signalled a momentous turning point in the relationship between Scotland and
England', leading in due course to centuries of peace and prosperity. Yet even
their leader, David McLetchie, was later to write: 'By the common consent of
historians, the century after 1603 was quite the worst in Scottish history, with
constitutional conflict, intellectual intolerance, sectarian violence and witch-
hunts.' Historians of the fourteenth century might wish to disagree. By January
2003, little had been agreed other than that the town of Berwick would mark

---

[2] www.visitscotland.com/aboutscotland/history/historyunionofthecrowns

the occasion with a programme of events largely designed to boost tourism in the area. Indeed, the local Liberal Democrat MP, Sir Archy Kirkwood, did advance the argument that 1603 'was a blessing for everyone, bringing peace and prosperity to this area in particular'. Meanwhile, it was February 2003, following questions in the House of Commons, before the Scottish Executive plucked up enough courage to establish an advisory group in the face of continuing SNP objections that it was attempting to 'rewrite history in the style of the old Soviet Union'. When that advisory group announced its preliminary plans in March it was immediately attacked for targeting children with 'pro-union propaganda'. On 30 March, *The Guardian*, that most English of newspapers, ran a story under the title 'UK's birthday marked by a lack of celebration' in which the focus was entirely on the Scottish parliament's unwillingness to recognise the event. In the mind of that newspaper's columnist this reticence was a consequence of the apparent decline in British identity among Scots. The fact that England and the Westminster parliament also ignored the occasion was not thought worthy of comment. In the end, only Berwick, the ping-pong town of the Anglo-Scottish wars of the Middle Ages, seized the opportunity to exploit the occasion at the beginning of April, though the Queen herself celebrated the union at a dinner in Edinburgh on 2 July, following her visit to the Scottish parliament. The short-lived advisory committee was wound up.[3]

This background of muddle and farce is amusing, although it does highlight some of the cultural warfare currently attaching itself to Scottish History. At the centre of this civil conflict between rival Scottish factions is the relationship with England, indeed some might argue that the very question of Scottish identity is defined in terms of that relationship. Of course, it is intensely irritating to the Scots that the English are not even aware of the fact that there is a relationship. Here, perhaps, lies a reason for the utter invisibility of any marking of the Union of the Crowns in England beyond the limits of plucky Berwick. However, indifference is a state of mind that is more acceptable than hostility, the posture commonly assumed to exist between both kingdoms before 1603.

---

[3] *The Times*, 27 May 2002, p. 13; 8 November 2002, p. 9; 20 January 2003, p. 2; 3 March 2003, p. 6; 1 April 2003, p. 19; *The Scotsman*, 27 May 2002, p. 7; 13 September 2002, p. 3; 21 January 2003, p. 2; 24 March 2003, p. 11; 5 June 2003, p. 19; 2 July 2003, p. 6; *The Herald*, 8 November 2002, p. 5; 7 February 2003, p. 8; 9 July 2003, p. 9; *Scotland on Sunday*, 10 November 2002, p. 20; 23 March 2003, p. 22; *Guardian Unlimited*, 30 March 2003 at http://observer.guardian. co.uk/politics/story/0,6903,925694,00.html; *Scottish Executive News Online*, 2 March 2003 at http://www.scotland.gov.uk/pages/news/2003/03/SETCS152.aspx; *BBC News UK Edition*, 2 March 2003 at http://news.bbc.co.uk/1/hi/scotland/ 2812579.stm; 7 April 2003 at http://news.bbc.co.uk/ 1/hi/england/2923587.stm; *The United Kingdom Parliament*, 13 February 2003 at http://www. parliament.the-stationery-office.co.uk/pa/cm200203/cmhansrd/cm

In looking at the prospects for success in 1603 it might be useful to review, briefly, the medieval inheritance of Anglo-Scottish relations. Undoubtedly, the fourteenth-century Wars of Independence hugely influenced the development of late medieval Scotland, leaving the Scots with a legacy of popular distrust of England. Rising levels of literacy created an expanding market among the public for Blind Harry's *The Wallace* and John Barbour's *Bruce*, ensuring that the conflict with England was relived by each new generation of readers. By contrast, in England the wars were largely forgotten or ignored outside the northern counties. From the later fourteenth century the threat to Scotland of English conquest receded, and over the course of the succeeding decades the Scots gradually won an unglamorous, drawn-out and sporadic Border war.[4] The marriage of James IV and Margaret Tudor in 1503 appeared to usher in a new phase of Anglo-Scottish co-operation, although this proved to be an over-optimistic ambition. Instead, the first half of the sixteenth century saw a retreat into suspicion, hostility and intermittent warfare. In the 1540s, Henry VIII resurrected antiquarian English claims to overlordship, indulging in a wasteful series of campaigns to reduce Scotland to a form of dependency.[5] From a Scottish perspective, the late medieval inheritance, therefore, was a memory of warfare and of English aggression.

Yet, by 1603 the English as enemy was fading in terms of lived experiences and was becoming a culturally constructed memory informed by a particular brand of patriotic history. Thus even in the early seventeenth century Scottish noble families continued to glorify the martial deeds of their ancestors in wars against the English, but this outburst of patriotism had little to do with contemporary politics, or attitudes towards their English neighbours. When in the early 1600s the 66-year-old Sir James Melville of Halhill wrote his memoirs he must have been one of only a few men alive who could remember the 'furious wair betwen the twa contrees' when he was a boy.[6] It

---

[4] For the Wars of Independence and their aftermath see R. Nicholson, *Scotland: the Later Middle Ages* (Edinburgh, 1974); A. Grant, *Independence and Nationhood: Scotland 1306–1469* (London, 1984); G. Barrow, *Robert Bruce and the Community of the Realm* (Edinburgh, 1982); C. MacNamee, *The Wars of the Bruces: Scotland, England and Ireland 1306–1328* (East Linton, 1997); F. Watson, *Under the Hammer: Edward I and Scotland 1286–1307* (East Linton, 1998); A. J. MacDonald, *Border Bloodshed: Scotland and England at War 1369–1403* (East Linton, 2000); M. Brown, *The Black Douglases* (East Linton, 1998); A. Goodman, 'The Anglo-Scottish marches in the fifteenth century: a frontier society', in R. A. Mason (ed.), *Scotland and England 1286–1815* (Edinburgh, 1987), pp. 18–33; C. Neville, *Violence, Custom and Law: the Anglo-Scottish Border Lands in the Later Middle Ages* (Edinburgh, 1998).
[5] For the warfare see G. Phillips, *The Anglo-Scots Wars 1513–1550* (Woodbridge, 1999); M. Merriman, *The Rough Wooings: Mary Queen of Scots 1542–1551* (East Linton, 2000).
[6] K. M. Brown, *Noble Society in Scotland: Wealth, Family and Culture from Reformation to Revolution* (Edinburgh, 2000), pp. 222–4; R. Gordon, *Genealogical History of the Earldom of Sutherland* (Edinburgh, 1813); D. Reid (ed.), *David Hume of Godscroft's The History of the House of Douglas*, 2 vols (Scottish Text Society, 4th series, Edinburgh, 1996), pp. 25–6; J. Melville, *Memoirs of His Own Time, 1549–93*, ed. T. Thomson (Bannatyne Club 18, 1827), p. 9.

is worth recalling that by the time James VI came into his English inheritance there had been no serious warfare between his two kingdoms for over half a century. Leaving aside minor Border incidents, the last significant battle had been Pinkie in 1547 and the last English occupying troops had departed Scotland following the Treaty of Norham in 1551. To regard England as Scotland's natural enemy in 1603 would be akin to contemporary Britons looking at Germany as a hereditary enemy, a point of view found only in the more distasteful ranks of English football supporters. Instead, for early modern Scots and English their shared history was one of an increasingly close working relationship. English armies intervened to aid Scottish Protestants in 1560 and to help the King's Party in the civil warfare of the early 1570s. A handful of Scottish nobles were in receipt of English pensions from the 1560s and James VI became a pensioner of Elizabeth I in the 1580s. The Anglo-Scottish League was signed in 1586, smoothing the way for Mary's execution in the following year, and ensuring a semi-coordinated response to the Spanish Armada in 1588. During the 1590s, inter-governmental agreements over Border incidents tightened up procedures for dealing with violent crime and theft, paving the way for the Border commission that followed union.[7] A shared language, a common Protestantism, and improved trade all served to reduce tensions and remove barriers, while ideas about Britain had achieved a sufficient degree of exposure over the course of the sixteenth century to be familiar at least in educated and court circles, although it is difficult to gauge how far those ideas impacted on practical politics.[8] The road-map to peace was well trodden long before James VI crossed the Tweed in the spring of 1603, and

---

[7] M. Lee, *John Maitland of Thirlestane and the Foundation of Stewart Despotism in Scotland* (Princeton, 1959); K. M. Brown, 'The price of friendship: the "well affected" and English economic clientage in Scotland before 1603', in Mason (ed.), *Scotland and England*, pp. 139–62; J. Goodare, 'James VI's English subsidy', in J. Goodare and M. Lynch (eds), *The Reign of James VI* (Edinburgh, 2000), pp. 110–25; T. I. Rae, *The Administration of the Scottish Frontier 1513–1603* (Edinburgh, 1966), pp. 193–224.

[8] J. Dawson, 'Anglo-Scottish Protestant culture and integration in sixteenth-century Britain', in S. Ellis and S. Barber (eds), *Conquest and Union: Fashioning a British State 1485–1725* (London, 1995), pp. 87–114; R. A. Mason, 'The Scottish Reformation and the origins of Anglo-Scottish imperialism', in R. A. Mason (ed.), *Scots and Britons: Scottish Political Thought and the Union of 1603* (Cambridge, 1994), pp. 161–86. On sixteenth-century ideas about Britain see A. H. Williamson, *Scottish National Consciousness in the Age of James VI* (Edinburgh, 1979); A. H. Williamson, 'Scotland, antichrist and the invention of Great Britain', in J. Dwyer, R. A. Mason and A. Murdoch (eds), *New Perspectives on the Politics and Culture of Early Modern Scotland* (Edinburgh, 1982), pp. 34–58; R. A. Mason, 'Scotching the Brut: politics, history and national myth in sixteenth-century Scotland', in Mason (ed.), *Scotland and England*, pp. 60–84; R. M. Merriman, 'James Henrisoun and "Great Britain": British union and the Scottish common-weal', in Mason (ed.), *Scotland and England*, pp. 85–112; R. A. Mason, *Kingship and the Commonweal: Political Thought in Renaissance and Reformation Scotland* (East Linton, 1998), chs 2 and 9.

if regal union represented an Anglo-Scottish marriage, this middle-aged couple had been living together for the better part of forty years.

What of the opening decades of regal union? Among the more distinguishing, and undervalued, characteristics of early Stuart Britain is its freedom from war, a feature of the period that contributed to the success of the regal union.[9] Scotland had no experience of international conflict between 1551 and the very limited involvement in Charles I's wars with France and Spain in 1625–9. By the 1630s, very few European states could claim along with Scotland to have enjoyed such a prolonged period of freedom from international warfare on its own territory. In fact, the Scots had not enjoyed such a long era of sustained international peace since the thirteenth century, nor would they experience it again until the end of the Napoleonic Wars. For England, the peace dividend with Scotland brought about the final closing of the feared 'postern gate' in 1586, a major achievement for Tudor diplomacy that made the country a good deal more secure. It was much more difficult for any other country to attempt to destabilise or weaken England by using Scotland as a proxy as had been done by France repeatedly until 1560, and as Spain attempted to do in the 1580s and 1590s.[10] James VI and I determined to end England's costly wars, while the series of treaties with Spain, France, and the United Provinces, the conclusion of the rebellion in Ireland, and the cultivation of a network of relationships throughout the Baltic region arguably amounted to the imposition of a Scottish foreign policy that kept England at peace for most of the remainder of James's reign.[11]

However, peace was unpopular with a significant cross-section of public opinion in England that resented the retreat from militant Protestantism and maritime aggression. The festering resentment at the abandonment of Elizabethan potency finally resulted in unsuccessful wars with both France and Spain in 1625–9.[12] There was no such pressure for foreign entanglement

---

[9] This point is made in C. Russell, 'James VI and I and rule over two kingdoms: an English view', *Historical Research* 76 (2003), p. 153.

[10] For an overview of the extent to which Elizabethan England was consumed by warfare see P. E. J. Hammer, *Elizabeth's Wars* (Basingstoke, 2003).

[11] M. Lee, *Great Britain's Solomon: James VI and I in His Three Kingdoms* (Urbana, 1990), pp. 261–98; S. Murdoch, *Britain, Denmark-Norway and the House of Stuart 1603–1660: a Diplomatic and Military Analysis* (East Linton, 2003); S. Murdoch, 'Diplomacy in transition: Stuart-British diplomacy in northern Europe, 1603–1618', in A. I. Macinnes, T. Riis, and F. Pederson (eds), *Ships, Guns and Bibles in the North Sea and Baltic States* (East Linton, 2000), pp. 93–114; S. Murdoch, 'Scottish ambassadors and British diplomacy', in S. Murdoch (ed.), *Scotland and the Thirty Years War 1618–1648* (Leiden, 2001), pp. 27–50; W. B. Patterson, *James VI and I and the Reunion of Christendom* (Cambridge, 1997).

[12] C. Russell, *Parliaments and English Politics, 1621–1629* (Oxford, 1979), pp. 70–203; T. Cogswell, *The Blessed Revolution: English Politics and the Coming of War, 1621–1624* (Cambridge, 1989).

from Scotland. The Scottish government's attitude to war was shaped largely by its adverse impact on European trade, and it preferred to watch from the sidelines while colluding in the supply of thousands of Scottish mercenaries to serve in the Thirty Years War.[13] Meanwhile, English imperial ideas and naval adventurism were aligned with the shared desire in both kingdoms to civilise barbarians, resulting in the emergence of a raft of colonial projects embracing the Scottish Highlands, Ireland, and North America. The failed colonisation of Lewis in 1605, the settlement of Jamestown in 1607, the statutes of Iona in 1609, the Ulster plantation of 1610, and the founding of colonies at Newfoundland in 1610, Bermuda in 1612, and Nova Scotia in 1620 amount to the beginnings of an Anglo-Scottish adventure in empire building. At the same time, Scots continued to migrate and establish communities throughout northern Europe that maintained strong relations with their home communities.[14] On the other hand, Scotland's foreign relations increasingly were determined by English policy needs, hence its reluctant if marginal involvement in an English war with France and Spain in the mid-1620s, as well as the brittle relations with the Dutch caused by an Anglocentric court-driven policy on fishing.[15] This issue of subordinating Scotland's own needs to those of an English-dominated court would continue to eat away at the foundations of regal union for the remainder of the century, culminating in the 1703 parliament's support for the Act anent Peace and War that placed foreign policy in its hands, triggering English determination to negotiate a parliamentary union.

The absence of domestic strife in early Stuart Britain is also notable, and is too often overshadowed by the imaginary clouds on the distant horizon. Although late Tudor England was rife with plots and fears of plots, outright

[13] M. Lee, *Government by Pen: Scotland Under James VI and I* (Urbana, 1980), pp. 195–217; S. Murdoch, 'James VI and the formation of a Scottish-British military identity', in S. Murdoch and A. Mackillop (eds), *Fighting for Identity: Scottish Military Experience c.1550–1900* (Leiden, 2002), pp. 3–32; S. Murdoch, 'Scotsmen on the Danish-Norwegian frontiers, 1589–1680', in S. Murdoch and A. Mackillop (eds), *Military Governors and Imperial Frontiers c.1600–1800* (Leiden, 2003), pp. 1–28.

[14] Lee, *Great Britain's Solomon*, pp. 196–232; K. R. Andrews, N. P. Canny, and P. E. H. Hair (eds), *The Westward Enterprise: English Activities in Ireland, the Atlantic and America, 1480–1650* (Liverpool, 1978); C. Brady and R. Gillespie (eds), *Natives and Newcomers: the Making of Irish Colonial Society 1534–1641* (Dublin, 1986); N. P. Canny, *Kingdom and Colony: Ireland in the Atlantic World 1560–1800* (Baltimore, 1988); J. H. Ohlmeyer, ' "Civilising of those rude partes": colonization within Britain and Ireland, 1580s–1640s', in N. Canny (ed.), *The Origins of Empire* (Oxford, 1998), pp. 124–47; D. Armitage and M. J. Braddick (eds), *The British Atlantic World 1500–1800* (Basingstoke, 2002); S. Murdoch and A. Grosjean (eds), *Scottish Communities Abroad c.1600–1707* (Leiden, 2005).

[15] M. Lee, *The Road to Revolution: Scotland under Charles I, 1625–37* (Urbana, 1985), pp. 79–88, 102–5, 170–1; A. I. Macinnes, *Charles I and the Making of the Covenanting Movement 1625–1641* (Edinburgh, 1991), pp. 108–13.

rebellion ceased after the Northern Rising of 1569, apart from the pathetic Essex Plot of 1601. Yet, while Scotland had not experienced a contested succession since 1329, England had a much less stable record of regime change. Fortunately, the removal of Mary, and James VI's acceptance of his mother's execution along with his patient wait for the throne to fall into his lap, contributed greatly towards that domestic stability. There was no war over the succession when Elizabeth finally died, and the Stuart kings presided over thirty-nine years of uninterrupted domestic peace before the outbreak of civil war in England in 1642, a rebellion-free period that is longer than at any time under the Tudors. The Gunpowder Plot of 1605, even with its anti-Scottish dimension, served to bind the new dynasty to the English people.[16] Clearly there were deep divisions between both Stuart kings and their critics in the English parliament, but it is unhelpful to read too much into the factional disputes that crippled these parliaments in the 1620s. Furthermore, while the forced loan of 1626 created immense local unrest in the reign of Charles I, that popular discontent never amounted to the kind of bloody popular insurrection experienced in France.[17] Of course, there is a huge debate over the extent to which the political ideas of James VI and I and his supporters set the Stuart monarchy on a road to conflict with an alternative English school of political thought, but what is incontestable is that the disagreements were contained peacefully for the better part of four decades.[18]

In Scotland, the minor uprisings in Orkney in 1612 and Islay in 1614–15 aroused barely a ripple of interest outside those islands, and the absence of rebellion between the failed Edinburgh insurrection of 1596 and the successful revolution of 1637 was the longest up to that point in Scotland's history. Without an English monarch stirring up Scottish nobles to rebel, and with the king safely ensconced in London, there was little chance of the many palace coups and regional uprisings that previously characterised James VI's chaotic reign. On the other hand, discontent such as was stirred up by the 1625 revocation and the teind commission could no longer be dealt with as directly as before 1603, allowing the Crown to be lulled into a false sense of

---

[16] J. Hurstfield, 'The succession struggle in late Elizabethan England', in J. Hurstfield, *Freedom, Corruption and Society in Elizabethan England* (London, 1973), pp. 104–36; J. Wormald, 'Gunpowder, treason and Scots', *Journal of British Studies* 24 (1985), pp. 187–209.

[17] Cogswell, *Blessed Revolution*; Russell, *Parliaments and English Politics*; K. Sharpe, *The Personal Rule of Charles I* (New Haven and London, 1992); R. Cust, *The Forced Loan and English Politics 1626–1628* (Oxford, 1987).

[18] J. Wormald, 'James VI and I, *Basilikon Doron* and *The Trew Law of Free Monarchies*: the Scottish context and the English tradition', in L. L. Peck (ed.), *The Mental World of the Jacobean Court* (Cambridge, 1991), pp. 36–54; J. P. Sommerville, *Royalists and Patriots: Politics and Ideology in England 1603–1640* (Harlow, 1999); G. Burgess, *The Politics of the Ancient Constitution: an Introduction to English Political Thought 1603–1642* (Basingstoke, 1992); G. Burgess, *Absolute Monarchy and the Stuart Constitution* (Yale, 1996).

security.[19] This was especially dangerous because the robust ideas about political resistance that had thrived in the later sixteenth century had not disappeared; instead, they had gone underground under pressure from James VI's aggressive defence of divine right monarchy. It was not difficult for those resentful and distrustful of Charles I to reconnect with those ideas when seeking justification for opposing the king in the late 1630s.[20] Distrust of the king also created new kinds of relationships between English and Scottish dissidents, a pattern experienced before, for example in the mid-fifteenth century, except that now the dissidents had a common enemy in Charles I.[21] Finally, although rebellion was always most likely in Ireland, and there were well-founded rumours of imminent risings in Ulster in 1611 and Leinster in 1629, the peace was maintained in spite of the provocative nature of English policies.[22] Peace was also more assured because of the fact that Highland mercenaries were now unable to intervene with the tacit approval of the King of Scotland.

Of course, the new British state system with its composite monarchies was not unique, and multiple monarchies existed elsewhere in Europe. The realisation of Stuart ambitions required some adjustment in the governing of the constituent parts of their three kingdoms, but while there was only one king those three realms did remain distinct from one another.[23] The fact that the Stuart kings chose to rule from London ought to be unremarkable and in

[19] Lee, *Road to Revolution*; Macinnes, *Charles I and the Making of the Covenanting Movement*.
[20] For a taste of the royalist arguments see J. H. Burns, *The True Law of Kingship: Concepts of Monarchy in Early Modern Scotland* (Oxford, 1996); R. A. Mason, 'A king by divine right: George Buchanan, James VI and the presbyterians', in Mason (ed.), *Scots and Britons*, pp. 112–37; Wormald, 'James VI and I, *Basilikon Doron* and *The Trew Law of Free Monarchies*'. On the continuity of ideas of resistance in Scotland see R. A. Mason, '*Rex Stoici*: George Buchanan, James VI and the Scottish polity', in Dwyer, Mason, and Murdoch (eds), *New Perspectives*, pp. 9–33; E. J. Cowan, 'The making of the national covenant', in J. Morrill (ed.), *The Scottish National Covenant in its British Context 1638–1651* (Edinburgh, 1990), pp. 68–89; E. J. Cowan, 'The political ideas of a covenanting leader: Archibald Campbell, marquis of Argyll 1607–1661', in Mason (ed.), *Scots and Britons*, pp. 241–61; J. D. Ford, '*Lex rex justo posita*: Samuel Rutherford on the origins of government', in Mason (ed.), *Scots and Britons*, pp. 262–92.
[21] How mature these relationships were before 1640 is uncertain, but see C. Russell, 'The Scottish party in English parliaments, 1640–2', *Historical Research* 159 (1993), pp. 35–52.
[22] N. Canny, *Making Ireland British 1580–1650* (Oxford, 2001), pp. 165–460.
[23] J. Wormald, 'James VI and I: two kings or one?', *History* 68 (1983), pp. 187–209; J. Wormald, 'The creation of Britain: multiple kingdoms or core and colonies', *Transactions of the Royal Historical Society*, 6th series, 2 (1992), pp. 173–94; J. Wormald, 'James VI, James I and the identity of Britain', in B. Bradshaw and J. Morrill (eds), *The British Problem c.1534–1707: State Formation in the Atlantic Archipelago* (Basingstoke, 1996), pp. 148–71; C. Russell, 'Composite monarchies in early modern Europe: the British and Irish example', in A. Grant and K. Stringer (eds), *Uniting the Kingdom? The Making of British History* (London, 1995), pp. 133–46; A. I. Macinnes, 'Regal union for Britain, 1603–1638', in G. Burgess (ed.), *The New British History: Founding a Modern State 1603–1715* (London, 1999), pp. 33–64.

itself was not a cause for concern since peripatetic kingship was ceasing to be a feature of early modern government. At the London court, James VI and I's preference for Scots in a powerful bedchamber and privy chamber and the largesse distributed to them undoubtedly created understandable tensions. There were certainly name-calling, a few fist fights and a good deal of ill-feeling, but there was no Sicilian Vespers. What matters is that those tensions were successfully managed, due in large part to English tolerance and their desire to make the Stuart succession work. From a Scottish point of view, the huge expansion of the court provided the king with enormous reservoirs of patronage that was used to draw much greater numbers of nobles into a client relationship with the king than had been possible before 1603. By the 1630s, the issue of overwhelming Scottish influence at court had disappeared, and while individual Scots like the 3rd Marquis of Hamilton were important office-holders, an acceptable equilibrium had been achieved. Those Scots who were required to attend court did gain access to the king, while the great majority of English courtiers understandably showed no interest at all in events in the northern kingdom. Why should they have been interested? Meanwhile, the process of élite integration that James VI and I encouraged among his nobles had some modest success in creating networks of aristocratic patronage and kinship that were trans-national.[24] By the mid-1630s many Scots had come to view the court as out-of-touch, as crypto-Catholic and as corrupt, but the fact that it was not criticised on account of its Englishness is significant.[25]

The structures put in place for the government of the new Britain had minimal or little impact on Anglo-Scottish relations, and what is surprising is

---

[24] N. Cuddy, 'The revival of the entourage: the bedchamber of James VI in administration and politics, 1603–1625', in D. Starkey (ed.), *The English Court from the Wars of the Roses to the Civil War* (Harlow, 1987), pp. 173–225; N. Cuddy, 'Anglo-Scottish union and the court of James I, 1603–1625', *Transactions of the Royal Historical Society*, 5th series, 39 (1989), pp. 107–24; K. M. Brown, 'The Scottish aristocracy, anglicization and the court, 1603–38', *Historical Journal* 36 (1993), pp. 543–76; J. H. Ohlmeyer, *Civil War and Restoration in the Three Kingdoms: the Career of Randal MacDonnell Marquis of Antrim, 1609–1683* (Cambridge, 1993), pp. 18–76; J. Scally, 'The Political Career of James, Third Marquis and First Duke of Hamilton (1606–1649) to 1643' (unpublished Ph.D. thesis, University of Cambridge, 1992). There were occasional outbursts of anti-Scottish sentiment: see S. Clucas, 'Robert Cotton's *A Short View of the Life of Henry the Third*, and its presentation', in S. Clucas and R. Davies (eds), *The Crisis of 1614 and the Addled Parliament* (Aldershot, 2003), pp. 179–80.

[25] Although a stark court–country divide is no longer entirely persuasive, there was a view of the court as corrupt and under Roman Catholic influence that was shared by Scots and English. On popery, see R. Clifton, 'Fear of popery', in C. Russell (ed.), *The Origins of the English Civil War* (London, 1973), pp. 144–67; C. Hibbard, *Charles I and the Popish Plot* (Chapel Hill, 1983); P. Lake, 'Anti-popery: the structure of a prejudice', in R. Cust and A. Hughes (eds), *Conflict in Early Stuart England* (Harlow, 1989), pp. 134–67. For some discussion of an emerging court élite in Scotland, see K. M. Brown, 'Courtiers and cavaliers: service, Anglicisation and loyalty among the royalist nobility', in Morrill (ed.), *Scottish National Covenant*, pp. 155–92.

how little governmental change took place. For England the regal union had no visible effect on the administration or financing of the state even if royal finances were affected by the new king's behaviour.[26] A handful of Englishmen were appointed to the Scottish Privy Council, while a little over 20 per cent of the membership of the English Privy Council was composed of Scots, reflecting the king's desire for a forum in which he could discuss the affairs of all his kingdoms. However, the former were nominal only and the latter rarely attended in numbers, leaving each kingdom with what were distinct executive arms of government. Furthermore, there was relatively little direct engagement between the two conciliar bodies even if the administrative framework provided by union, and the Crown's British ideology, ensured a useful level of co-operation between individual councillors of the two kingdoms. This is most apparent in the joint approach to the Borders, but it appears in other less obvious areas such as in dealing with travel licences, or in sorting out commercial difficulties. Under James VI and I the Scottish Privy Council was highly effective, even if latterly it became a little tired, but it clearly declined in terms of competence and independence after 1625. However, there was never any question of interference in Scotland by English councillors; the fault lay entirely with the king.[27]

The failure of James VI and I's plans for a union of legislatures should not unduly overshadow any discussion of Anglo-Scottish relations. The Scots probably would have accepted a parliamentary union had terms been negotiated, but the English would only consider a union if it included the conditions the Scots were unlikely to accept, that is not only one enlarged parliament but also an incorporating union of religion and civil law. But while the debate over union between 1604 and 1608 soured the king's relations with the House of Commons, there was little animosity between the two parliaments. In contrast to the early eighteenth century, when the two assemblies developed outright suspicion of and hostility towards one another, the parliaments of the early Stuart kings were not stages on which anti-English or anti-Scottish views were widely or regularly expressed. Men like Sir Edwin Sandys might have given voice to English anger and fear, but they were no

---

[26] B. P. Levack, *The Formation of the British State: England, Scotland, and the Union 1603–1707* (Oxford, 1987); A. Fletcher, *Reform in the Provinces: the Government of Stuart England* (London, 1986); M. Braddick, *The Nerves of State: Taxation and the Financing of the English State, 1558–1714* (Manchester, 1996); J. Cramsie, *Kingship and Crown Finance under James VI and I 1603–1625* (Woodbridge, 2002).

[27] Lee, *Government by Pen* offers the best single account of Scottish government in this period; Levack, *Formation of the British State*, pp. 62–4; Brown, 'The Scottish aristocracy, anglicization and the court', pp. 543–76, esp. pp. 555–6; M. Lee, 'Charles I and the end of conciliar government in Scotland', *Albion* 12 (1980), pp. 315–36.

more anti-Scots than contemporary Eurosceptics are anti-European. In large part, a studied indifference characterised the attitude of these national assemblies to the other kingdom.[28] However, there is little doubt that the increasingly imperious treatment of the Scottish parliament by James VI and I and Charles I was in large part a consequence of regal union, evident in the enhanced patronage that made management of parliament easier, and in the king's lack of exposure to the criticism of the Estates.[29] Of course, from 1640 the two national parliaments discovered they had much in common in their disagreements with Charles I.

Although English lawyers displayed a level of hostility to parliamentary union on account of the implicit threat to the Common Law of England, there was certainly no interest in foisting that law on Scotland. The law courts of England and Scotland remained utterly indifferent to each other in spite of Sir Thomas Craig's argument that much of the legislative traditions of the two kingdoms had its roots in the same feudal law. This indifference towards Scotland's separate legal system allowed its legal profession to evolve independently and without any need to feel threatened.[30] This was in sharp contrast to the situation in Ireland where Jacobean administrators like Sir John Davies enforced the adoption of English law, a policy designed to deliberately undermine the Old English community and to attack Gaelic society. Furthermore, Irish lawyers were also excluded from practising on account of their Catholicism, and only the under-supply of qualified lawyers in Ireland resulted in a compromise in 1628 by which Irish lawyers could practise if they spent five years working at the Inns of Court in London and took an oath of allegiance to the Crown.[31]

[28] B. Galloway, *The Union of England and Scotland 1603–1608* (Edinburgh, 1986). Other than on the issue of union it is significant how little relevance Scotland had to English parliamentary history: see K. Sharpe (ed.), *Faction and Parliament: Essays on Early Stuart History* (London, 1978); Russell, *Parliaments and English Politics*; D. L. Smith, *The Stuart Parliaments 1603–1689* (Oxford, 1999).

[29] J. Goodare, 'The Scottish parliament of 1621', *Historical Journal* 38 (1995), pp. 29–51; and see the essays by V. Wells on the parliament of 1612 and J. Young on the parliament of 1633, in K. M. Brown and A. J. Mann (eds), *Parliament and Politics in Scotland 1567–1707* (Edinburgh, 2005).

[30] G. Donaldson, 'The legal profession in Scottish society in the sixteenth and seventeenth centuries', *Juridical Review* n.s. 21 (1976), pp. 1–19; B. P. Levack, 'Law, sovereignty and the union', in Mason (ed.), *Scots and Britons*, pp. 213–37; Levack, *Formation of the British State*, pp. 68–101; B. P. Levack, 'The proposed union of English and Scots law in the seventeenth century', *Juridical Review* n.s. 20 (1975), pp. 97–115; A. Murdoch, 'The advocates, the law and the nation in early modern Scotland', in W. Prest (ed.), *Lawyers in Early Modern Europe and America* (London, 1981), pp. 147–63; Russell, 'James VI and I and rule over two kingdoms', pp. 151–63.

[31] H. S. Pawlisch, *Sir John Davies and the Conquest of Ireland: a Study in Legal Imperialism* (Cambridge, 1985); D. Cregan, 'Irish recusant lawyers in politics in the reign of James I', in *Irish*

The most obvious difference to Anglo-Scottish relations lay in the Borders, or the 'Middle Shires' as James preferred to describe the region. The improved regulation of cross-border crime that was a feature of the five or six years before 1603 was dramatically accelerated. The arrival of a single authority bestriding both sides of the Border hugely eased the difficulties previously faced by local officers in England and Scotland. The joint Border commission was not established until 1605, but its work along with the creation of a mounted police force, and the personal authority of the Earl of Dunbar ensured that the campaign to normalise the region was remarkably successful. Deploying vicious methods to crack down on lawbreakers, the Border commission largely achieved its objectives within less than twenty years. Low-level thieving and rustling remained a feature of certain Border localities, but the mayhem of earlier decades had gone for ever. This is an achievement that is often taken for granted, but arguably it is the single biggest territorial advance of law and order in Britain between the pacifying of the Welsh marches in the early twelfth century and the solving of the Highland problem after 1746. The social as well as the economic benefits that accrued to communities from Northumberland to Dumfriesshire was one of the major achievements of Anglo-Scottish co-operation in the seventeenth century.[32]

The impact of improved Anglo-Scottish relations on the Highlands was less obvious, but English naval power in the Irish Sea along with English control of Ulster did reconfigure the world in which Highland clans operated. West Highland chiefs were now deprived of a market for their mercenaries in Ireland, reducing the need for the clans' military ethos; they were more vulnerable to seaborne attack; and they were subject to greater scrutiny by a Privy Council in Edinburgh that had more time and resources to devote to Highland affairs. The 1609 statutes of Iona did not suddenly, or even permanently, alter the sociology of Highland clans as was their intent. But their existence alongside other more traditional policies was an indication of a changing relationship with the Crown that brought a measure of improved law and order, at least until the outbreak of war in the 1640s.[33] It is highly

Jurist 5 (1970), pp. 306–20; J. Ohlmeyer, 'Irish recusant lawyers during the reign of Charles I', in M. O Siochru (ed.), *A Kingdom in Crisis: the Confederates and the Irish Civil Wars* (Dublin, 2000), pp. 61–87.

[32] J. Goodare and M. Lynch, 'The Scottish state and its Borderlands, 1567–1625', in Goodare and Lynch (eds), *Reign of James VI*, pp. 186–205; J. Goodare, *State and Society in Early Modern Scotland* (Oxford, 1999), pp. 254–85; R. T. Spence, 'The pacification of the Cumberland Borders, 1593–1628', in *Northern History* 13 (1977), pp. 99–122; S. J. Watts, *From Border to Middle Shire: Northumberland 1586–1625* (Leicester, 1975).

[33] M. Lynch, 'James VI and the "Highland problem"', in Goodare and Lynch (eds), *Reign of James VI*, pp. 208–28; J. Goodare, 'The statutes of Iona in context', *Scottish Historical Review* 77 (1998), pp. 31–57; Goodare, *State and Society*, pp. 254–85; A. Macinnes, *Clanship, Commerce and the House of Stuart, 1603–1788* (East Linton, 1996), pp. 56–87.

unlikely that any headway would have been made in the Highlands without enduring good relations with England. After all, it required the full might of the Hanoverian state to achieve a permanent reshaping of Highland society. Meanwhile, after 1610 the settlement of Ulster by Lowland Scots in a joint enterprise with the English offered a means to further break the dangerous contacts between the Gaelic communities on either side of the Irish Sea.[34]

The debate over parliamentary union exposed the low opinion that was held by some Englishmen of the Scottish economy. As Sir Henry Spelman, an English lawyer and antiquarian, put it, 'As for riches, what have they to enritche us withall? What merchandize of worthe?'[35] Put simply, Scotland was mistakenly perceived as poor and backward, and as offering no opportunities for profit, a view that was in sharp contrast to the potential wealth believed to lie in Ireland if only the country could be released from the incompetence of the uncivilised and unproductive natives. One useful consequence of this negative attitude was that Scots had little to fear from their much more prosperous neighbours; there was no interest in England in purchasing Scottish land, capturing Scottish markets, or partnering Scottish ventures. In spite of the complaints about pensions paid to Scots in the early years of the union, there was no sustained political pressure in England to make Scotland pay its way. Again the contrast with Ireland is telling, as Wentworth's policy of 'thorough' in the 1630s eventually returned a surplus to the king.[36] In fact, Scotland was prosperous in the early seventeenth century when the economy experienced a prolonged period of growth. International and domestic trade expanded, towns grew in size, credit facilities were eased, and landlords invested heavily in their estates and houses. Colonial opportunities were also opened up in Ireland and overseas. Scotland grew rich under its absentee kings, benefiting from the prolonged peace and domestic stability, and from the benign relationship with England. As for trade with England, here too there was some expansion. By the early 1620s, 22 per cent of Scottish customs revenue was raised from English imports, while London had grown to become one of the principal destinations for Scottish exports along with Veere, Rotterdam, and Königsberg.[37]

---

[34] Canny, *Making Ireland British*, pp. 187–242, 347–62; R. Gillespie, *Colonial Ulster: the Settlement of East Ulster, 1600–41* (Cork, 1985); M. Perceval-Maxwell, *The Scottish Migration to Ulster in the Reign of James I* (London, 1973); J. M. Hill, 'The origins of the Scottish plantation in Ulster to 1625: a reinterpretation', *Journal of British Studies* 32 (1993), pp. 40–70.
[35] From 'Of the union', in B. R. Galloway and B. P. Levack (eds), *The Jacobean Union: Six Tracts of 1604* (Scottish History Society, 4th series, 21, Edinburgh, 1985), p. 162.
[36] Canny, *Making Ireland British*; R. Gillespie, *The Transformation of the Irish Economy, 1550–1700* (Dundalk, 1991); M. Maccarthy-Morragh, *The Munster Plantation: English Migration to Southern Ireland, 1583–1641* (Oxford, 1986).
[37] S. G. E. Lythe, *The Economy of Scotland in its European Setting 1550–1625* (Edinburgh, 1960); T. M. Devine and S. G. E. Lythe, 'The economy of Scotland under James VI: a revision article',

In terms of culture, the greatly improved Anglo-Scottish relations of the early seventeenth century had a modest impact. Naturally the royal court in London reflected the interests and ideas of the new Scottish dynasty, and there was an outpouring of propaganda, manufactured to engender some sense of Britishness. However, even at court the esoteric nonsense and the pompous imagery made few inroads, and in the localities the British message made no impact at all.[38] There is no significant evidence of any wider changes in English culture as a consequence of Scottish influences.[39] In Scotland, the regal union brought no great rush to import English styles and fashions, although it probably gave the Scots language another push in the direction of spoken English. The rising wealth of the nobility and merchants ensured that there was a greater level of disposable income to invest in the arts and crafts than ever before, and it is certainly mistaken to imagine that the removal of the court meant that Scotland was abandoned to a Calvinist wasteland.[40] The

---

Scottish Historical Review 50 (1971), pp. 91–106; P. G. B. McNeill and H. L. McQueen (eds), *Atlas of Scottish History to 1707* (Edinburgh, 1996), pp. 262, 264–83, 312–13. For landed wealth, see Brown, *Noble Society in Scotland*, pp. 25–109. For urban growth and wealth, see M. Lynch, 'The crown and the burghs 1500–1625', in M. Lynch (ed.), *The Early Modern Town in Scotland* (London, 1987), pp. 55–80; J. J. Brown, 'Merchant princes and mercantile investment in early seventeenth century Scotland', in Lynch (ed.), *The Early Modern Town in Scotland*, pp. 125–46.

[38] G. Parry, *The Golden Age Restor'd: the Culture of the Stuart Court, 1603–42* (Manchester, 1981); R. M. Smuts, *Court Culture and the Origins of a Royalist Tradition in Early Stuart England* (Philadelphia, 1987); R. Strong, *Henry Prince of Wales and England's Lost Renaissance* (London, 1986); R. Strong, *Britannia Triumphans: Inigo Jones, Rubens and Whitehall Palace* (London, 1980); D. J. Gordon, *Hymenaei: Ben Jonson's Masque of Union* (Berkeley, 1980); S. J. Piggott, *Ancient Britons and the Antiquarian Tradition: Ideas from Renaissance to the Regency* (London, 1989); M. Butler, 'The invention of Britain and the early Stuart masque', in R. M. Smuts (ed.), *The Stuart Court and Europe: Essays in Politics and Political Culture* (Cambridge, 1996), pp. 86–112; Galloway, *Union of England and Scotland*; Galloway and Levack (eds), *Jacobean Union*. There was a perception that the Stuart dynasty and the Scots contributed to the debasement of court culture: see A. Bellany, *The Politics of Court Scandal in Early Modern England: News Culture and the Overbury Affair, 1603–1660* (Cambridge, 2002).

[39] On the wider cultural environment in England, see G. Parry, *The Seventeenth Century: the Intellectual and Cultural Context of English Literature 1603–1700* (Harlow, 1989); B. Ford (ed.), *Seventeenth-Century Britain: the Cambridge Cultural History* (Cambridge, 1989); K. Sharpe and S. N. Zwicker (eds), *Politics of Discourse: the Literature and History of Seventeenth-Century England* (Berkeley, 1987); K. Sharpe and P. Lake (eds), *Culture and Politics in Early Stuart England* (London, 1994); Peck (ed.), *Mental World*.

[40] For a taste of Scottish culture, see Brown, *Noble Society in Scotland*, pp. 181–270; C. McKean, *The Scottish Chateau: the Country House of Renaissance Scotland* (Stroud, 2001); D. Howard, *The Architectural History of Scotland: Scottish Architecture from the Reformation to the Restoration, 1560–1666* (Edinburgh, 1995); M. R. Apted, *The Painted Ceilings of Scotland 1550–1650* (Edinburgh, 1966); R. D. S. Jack (ed.), *The History of Scottish Literature, I: Origins to 1660* (Aberdeen, 1988); R. Houston, *Scottish Literacy and the Scottish Identity 1600–1800* (Cambridge, 1985); D. MacMillan, *Scottish Art 1460–1990* (Edinburgh, 1990); D. Thomson, *Painting in Scotland 1570–1650* (Edinburgh, 1975); J. Purser, *Scotland's Music: a History of the Traditional and Classical Music of Scotland from the Earliest Times to Today* (Edinburgh, 1992); R. Watson

king's subjects remained a polyglot collection of nations and tribes comprising the English in their localised variants, the Welsh, the Lowland Scots, the Gaelic Highlanders, the Norse-speaking Orcadians, and in Ireland the Gaelic Irish, the Old English, the New English, and the emerging Scots-Irish.[41]

However, Scottish animosity towards the creeping imposition of the forms and beliefs of the Church of England is a feature of the age, although the initiative for this development came from the Crown and not the English bishops. Following the union, English puritans soon found that James VI and I had little sympathy for their cause, but the king largely succeeded in balancing the competing interests within the church. It was Charles I's determination to impose Laudian reforms on the church that opened up much deeper and more dangerous religious rifts.[42] Meanwhile, James VI and I might not have had a blueprint for the reform of the Church of Scotland, but he did resent the retreat he had been forced to make from the 1584 Black Acts. By 1603, he had regained some ground, but the move to England created new opportunities for advancing his preference for Erastian bishops. Andrew Melville and his presbyterian colleagues were victims of the king's new-found security in London, and of the added impetus to the king's plans that came from his desire to achieve a degree of congruence between his two British churches. Yet, while the king received the encouragement and help of English bishops, the agenda was not set by them, nor was it forced on an entirely unwilling Scottish people, even if David Calderwood, his colleagues and supporters saw it in such terms. The king's manipulation of the general

(ed.), *The Poetry of Scotland: Gaelic, Scots and English* (Edinburgh, 1995). Even a form of Scottish court culture survived after 1603: M. Pittock, 'From Edinburgh to London: Scottish court writing and 1603', in E. Cruickshanks (ed.), *The Stuart Courts* (Stroud, 2000), pp. 13–28.
[41] C. Kidd, *British Identities Before Nationalism: Ethnicity and Nationhood in the Atlantic World 1600–1800* (Cambridge, 1999); H. A. MacDougall, *Racial Myth in English History: Trojans, Teutons and Anglo-Saxons* (Montreal, 1982); Williamson, *Scottish National Consciousness*; A. Williamson, 'Patterns of British identity: "Britain" and its rivals in the sixteenth and seventeenth centuries', in Burgess (ed.), *New British History*, pp. 138–73; K. M. Brown, 'Scottish identity in the seventeenth century', in B. Bradshaw and P. Roberts (eds), *British Consciousness and Identity* (Cambridge, 1998), pp. 236–58; W. Ferguson, *The Identity of the Scottish Nation* (Edinburgh, 1998), pp. 120–43; M. Lynch, 'A nation born again? Scottish identity in the sixteenth and seventeenth centuries', in D. Brown, R. J. Findlay, and M. Lynch (eds), *Image and Identity* (Edinburgh, 1998), pp. 82–104; N. P. Canny, 'Identity in Ireland: the emergence of the Anglo-Irish', in N. P. Canny and A. Pagden (eds), *Colonial Identity in the Atlantic World, 1500–1800* (Princeton, 1987), pp. 159–213; N. Canny, 'Irish, Scottish and Welsh responses to centralisation, c.1530–c.1640: a comparative perspective', in A. Grant and K. Stringer (eds), *Uniting the Kingdom?* (London, 1995), pp. 147–69; N. P. Canny, 'The formation of the Irish mind: religion, politics and Gaelic Irish literature, 1580–1750', *Past and Present* 95 (1982), pp. 91–116; A. Clarke, *The Old English in Ireland 1625–1642* (London, 1966).
[42] K. Fincham (ed.), *The Early Stuart Church, 1570–1640* (Harlow, 1994); P. Collinson, *The Religion of Protestants: the Church in English Society, 1559–1625* (Oxford, 1982); N. Tyacke, *Anti-Calvinists: the Rise of English Arminianism, c.1590–1640* (Oxford, 1987).

assembly and of parliament was made easier by the greater patronage at his disposal, but those Scottish clergy and nobles who acquiesced in, or embraced, the idea of an Erastian episcopacy were not responding to an Anglicising programme of church reform. Instead, they were reacting against the excessive behaviour of presbyterian activists and agreeing with the king's analysis of its causes. However, the liturgical policy pursued by James and by Charles I from the Five Articles of Perth in 1618 through to the introduction of the Prayer Book in 1637 was a consequence of a largely passive English influence. In pursuing the Five Articles, James VI and I was seeking to achieve a greater degree of outward conformity with the Church of England, and he was reflecting his own beliefs that had been recast after more than a decade's exposure to Anglican religion, a religion that was beginning to move in an Arminian direction. Again the issue is one of English influence rather than English designs. Arguably this is less true of the Prayer Book controversy where Charles I and William Laud were driving forward a policy that had the appearance of subordinating the Church of Scotland to Canterbury. Here in religion was the single most damaging evidence of Scotland's distinctive traditions being compromised, and significantly it was on this issue that the Covenanters placed greatest emphasis in their subsequent negotiations with English parliamentarians in the 1640s.[43]

Where does this rapid and necessarily superficial summary leave the 'blessed Union', a phrase found in the royal proclamation of 20 October 1604 intimating the alteration of the king's style to King of Great Britain?[44]

---

[43] M. Lynch, 'Calvinism in Scotland, 1559–1638', in M. Prestwich (ed.), *International Calvinism 1541–1715* (Oxford, 1985), pp. 225–55; D. G. Mullan, 'Theology in the Church of Scotland, 1618–c.1640: a Calvinist consensus', *Sixteenth Century Journal* 26 (1995), pp. 595–618; A. R. MacDonald, *The Jacobean Kirk 1567–1625: Sovereignty, Polity and Liturgy* (Aldershot, 1998); D. Mullan, *Episcopacy in Scotland: the History of an Idea 1560–1638* (Edinburgh, 1986); I. B. Cowan, 'The five articles of Perth', in D. Shaw (ed.), *Reformation and Revolution* (1967), pp. 160–77; J. D. Ford, 'The lawful bonds of Scottish society: the five Articles of Perth, the Negative Confession and the National Covenant', *Historical Journal* 37 (1994), pp. 45–64; J. D. Ford, 'Conformity in conscience: the structure of the Perth Articles debate in Scotland, 1618–38', *Journal of Ecclesiastical History* 46 (1995), pp. 256–77; D. Stevenson, 'Conventicles in the kirk, 1619–37', *Records of the Scottish Church History Society* 18 (1972–4), pp. 99–114; W. R. Foster, *The Church Before the Covenants: the Church of Scotland 1596–1638* (Edinburgh, 1975); D. G. Mullan, *Scottish Puritanism 1590–1638* (Oxford, 2000); M. Todd, *The Culture of Protestantism in Early Modern Scotland* (Yale, 2002); S. A. Burrell, 'The covenant idea as a revolutionary symbol: Scotland, 1596–1637', *Church History* 27 (1958), pp. 338–50; S. A. Burrell, 'The apocalyptic vision of the early covenanters', *Scottish Historical Review* 63 (1964), pp. 1–24; J. Coffey, *Politics, Religion and the British Revolutions: the Mind of Samuel Rutherford* (Cambridge, 1997); E. J. Cowan, 'The making of the national covenant', in Morrill (ed.), *Scottish National Covenant*, pp. 68–89.

[44] J. F. Larkin and P. L. Hughes (eds), *Stuart Royal Proclamations*, I: *Royal Proclamations of King James I, 1603–1625* (Oxford, 1973).

Unfortunately the regal union is too often discussed in terms of its failures, especially as it ended in revolution, civil warfare, and tyrannicide.[45] Even the argument that it endured for so long appears to offer only grudging acknowledgement of what was achieved. However, if we place this period in the longer context of Anglo-Scottish relations it is fairly remarkable. At its heart is a political realignment that brought England and Scotland into alliance and friendship through the Scottish Reformation in 1560, the Anglo-Scottish League of 1586, and James VI's peaceful accession to the English throne in 1603. That new relationship provided both kingdoms with far greater security than either had previously enjoyed, and in conjunction with Stuart policy for most of the period it conferred an unusually prolonged period of peace. The relationship also underwrote a far greater degree of domestic peace and stability, especially in Scotland. It allowed the two governments to co-operate where co-operation was most useful (on the Borders especially), created a genuinely multi-cultural royal court, ensured that national parliaments remained respectful of one another, facilitated economic growth that brought the Scots a greater level of prosperity than had been enjoyed for a very long time, and allowed greater cultural exchange without undermining the national identity of either side. Only in religion was the relationship strained by the Crown's increasing preference for Anglican practices. What the 1604 proclamation identified as 'An unities of Religion, the chiefest band of heartie Union' proved to be the undoing of the regal union in the form established by James VI and I.

As the political spats over the four-hundredth anniversary of regal union demonstrate, the events of 1603 are still capable of generating a range of responses. Comparing 1603 with 2003 also draws attention to the ways in which Anglo-Scottish relations have both altered and remained fixated by similar problems. Religion is no longer an issue, but the role of the monarch remains divisive. Like those seventeenth-century Englishmen upset by James VI and I's change of style, so today we have Scots irritated by the present Queen's title. The two parliaments are again feeling their way around one another even if for the present the UK Westminster parliament is clearly the fount of sovereign authority. There are arguments about differences in national identity in the two kingdoms, and the draining away of Scottish skills to England that began in 1603 continues unabated. However, unlike in the early seventeenth century large numbers of much-needed English migrants now move northwards. English MPs and political commentators continue to complain, with some justification, that there are too many Scots at court wielding too much power, and, less convincingly, that too much

---

[45] Arguably this is a fault of K. M. Brown, *Kingdom or Province? Scotland and the Regal Union 1603–1715* (Basingstoke, 1992), pp. 86–111.

English money is drained north. There remain Scots who lament the fact that the locus of power is in London and not in Edinburgh. Perhaps it is not so surprising that in spite of the successes of 1603, Westminster ignored the regal union in 2003, that the Queen politely kept her distance, and the Scots had a brawl over it.

4

The English, the Scots, and the Dilemmas of Union, 1638–1654

JOHN MORRILL

I

APPEARANCES CAN BE DECEPTIVE. The alliances of powerful groups in England and in Scotland between 1638 and 1654 might imply that there was a stormy love affair between the kingdoms going on. One could make a case for this approach. There were natural alliances between groups in the two kingdoms, such as that between the Crown and those wealthy Scottish peers who, reflecting on English brides and broad acres on either side of the Border, pointedly referred to themselves in 1638 as 'your Majesty's British nobility'.[1] There was the pact made between stern Calvinists on both sides of the Border who opposed the king's policies in church and state and who made common cause in the Solemn League and Covenant.[2] As a result of the Covenant, Scots and English sat side by side on the central executive committee that oversaw the wars in England and Ireland (the Committee of Both Kingdoms, 1644–7),[3] and at the Westminster Assembly, where six Scottish ministers and nine elders punched beyond their weight alongside over a

---

[1] P. Donald, 'The Covenant and British Politics', in J. Morrill (ed.), *The Scottish National Covenant in its British Context* (Edinburgh, 1990), p. 126.
[2] Morrill (ed.), *Scottish National Covenant*, pp. 14–21; E. J. Cowan, 'The Solemn League and Covenant' and other essays, in R. A. Mason (ed.), *Scotland and England 1286–1815* (Edinburgh, 1987), pp. 182–202 and *passim*. And for the best recent overview, see D. Scott, *Politics and War in the Three Stuart Kingdoms 1637–1649* (2004), esp. chs 1 and 3.
[3] J. S. A. Adamson, 'The triumph of oligarchy: the management of war, and the committee of both kingdoms, 1644–1645', in C. Kyle and J. Peacey (eds), *Parliament at Work: Parliamentary Committees, Political Power and Public Access in Early Modern England* (Woodbridge, 2002), pp. 101–27.

Proceedings of the British Academy, **127**, 57–74. © The British Academy 2005.

hundred English and Welsh members.[4] One might also point to the fact that as early as 1641, the king was pushed by the English and Scottish parliaments into agreeing to a treaty that promised a confederal union of the two kingdoms, and that that agreement was further discussed in 1643, 1645, 1646, and 1648.[5] As late as 1648, indeed, Cromwell crushed a Scottish army led by members of the Engagers—very much the *soi-disant* 'British nobility' of 1648. He then advanced into Scotland, halted before Edinburgh, and having satisfied himself that the founders of the 1643 Covenant could be trusted to govern Scotland in a way that secured godliness and represented no threat to England, he retreated back into England. He wrote home to Speaker Lenthall: 'I do think the affairs of Scotland are in a thriving posture, as to the interest of honest men; and Scotland like to be a better neighbour to you now . . .'.[6] When an English Army finally conquered Scotland in the years after 1649, the English might be said to have consulted the Scots on how best to unify the two commonwealths. The resultant union, according to a Protectoral Ordinance of April 1654 was the outcome of an invitation 'to the people of [Scotland] unto such a happy union', an invitation which was 'accepted' by 'their deputies convened at Dalkeith and again at Edinburgh'. It might seem that there was much striving for a new working relationship between major groupings in the two kingdoms over these years, much hope of a new and better relationship between the two peoples.[7] It might seem so, but it would be wrong. This was a period in which distrust, double-dealing, broken promises, and betrayal lay occasionally just below the surface, but more often jutted out through a meagre topsoil of harmony.

II

At no point in the history of Britain and Ireland has the whole archipelago experienced such sustained and brutal internal war as in the 1640s and early

---

[4] The standard current account is R. S. Paul, *The Assembly of the Lord* (Edinburgh, 1985), which includes a list of all the members at pp. 546–55 (with the Scots at pp. 554–5). But see now the transformative work of Chad van Dixhoorn, 'Reforming the Reformation: Theological Debate at the Westminster Assembly 1643–1652' (Ph.D. thesis, University of Cambridge, 2004). This contains a revelatory new edition of the minutes of the Assembly, transcripts of journals of the Assembly newly recovered, and a major reassessment of what happened there and why.

[5] J. Morrill, 'Three Kingdoms and One Commonwealth? The enigma of mid-seventeenth-century Britain and Ireland', in A. Grant and K. Stringer (eds), *Uniting the Kingdom?* (London, 1995), pp. 170–202.

[6] S. C. Lomas (ed.), *The Letters and Speeches of Oliver Cromwell with Elucidations by Thomas Carlyle* (with an introduction by C. H. Firth), 3 vols (London, 1904), I, p. 380.

[7] S. R. Gardiner, *Constitutional Documents of the Puritan Revolution 1625–1660*, 3rd edn (Oxford, 1906), pp. 418–22.

1650s. The English people was at war with itself and a king was tried, convicted, and executed, the Crown deemed 'unnecessary, burdensome and dangerous to the liberty, safety and public interest',[8] and the House of Lords declared to be 'useless and dangerous to the people of England'.[9] Perhaps one in five of all adult males bore arms and perhaps one in twenty adult males died in battle or of campaign-related causes. And yet in the course of these wars internal to England in the 1640s, perhaps one in four of those serving in arms came from Scotland and Ireland.[10] The Scottish people was more spasmodically at war with itself, though a larger proportion served in England and Ireland than in Scotland so that a similar proportion of the adult population served in arms and died.[11] Each of the peoples of Ireland was at war with itself and with the others, and almost every inhabitant of Ireland was at some point vulnerable to attack by British armies. At least one in ten died in the conflict and perhaps as many as 20 per cent went into exile or were transported.[12] These were wars of religion as much as any wars in early modern Europe were wars of religion—that is to say they were about many things other than religion, but confessional poles were those around which all kinds of other issues clustered. And they were also wars in which most of the leaders were desperate to redefine the constitutional relationships that bound together the three component polities of England (and Wales), Scotland, and Ireland.[13] Yet separation and independence was an issue for very few. The only group with a serious commitment to breaking up rather than reshaping the state system created since 1534 were those who governed England in the years immediately after the establishment of the English (and Irish) Commonwealth, who wished to wash their hands of Scotland.[14]

[8] Gardiner, *Constitutional Documents*, p. 385.
[9] Ibid., p. 387.
[10] C. Carlton, 'The impact of the fighting', in J. Morrill (ed.), *The Impact of the English Civil War* (London, 1991), pp. 17–31; and more generally, C. Carlton, *Going to the Wars: the Experience of the British Civil Wars, 1638–1651* (London, 1992), esp. pp. 201–30 and *passim*.
[11] The best general overview is S. Reid, *Scots Armies of the Civil War 1639–1651* (Norwich, 1982). For a short summary of the armies and their campaigns, see E. Furgol, 'Civil War in Scotland', in J. P. Kenyon and J. Ohlmeyer (eds), *The Civil Wars: a Military History of England, Scotland and Ireland 1638–1660* (Oxford, 1998), pp. 41–72.
[12] P. Lenihan, *Confederate Catholics at War, 1641–1649* (Cork, 2001), pp. 221–30.
[13] Morrill, 'Three Kingdoms', pp. 170–192.
[14] See below, and for Irish separatism see J. Casway, 'Gaelic Maccabeanism', in J. Ohlmeyer (ed.), *Political Thought in Seventeenth-Century Ireland* (Cambridge, 2000), pp. 176–90.

III

By 1638, Anglo-Scottish relations were already at a low ebb. There was a widespread English perception that the Scots had gained far more from the 1603 Union of the Crowns than the English had: a disproportionate number of lucrative positions at court; the acquisition of too many English heiresses and too much English land; and the securing of a disproportionate share of the property confiscated from Irish rebels, especially in the north of Ireland. Most Scots were equally sure that the union had been a disaster for Scotland. It was leading to creeping Anglicisation, especially of the church, to a king in Charles I who had challenged the titles that many of the nobles held to the land they had secured during the Reformation, who showed scant regard for the rule of law, and who replaced James VI and I's 'government by pen' by government by fiat.[15]

It was a religious issue that lit the fuse. Charles's attempt to impose a version of the 1549 English Prayer Book on the Scots without consultation or consent provoked a national strike.[16] A majority of the nobility, most of the clergy, and the leaders of many urban and rural communities declared in the National Covenant that they would not implement Charles's policies. In the past—as in the late 1620s over the king's attempt to impose new conditions on all those who had gained lands from Crown and church over the previous century—such protests had been effectual. The king had no power to enforce that which his enforcers swore a solemn oath they would not enforce. They had not reckoned on a King of Britain and Ireland using the resources of all his kingdoms against them. An English army and an English navy, an Irish army, and Highlanders who preferred malign neglect at Whitehall to malign theocracy from Edinburgh were brought to bear against the predominantly Lowland Covenanters. It is important to note that the king started the War of the Three Kingdoms by declaring war on the Covenanters.[17] Faced by his threat of force, the Scots mobilised more efficiently than the king. But Charles's plan to use the resources of all his kingdoms to overcome opposi-

---

[15] The most recent discussions are M. Lee, *Government by Pen: Scotland under James VI and I* (Urbana, 1980) and his *The Road to Revolution: Scotland under Charles I* (Urbana, 1985), and a succession of brilliant essays by Jenny Wormald, most notably 'James VI and I: two kings or one', *History* 68 (1983), pp. 187–209.

[16] The fullest analyses of the crisis of 1637–8 are P. Donald, *An Uncounselled King: Charles I and the Scottish Troubles, 1637–1641* (Cambridge, 1990); Morrill (ed.), *Scottish National Covenant*; J. Morrill, 'A British Patriarchy? Ecclesiastical Imperialism under the early Stuarts', in A. Fletchers and P. Roberts (eds), *Religion, Culture and Society in Early Modern Brtain* (Cambridge, 1993), pp. 209–37. I hope in a forthcoming article to establish the claim that there was a Laudian enterprise to introduce versions of the conservative 1549 Prayer Book in all three kingdoms.

[17] Morrill, 'Three Kingdoms', pp. 177–80. See also J. Morrill, *The Nature of the English Revolution* (London, 1993), pp. 260–4.

tion in one part of it was a vital demonstration to the Scots of the hazards of the Union of 1603. No longer was there the comforting thought that a Scottish king had become King of England. Now a king more English than the English ruled Scotland without regard to its ancient laws, ancient liberties, and modern religious sensibilities.[18]

The initial Scottish response was to strip the King of England of his powers in Scotland. In future, all his authority would be exercised through Scotsmen chosen for him and through institutions that met independently of his will and influence. This was not tolerable to a man like Charles and he made a second and even more disastrous attempt to use the resources of all his kingdoms to impose himself on Scotland. This time the Scots did not merely defend the borders against him. They marched into England, occupied the north-east as far south as Newcastle and demanded a settlement guaranteed by the parliaments of both kingdoms and a settlement that redefined the relationship between them.[19] By occupying the north-east of England for more than a year, the Scots gave to the English parliament the opportunity to dictate solutions to the grievances of England. They created the circumstances out of which England was to have its own civil war. But they also sowed the seeds of their own civil wars (1644–5 and 1650–2) and they found themselves drawn into interventions in the civil wars in Ireland and in England that committed one in ten adult Scottish males to service outside the borders of Scotland.[20]

IV

Between 1638 and 1654, Scottish armies marched into England (they never used the word 'invaded') on five separate occasions, and there were significant numbers of Scottish troops in formal occupation of large parts of northern England for almost half of the 1640s. There were no English troops in Scotland until 1648, but in the 1650s the Scottish Lowlands (but not the Scottish Highlands) were occupied by 10,000 or more English troops. To look at it another way: in the year 1645 there was not only a civil war in England, a civil war in Scotland, and a civil war in Ireland. There was (at the beginning

[18] Donald, *An Uncounselled King*, modified by J. Scally, 'Counsel in Crisis: James, third Marquess of Hamilton and the Bishops' Wars', in J. Young (ed.), *Celtic Dimensions of the British Civil Wars* (Edinburgh, 1997), pp. 18–34; C. Russell, *The Fall of the British Monarchies 1637–1643* (Oxford, 1991), chs 1–4.

[19] The fullest account of the campaigns is in M. Fissell, *The Bishops' Wars: Charles I's Campaigns against Scotland 1638–40* (Cambridge, 1994).

[20] See here especially D. Stevenson, *Alistair MacColla and the Highland Problem in the Seventeenth Century* (Edinburgh, 1980), esp. ch. 1.

of the year) a Scottish army stationed in the north Midlands that was the largest single army in England. There was a Scottish army in Ireland and the remnants of an English army there too. There was an army in Scotland upholding the king's interest there that was more than half Irish; and the king was actively negotiating for an Irish Catholic army to be shipped to England. Between 1642 and 1652 perhaps one in three of all those subjects of Charles I who bore arms in these wars fought in a kingdom other than their own. There is a dilemma about whether to refer to events of these years as the *War* of the Three Kingdoms or the *Wars* of the Three Kingdoms. There is no case for referring to this period as the period of the English Civil War.

V

In the years 1640 and 1641 Charles I lost effective control of all his kingdoms, in what Conrad Russell has called a 'billiard-ball effect'.[21] The Scots compelled him (in a treaty guaranteed by the English parliament) to agree to meet parliament every third year; to agree that all those who made and enforced policy in and for Scotland would be approved by the Scottish parliament or by other representatives of the Estates; to accept not only full-blown presbyterianism but a strict separation of church and state. By the autumn of 1641 the Catholic community of Ireland wanted its own version of the Scottish deal. They sought a reformed and regular parliament which would be dominated by Catholics; government of the inhabitants of Ireland by Irish-born men appointed or approved by an autonomous Irish parliament. And they demanded a fully independent Irish Catholic church enjoying, within an (initially at least) pluralistic polity, all the rights the church might expect to enjoy in a Catholic confessional state. Fear that a weak king might be unable to prevent a vindictive English parliament from seeking to create and then to impose a Protestant confessional state led to a series of major rebellions. These in turn led to the creation of just such a Catholic state, which sought to sever all links with England but not with the house of Stuart. The English too took the Scottish settlement to heart. They secured the passage of a Triennial Act, and insisted with ever-greater urgency on the creation of mechanisms to ensure that the king listen both to the men of 'ancient riches' and those in whom the dominant groups in the two Houses could feel confidence. In all the kingdoms the men held responsible for past misgovernment were driven from office and the institutions that were taken to be the most perni-

---

[21] C. Russell, 'The British Problem and the English Civil War', *History* 72 (1987), reprinted in P. Gaunt (ed.), *The English Civil War: the Essential Readings* (Oxford, 2000), at p. 94.

cious instruments of their misgovernment (Star Chamber and High Commission in England, Castle Chamber and High Commission in Ireland, and High Commission in Scotland) were abolished. What many of the Scots and some Irish Catholics sought, however, was not merely a transformation of the institutions of the kingdoms of Scotland and Ireland, but a changed constitutional relationship between the kingdoms. Clause 8 of the Treaty between England and Scotland in 1641, for example, envisaged the creation of a confederal constitution, with simultaneous meetings of parliament in each kingdom attended by delegates from the other kingdom with a power to veto legislation hostile to the interests of their own people. It also envisaged the permanent existence of *conservatores pacis*, standing bodies of commissioners from both kingdoms with authority over crucial issues, such as the making of war and peace and the arbitration of disputes between the kingdoms.

The Scots also sought joint control of a new *British-Protestant* ascendancy in Ireland. Believing that both Charles I and the Long Parliament had committed themselves to such a confederal constitution, the Scots army returned home in the high summer of 1641 and disbanded. They set up the appropriate bodies and waited—in vain—for the English to respond. The promised changes were reiterated in the Solemn League and Covenant between the Long Parliament and the Scottish parliament in 1643 and in the Engagement between the king and the Scottish parliament in 1648. Although it was second in importance in their minds to the introduction of presbyterian uniformity in all three kingdoms, confederalism mattered to the Scots.[22]

VI

From 1648 until at least 1651 almost all those Scots whose views are recoverable wanted to create a confederal union of the two kingdoms, although a few radicals dreamt of a broader union of Britain and the Netherlands in which English power would be diluted.[23] For the period down to January

---

[22] For Ireland, see N. Canny, *Making Ireland British 1580–1650* (Oxford, 2001), ch. 8, and more generally the works discussed in ch. 8.1 at pp. 461–9 ('The Irish insurrection of 1641: the historiographical background'). For Scotland, see K. Brown, *Kingdom or Province? Scotland and the Regal Union 1603–1715* (Basingstoke, 1992), ch. 5; R. Mason (ed.), *Scotland and England 1286–1815* (Edinburgh, 1985), chs 4–6; E. J. Cowan, 'The political ideas of a Covenanting leader: Archibald Campbell, Marquis of Argyll 1607–1661', in R. Mason (ed.), *Scots and Britons: Scottish Political Thought and the Union of 1603* (Cambridge, 1994), pp. 241–62; Morrill, 'Three Kingdoms', pp. 180–4.

[23] See Arthur Williamson, 'Union with England Traditional, Union with Britain Radical: Sir James Hope and the mid seventeenth-century British State', *English Historical Review* 110

1649, most of the English resisted any redefinition of the constitutional relationship between the two kingdoms or commonwealths. After that those who
governed in England tried to break the link between England and Scotland
that had been created by the Union of the Crowns. The English parliament
abolished monarchy in England and Ireland *but not in Scotland*. The act abolishing the office of king began: 'whereas Charles Stuart, late king of
England, Ireland, and the territories and dominions thereunto belonging
. . .'. It pointedly ignored the Scots throughout the rest of the act.[24] The
Rump made no efforts to persuade the Scots to abolish monarchy. They were
perfectly willing to contemplate and live with a return to the situation that
had existed before 1603, with Scotland under the house of Stuart and the
English with their own arrangements. It was the Scots who were unable to
imagine an independent future for themselves and insisted on first proclaiming and then crowning Charles II as King of Britain and Ireland and gam-
bling all on making good that larger claim. The Scots were encouraged to
resume their independence as a people and a polity, free to remain as a separate kingdom to the north of the Commonwealth of England and Ireland.
But they refused. As late as 1651, when the Rump struck a new Great Seal, it
displayed a map of England, Wales, and Ireland but omitted the outline of
Scotland. If there was any desire for independence in this period rather than
a desire for devolution, it is be found more in England than in Scotland and
Ireland. The Scots—led now by the men who had refused to fight for Charles I
in 1648 and who adhered rigidly to the Covenants—did not respond by
proclaiming Charles as King of Scotland. Rather they proclaimed him 'the
righteous air [heir] and Lawfull successor' to the kingdoms of 'Britain,
France and Ireland'.[25] The English conquest of Scotland that began in 1650
and which culminated in 1653 with an incorporative union imposed by the
English was very much a second best for the English.[26] It was not the con-
sensual agreement portrayed by English propagandists. Commissioners of
the shires and burghs were summoned to Dalkeith, and only those who
embraced an incorporative union were allowed on to the delegation to go to
London. They arrived believing they were coming to a round-table conference to debate the future of the union. They were allowed to speak to the
English commissioners, who then sent them away while they drafted the
Articles of Union to be promulgated initially by the Protectoral Council and

---

(1999), pp. 303–22, and (more generally) his 'Patterns of British identity: "Britain" and its rivals
in the sixteenth and seventeenth centuries', in G. Burgess (ed.), *The New British History:
Founding a Modern State 1603–1715* (London, 1999) pp. 138–73.

[24] Gardiner, *Constitutional Documents*, p. 385.

[25] *Acts of the Parliaments of Scotland*, VI, pt ii, pp. 156–7.

[26] Derek Hirst, 'The English Republic and the Meaning of Britain', *Journal of British History*
66 (1994), pp. 451–86, reprinted in B. Bradshaw and J. Morrill (eds), *The British Problem*

then by a parliament in which 7 per cent represented Scotland, many of those Englishmen. A shotgun marriage indeed, or less anachronistically, a pike and musket marriage.

VII

Alongside and largely underpinning the persistent Scottish demand for a confederal settlement, and a factor in the English preference for either an integrative union or no union at all was, of course, religion. Between 1638 and 1641, the Scots demanded an end to all Anglicisation of their reformed church, and they set out to achieve this by establishing a rigid separation of church and state and making the church safe from all royal intervention or influence. Such a settlement, however, ultimately relied upon a compliant state, and faith in that compliance quickly waned. So, between 1643 and 1654, those who governed in Scotland were committed to a union of the churches of England, Scotland, and Ireland. They demanded one confession of faith, one form of worship, a common form of church government and discipline, and a firm theocratic polity for the confederated kingdoms. But those who dominated the government of England became more and more committed to a much looser form of Protestant polity, one that permitted committed Protestants with tender consciences to set up their own exclusive religious communities outside a national church that was Congregationalist, disestablished, Erastian. Support for what was widely and dismissively described as a rigid or Scottified presbytery in England became smaller and shriller.[27]

By the time of the negotiations for the Solemn League and Covenant in 1643, the Scots demanded presbyterianism as the basic price of their military intervention in the English wars. The English, notoriously, inserted weasel words into the treaty, by committing themselves to the reform of religion throughout the Stuart dominions 'according to the word of God and the example of the best reformed churches'.[28] The Scots took this to be Geneva and Scotland; the Congregationalist and Erastian casuists in England took it to mean Massachusetts. Even those English Parliamentarians who were willing to use the language of presbytery and synodical government were

---

1534–1707 (Basingstoke, 1996), pp. 192–219. See also my forthcoming essay 'The rule of saints and soldiers: the wars of religion in Britain and Ireland 1638–60', in J. Wormald (ed.), *The Shorter Oxford History of the British Isles: the Seventeenth Century* (Oxford, forthcoming).

[27] J.-L. Kim, 'The Debate on the Relations between the Churches of Scotland and England during the British Revolution (1633–1647)' (Ph.D. thesis, University of Cambridge, 1997, printed in Daegu, 1999).

[28] Gardiner, *Constitutional Documents*, p. 268.

hostile to clerical authority and determined to ensure lay control of the church at local and national level.[29] Robert Baillie is not the most aphoristic of Scots, but two of his sayings are amongst the most pungent of the whole period. The English, he asserted bitterly, were willing to concede presbyterianism, but only a 'weak erastian presbytery'. And, commenting on the Solemn League and Covenant, he said of the English: 'they for a civil league and we for a religious covenant'.[30] Often enough in history, treaties deliberately use ambiguous language to paper over cracks. Sometimes the subsequent calamities that mark the unravelling of such agreements make matters worse. The Solemn League and Covenant belongs to that school of failed diplomacy.

Even when they were allies, then, groups in England and Scotland always wanted different things. And if this was true of their relations with one another, it was also true of their relations with the third of Charles I's kingdoms, Ireland.

VIII

There were two largely separate rebellions in Ireland in late 1641. The first, by the Old English of the Pale and Munster was in essence an attempt to secure for that largely Catholic community the same political and religious autonomy that the presbyterians had secured in Scotland. It aimed to create an Irish kingdom independent of interference from Whitehall and from Westminster, and to halt a century of creeping Anglicisation. The other rebellion was by the dispossessed and the exiled Gaelic Irish communities of Ulster, the perforation of ulcers of resentment created by the expropriations and plantation of the 1610s and the harassment of the remaining Catholic population since. The rebels proclaimed that their targets were only the English, but Scottish settlers took their share of murder and atrocity. It is impossible now to determine how many Protestants were killed, maimed, driven out. The figure for the eighteen months after October 1641 is more likely to be 3,000 killed and 3,000 dispossessed than the tens, even hundreds of thousands claimed at the time—a figure endorsed by committees of the Long Parliament. It was still an outbreak of vengeance that required an instant response.[31] And the Covenanters were the first to get an army to Ulster to end the massacres and

---

[29] For an admirable recent summary, see A. Woolrych, *Britain in Revolution 1625–1660* (Oxford, 2002), pp. 268–72.

[30] W. Ferguson, *Scotland's Relations with England: a Survey to 1707* (Edinburgh, 1977), p. 126.

[31] For some recent discussions, see M. Perceval-Maxwell, *The Outbreak of the Irish Rebellion of 1641* (Dublin, 1994); N. P. Canny, 'What really happened in Ireland in 1641?', in J. Ohlmeyer (ed.), *Ireland from Independence to Occupation 1641–1660* (Cambridge, 1995), pp. 24–42; B. MacCuarta, *Ulster 1641: Aspects of the Rising* (Belfast, 1993).

to punish the rebels. For a decade, Munro's brigade struggled to protect the Scottish settlers. To do so, he exercised a policy of reprisal that set the tone for others. When he encountered his first Catholic rebels on 30 April 1642, he hanged all those whom he took prisoner. When he reached Newry, he reported that he had rounded up all the townsmen and interrogated them: 'the indifferent being severed from the bad whereof 60 with two priests were shot and hanged, the indifferent are banished'. But he also increasingly skirmished with English troops as both scavenged for food and sought to occupy as much territory as possible.[32] The English reneged on their promises to underwrite the costs of the Scottish expedition even more completely than they reneged on their promises to pay the Scottish army in England. It was another cause of sourness.

Worse still was the Scots insistence that the post-war settlement of Ireland would lead to power-sharing by the English and the Scots in Ireland.[33] The Solemn League and Covenant is entitled 'a solemn league and covenant for Reformation and defence of religion, the honour and happiness of the King, and the peace and safety of the three kingdoms of England, Scotland and Ireland'.[34] Throughout, a settlement in all three is enunciated, and the involvement of *both* parliaments (that is, Edinburgh and Westminster) in the settlement of Ireland is asserted. Like so much else, the English quickly reverted to seeing Ireland as an English problem to be solved by the English without reference to the Scots.[35] Notoriously, when John Milton, as official propagandist of the English Commonwealth, was commissioned in 1649 to write about the gathering coalition of Royalists and Catholics in Ireland (the pact between Ormonde and O'Neill), he devoted most of his space to denouncing not the wickedness of the papists of Ireland, but the intolerance of the Scottish presbyterians of Belfast. Ireland, far from helping to create a common cause between the parliamentary majorities in England and Scotland, became a further cause of mistrust and recrimination.[36]

---

[32] D. Stevenson, *Scottish Covenanters and Irish Confederates: Scottish-Irish Relations in the Mid-seventeenth Century* (Belfast, 1991), pp. 103–30, esp. p. 106.

[33] Morrill, 'Three Kingdoms', pp. 180–3.

[34] Gardiner, *Constitutional Documents*, p. 267.

[35] J. S. A. Adamson, 'Strafford's Ghost: the British context of Viscount Lisle's lieutenancy in Ireland', in Ohlmeyer (ed.), *Ireland from Independence to Occupation*, pp. 128–59; P. Little, 'The English parliament and the Irish constitution 1641–1649', in M. O'Siochru (ed.), *Kingdoms in Crisis: Ireland in the 1640s* (Dublin, 2001), pp. 106–21.

[36] John Milton, *Articles of peace, made and concluded with Irish rebels . . . And a representation of the Scotch Presbytery at Belfast* (1649). My understanding of this piece has been transformed by discussions with Dr Joad Raymond, following a paper he gave at my graduate seminar on this tract in 1999.

IX

I have noticed earlier that there is a tension between calling the events of 1638–54 the War of the Three Kingdoms and the Wars of the Three Kingdoms. The case for the former is that the king himself and his supporters everywhere, the leading Covenanters, the Engagers in 1648, and Cromwell and his allies after 1649 thought three-dimensionally. Their strategic thinking *always* planned to optimise the resources at their disposal in three kingdoms to secure their political and religious goals. Let us consider the Covenant itself and the king's response both in making the Cessation in Ireland and in authorising Montrose's Scottish–Irish war in Scotland; or let us reconsider the early months of 1645. As the Long Parliament reorganised its armies to create the New Model, Charles was secretly negotiating for an Irish Catholic army and was redirecting Montrose's priorities. The reorganisation and division of the king's armies in England was predicated upon this archipelagic strategy. Or let us recall the so-called second civil war of 1648—at its heart was the plan for a Scottish irruption into England, and the arrival of Catholic troops from Ireland under English and Scottish officers and a *levée en masse* of English royalists.[37] Of the twenty largest battles across the isles in the period 1642–51, more than half had a significant proportion of men fighting outside their own territory.[38]

The case for calling it the Wars of the Three Kingdoms is much stronger. The plural reminds us of chronological phases. Traditional English historiography speaks of three civil wars (1642–6, 1648, 1649–51). There was no internal war in Scotland except in the years 1643–5 and 1649–54. Fighting in Ireland was intermittent, at least until 1649. Different codes and conduct of war existed in each of the territories: a wholly different moral economy of atrocity and massacre. Scots did not hang their English opponents as they hanged the Irish, or even as Montrose treated the inhabitants of Aberdeen. Cromwell did not behave at Pembroke as he did at Drogheda.[39] When English troops were killed in England in the 1650s, every legal effort was made to bring the culprits to trial and to the noose. In Scotland, when an English soldier was killed, the community from which the culprits sprang was required to hand them over or face arbitrary fines. In Ireland, when an English soldier was killed, the community from which the culprits sprang was required to

---

[37] R. Ashton, *Counter-Revolution: the Second Civil War and its Origins 1646–1648* (London, 1994); Woolrych, *Britain in Revolution*, pp. 402–60; Morrill, 'Three Kingdoms', pp. 184–5.
[38] i.e. in England: Nantwich, Marston Moor, Preston, Worcester; in Scotland, Tippermuir, Auldearn, Kilsyth, Philiphaugh, Dunbar; in Ireland, Dungan's Hill, Benburb, Rathmines.
[39] For Cromwell at Drogheda, the best current account is by J. S. Wheeler, *Cromwell in Ireland* (Dublin, 1999), pp. 64–88.

hand over the culprits for summary execution or else that community would see its dwellings and buildings torched and hostages transported to the Barbados. Different theatres, different kinds of war.[40]

X

John Pocock has produced a conceptual framework for understanding these conflicts. He suggests that we draw down concepts developed by the Romans to understand the phenomenon of internal war within their empire (and therefore known through Latin writings to the actors in the War(s) of the Three Kingdoms):

> It was a war among (and not between) the kingdoms comprising a multiple monarchy, and to find an appropriate label we should turn to the ancient Roman distinction between *bellum civile* and *bellum sociale* . . . A *bellum civile* was a war between *cives*, citizens of the same polity; a *bellum sociale* a war between *socii*, polities associated in a system comprising a multiplicity of states. The great *bellum sociale* of antiquity turned on the eligibility of Italian *socii* to be treated as *cives Romani*; it was a formal similarity with the Scottish endeavour to establish by military means that English and Scots should be members of a uniform ecclesiastical polity . . .[41]

Applying his model, we find that elements of both kinds of war can be found in each kingdom. The king, the Scots (nobility and kirkmen), the Protestant communities of Ireland, and many of the leading figures in the Confederation of Kilkenny had as a principal objective a radical shift in the relationship of the kingdoms one to another as a result of the war, and fundamental changes in the rights of the peoples in relation to one another. They were fighting a *bellum sociale*. Most of them, most of the time, were also fighting a *bellum civile*, and other leaders in England and in Ireland were fighting predominantly a *bellum civile*. But it may be that Pocock leaves out of account a third kind of internal war for which I do not know the Latin term: a war of independence (as exemplified by the Jewish Revolt of AD 67–70). As far

---

[40] See J. Morrill, 'The Britishness of the English Revolution', in R. Asch (ed.), *Three Nations: a Common History? England, Scotland, Ireland and British History c.1600–1920* (Bochum, 1993), pp. 90–115. See also B. Donagan, 'Atrocity, war crime and treason in the English Civil War', *American Historical Review* 99 (1994), pp. 1137–66. The most thorough and probing study is being prepared as a Cambridge Ph.D. by Inga Volmer and I have benefited from discussing these matters with her and reading her thesis submitted for the M. Phil. in Historical Studies in Cambridge, available in the History Faculty Library (and not the University Library) in Cambridge.

[41] J. Pocock, 'The Atlantic archipelago and the war of the three kingdoms', in B. Bradshaw and J. Morrill (eds), *The British Problem c.1534–1707: State Formation in the Atlantic Archipelago* (Basingstoke, 1996), p. 186.

as I know, no one in Scotland was fighting for independence from the house of Stuart or for looser ties with England; on the contrary from 1640 to 1654 they were fighting for a confederal union of the kingdoms and churches. All the Protestants of Ireland wanted a redefined relationship between the kingdoms; and most of the Catholics wanted to create an Irish kingdom independent of the English parliament and courts but subject to the royal house of Stuart. However, it is becoming increasingly clear that there was— especially amongst the previously dispossessed Catholic septs of Ulster—a willingness, perhaps even a determination, to free Ireland from English and Stuart control. There was equally a determination to recreate a Celtic realm initially under foreign Protectorship until such time as it might be possible to recreate the ancient Celtic high kingship. And in 1649 the Rump of the English parliament and its Council of State wished to secede from Scotland, to de-couple the dynastic Union of 1603 and to allow Scotland to float free as an independent monarchy to the north of an English and Irish Commonwealth.[42]

Now, the point of this refining of Pocock's argument is to be clearer than he sometimes is about distinguishing two distinct processes: the structural stress engendered by the process of converting a dynastic agglomerate into a state system; and the fevers induced by the partly successful processes of acculturation of the Celtic peoples of the Atlantic archipelago into lowland English systems of law and inheritance, language, religion. The result was the creation of new English, Irish, Scottish, and Welsh identities very different from older English, Irish, Scottish, and Welsh identities. It also resulted in the creation within the peoples of the island of Britain, but not amongst most of the peoples of the island of Ireland, of an additional *British* identity. The wars of the 1640s and the early 1650s are for many an attempt to command the first of those processes, the creation of a state (and in that sense to be part of a holistic enterprise), and to withstand the second of them, to become more English (and in that sense to seek to refuse to be part of that enterprise).

XI

I have one more observation to make about the tangled web of Anglo-Scottish relations between 1638 and 1654 and that relates to the way the

---

[42] I have discussed this in rather different ways in 'The War(s) of the Three Kingdoms', in Burgess (ed.), *New British History*, pp. 65–91 and Morrill, 'Rule of saints and soldiers'.

English and the Scots reacted to the crisis of the winter of 1648–9 and the wholly English act of regicide.

The execution of Charles I on 30 January 1649 was an English event with archipelagic consequences. There was no pressure for regicide in Scotland and Ireland: those English army officers and the scattering of civilian supporters they enlisted showed no interest in notifying—let alone consulting—anyone in Charles's other kingdoms before they put him on trial and decapitated him.

The regicide was driven forward by a conviction that by restarting the civil war in 1648 the king had committed sacrilege, had sought to overturn the judgement that God had so clearly delivered in the First War of 1642–6.[43] He was a 'Man of Blood'[44] who had spilt the innocent blood of God's people, a man whom God would call to account, and at human hands. But the regicide was not a *republican* act. The documents that built up the case for regicide criticised Charles I and his eldest son, but not the office or the family. There is strong evidence that until the very last minute the army leaders hoped to persuade Charles to abdicate in favour of one of his younger sons.[45] It is not that they thought him unworthy of death; rather, they were appalled at the prospect of making regicide stick. They clearly anticipated massive English, archipelagic, and international outrage and envisaged having to face overwhelming military reprisals. And it was to limit the scale of this disaster that the Rump Parliament made a stunning offer to the Scots in the immediate wake of regicide. It abolished monarchy in England and Ireland *but not in Scotland*.[46] The Union of the Crowns was portrayed as a disaster for both peoples, and the Scots were encouraged to resume their independence as a people and a polity, free to remain as a separate kingdom to the north of the Commonwealth of England and Ireland. It was an offer completely spurned by the entire Scottish political establishment. Their parliament proclaimed Charles II as King of Britain and Ireland and they spent much of the next five years trying to restore him to all his kingdoms. They were bound in a Covenant with God that they could not unilaterally abrogate; and the

---

[43] This is the argument of J. Morrill and P. Baker, 'Oliver Cromwell, the Regicide and the Sons of Zeruiah', in J. Peacey (ed.), *The Regicides and the Execution of Charles I* (Basingstoke, 2001), pp. 14–35.

[44] A reference to the Old Testament book of Numbers, ch. 35, v. 33. See also P. Crawford, 'Charles I, That Man of Blood', *Journal of British Studies* 16 (1977), pp. 41–61.

[45] Most clearly seen in *The Remonstrance of the Army* (25 November 1648).

[46] Gardiner, *Constitutional Documents*, pp. 384–7; D. Hirst, 'The English Republic and the meaning of Britain', in Bradshaw and Morrill (eds), *The British Problem*, pp. 451–86. Of course the English parliament could not make law for Scotland; but neither could the Scottish parliament make law for England—but it chose to do so when it pronounced Charles II King of Great Britain and crowned him as such at Scone: Morrill (ed.), *Scottish National Covenant*, pp. 20–2.

Covenant was a British and Irish and not just a Scottish document, with obligations relating to all of Britain and Ireland.

The pronouncements of those who urged or carried out the regicide and who then carried out the abolition of the monarchy after weeks of agonising are largely free of the language of republicanism. That language would afterwards be used by some of the propagandists for the regime which had replaced Charles, but that is another matter.[47] Whatever the chattering classes thought in the later 1640s, the men of action did not intend or want to replace monarchy as well as Charles I. The establishment of a kingless commonwealth was a bolt out of the blue. The Scots commissioners in London sent a series of briefing documents back to Edinburgh. They were unambiguous that the Rump intended to try Charles I and might execute him. The best they could do for him was play for time, and that they certainly tried to do.[48]

But these same commissioners in their thorough briefings did not warn the Estates to expect the abolition of monarchy. Argyll and his friends were bracing themselves for a decision of even greater difficulty for them: what to do if and when the English parliament broke the hereditary succession and tried to impose one of Charles's younger sons on the throne. They prepared an oath to bind all of Scotland to the Prince of Scotland (as they termed Prince Charles).[49] They were anticipating the crisis of 1701–7.[50]

Yet the Scots had miscalculated. Because Charles would not abdicate, he had to be executed. And because he was executed he could not be replaced, for the sheer scale of meeting the anticipated reaction forbade it. The establishment of a free commonwealth was a poor second best to the replacement with his consent of an inflexible adult king by a pliable child king. And the dream of a monarchical restoration stayed with that clear majority of defeated Royalists and demoralised presbyterian Parliamentarians that

---

[47] As in the pronouncements by John Cook, who published in 1650 a version of the speech he would have made at the trial of Charles I if the king had consented to plead: *King Charles His Case* (1648). Cook was the king's chief prosecutor. See also Cook's *Monarchy no creature of God's Making* (1652). Cook's republican rhetoric is analysed by Glenn Burgess, 'Regicide: the execution of Charles I and English political thought', in R. von Friedeburg (ed.), *Murder and Monarchy: Regicide in European History 1300–1800* (Basingstoke, 2004), pp. 212–36.

[48] Printed in the *Acts of the Parliaments of Scotland*, VI (1819), pp. 337–8, 347–8, 358–9, 62. See the discussion in D. Stevenson, *Revolution and Counter-Revolution in Scotland, 1644–1651* (Edinburgh, 1977), pp. 128–30.

[49] *Acts of the Parliaments of Scotland*, VI, pt ii, p. 362.

[50] A reference to the struggle following the English parliament's passage of the Act of Settlement in 1701 which (passing over almost fifty Catholic claimants) offered the reversion of the Crown to the Electress Sophia of Hanover and her descendants. This act was not binding on Scotland and it gave the Scots the opportunity to break the Union of the Crowns or to extract major concessions from the English in return for the passage of a similar act through the Scottish parliament, the negotiation which led to the Treaty of Union.

remained loyal to the house of Stuart. Such a vision was also shared amongst that pragmatic minority of defeated Royalists, marginalised political presbyterians, and time-serving lawyers. It was even shared by elements in the army, who worked in and under every regime of the 1650s, who sought to restore monarchy in the house of Cromwell.[51]

But if regicide was a minority English choice with no resonance elsewhere in Charles I's state system, and if regicide came to carry as a consequence what could be called an unsought 'strong republicanism' (that is, a renunciation of the title and office of king), then it led on to a much wider exploration throughout the polity of what could be called 'weak republicanism'. This is not the same thing as civic republicanism, that admiration of the superior example of just government afforded by a study of the political ideas of antiquity and the Renaissance. Rather it is a radical constitutionalism that saw liberty itself as consisting in a body believing itself to be mandated by God to speak for a free people and to decide what powers it was prudent to confer on a king. And it saw that mandated people as having the God-given right to decide who should be permitted to exercise those powers and under what sanctions. It also claimed that monarchy could (and should) be suspended until all those conditions were met. In that sense, the islands were full of 'weak republican' noises between 1647 and 1660.[52]

It is of course true that as soon as the Scottish parliament heard that the English had executed their king, they unanimously proclaimed Charles II as the 'rightful and Lawfull successor' to the kingdoms of 'Britain, France and Ireland by the providence of God and by the Lawfull right of undoubted succession and descent'. But in a less quoted passage, they went on to say that:

> Because his Majesty is bound by the law of God and fundamentall lawis of this kingdome to rule in righteousness and equitie . . . it is heereby declared that before he can be admitted to the exercise of his royall dignitie he shall give satisfactioun to this kingdome in those things that concerne the security of religioun, the union betwix the kingdomes and the good and peace of his [various] kingdomes according to the solemn league and covenant.[53]

And to ram that point home, two days later on 7 February 1649 an Act anent Securing of Religion and Peace of the Kingdom changed the coronation oath and exacted other guarantees that the king would establish both

---

[51] Morrill and Baker, 'Oliver Cromwell, the Regicide and the Sons of Zeruiah', pp. 30–5.

[52] For a range of views on this, see David Norbrook, *Writing the English Republic 1627–1660* (Cambridge, 1999); S. Barber, *Regicide and Republicanism 1646–1659* (Edinburgh, 1998); B. Worden, 'English Republicanism', in J. Burns and M. Goldie (eds), *The Cambridge History of Political Thought*, III: *1450–1700* (Cambridge 1991), pp. 453–85.

[53] *Acts of the Parliaments of Scotland*, VI, pt ii, p. 363.

true religion and the constitutional forms of a confederated monarchy.[54] Until such time as these guarantees were forthcoming he was suspended from the exercise of the authority. By Scottish constitutional theory in 1649 Charles II had a right to a royal title but not a royal office. This position united the Covenanters in 1649, but determining what represented adequate guarantees was to divide them absolutely and irreconcilably over the following fifteen months, leading to the emergence of the Resolutioners, who were willing to take Charles II's promises of compliance at face value, and the Remonstrants, who were not.[55]

This might be thought a particularly soft kind of weak republicanism.[56] But if we are going to extend the definition beyond a commitment to kinglessness, it is difficult to draw a line short of this. And if we disallow this, then we must disallow almost all that we normally call Leveller or Army republicanism in England. Harder forms of republicanism did emerge in Scotland; but only under the intense pressure of royal betrayal and the military conquest and absorption into a greater England.

The wars of the 1640s fragmented the political communities in England and in Scotland. But as the various groups struggled to find allies across as well as within historic frontiers, it was the failure of minds to meet that stands out. There was no English enthusiasm for a union of kingdoms or commonwealths, and the union that did result was reluctant and uncelebrated. Within Scotland there was an absolute commitment to protecting Scottish law and the Scottish Reformation from the twin evils of English popery and English religious anarchy. But as you cannot prevent radiation leaks by erecting fences, so the Scots could not protect their Reformation without closing down nuclear reactors in England. The Scots did not seek independence of England but devolution within a dual monarchy. It is what they were to seek again in 1707 and throughout what might be termed the War of the Two Dynasties from 1689 to 1746. To end on a note of provocation: it is arguably still the primary discourse of the present day.

Note. This essay draws on material used elsewhere, notably in an essay entitled 'Rethinking Revolution in Seventeenth-Century Britain', in Kazuhito Kondo (ed.), *State and Empire in British History: Proceedings of the Fourth Anglo-Japanese Conference of Historians* (Tokyo, 2003).

[54] J. R. Young, *The Scottish Parliament 1639–1661: a Constitutional and Political Analysis* (Edinburgh, 1996), pp. 224–5.
[55] Stevenson, *Revolution and Counter-Revolution*, chs 4–6; J. D. Grainger, *Cromwell against the Scots: the Last Anglo-Scottish War 1650–2* (Edinburgh, 1997), esp. chs 1 and 4.
[56] I discuss how this argument can be applied to Ireland in 'Rule of saints and soldiers'. For a tantalising glimpse of the way the O'Neills were conceiving of the restoration of Gaelic High Kingship in Ireland, see Casway, 'Gaelic Maccabeanism'.

5

Judicial Torture, the Liberties of the Subject, and Anglo-Scottish Relations, 1660–1690

CLARE JACKSON

IN 1689, THE WHIG POLEMICIST, JAMES WELWOOD, published an anonymous pamphlet claiming that 'if one wanted to draw the scheme of one of the most despotic governments in the world', one would not need to search as far afield as 'Constantinople, Moscow or some of the eastern Courts for a Copy to design after'. For, according to Welwood, 'Scotland alone' might sufficiently furnish an appalled observer 'with all the ideas of oppression, injustice and tyranny concentred for the space of twenty years and upwards in that kingdom.'[1] Another anonymous pamphlet published the same year, entitled *The Sco[t]tish Inquisition*, likewise described the brutal manner in which Charles II's ministers enforced political obedience and religious conformity, even resorting to extort 'all by Torture with their engines of Cruelty, the Boots, fired Matches betwixt the Fingers, and Thumbkins, and after torturing hanged several, tho' thereby they could extort nothing'.[2] Such contemporary descriptions seemingly confirmed that Restoration Scotland was indeed a desperately barbarous, primitive, and oppressive place, where scant regard was accorded to civil liberties, no writ of habeas corpus ran, and where physical torture was not only legal, but also regular judicial practice. Succeeding generations indeed identified that era as the 'darkness before the

---

[1] [James Welwood], *Reasons why the Parliament of Scotland Cannot comply with the Late King James' Proclamation, Sent lately to that Kingdom, &c.* (London, 1689), sig. B2r.
[2] Anon., *The Scotish [sic] Inquisition; Or, A Short Account of the Proceedings of the Scotish Privy-Counsel, Justiciary Court, and those Commissionated by them, whereby the Consciences of good Men have been Tortured, the Peace of the Nation these several Years past exceedingly Disturbed, and Multitudes of Innocent People cruelly Oppressed, and inhumanely Murdered* (Edinburgh, 1689), pp. 1–2.

Proceedings of the British Academy, **127**, 75–101. © The British Academy 2005.

dawn' of happy civilisation.[3] Following the incorporating Anglo-Scottish Union of 1707, judicial torture was entirely proscribed by the British parliament of Queen Anne in 1708, and among those Enlightenment commentators who subsequently celebrated its statutory abolition was Baron David Hume, for whom judicial torture remained 'a vestige of barbarity'.[4]

While traditional tendencies to denigrate the Restoration era as one of parochial politics and ecclesiastical extremism remain open to challenge,[5] this chapter reconsiders Hume's 'vestige of barbarity': the role of judicial torture in late seventeenth-century Scotland. It begins by examining the practice of judicial torture in its broader legal, political, and philosophical contexts before turning to consider three specific instances wherein torture was sanctioned. The first concerns the torture in 1676 of the Covenanting preacher, James Mitchell, following his alleged attempt to assassinate the head of the established church, Archbishop James Sharp of St Andrews. The second examines the torture of William Spence and William Carstares in 1684 on suspicion of treasonable attempts to foment an Anglo-Scottish rebellion against Charles II's authority, and the final case considers the torture in 1690 of an English political agitator, Henry Neville Payne, in connection with Anglo-Scottish Jacobite intrigues being concerted against the government of William and Mary.

In addition to examining the role of judicial torture within a domestic Scottish context, revisiting these cases also reveals that while judicial torture remained legal in late seventeenth-century Scotland, but not in England, its use could be interpreted by commentators elsewhere in the Stuart multiple monarchy as an alarming archetype of arbitrary models of governance. In this context, the politics of early modern multiple monarchy ensured that political allegiances frequently transcended national loyalties. For while the Stuart monarchs' opponents feared the existence of an Anglo-Scottish court conspiracy that aimed to suppress all forms of political resistance and religious dissent, members of Charles II's administration, and that of his brother, were equally concerned that political and religious factions in both

---

[3] The phrase is taken from David Stevenson, 'Twilight before night or darkness before dawn? Interpreting seventeenth-century Scotland', in Rosalind Mitchison (ed.), *Why Scottish History Matters* (Edinburgh, 1991), pp. 37–47.

[4] David Hume, *Commentaries on the Laws of Scotland respecting Crimes*, 2 vols (Edinburgh, 1986), I, p. 542. The Whig historian, Gilbert Stuart, likewise regarded the persistence of judicial torture in the late seventeenth century as a 'disgrace of humanity' that was exploited by a Scottish Privy Council whose 'odious prerogative' legitimated procedures that served to 'exceed the star-chamber of England in every thing that is most daringly and most exquisitely profligate': Gilbert Stuart, *Observations concerning the Public Law, and the Constitutional History of Scotland: With occasional remarks concerning English Antiquity* (Edinburgh, 1779), p. 279.

[5] See most recently, Clare Jackson, *Restoration Scotland, 1660–1690: Royalist Politics, Religion and Ideas* (Woodbridge, 2003).

Scotland and England would succeed in co-ordinating their resistance with devastatingly destabilising consequences. As the Scottish Lord Advocate, Sir George Mackenzie of Rosehaugh, perceived in 1685, the Stuart multiple monarchy was 'divided not in nations, but opinions, the old animosities among Scots, English and Irish being forgot and buried'. As Mackenzie explained, 'the modern differences ... [were] between Episcopal and Fanatic, Cavalier and Republican, or as some term it, Whig and Tory'.[6] And Tory fears were indeed vindicated that year, when a potentially critical challenge to James VII and II's authority was averted, following the suppression of an armed insurrection launched by Archibald Campbell, 9th Earl of Argyll, in the west of Scotland. Aware that Argyll's rising had originally been planned to coincide with another rebellion in the west of England by Charles II's natural son, the Earl of Monmouth, the English puritan diarist, Roger Morrice, reported a demand made in the English House of Commons to 'call to mind the Loyall Example of Scotland that had made it death to goe to Conventicles'. Insisting that the English legislature should not be less zealous in its attempts to secure political and religious loyalty than the Scots parliament, another English MP had evidently suggested imitating Scots practice further and 'moved that racks [of torture] might be established by law in England to force prisoners to confess'.[7]

I

Despite Morrice's report of calls for the reintroduction of torture racks into England, torture played no part in the juridical world of Restoration England. It was not only prohibited by English common law, but the English Privy Council was denied the right to issue torture warrants when English conciliar justice ceased in 1640.[8] Torture was, however, much more common in Continental Europe, where it remained central to early modern criminal law. As John Langbein has shown, its importance was ensured by the requirement of the Romano-canonical law of proof that all capital crimes had to be proven by the testimony of either two reliable eyewitnesses or the defendant's

---

[6] Sir George Mackenzie, *A Defence of the Antiquity of the Royal Line of Scotland: With a true Account When the Scots were Govern'd by Kings in the Isle of Britain* (London, 1685), p. iii.

[7] Dr Williams' Library, London: Roger Morrice's 'Entr'ing Book', Vol. 'P', f. 468 (14 June 1685).

[8] For a narrative account of the use of torture in English conciliar justice, see James Heath, *Torture and English Law: an Administrative and Legal History from the Plantagenets to the Stuarts* (Westport, Conn., 1982). For an account of the different methods of torture deployed in England and Scotland, see R. D. Melville, 'The use and forms of judicial torture in England and Scotland', *Scottish Historical Review* 2 (1905), pp. 225–48.

confession.[9] Since it was often the case that two eyewitnesses were unlikely to have been present at the scene of a serious crime, torture could provide an effective means to secure confession. By the same token, an equally high premium was placed on the capacity of torture to establish innocence within Continental courtrooms. For if a suspect denied involvement and thereafter withstood judicial torture, all other proofs were traditionally purged and the subject was acquitted and normally liberated.

In Scotland, however, the use of torture was somewhat different since, like England, Scotland followed a system of trial by jury whereby the final determination of a suspect's guilt or innocence was entrusted to a jury, who could convict on circumstantial evidence. Accordingly, the same premium was not placed on securing confessions as on the Continent. Moreover, as torture was prohibited by Scots common law, its use could only be justified as a method of eliciting pre-trial information by invoking the authority of Roman law. The use of judicial torture in Restoration Scotland thus remained primarily an extra-judicial procedure, employed for interrogative purposes in a manner similar to the situation that prevailed in early seventeenth-century England when, as Sir Francis Bacon had informed James VI and I, '[i]n the highest cases of treason, torture is used for discovery and not for evidence' in order 'to identify and forestall plots and plotters'.[10] In this context, interrogative torture also differed entirely from forms of afflictive or corporal punishment, whereby pain was legally inflicted for punitive purposes.

Contrary to popular perceptions that state torture was arbitrary and unlawful, the practice of judicial torture in Restoration Scotland was carefully regulated and documented. Warrant to torture could only be sanctioned by the Scottish parliament, or by the Scottish Privy Council, if parliament was not in session. Resort to judicial torture was not particularly frequent, for as Brian Levack's analysis of the thirty-four torture warrants issued by the Privy Council between 1590 and 1690 indicates, torture was only authorised in cases of the utmost gravity, involving suspected treason, sedition, witchcraft, and murder.[11] Notwithstanding, unwarranted torture did occur and Levack has revealed the extent to which central governmental authorities frequently found themselves powerless to prevent illegal torture being perpetrated by local magistrates, particularly in cases of suspected witchcraft.

---

[9] See John H. Langbein, *Torture and the Law of Proof: Europe and England in the Ancien Régime* (Chicago, 1977); see also Mirjan Damaska, 'The death of legal torture', *Yale Law Journal* 87 (1977–8), pp. 860–84.
[10] Quoted by Peter Pesic, 'Wrestling with Proteus: Francis Bacon and the "torture" of nature', *Isis* 90 (1999), pp. 81–94 at p. 91. See also Elizabeth Hanson, 'Torture and truth in Renaissance England', *Representations* 34 (1991), pp. 53–84.
[11] See Brian P. Levack, 'Judicial torture in the age of Mackenzie', in Hector L. McQueen (ed.), *The Stair Society: Miscellany IV* (Edinburgh, 2002), pp. 196–7.

When correctly authorised by the Privy Council or parliament, however, resort to judicial torture was defended on the essential grounds of safeguarding state security. Although someone who later acquired the unenviable sobriquet 'Bluidy Mackenzie' might be expected to defend such barbarous practice, as Lord Advocate, Sir George Mackenzie of Rosehaugh acknowledged in his *Laws and Customs of Scotland in Matters Criminal* (1678) that 'Torture is seldom used with us' and described the Privy Council as being 'tender' in its use.[12] Elsewhere, he insisted that torture was nevertheless 'warranted by our uncontroverted Law',[13] and that since the 'preservation of Order and Society makes Severity prevaile', torture was 'allowed to support this order'.[14] Security considerations aside, Mackenzie further justified the use of interrogative torture on the grounds that 'Torture is intended for bringing the Verity to Light'.[15] For, epistemologically, the defence of torture was predicated on a belief in the discernible reality of truth and in the corporeal location of that truth. Hence torture represented a judicial procedure whose intended outcome was the discovery of truth in suspected criminal activity. The physical inability of suspects to withhold objective truth ensured that the struggle between torturer and tortured revolved around the point at which the body would yield access to that truth. In this context, the phraseology of the Privy Council warrants ordering, for example, the torture of a former servant of the Earl of Argyll, William Spence, resolved 'to use all methods necessar . . . for expiscating the truth in so important a matter'; the verb 'expiscate' meaning literally 'to fish out'.[16] Moreover, the extent to which physical incapacity under torture would prevail over deluded self-possession was impressed on Spence's co-accused, William Carstares, when Lord Advocate Mackenzie had visited Carstares in an English prison to warn him that unless he co-operated with interrogation in London, 'the Boot in Scotland should

---

[12] Sir George Mackenzie, 'The Laws and Customs of Scotland, In Matters Criminal. Wherein is to be seen how the Civil Law, and the Laws and Customs of other Nations doth agree with, and supply Ours', in *The Works of that Eminent and Learned Lawyer, Sir George Mackenzie of Rosehaugh*, ed. Thomas Ruddiman, 2 vols (Edinburgh, 1718–22), II, p. 261.

[13] Sir George Mackenzie, *A Vindication of the Government in Scotland. During the Reign of King Charles II. Against Mis-representations made in several Scandalous Pamphlets &c.* (London, 1691), p. 24.

[14] British Library (hereafter BL) Add. MSS 18, 236, Sir George Mackenzie of Rosehaugh, 'A Discourse on the 4 First Chapters of the Digest to Shew the Excellence and usefullnesse of the Civill Law', f. 5v.

[15] Mackenzie, 'Laws and Customs', in *Works*, II, p. 261.

[16] *Register of the Privy Council of Scotland*, 3rd series, IX: *1684*, ed. Henry Paton (Edinburgh, 1924), p. 73. Lisa Silverman has drawn attention to the similarly ritualistic type of bodily phraseology incorporated in directions to torture in early modern France, showing that the verb 'tirer' was most commonly deployed 'pour tirer la verité de sa bouche' (to draw the truth from his mouth): Lisa Silverman, *Tortured Subjects: Pain, Truth and the Body in Early Modern France* (Chicago, 1991), p. 81.

drive out of me' information that Mackenzie believed Carstares to be withholding wilfully.[17]

II

The controversial use of physical torture as an extra-judicial procedure assumed prominence in the case of James Mitchell, whose trial in January 1678 for the capital crime of the attempted murder of a Privy Councillor was later deemed by the judge, Sir John Lauder of Fountainhall, as 'one of the most solemne Criminall tryalls [there] had been in Scotland thesse 100 years'.[18] The trial represented the culmination of a protracted series of events that had started a decade earlier when Mitchell had launched an unsuccessful assassination attempt against Archbishop James Sharp of St Andrews in July 1668 that had seriously wounded Sharp's companion, Bishop Andrew Honyman of Orkney. At the time, Sharp had privately acknowledged his escape to have been 'indeed marveilous and extraordinary', but remained convinced that 'the design was against me', contrived by Covenanting veterans of the suppressed Pentland Rising of 1666 who had now 'resolved upon another more ugly, yet more expeditious and effectual method for destroying the government'.[19] Although Mitchell evaded capture by escaping overseas, on his return to Edinburgh in 1674, he was arrested and examined by a Privy Council committee before whom he acknowledged participating in the Pentland Rising and also accepted responsibility for the assassination attempt, having apparently received an assurance that his life would be spared were such a confession forthcoming. Since Mitchell refused to repeat or acknowledge his confession before a group of Justiciary Court judges, however, insufficient corroborating evidence prevented prosecution. Mitchell thus remained in prison until he staged an unsuccessful escape attempt in December 1675, after which the Privy Council ordered that he 'be putt to the question and tortur'.[20]

---

[17] Robert Story, *William Carstares: a Character and Career of the Revolutionary Epoch (1649–1715)* (London, 1874), p. 77.

[18] Sir John Lauder of Fountainhall, *Historical Notices of Scotish [sic] Affairs, Selected from the Manuscripts of Sir John Lauder of Fountainhall, Bart., one of the Senators of the College of Justice*, ed. David Laing, 2 vols (Edinburgh, 1848), I, p. 185.

[19] National Library of Scotland, MS 2512, f. 118, 'Archbishop Sharp to the earl of Lauderdale, 23rd July, 1668'. That Mitchell was able to flee the scene of crime unapprehended was regarded by presbyterian sympathisers as evidence of prevalent popular antiepiscopalianism. According to James Kirkton, for example, after the assassination attempt, '[t]he cry arose, a man was killed. The people's answer was, It's but a bishop; and so there was no more noise': James Kirkton, *The Secret and True History of the Church of Scotland, from the Restoration to the Year 1678*, ed. Charles Kirkpatrick Sharpe (Edinburgh, 1817), p. 277.

[20] *Register of the Privy Council, IV: 1673–1676*, ed. P. Hume Brown (Edinburgh, 1911), p. 509.

Meanwhile, the newly appointed Lord Advocate, Mackenzie of Rosehaugh, reported '[n]ew discoveries . . . made of a design to kill the Archbishop' and renewed energy was directed towards inducing Mitchell to acknowledge his former confession of involvement in the Pentland Rising, if not also responsibility for the assassination attempt.[21] Accordingly, on 24 January 1676, Mitchell was tortured with 'the boot', which was a wooden or iron casing that encircled the leg from the ankle to the knee. A hammer or mallet was then used to drive wooden wedges into the boot between the casing and the leg, often resulting in the leg being crushed.[22] After answering a series of factual questions, Mitchell refused to supply further elaboration or to acknowledge his retracted confession and endured nine strokes of the mallet before fainting 'through the extremity of pain'.[23] When further torture on his other leg was then suggested, some of Mitchell's associates were reported to 'drop in a letter' to Archbishop Sharp, warning that should Mitchell's torture continue, 'he should have a shott from a steddier hand', whereupon threats of renewed torture were abandoned and Mitchell was remanded in prison.[24]

Although the judicial purposes of Mitchell's torture proved unsuccessful, its political impact immediately extended beyond Scots boundaries to furnish alarmed English commentators with a terrifying spectacle of the brutality of judicial procedures in Charles II's northern kingdom. In an audaciously subversive Latin manuscript poem narrating Mitchell's torture, entitled 'Scaevola Scoto-Britannicus', the English poet and puritan MP for Hull, Andrew Marvell, dubbed Mitchell 'Scaevola' in an allusion to the Roman patriot, Gaius Mucius Scaevola, who in 509 BC had plotted to kill the Etruscan king storming Rome, Lars Porsena, but had, like Mitchell, attacked the wrong man, killing Porsena's secretary instead. Regarding events in 'nostra Scotia' (our Scotland) as a portent for the way in which the rest of

---

[21] Sir George Mackenzie, *Memoirs of the Affairs of Scotland from the Restoration of King Charles II. A.D. M. DC. LX*, ed. Thomas Thomson (Edinburgh, 1821), p. 328.

[22] Concerned that Lord Macaulay's accounts of judicial torture consistently caricatured the Scots as 'savages by comparison' with their English neighbours, the nineteenth-century Tory historian, Mark Napier, emphasised the barbarity of Elizabethan instruments of torture to claim, somewhat unconvincingly, that '[t]he Scotch boot was a mere flea-bite compared to the iron embrace of the English Scavenger's Daughter': Mark Napier, *Memorials and Letters Illustrative of the Life and Times of John Graham of Claverhouse, Viscount Dundee*, 3 vols (Edinburgh, 1859), II, p. 101n. Claiming that accounts by 'the drivelling Wodrow and the dictatorial Macaulay' exaggerated the preponderance of torture in Scotland, Napier instead acclaimed Fountainhall's treatment of torture as serving to 'reduce their crude and vague anathemas within the bounds of justice and common sense' (Ibid., II, p. 104n).

[23] 'Of the process and execution of Mr. James Mitchell, January 1678', in Robert Wodrow, *The History of the Sufferings of the Church of Scotland from the Restoration to the Revolution*, ed. Robert Burns, 4 vols (Glasgow, 1828–30), II, p. 458.

[24] Robert Law, *Memorialls: Or, The Memorable Things that fell out within this Island of Brittain from 1638 to 1684*, ed. Charles Kirkpatrick Sharpe (Edinburgh, 1819), pp. 85–6.

Charles II's British subjects could expect to be governed, Marvell's poem perceptively captured the dual manner in which Scotland could be appropriated by external observers as both an alien, barbarous, and foreign land, yet also one that remained sufficiently familiar to represent a realistic and imminent threat. Hence, as Marvell warned, 'Scaevola si Thuscum potuit terrere Tyrannum, / Fortius hoc specimen Scotia nostra dedit' (If ever Scaevola was able to frighten the Etruscan tyrant, our own Scotland has afforded in this an even more impressive example).[25] Referring to Mitchell's claim that the assassination attempt on Sharp had been intended as retribution for the government's execution of those involved in the Pentland Rising (or, in Mitchell's words, 'the blood of the saints ... is yet reeking hot at the Croce of Edinburgh'),[26] Marvell related how Mitchell was now discovering that 'Ocrea torquet idem, mitra beatque scelus' (The boot punishes and a mitre blesses the same crime). Although Marvell recognised Mitchell's bullet had miscarried to wound an innocent bishop, 'Insons si Praesul quilibet esse potest' (If any bishop can be innocent), Marvell boldly accounted the only difference between a bishop and a murderer to be 'Inter Luciferum Furciferumque quod est' (The difference between a Lucifer and a gallows rogue). Admiring Mitchell's Stoic endurance of the agonising torture, Marvell recounted how 'Intima contuso et dum ringitur osse medulla / Calceus urit ubi cernere nemo queat, / Ut vacat!' (And while the inmost marrow is twisted in the bruised bone, the bone burns, where no one can see the boot pinch, how unconcerned he seems!), to the extent that 'Non poenas illum sed dare jura putes' (You would think him not to be suffering the sentence but imposing it). Reminding his readers that, like his classical predecessor, 'Hic è tercentum Mutius unus erat' (This was one Mucius from three hundred [would-be assassins]), Marvell's conclusion that 'Explosa nequiit quem sternere glande Michellus, / Explodet saevum Scotia Pontificem' (The cruel bishop whom Mitchell could not quell with his exploded bullet, Scotland herself will lay waste) was later to reverberate as an eerily accurate premonition when Sharp was brutally murdered by extremist Covenanting nonconformists in 1679.[27]

---

[25] Andrew Marvell, 'Scaevola Scoto-Britannicus', in Nigel Smith (ed.), *The Poems of Andrew Marvell* (London, 2003), pp. 419–20. With reference to Marvell's poem, I am grateful to Professor John Kerrigan for allowing me to read a chapter entitled 'Our Scotland, 1660–1699: Marvell, Mackenzie, Cleland' from his forthcoming study of seventeenth-century literature and 'the British Problem'. Marvell's admiration for the suffering of the Scots presbyterians was confirmed in one of the last letters he wrote in June 1678 to his nephew, William Popple. Contending that '[t]he Patience of the Scots, under their Oppressions is not to be paralleled in any History', Marvell observed how they 'still continue their extraordinary and numerous, but peaceable, Field Conventicles': H. M. Margoliouth (ed.), *Poems and Letters of Andrew Marvell*, 3rd edn, 2 vols (Oxford, 1971), II, p. 357. More recently, Mitchell's torture was also recounted in grim detail in James Robertson's novel, *The Fanatic* (London, 2000).

[26] Fountainhall, *Historical Notices*, I, p. 182.

[27] Marvell, 'Scaevola Scoto-Britannicus', pp. 419–20.

Although Mitchell was not tortured again by Charles II's authorities, the ambiguous status of his retracted confession remained central to the prosecution's case when he was eventually placed on trial in January 1678. Attending the trial, the Duke of Lauderdale's Anglican chaplain, George Hickes, found the courtroom 'full of disaffected villans' who spat on his clerical habit and 'pelted me now & then, wth such things as bits of apple, & crusts of bread'.[28] Arguing 'that Confessions are of all Probations the most Infallible' since '[o]ther Proofs are elicited by Men, but this is procur'd by God himself', Mackenzie specifically insisted that Mitchell's original confession had not been 'extorted from him by Racks and Instruments'.[29] Moreover, representing 'the greatest' witnesses 'that ever appeared in a criminall cause with us', the Scottish Chancellor, John Leslie, Duke of Rothes, the Parliamentary High Commissioner, John Maitland, Duke of Lauderdale, his brother Charles Maitland of Halton, and Archbishop Sharp himself all denied that Mitchell's confession had been obtained in exchange for an assurance that his life would be spared. When Sharp's testimony was challenged, however, the archbishop evidently 'fell in a mighty chaff and passion, exceedingly unbecoming his station, and the circumstances he was then stated in, and fell a scolding before thousands of onlookers'.[30] Following a request from Mitchell's defence counsel, Sir George Lockhart of Carnwrath, the relevant excerpts from the Privy Council Registers were then produced in court and indicated that Mitchell had indeed acknowledged responsibility for the assassination attempt only 'upon assurance given him by one of the Committee, as to his life, who had warrand from the Lord Commissioner and the Council

---

[28] BL Lansdowne MSS 988, f. 155r, 'George Hickes to Dr. Patrick or Dr. Oughram, 10th January 1678'.

[29] W. G. Scott-Moncrieff (ed.), *The Records of the Justiciary Court, Edinburgh, 1661–1678*, 2 vols (Edinburgh, 1905), II, p. 318; Sir George Mackenzie, *An Idea of the Modern Eloquence of the Bar. Together with a Pleading out of every Part of Law* (Edinburgh, 1711), p. 147. In his 'Laws and Customs of Scotland in Matters Criminal', published in the same year as Mitchell's trial, Mackenzie clarified that 'Confession, though extrajudicial, may be sufficient (if adminiculated) to subject the Confessor to the Torture; but this is rarely practised with us'. He did, however, 'remember to have seen Mitchel lately tortured, upon his retracting a Confession emitted by him in Presence of his Majesty's Privy Council': 'Laws and Customs', in *Works*, II, p. 249. More generally, however, Mackenzie insisted that 'a Confession extracted by Torture, is in no Law sufficient' for unless 'it be adhered to, after the Person is removed from the Rack, for two, or three Days, it makes no Faith' (Ibid.). Regarding Mackenzie's point about the premium placed on conscience, a moral correlate between the use of judicial torture and the operation of individual conscience was later drawn, for example, by Gottfried Wilhelm Leibniz, who argued that 'the conscience of evil-doing tortures the evil of itself, and so our nature was formed by the admirable plan of our Author that if there be no other, certainly there will be this penalty for sinners: guilt at the action' (quoted by Peter Pesic, 'Nature on the rack: Leibniz's attitude towards judicial torture and the "torture" of Nature', *Studia Leibnitiana* 29 (1997), p. 194).

[30] Fountainhall, *Historical Notices*, I, p. 184.

to grant the same'.[31] Although the Justiciary Court judges ruled the evidence obtained in the Privy Council register to be inadmissible having been 'cancelled by the Depositions of the Duke of Lauderdale . . . and other members of the Committee and Council',[32] the testimonies of Rothes, Lauderdale, Halton, and Sharp inevitably incurred immediate suspicion and Lauderdale 'stormed' in protest that he had agreed to appear in court 'to depone, but not to be staged for perjurie'.[33] Notwithstanding widespread dissension, Mitchell was convicted unanimously and sentenced to execution the following day.[34]

As suspicions of judicial malpractice festered, Mitchell's trial provoked popular dissent throughout Charles II's multiple monarchy. As Fountainhall recorded, events 'made a wonderfull noice' within Scotland, since most observers 'generally believed the law was streatched to get his [Mitchell's] neck streatched' as 'satyres and bitter verses flew about like hornets, in great swarmes . . . speaking much acrimony, and ane almost universall discontent'.[35] Alarmed by the content of such invectives, Lauderdale's chaplain, Hickes, decided to retaliate by attacking the 'Reports which these Instruments of Mischief send to London', denouncing 'these Coiners and Dispersers of false News' as 'a grievous Plague to both Church and State.'[36] In response, Hickes produced his own narrative of Mitchell's trial, this time deeming Mitchell to be a 'Ravillac Redivivus' in a reference to the fanatical Catholic, François Ravillac, who had assassinated King Henri IV of France in 1610. Accordingly, Hickes also reproduced several of Mitchell's written defences to indicate how his 'Soul had entered into the secret of the

---

[31] Scott-Moncrieff (ed.), *Records of the Justiciary Court*, II, p. 338. Extracts of the register relating to Mitchell's case can be found in National Archives of Scotland (hereafter NAS) GD 33/65/32, 'Paper . . . [with] reference chiefly to apprehension of James Mitchell &c.' and NAS GD 33/65/34, 'Privy Council paper being an Act of Council regarding the case of Jaˢ Mitchell &c.'.

[32] Scott-Moncrieff (ed.), *Records of the Justiciary Court*, II, p. 339.

[33] Fountainhall, *Historical Notices*, I, p. 184. Regarding the evidence supplied in the Privy Council register, Fountainhall recorded the views of some onlookers that Lockhart's 'late producing the Acts of Secret Councell was ane oversight; others judged it a designe to entrap the Duke and other witnesses' (Ibid., I, p. 185).

[34] For the original verdict, see NAS JC 39/30, 'Verdict of assize at trial of James Mitchell for the attempted murder of Archbishop Sharp in 1668'.

[35] Fountainhall, *Historical Notices*, I, p. 185. As Fountainhall acknowledged, the popular impact of the mismanaged trial was such that even many government supporters 'desired they had never dipt in it, but only keipt him [Mitchell] in perpetuall imprisonment' (Ibid.).

[36] [George Hickes], *Ravillac Redivivus, Being a Narrative of the late Tryal of Mr. James Mitchel a Conventicle-Preacher, Who was Executed the 18th of January last, for an attempt which he made on the Sacred Person of the Archbishop of St. Andrews . . . In a Letter from a Scottish to an English Gentleman* (London, 1678), p. 3.

Jesuites' on the grounds that Mitchell had 'not only acted like one of their Assassins, but had written his Apology with their poysoned ink'.[37]

III

While Marvell's 'Scaevola Scoto-Britannicus' presented a poetically evocative account of Mitchell's torture, another equally dramatic account of torture in Restoration Scotland was penned several years later by another English puritan. In October 1684, Roger Morrice reported in his 'Entr'ing Book' the Scottish Privy Council's decision to interrogate various prisoners suspected not only of possible complicity in the 'Rye House Plot' that had been foiled the previous year, but also of continued treasonable attempts to foment a joint Anglo-Scottish rebellion against Charles II's government. Among those suspects was William Spence, a former servant of Archibald Campbell, 9th Earl of Argyll. Having been arrested in London in October 1683, Spence had initially been questioned by several Scots Privy Councillors, including the Lord Advocate, Mackenzie of Rosehaugh, before being returned to Scotland where he had been kept as a chained prisoner in Edinburgh Castle for nearly a year. Since Spence had proved obdurately uncooperative during previous interviews in both London and Edinburgh, the Privy Councillors had decided to put Spence to torture. As Morrice's Entr'ing Book recorded, the Privy Councillors thus:

> re-examined Mr. Spence, and booted him giving 18 knocks with the Mallet upon the Wedge, whereas they use to give but six or seaven only, and after that charged fower soldiers (nay, swore them), to continue with him constantly, and to keep him from sleeping, which they did without intermission for 9 or 10 days and nights, when he was ready to die upon the floor for want of sleepe, they often pinched him, and touched him with hott things to prevent it &c. insomuch that he was almost distracted. They threw water upon his broken legg [and] the balls of his eyes swolen as big as Tennis balls. After that they tormented him by the thumbs stretching them towards the same length as his fingers.[38]

Although Morrice's entry regarding Spence's torture appeared in October 1684, the torture had actually occurred between 25 July and 21 August. According to Morrice, the boot wedge was driven in eighteen times, contrary to a customary six or seven and a contemporary presbyterian diarist, John

---

[37] Ibid., p. 41. As far as Mitchell's physical appearance was concerned, Hickes accounted him to be 'a lean, hollow-cheeck'd man, of a truculent Countenance, and had the air of an Assassin as much as a man could have' (p. 7).

[38] Morrice, 'Entr'ing Book', Vol. 'P', ff. 441–2 (16 October 1684).

Erskine of Carnock, confirmed that Spence 'received many strokes until his leg was quite crushed'.[39] Morrice also reported that water was thrown on Spence's 'broken legg', while a surgeon, John Baillie, received a fee of £5 sterling from the Privy Council in September 'for what he did and furnished towards the cure of Mr. Spence'.[40]

Despite enduring the boot on 26 July, Spence remained 'very obnoxious and suspect of prevarication', according to Fountainhall.[41] Accordingly, responsibility for Spence was entrusted to General Thomas Dalziel who imprisoned him in the Guildhall at Edinburgh's Canongate and subjected him to a policy of sleep deprivation, setting him 'upon a form where he had nothing to lean on'.[42] As Foutainhall observed, Spence was not only dressed in a rough hair-shirt to keep him awake, but was also regularly pricked 'as the witches are used.'[43] In this sense, 'pricking' referred to the common belief that proof of diabolic activity could be obtained through the 'insensible witch's mark', whereby a guilty witch would not bleed or bruise in response to needle punctures. Although Morrice reported that Spence was forcibly kept awake for nine or ten nights, Fountainhall's account indicates five, while Erskine's diary states that Spence was deprived of sleep until 2 August, suggesting seven. During this period, Fountainhall also recorded that Spence refused food 'of purpose, that he might require the lesse sleip'.[44] In a letter of 3 August, General Dalziel reported visiting Spence who 'reaves [raves] much' and 'knowes not what he sayes', adding that a physician and a surgeon appointed to inspect Spence had advised that 'if he be not eas'd with some sleep he will goe mad'.[45]

Accordingly, Spence was returned to the Tolbooth and permitted some sleep. On 7 August, however, the Privy Councillors found that he remained 'altogether refractory and obstinate' and ordered he be put to renewed torture, but this time by a 'new engyne' of torture, known as the 'thumbscrews' which resembled a miniature pair of steel stocks with a strong central screw. The suspect's thumbs were inserted into the twin apertures and the upper bar screwed downwards until the thumbs were crushed. According to Erskine,

[39] John Erskine of Carnock, *Journal of the Hon. John Erskine of Carnock 1683–7*, ed. W. Macleod (Edinburgh, 1893), p. 78.
[40] *Register of the Privy Council, IX: 1684*, p. 352.
[41] Fountainhall, *Historical Notices*, II, p. 545.
[42] Erskine, *Journal*, p. 78.
[43] Fountainhall, *Historical Notices*, II, p. 545.
[44] Ibid.
[45] NAS GD 124/15/176, 'Letter to the earl of Mar from General Thomas Dalziel, 3rd August 1684'. According to Erskine, although the surgeon initially appointed to treat Spence after his torture had 'out of compassion left him with a glass of ointment . . . to put on his leg at diverse times', it had been removed by the soldiers guarding Spence, although Erskine was unsure 'whether by order or not': Erskine, *Journal*, p. 78.

this pressure was applied on Spence until his 'broken bone was appearing thro' the skin'.[46] Despite having endured such torture 'for a long time', Spence remained unyielding, but on being threatened again by the boot, Fountainhall reported that Spence 'being frighted, desired tyme, and he would declare what he knew'.[47] Thereafter Spence agreed to decipher two encoded letters that had been sent from the Netherlands by his erstwhile master, Argyll, but which had been intercepted by Charles II's agents. In return for his co-operation, the Privy Councillors formally granted Spence a royal remission and pardon for any treasonable activity in which he may have been previously involved. It was also ordained that Spence should not be tortured or interrogated further about the matter and that neither the contents of the two intercepted letters, nor Spence's own testimony, would 'prejudge himself nor any person delated by him in his said answears'.[48] Accordingly, Spence explained and decoded the intricate cipher employed by Argyll. In addition to supplying detailed information concerning Argyll's plans to stage an armed Anglo-Scottish uprising against Charles II's government, Spence also identified a 'Mr. Red' cited in the correspondence as his co-accused, William Carstares.[49] Thereafter, Spence remained in custody, but was given the freedom of Edinburgh Castle, before being liberated later that month.

Despite the Privy Council's assurances that Spence's testimony would not be used against either himself or a third party, Carstares was then put to torture on 5 September. According to Erskine, the thumbscrews were applied to Carstares and 'kept on him about an hour and a half, his hands being behind his back'.[50] Despite remaining silent, when threatened with the boot, the following day, Carstares capitulated and agreed to supply a formal deposition wherein he named a series of prominent presbyterian nonconformists

[46] Erskine, *Journal*, p. 79. For more information on thumbscrews, see Alexander J. S. Brook, 'Notice of a Pair of Thumbikins . . . with some Notes concerning the Application of Torture in Scotland', *Proceedings of the Society of Antiquaries of Scotland*, 3rd series, 25 (1890–1), pp. 463–75.

[47] Fountainhall, *Historical Notices*, II, p. 548.

[48] *Register of the Privy Council*, IX: *1684*, p. 119.

[49] For a more detailed account of the cipher employed by Argyll, see Joseph McCormick (ed.), *State-Papers and Letters, addressed to William Carstares . . . To which is prefixed the Life of Mr. Carstares* (Edinburgh, 1779), p. 107. In one letter, each word was placed in a separate space and the total letter comprised 128 horizontal lines with eight vertical columns of words. Each column had been reproduced in vertical order, so that the second word in the original letter was moved to the 129th place from that which preceded it, generating an evidently meaningless message. Certain key names and subjects were further concealed by numerical ciphers and the use of nonsensical words, so that England and Scotland were, for example, referred to as 'Birch' and 'Brand' respectively. The letter was accompanied by a separate communication, indicating that 'Mr. B.' would pay a total sum of 128 guilders and 8 stivers, indicating a covert allusion to the cipher employed.

[50] Erskine, *Journal*, pp. 81–2.

allegedly cognisant of the conspiracy, thereby prompting a series of new arrests.[51] Carstares was thereafter transferred to Stirling Castle until he was recalled to swear the accuracy of his deposition on oath before the Privy Council on 22 December, whereupon he received assurance that his testimony had been obtained for information purposes and would not be used as judicial evidence. On being freed, Carstares discovered that his deposition had, however, been published by the authorities with no indication of the physical coercion involved in its supply or of the extenuations and qualifications with which Carstares claimed to have couched his responses.[52] Meanwhile, objection was voiced by some Privy Councillors to the successive torturing of those randomly named by those other suspects who thereby acquired immunity from prosecution by agreeing to supply information. As William Douglas, 3rd Duke of Hamilton, alleged, 'at this rate, they might, without accusers or witnesses, take any person off the street, and torture him'.[53]

The day after Carstares swore the accuracy of his deposition, the trial began of Robert Baillie of Jerviswood, whose name had not only been supplied by Carstares, but whose trial provided Charles II's minsters with a crucial opportunity to convince a sceptical Scottish populace about the reality of the threat posed to civil order by disaffected presbyterian Covenanters. As Fountainhall observed, 'the reputation of our Governors lay deeply at the stake, in convincing the world of the truth and reality of this plot discovered by them'. Hence 'they were hugely concerned to obviate anything that seemed in the least to infringe, invalidate, or take off the credibility of the plot in the minds of the people.' A quick verdict was likewise deemed all the more urgent, for not only were 'the holy days of Zuile [Yule] approaching' but Baillie's physical health was known to be precarious and the authorities remained keenly mindful 'of their reputation in discovering this Scots plot ... for if it had miscarried, it would have made the people believe it was but a sham, forged plot'.[54]

Proceedings against Baillie were accordingly conducted with abnormal haste and other individuals cited in Carstares's deposition were compelled to

---

[51] Among the new detainees were Walter Scott, Earl of Tarras, James Murray of Philiphaugh, Hugh Scott of Galashiels, and Sir James Dalrymple; for further information, see Richard L. Greaves, *Secrets of the Kingdom: British Radicals from the Popish Plot to the Revolution of 1688–89* (Stanford, 1992), p. 244.

[52] Carstares's deposition appeared as *The Deposition of Mr. William Carstares. When he was Examined before the Lords of Secret Committee, given in by him, and renewed upon Oath, the 22 of December 1684, in presence of the Lords of his Majesty's Privy Council* (Edinburgh, 1684); for Carstares's grievances regarding its publication, see Wodrow, *Sufferings of the Church of Scotland*, IV, p. 99.

[53] Sir John Lauder of Fountainhall, *The Decisions of the Lords of Council and Session from June 6th, 1678 to July 30th, 1712*, 2 vols (Edinburgh, 1759), I, p. 303.

[54] Ibid., I, p. 327.

testify in person, such as Walter Scott, Earl of Tarras, who had himself also been indicted for treason. Although Baillie's defence counsel objected that Tarras's testimony was compromised by virtue of his being *socius criminis*, this objection was repelled by the prosecution on the reason of state grounds that to disallow such evidence would be 'to allow Treason, since no man can prove a Plot, but he that is upon it'.[55] Deeming Baillie to be 'the Ring-leader of all those, who in this Kingdom concurred with the English Conspirators', Lord Advocate Mackenzie insisted that 'if he be not convicted, there should be no man punished for this Conspiracie'. Concluding his prosecution, Mackenzie further warned the jury to 'Remember the danger likewise of emboldening Conspiracies against the Kings Sacred Life, and of encouraging a Civil War, wherein yourselves and your Posterity may bleed' and counselled them to avoid 'making the least difficulty to find a man Guilty, by the strongest Proofs that ever were adduced in so latent a Crime as Conspiracy is'.[56] Complying with this advice, the jury convicted Baillie on 24 December and he was sentenced to immediate execution and quartering, proceedings being conducted so precipitously, it was alleged, on account of Baillie's frail health and the government's fear 'lest his death should be too quick for them'.[57] Yet while Baillie's execution enabled Charles II's ministers to spend Christmas 1684 congratulating themselves on the elimination of a known dissident, suspicions quickly arose that Baillie had, in fact, served primarily as an unfortunate scapegoat for the government's political agenda. As several commentators, including Fountainhall, acknowledged, Carstares's deposition had only 'cited many that were upon the knowledge', in general terms, 'of a current plot in Scotland these ten years past'.[58] Even Mackenzie had concluded his prosecution speech at Baillie's trial by conceding to the jury that he had 'insisted so much upon this Probation, rather to convince the World of the Conspiracy, than you that this Conspirator is Guilty'.[59]

---

[55] *The Tryal and Process of High-Treason and Doom of Forfaulture Against Mr. Robert Baillie of Jerviswood, Traitor* (Edinburgh, 1685), p. 9. On its title page, this published account of the trial announced that it was printed 'By His Majestie's special Command. As a further proof of the late Fanatical Conspiracy'.

[56] Ibid., pp. 30, 36.

[57] Gilbert Burnet, *Bishop Burnet's History of His Own Time: From the Restoration of Charles II to the Treaty of Peace at Utrecht, in the Reign of Queen Anne* (London, 1838), p. 380. As Fountainhall recorded, after Baillie's death, copies of Baillie's scaffold speech circulated widely, provoking Charles II's ministers to suggest giving Baillie's wife 'his four quarters to bury, if she could suppress and bring in all the copies of it, that it might not fly abroad; yet others thought this was the high way to set curiosity on edge, to search for, and propale it': Fountainhall, *Decisions*, I, p. 327.

[58] Fountainhall, *Decisions*, I, 302.

[59] *Tryal and Process*, p. 36. In his journal, Erskine of Carnock recorded how Baillie himself had reminded Mackenzie in court 'how he had said to him lately that he was now convinced he was

More seriously, the conduct of Baillie's trial contained several serious irregularities, the majority of which related, directly or indirectly, to the testimonies supplied by Spence and Carstares under torture. In the first place, the Privy Councillors had assured both individuals that their testimonies had been obtained for information and would not be used as evidence to implicate either themselves or any third party. And while Carstares had been exempted from testifying at Baillie's trial in person, his deposition *had* been cited, despite protests from Baillie's defence counsel. In the absence of precise rules of evidence in late seventeenth-century Scots law, it was, however, difficult to exclude statements obtained by torture.[60] Citing reason of state grounds for its inclusion as adminicular, or supporting, evidence, Mackenzie had acknowledged that testimonies taken *in absentia* were inadmissible in Roman law. Nevertheless, he had argued that this did not mean 'that our Juries, whom the Law allows to be a Law to themselves, and to be confin'd by no Rule, but their Conscience' might not trust the contents of such depositions when they were satisfied that such evidence had been supplied in otherwise formal circumstances.[61] For his part, Mackenzie reassured the jury that he regarded Spence's deciphering of Argyll's correspondence and Carstares's sworn deposition as 'the two surest proofs that Law ever invented, or the Nature of Human Affairs can allow'.[62]

A second type of legal irregularity surrounded the dubious jurisdictional competence by which the torture of Spence and Carstares had originally been authorised. For both had been initially apprehended in England before being returned to Scotland, where they had been interrogated about activities that had allegedly taken place in England and the Netherlands. In Carstares's case, although born in Scotland, he had lived in England since 1672 and he thus argued that his forcible return to Scotland was a deliberate contraven-

---

innocent', whereupon Mackenzie had replied, 'I said I thought you was [*sic*] indeed innocent of any design against the king': Erskine, *Journal*, p. 101. During the trial, Mackenzie had also acknowledged 'all the noise we have heard' surrounding the judicial proceedings, including allegations that the case was 'but a Cheat, the Kings Judges have been Murderers, all the Witnesses have been Knaves, and such as dyed for it, have been Martyrs': *Tryal and Process*, p. 30.

[60] Insisting that he had received formal assurance 'that my Testimony should not be made use off at the bar of any Judicator ag^t any persone whatsomever', Carstares later informed his mother that when he had subsequently remonstrated at the citation of his deposition during Baillie's trial, 'my Lord Chanc^{lor} was pleased to acknowledge before my Lord Treas^r and some of others of the secret Committee that what was done was a breache w^t me': NAS GD 406/1/10811, 'Wm Carstares to his mother [Janet Mure] setting down what he had said when examined about Argyll's rebellion, 1684'.

[61] *Tryal and Process*, p. 34. As Mackenzie clarified, the depositions in this instance were 'not meer Testimonies . . . emitted without an Oath, and a Judge', but had been 'taken under the awe of an Oath, and by the direction of a Judge' (Ibid.).

[62] Ibid., p. 30.

tion of the English Habeas Corpus Act of 1679 which he claimed to have been 'made expressly for the security of the liberty of Scots and Irish men'.[63] For as Carstares correctly insisted, the act had been passed to prevent 'illegal imprisonments beyond the seas', specifically enjoining that 'noe Subject of this Realm that now is or hereafter shall be an Inhabitant or Resident of this Kingdome of England . . . shall or may be sent Prisoner into Scotland Ireland Jersey Guernsey &c'.[64] Hence Carstares regarded his return to Scotland as 'such a breach of law as cannot be palliated', later confirming that 'in all my examinations in Scotland, I was not so much as accused of a crime committed in that kingdom'. For Carstares, it was 'plain that I and others were sent home, because it was judged that violent tortures which the laws of England— at least the custom—does not admit of, would force to anything'.[65] Once in Scotland, he continued to challenge the 'popish counsels prevailing there' by disputing the validity of the Privy Council's torture warrant. Despite establishing that he was not accused of any crimes committed in Scotland, he was, however, informed by Lord Advocate Mackenzie that if he 'had been guilty of contriving against his majesty's government at Constantinople', he would face the same prosecution from Charles II's authorities, to which Carstares claimed to have countered, in vain, that the crimes of which he was evidently accused 'were said to be committed in England, where his majesty's laws were equally in force for the security of his government, which at Constantinople they were not'.[66]

Rhetorical flourishes aside, Mackenzie doubtless acknowledged the force of Carstares's objections, since the status of Scots prisoners detained in England had been discussed extensively by Charles II's ministers following the arrest of Spence, Carstares, and several other prominent Scots the previous year. In August 1683, the Scottish Secretary, Alexander, Earl of Moray, had confirmed from London that the case of the Scots suspects had been 'fullie debeated [sic]' in the English 'Cabinit Councill', when Charles II had deemed it 'by no meanes fitt to send up thes Scots prisoners to be tried hear, seeinge no probabilitye of reatching them', while simultaneously recognising that any attempt to return them to Scotland 'uould occatione much noice, especially iff it proued to no effecte, and in that case uould be mor hurtfull then profitable to the Kings service'.[67] As Lord Advocate, Mackenzie of

---

[63] Wodrow, *Sufferings of the Church of Scotland*, IV, p. 98.

[64] 'An Act for the better securing the Liberty of the Subject and for Prevention of Imprisonments beyond the Sea' (1679), in *Statutes of the Realm . . . Volume the Fifth [1625–1680]* (London, 1819), p. 937.

[65] Story, *William Carstares*, p. 78.

[66] Wodrow, *Sufferings of the Church of Scotland*, IV, p. 98.

[67] Historical Manuscripts Commission, *Report on the Buccleuch & Queensberry Manuscripts (15th Report, Appendix, Part VIII)*, 2 vols (London, 1897), I, pp. 30–1. In a letter to the Scottish

Rosehaugh had evidently attempted to persuade Charles II 'that ther was a necessarie formality to be used in it, and peapers [*sic*] to pass', but such scruples were discounted at a subsequent meeting of Scots Privy Councillors in London, when John Drummond of Lundin advised the king 'that it was of ill consequence, wher he was free and unbounded, to tye himself to formes'.[68] Ironically, Lundin succeeded in convincing Charles II to return the prisoners to Scotland by citing the previous occasion in 1674 when Carstares had been arrested 'in Ingland for a crime committed in Ingland', but had been 'by the King's order, without communicating of it to his councell in any of the Kingdoms, sent to Scotland', where he had been imprisoned without charge or trial in Edinburgh Castle for five years before being released in 1679.[69]

Aside from such serious legal irregularities, broader moral and theological difficulties also arose from the fact that Carstares had been compelled to swear the accuracy of his deposition on oath. Since torture was ostensibly intended to elicit information, rather than to supply judicial evidence, administering oaths was generally regarded as an inappropriate contravention of a subject's privilege against self-incrimination and the absence of formal criminal charges to which an individual could be expected to respond. Hence both Spence and Carstares had consistently refused to swear oaths consenting to answer *super inquirendis* any questions that were posed during torture, as opposed to a pre-circulated written list of specific enquiries.[70]

Chancellor, the Earl of Aberdeen, dated 14 August 1683, Sir Andrew Forrester likewise requested information as to 'whether any thing is to be layd to their charge in Scotland; to the end that, if the law can not reatch them here, they may be sent with some other Scottsmen, who are like to be ordered to goe down to be tried there': John Dunn, *Letters Illustrative of Public Affairs in Scotland, Addressed by Contemporary Statesmen to George, Earl of Aberdeen* (Aberdeen, 1851), p. 131.

[68] *Buccleuch & Queensberry Manuscripts*, I, p. 159. In his 'Entr'ing Book', Roger Morrice likewise recorded how the detained Scots had been examined by Mackenzie who 'reported he found none of them less or more concerned in the rebellion in Englan[d], only some (who were not concerned in the Scotch rebellion) had fled hither rather then take the Test before the judges itenerant in their circuit in Scotland'. According to Morrice, Mackenzie's report was, however, ill received by Charles II's ministers 'which troubled him [Mackenzie] very much': Morrice, 'Entr'ing Book', Vol. 'P', f. 383 (27 October 1683).

[69] *Buccleuch & Queensberry Manuscripts*, I, p. 159.

[70] When threatened with torture if he did not acknowledge his retracted confession in 1676, James Mitchell had also insisted that he did not consider himself 'obliged by the law of God, nature, or the nation, to become mine own accuser': Wodrow, *Sufferings of the Church of Scotland*, II, p. 456. In 1651, the English philosopher Thomas Hobbes had likewise argued that since 'Torture is to be used but as a means of conjecture, and light, in the further examination, and search of truth', testimonies emitted under torture 'ought not to have the credit of a sufficient Testimony', since whether or not an individual spoke truthfully or mendaciously, 'he does it by the Right of preserving his own life': Thomas Hobbes, *Leviathan*, ed. Richard Tuck (Cambridge, 1991), p. 99. More widely, one of the original functions of torture had been to allow the accused to convict or acquit themselves on the basis of their own truthful testimony. Once the capacity

Finally, a wider moral anxiety surrounded the fact that the testimonies supplied by both Spence and Carstares had been coerced, being emitted under conditions of intense physical and mental duress. During Carstares's torture, one Privy Councillor, Hamilton, had even 'retired, and refused to be present', correctly recognising that 'if the party should die in the torture, the Judges were liable for murder, [or] at least were severely censurable'.[71] Moreover, judicial testimony was also only regarded as reliable if supplied by persons of a sound mind. Having deprived Spence of sleep for over five nights, even General Dalziel had recognised that Spence 'knowes not what he sayes', reporting the professional medical advice that unless Spence was allowed to sleep 'he will goe mad' which would mean that 'all hope of confession is gone'.[72] Finally, Spence had himself only been tortured after the Privy Council's plans to torture another prisoner, William Gordon of Earlston, were abandoned after Gordon's sanity was questioned. For, as Fountainhall reported, having been brought to the torture chamber, 'through fear or distraction', Gordon had 'roared out like a bull, and cried and struck about him, so that the hangman and his man durst scarce lay hands on him', before 'at last he fell in a swoon'.[73]

IV

The physical brutality and alleged arbitrariness of political proceedings under Charles II and James VII and II ensured that the period later became popularly synonymous with the barbarous 'Killing Times' depicted in subsequent presbyterian martyrologies. Moreover, when external observers, such as Roger Morrice, were even moved to dub Scotland 'the Island of [the] Boot' in June 1685, it might have been expected that judicial torture would have been abolished as part of the Williamite Revolution of 1689.[74] The emergence of new sources of political dissension in the form of Jacobite opposition to the new administration served, however, to place a renewed premium on the

---

of torture to purge proofs against the accused began to be undermined, however, torture became primarily an evidentiary procedure, entirely different from judicial procedures, such as the 'trial by ordeal', which had conflated the supply of evidence with indications of guilt or innocence: see Robert Bartlee, *Trial by Fire and Water: the Medieval Judicial Ordeal* (Oxford, 1986) and Margaret H. Kerr, Richard D. Forsyth, and Michael J. Plyley, 'Cold water and hot iron: trial by ordeal in England', *Journal of Interdisciplinary History* 22 (1992), pp. 573–95.
[71] Fountainhall, *Decisions*, I, p. 303. In his 'Laws and Customs of Scotland in Matters Criminal' of 1678, Mackenzie had earlier confirmed that '[t]hese who torture, if the Person tortured die, are punishable, as Murderers': 'Laws and Customs', in *Works*, II, p. 261.
[72] NAS GD 124/15/176, 'Letter to the earl of Mar from General Thomas Dalziel, 3rd August 1684'.
[73] Fountainhall, *Historical Notices*, II, p. 465.
[74] Morrice, 'Entr'ing Book', Vol. 'P', f. 468 (18 June 1685).

preservation of state security. Accordingly, although the Claim of Right presented by the Convention of Estates to William and Mary in April 1689 stated that 'the useing Torture without Evidence, or in ordinary Crymes, is contrary to Law', the option remained for the king's Scottish ministers to sanction torture in extraordinary circumstances if they were already in the possession of incriminating evidence.[75] The retention of torture as an interrogatory procedure was perceived by servants of the discredited regimes of Charles II and his brother, such as Mackenzie of Rosehaugh, as a retrospective vindication of their actions and a negation of vociferous Covenanting allegations that torture was 'inconsistent with all humanity'. For as Mackenzie argued in 1691, if torture was inconsistent with humanity, its humanity could not be reversed by reserving its warrant to parliamentary authority nor by insisting that it should not be inflicted without just cause, 'since every Man may easily pretend that what he does is done upon just Motives'.[76]

The continued legality of judicial torture could not, however, entirely dispel an increasing official queasiness about its usage, which became evident in the case of the last person to be tortured in Scotland, who was, ironically, an Englishman. A veteran Catholic playwright, polemicist, and agitator, Henry Neville Payne had become associated with the group of disillusioned Scottish presbyterian magnates congregated around Sir James Montgomery of Skelmorlie, whose frustrated personal ambitions had compounded a broader political disenchantment to encourage covert liaisons with English Jacobite agitators.[77] Payne himself was arrested as 'a traffiqueing papist' on his arrival in Scotland on 4 August 1690,[78] having been 'informed he was to be indyted for high Treson [sic]' and deeming it not 'saiff to stay [for] a tryall' in England, according to one of Montgomery's accomplices, John Murray, Earl of Annandale.[79] Following Payne's detention, however, the English

---

[75] Thomas Thomson and Cosmo Innes (eds), *The Acts of the Parliaments of Scotland*, 12 vols (Edinburgh, 1814–75), IX, p. 39. As the Whig historian, Lord Macaulay, later observed, '[n]othing in the proceedings at Edinburgh astonishes an Englishman more than the manner in which the Estates dealt with the practice of torture': Thomas Babington Macaulay, *The History of England from the Accession of James the Second*, 4 vols (London, 1864), III, p. 22.

[76] Mackenzie, *Vindication of the Government in Scotland*, p. 24.

[77] For more information about Payne, see Willard Thorp, 'Henry Nevil Payne, dramatist and Jacobite conspirator', in Hardin Craig (ed.), *Essays in Dramatic Literature: the Parrott Presentation Volume* (Princeton, 1935), pp. 347–81.

[78] *Register of the Privy Council*, XV: *1690*, ed. E. W. M. Balfour-Melville (Edinburgh, 1967), p. 274.

[79] *Leven and Melville Papers: Letters and State Papers Chiefly Addresed to George, Earl of Melville, Secretary of State for Scotland 1689–1691*, ed. W. H. L. Melville (Edinburgh, 1843), p. 513. For further information about Anglo-Scottish Jacobite intrigues and the 'Montgomery Plot', see P. A. Hopkins, 'Sir James Montgomery of Skelmorlie', in Eveline Cruickshanks and Edward Corp (eds), *The Stuart Court in Exile and the Jacobites* (London, 1995), pp. 39–59 and his *Glencoe and the End of the Highland War*, 2nd edn (Edinburgh, 1998).

authorities evidently became attracted by the potential to extract greater amounts of intelligence by means of the alternative methods of inquisitorial procedure available in Scotland. Hence pressure to torture Payne came primarily from London, where the Solicitor-General for Scotland, Sir William Lockhart, argued that 'his treason against the King of Scotland is a sufficient reason to try him ther', despite Payne's protestations that he was protected by an English parliamentary indemnity.[80]

While receiving regular directions from London to 'have no pitie on him', being 'a desperat cowardlie fallou', the Scots Privy Council simultaneously faced opposition to the idea of torturing Payne from his fellow Jacobite sympathisers in Scotland, including Sir Aeneas Macpherson of Cluny.[81] In his own *Vindication*, published in 1692, Macpherson claimed to have succeeded in delaying Payne's torture by visiting the Lord Advocate, Sir John Dalrymple of Stair, to leave an anonymous 'note in the lock-hole of his door'. This communication evidently warned Dalrymple of popular hostility to 'a set of men' who 'make it y^r business to drive matters to extremity, not so much in favours [*sic*] of the present Government as to excuse the supposed failures and extravagances of the last'. Hence the note criticised Dalrymple's keenness 'to bring men of quality to torture under a Government that justlie values itself upon reforming all abuses of that kind'.[82] Since the letter also threatened Dalrymple's life, Macpherson alleged that the Privy Council thereafter decided against putting Payne to torture, having concluded that 'it was not improbable that he who wrote the line, might have the heart to execute it' and should this eventuality occur, 'the government was likely to lose more by Sir John's death, then could be gained by Mr Paine's discoveries'.[83] When later arrested and imprisoned in Edinburgh Tolbooth, alongside Payne, however, Macpherson found himself threatened by torture, whereupon he composed an 'Address and Remonstrance' against the procedure,

[80] *Leven and Melville Papers*, p. 504. The greatest personal pressure appeared to come from Queen Mary, for as Lockhart related, 'when the Queen do[e]s not hear that all is well, she dou[b]ts the worst' (Ibid., p. 520). In 1693, Payne's alleged co-conspirator, Montgomery of Skelmorlie, expressed his outrage '[t]hat a free-born Englishman, hath been tortured in Scotland by order from England, against all Law, and Example': [Sir James Montgomery of Skelmorlie], *The People of England's Grievances offered to be Enquired into, and Redress'd by their Representatives in Parliament* (n.p., 1693), p. 2.

[81] *Leven and Melville Papers*, p. 503.

[82] Sir Aeneas Macpherson, 'The Vindication off Sir Aeneas Macpherson', in A. D. Murdoch (ed.), *The Loyal Dissuasive and other Papers concerning the affairs of Clan Chattan* (Edinburgh, 1902), pp. 185–6.

[83] Ibid., p. 186. That such a letter was sent is confirmed by the Privy Council's record of '[a] letter produced and read in Councill from ane unknown hand direct to the Lord Advocat threatning to murder his lorship in case Henry Navill Paine were put to tortur': *Register of the Privy Council*, XV: *1690*, p. 358.

arguing that it was an inappropriate method to be deployed against someone
of his own gentlemanly social status, who also happened to be a member of the
Faculty of Advocates. Deeming torture to be 'in it self barbarous, and not used
in any Christian Kingdom or Commonwealth', apart from Spain and France,
Macpherson denied that even in France any 'gentleman was tortured in that
wise and warlike country', while in ancient Rome, slaves and aliens 'might be
bound or buffeted, but no denizens, no citizen of Rome'.[84] Reminding the
Privy Council that torture had been 'reckoned among those streatches and
grievances for which King James was forfaulted', Macpherson contended
that it could hardly 'be practised and repeated without a manifest contradiction under the present settlement'. Moreover, should such practices persist,
Macpherson warned that the Scots populace 'may look a squint to a new
change, and be content to see his present Majestie follow the fate of his
predecessor'.[85]

Although Macpherson was later liberated, Payne was eventually tortured
on 10 and 11 December 1690 under the supervision of the Earl of Crawford,
as President of the Convention Parliament. Writing to the Earl of Melville,
as Scottish Secretary, on 12 December, Crawford recounted how he had
enjoined the simultaneous use of both the boot and the thumbscrews on both
of Payne's thumbs and one of his legs 'with all the severity that was consistent with humanity, even unto that pitch, that we could not preserve life, and
[would] have gone further'. Such pressure had, however, been applied 'without the least success', since Payne had remained 'so manly and resolute under
his suffering, that such of the Council as were not acquainted with all the evi-
dences, were brangled [unconvinced], and begun to give him charitie, that he
might be innocent'. Even Crawford confessed his own surprise 'that flesh and
blood could, without fainting, and in contradiction to the grounds we had
insinuat of our knowledge of his accession in the matter, endure the heavie
penance he was in for two houres'. For his part, Crawford concluded that
such fortitude was attributable to Payne's 'religion, and it's dictates' and
Payne's assumption 'that he must thereby save his soule, and be canoniz'd
among their saints'.[86] Corroboration of Crawford's account was supplied
by the surgeon and apothecary appointed to attend Payne's torture, George

---

[84] Sir Aeneas Macpherson, 'Address and Remonstrance . . . ag^t the torture to the Commission
and Council of Scotland', in Murdoch (ed.), *Loyal Dissuasive*, p. 202. In his 'Laws and Customs
of Scotland in Matters Criminal', Mackenzie accepted that minors under the age of fourteen
should not be tortured, nor the very elderly, but observed that while such exemptions were in
some other jurisdictions 'extended to Women, sick Persons, and such as had been eminent in any
Nation for Learning or any other Arts', he insisted that 'all this is arbitrary with us': 'Laws and
Customs', in *Works*, II, p. 261.

[85] Macpherson, 'Address and Remonstrance', p. 203.

[86] *Leven and Melville Papers*, pp. 582–3.

Stirling. As Stirling reported, the thumbscrews had been applied on both of Payne's thumbs on 10 December 'for the Space of near two hours [g]raduallie swizing [squeezing] prittie severlie'. When reapplied the following day, Stirling observed that Payne's 'thumbs became [a]s thin [a]s the back of [a]ne ordinarie Knife' and as 'Whyte as any member is Without lyfe'. At the same time, the boot was applied to one of Payne's legs 'graduallie Dryving Wagges' to ensure that 'the external Malleol [*malleolus*] was made Smooth and equall with the shin bone' which occasioned 'a great Swelling [a]nd Inflamationes in both the hands leg and foot', producing 'ane sharp fever for som dayes' as well as a 'Couple of Ulcers which were tedious to be cured'.[87]

Given Payne's refusal to confess any criminal involvement or to supply additional information, the Privy Councillors were unsure how to proceed further. Petitioning King William in January 1691 for advice, they respectfully reminded him that since 'the delaying to put persones in prison to tryall is declaired to be contrare to law', they construed that either the Lord Advocate should be instructed to prosecute Payne, or if William preferred, he should 'cause transport him to Ingland, he being a native of that kingdom'.[88] Denied any formal protection of habeas corpus, Payne was, however, detained until a trial was eventually arranged for 13 June 1693, at which point, according to Burnet, Payne informed several Privy Councillors 'that as long as his life was his own, he would accuse none, but he was resolved he would not die; and he could discover enough to deserve his pardon'. As Burnet related, Payne's claims 'struck such terror into many of them, whose sons or near relations had been concerned with him' that, following a hasty attempt to divert Payne's case from being heard in parliament to the Justiciary Court, the 'enquiry was stifled'.[89] Having squandered 'the true opportunity of putting an end to plotts in this kingdom', the Scottish Secretary, James Johnstoun, thereafter confided to John Locke that not only did Payne owe 'his Safety to the dimensions of his crime', but 'the reason was plain, that many were concerned, and guilt was stronger than Shame'.[90] Thereafter Payne was transported to Dumbarton Castle where he remained in prison until he was finally released in February 1701.[91]

---

[87] NAS GD 26/7/60(4), 'Report of George Stirling, surgeon and apothecary, 13th January 1691'.

[88] *Leven and Melville Papers*, p. 592.

[89] Burnet, *History of his Own Time*, p. 597.

[90] E. S. de Beer (ed.), *The Correspondence of John Locke*, (Oxford, 1989) VIII, pp. 433–4. As Johnstoun perceived, 'this Nation [Scotland] was a two edged tool which may happen to Cutt deep one time or other either for the present Settlement or against it'.

[91] During Payne's imprisonment at Dumbarton, he evidently became interested 'in preparing ane experiment for river navigation' on the Clyde and in 1699 gained the Privy Council's permission for limited freedom to investigate whether or not 'safer, larger and swifter vessels may be made with far less charge than any now in use': Robert Chambers, *Domestic Annals of Scotland from the Revolution to the Rebellion of 1745*, 3 vols (Edinburgh, 1861), III, p. 218.

While Payne's torture, like that of Mitchell's in 1676, failed in its judicial objective, the case again aroused interest outside Scotland. Within the Earl of Nottingham's manuscripts is an anonymous memorandum entitled 'The Case of Henry Neville Payne', evidently penned shortly after the Jacobite defeat at the battle of the Boyne in July 1691 by an author claiming to be 'an enemy to the government of the bowstring, to civill as religious inquisition'. Having heard of Payne's 'fertile invention, his vivacious pen, his universall genius' and 'how true an English man he is', the author challenged the legality of the Scottish Privy Council's actions. While accepting its competence to torture 'for discovery of some barbarious [*sic*] murther or conspiracie against the State', the author insisted, however, that more substantial probative evidence was required than the unreliable and unsworn allegations supplied by one of Payne's alleged co-conspirators, Annandale. More generally, although the anonymous author acknowledged that the use of judicial torture had increased since 1660, 'yet none of the arbitrary ministers of those reigns, of which wee have soe loudly, and in this perticular [*sic*] with too much reason complained' had ever contemplated applying 'torture to any foreigner' concerning treasonable conspiracies either in Scotland or elsewhere. Moreover, since Payne had been detained immediately upon arriving in Scotland, the author drew attention to the fact that 'it was not so much as pretended that he had committed any crime in that kingdom'. Reading William's personal order that Payne be tortured as 'an unpresidented unparallel'd instance of ilegall and arbitrary power', the author denied that the history of Scotland or any other country could 'cite anything to equall this usage of a subject without any pretext of law'. Observing that torture was often accounted to be more grievous than corporal punishment, on the grounds that it could be both more painful and able to be inflicted on the innocent alongside the guilty, the anonymous author warned the Williamite administration in Scotland that 'Gibbets and halters are not so dreadfull expressions of tyranny as boots and thumakins' since '[a]ny man would choose to be murthred than wracked'.[92]

V

A range of broader juridical, political, moral, and epistemological anxieties were thus increasingly attaching themselves to the practice of judicial torture in Restoration Scotland. In juridical terms alone, while the Roman jurist, Ulpian, had warned that torture was 'a chancy and risky business and one

---

[92] Anon., 'The Case of Henry Neville Payne', in Historical Manuscripts Commission, *Report on the Manuscripts of the late Allan George Finch Esq., of Burley-on-the-Hill, Rutland*, III: *1691*, ed. Francis Bickley (London, 1957), pp. 368–70.

which may be deceptive',[93] in 1678 Lord Advocate Mackenzie of Rosehaugh likewise acknowledged that torture was 'seldom used with us, because some obstinate Persons do oftimes deny Truth, while others who are frail and timorous, confess, for Fear, what is not true'.[94] For this reason, confessions emitted through coercion were increasingly regarded as less indicative than other forms of proof, including circumstantial evidence. When prosecuting James Mitchell that same year, Mackenzie had specifically pointed out that Mitchell's retracted confession had not been 'extorted from him by Racks and Instruments',[95] while the attempt by Mitchell's defence counsel to allege that 'it was a confession elicit by torture, and so revockable was repelled, because when he confest, their was nather torture nor threats adhibit'.[96] After Baillie of Jerviswood's trial in 1684, the judge, Sir John Lauder of Fountainhall, had echoed such concerns, conceding that 'what Carstares and the rest have said, is but an imperfect narrative of this plot', since those questioned 'told no more than what was squeezed out of them by special interrogators, torture and fear of more'.[97] Finally, recounting Payne's torture in 1690, the Earl of Crawford had confessed that his 'stomach is truely so farr out of tune, by being witness to an act so far cross to my natural temper' that it was only the gravity of the Jacobite threat that had 'prevailed over me to have in the Councils name been the prompter of the executioner to encrease the torture to so high a pitch'.[98]

As Crawford's comments indicate, the use of judicial torture in Restoration Scotland conformed to William Blackstone's eighteenth-century characterisation of torture as 'an engine of state, not of law'.[99] Moreover, as the cases

---

[93] Theodor Mommsen, Paul Kruger, and Alan Watson (eds), *The Digest of Justinian*, 4 vols (Philadelphia, 1985), IV, p. 841 (Title 48.18).

[94] Mackenzie, 'Laws and Customs', in *Works*, II, p. 261. Here Mackenzie was effectively paraphrasing Ulpian, who had pointed out that 'there are a number of people who, by their endurance or their toughness under torture, are so contemptuous of it that the truth can in no way be squeezed out of them. Others have so little endurance that they would rather tell any kind of lie than suffer torture; so it happens that they confess in various ways, incriminating not only themselves, but others also': Mommsen, Kruger, and Watson (eds), *Digest of Justinian*, IV, p. 841.

[95] Mackenzie, *Idea of the Modern Eloquence of the Bar*, p. 147.

[96] Fountainhall, *Historical Notices*, I, p. 183.

[97] Fountainhall, *Decisions*, I, p. 327. Elsewhere in his *Decisions*, Fountainhall reported debates regarding the right to torture witnesses as well as the accused, confirming that torturing witnesses was 'indeed agreeable to the R[oman] law, but does not suit the genius of our nation, which looks upon the torture of the boots as a barbarous remedy; and yet of late it hath been frequently used among us' (Ibid., I, p. 142).

[98] *Leven and Melville Papers*, p. 583.

[99] William Blackstone, *Commentaries on the Laws of England*, 4 vols (Oxford, 1765–9), IV, p. 321. Elsewhere, Jeremy Bentham emphasised the multi-faceted character of any discussion of the justification of judicial torture and the need for a range of different and conflicting legal, conceptual, psychological, and moral standpoints to be adopted. For, as Bentham warned,

examined in this chapter indicate, torture proved more effective for the authorities when deployed to elicit information, rather than to supply judicial evidence. For although torture failed to yield the desired confessions of criminal involvement from Mitchell and Payne in 1676 and 1690 respectively, when applied to Spence and Carstares in return for immunity from prosecution in 1684, sufficient intelligence was gathered to facilitate Baillie's trial, the swift and brutal outcome of which undermined the morale of Covenanting resistance and partially explains the failure of Argyll's rising six months later.[100]

To conclude, if judicial torture is regarded as 'an engine of state, not of law', primarily deployed to protect civil society, rather than to punish known crimes, then some chilling contemporary parallels emerge. Confronted by global threats from unknown terrorist enemies, an expanding jurisprudential literature is currently addressing the issue of whether or not blanket prohibitions on torture require recalibration. Citing the notorious 'ticking-bomb scenario', it remains debatable as to whether invoking a 'necessity defence' to sanction forcible interrogation is less morally blameworthy than the loss of many hundreds, or even thousands, of innocent lives in a terrorist attack.[101] Moreover, should such an attack take place, the prospect of numerous lawsuits from pursuers claiming that a state did not exploit all available avenues to forestall such an attack ensures that judicial torture continues to feature in any language of proportionality analysis. On a different note, the issues of contested jurisdiction that arose in relation to the torture of Spence, Carstares, and Payne for crimes allegedly committed outside Scotland also presages increasing current interest in issues of transnational criminal culpability and civil liability.[102] For just as alarmed Englishmen such as Andrew Marvell and Roger Morrice were unable to disregard the practice of judicial

---

'[t]here is no approving it in the lump, without militating against reason and humanity, nor condemning it without falling into absurdities and contradictions' (quoted by W. L. and P. E. Twining in 'Bentham on Torture', *Northern Ireland Legal Quarterly* 24 (1973), pp. 305–56, at p. 337).

[100] Notably, the torture of Spence and Carstares occurred at the peak of the so-called 'Killing Times', when threats to Scottish state security were at their highest. For although all the leading English Whig plotters, such as the Earl of Shaftesbury, the Earl of Essex, and Lord John Russell had been removed through death, alleged suicide, or execution, Scottish fears of rebellion by the 9th Earl of Argyll remained acute throughout the early 1680s and were vindicated in the summer of 1685.

[101] From an extensive literature, see for example, 'Is torture ever justified?', *The Economist* (11–17 January 2003), pp. 21–3; Winifred Bruger, 'May governments ever use torture? Two responses from German law', *American Journal of Comparative Law* 48 (2000), and John T. Parry and Welsh W. White, 'Interrogating suspected terrorists: should torture be an option?', *University of Pittsburgh Law Review* 63 (2002), pp. 743–66.

[102] See, for example, Craig Scott (ed.), *Torture as Tort: Comparative Perspectives on the Development of Transnational Human Rights Litigation* (Oxford, 2001).

torture in Charles II's Scotland, the expanded extraterritorial jurisdiction of bodies such as the International Criminal Court similarly guarantees that judicial torture remains a relevant issue for us all.

Note. The author would like to thank John Cairns and Mark Goldie for their comments on an earlier draft of this chapter.

6

Taking Stock: Scotland at the End of the Seventeenth Century

CHRISTOPHER A. WHATLEY

THE TASK OF ASSESSING THE CONDITION OF SCOTLAND at the end of the seventeenth century and the beginning of the eighteenth century is an important one. This of course was the period in which the regal union of England, Wales, and Scotland imploded, to be replaced in 1707 by incorporating union. It is more, however, than simply a matter of interest for the historical record that we should take stock of Scotland's economic circumstances— broadly interpreted—at this juncture in Scottish political and constitutional history. For one thing, of course, in ways that will be outlined later, conditions within Scotland fed the implosion. Related to this is the question of how *far* and in what manner economic conditions influenced political attitudes—and action—in Scotland in the years up to 1707 and more particularly during the autumn of 1706 when the terms of incorporating union were resolved. There is also the debate about the reasons for Scotland's remarkable development in the decades which followed the Union of 1707, although this did not happen immediately. There are competing views on both of these topics. If however we can contribute authoritatively to the first of these debates, the focus of this chapter, we need to be clearer than perhaps we are at present about the strengths and weaknesses of Scotland's economic position around the beginning of the reign of Queen Anne. What follows is an attempt to provide greater clarity, not by offering a radically new thesis,[1] but by re-presenting existing knowledge, and complementing this with recent and new research findings. The chapter will conclude by drawing some connections between economic conditions and the incorporating union.

---

[1] The argument here recovers the main lines established in T. C. Smout, *Scottish Trade on the Eve of Union*, 1660–1707 (Edinburgh and London, 1963), pp. 239–56.

Proceedings of the British Academy, **127**, 103–125. © The British Academy 2005.

It is clearly no longer acceptable to write off seventeenth-century Scotland. It was certainly no parochial backwater, obsessed by religious disputation (although in Scotland as much as anywhere else in Europe and more so than in England, religion continued to be a prominent factor in determining the attitudes and behaviour of individuals and governments, both nationally and in the localities).[2] Voluminous quantities of research publications have appeared over the past quarter-century which serve to dispel earlier generations of historians' gloom-laden judgements on the century of the regal union. Investigations ranging from agrarian change through intellectual developments to the architectural triumphs of William Bruce and James Smith have portrayed a much more advanced society than was once thought to have been the case, and one which at the upper social levels drew strongly on best practice in Europe.[3]

It is legitimate, however, to subject this work to critical scrutiny and ask whether in an effort to redress the historiographical balance, the scales in favour of pre-union Scotland have not been tipped too far. Attention has strayed from the issue of the strength of the material base, the wealth of the nation and its capacity to support its people and provide the infrastructure necessary for civil society to thrive.[4] There is virtual unanimity that the seventeenth century ended in an economic trough. Yet this has been characterised as temporary, of little or no consequence as far as the making of the incorporating union was concerned, a 'blip' in a rising trajectory which would come to fruition with the Scottish Enlightenment and the economic triumphs of the final two decades of the eighteenth century.[5] It is a judgement which— at first sight—is supported by comparison with the Irish economy in the same period.[6] It is clear that many of the lines of future success were laid pre-

[2] P. Seaward, *The Restoration* (London, 1991), p. 16; B. Lenman, 'The limits of godly discipline in the early modern period with particular reference to England and Scotland', in K. von Greyerz (ed.), *Religion and Society in Early Modern Europe, 1500–1800* (London, 1984), pp. 124–45; see too M. J. Braddick, *State Formation in Early Modern England, c.1550–1700* (Cambridge, 2000), pp. 361–71.

[3] For a short survey of the historiography, see D. Stevenson, 'Twilight before night or darkness before dawn? Interpreting seventeenth-century Scotland', in R. Mitchison (ed.), *Why Scottish History Matters* (Edinburgh, 1991), pp. 37–47; K. M. Brown, 'Reformation to the Union, 1560–1707', in R. A. Houston and W. W. J. Knox (eds), *The New Penguin History of Scotland* (London, 2001), pp. 182–275 (includes a full bibliography).

[4] See N. T. Phillipson, 'Lawyers, landowners, and the civic leadership of post-union Scotland', *Juridical Review* n.s. 21, 2 (1976), pp. 106–9.

[5] T. M. Devine, 'The Union and Scottish development', *Scottish Economic and Social History* 5 (1985), p. 25; M. Lynch, *Scotland: a New History* (London, 1991), p. 309.

[6] L. M. Cullen, 'Incomes, social classes and economic growth in Ireland and Scotland, 1600–1900', in T. M. Devine and D. Dickson (eds), *Ireland and Scotland 1600–1850* (Edinburgh, 1983), pp. 248–60. This argument owes much to hindsight and something to the conflation of periods, it understates the contemporary importance of foreign trade, assumes that overseas

1707,[7] although whether the economic result would have been so spectacular without the opportunities provided by Scotland's incorporation within the British state is questionable. Scots with particular interests to defend and promote certainly did their best to make sure the union worked in their favour.[8] Recently however, a tantalising case has been made that such was the strength of Scottish entrepreneurial engagement in the Americas that the Scots were provided with a real opportunity to break out of the European mercantilist cage and maintain the regal union without political incorporation.[9]

Contemporaries appear to have been less sanguine than modern historians about Scotland's fortunes during the seventeenth century and, it will be argued here, with good reason. Scottish inquisitiveness, travel to England and through Europe inspired emulation but also had the effect of exposing Scotland's inadequacies. There were those who were convinced that the entire period of regal union had been harmful to Scottish interests. John Clerk reflected that while the stock of money in Scotland was once less than at present, 'yet we had such a Proportionable share of the riches of Europe, as served us to make no Contemptible Figure, both at home and abroad'.[10] This was not the conclusion that was drawn when England was compared with other nations. That England seemed to be racing ahead was galling enough, but even more so were the achievements of smaller states like Denmark, Savoy, Sweden, and Tuscany.[11] It was *relative* decline that irked Clerk as much as the more overtly patriotic Lord Belhaven who was moved around 1695 to write of the distasteful sight of 'all our neighbour nations', some of which were 'not to be compared with us some hundredth years ago, now raising their honour,

---

trade difficulties were exaggerated by pro-unionists, inflates Scottish strengths and plays down those aspects of Irish society which were in advance of Scotland, for example the greater force of commercialisation and the modernisation of Dublin.

[7] The importance of the seventeenth-century cultural base has been emphasised in A. Broadie, *The Scottish Enlightenment* (Edinburgh, 2001), pp. 6–14 and D. Allan, *Virtue, Learning and the Scottish Enlightenment* (Edinburgh, 1993); see too the first four chapters in R. H. Campbell and A. S. Skinner (eds), *The Origins and Nature of the Scottish Enlightenment* (Edinburgh, 1982).

[8] C. A. Whatley, *Scottish Society, 1707–1830: Beyond Jacobitism, Towards Industrialisation* (Manchester, 2000), chs 2 and 3; Bob Harris, 'The Scots, the Westminster parliament, and the British state in the eighteenth century', in J. Hoppit (ed.), *Parliaments, Nations and Identities in Britain and Ireland, 1660–1850* (Manchester, 2003), pp. 124–45.

[9] A. I. Macinnes, M. D. Harper, and L. G. Fryer (eds), *Scotland and the Americas, c.1650–c.1939: a Documentary Source Book* (Edinburgh, 2002), pp. 1–14.

[10] National Archives of Scotland (NAS), Clerk of Penicuik MSS, GD 18/3129, J. Clerk, *The Circumstances of Scotland Considered, With Respect to the present Scarcity of Money: Together with some Proposals For Supplying the Defect thereof, And rectifying the Balance of Trade* (1705), pp. 3–4.

[11] NAS Clerk of Penicuik MSS, GD 18/3130, Notes, 'the necessity there was for a union', n.d.

enlarging their territories, increasing their riches and consequently their power'.[12]

Contemporary critiques were not confined to unrepresentative and hysterical gloom-mongers, or individuals with particular axes to grind.[13] References to economic hardship constantly recur whether the sources were public or private. The pain was not felt equally acutely throughout Scotland or across the classes or indeed over time (there were periods when, following a disrupting event, the pattern of everyday life seemed to recover quickly),[14] but virtually everywhere and at all social levels for which records survive there was an awareness that something was badly wrong. This was not economic defeatism, but a recognition of economic reality, from all sides of the political spectrum.[15] Although anxieties of various sorts also manifested themselves in England in the 1690s (from causes similar to those which worried Scots), England was materially stronger and therefore in a better position to cope with adversity. England too had begun to make a substantial mark as a world-ranking commercial and military force.[16]

It is intended here to argue that by the end of the century the achievements of the previous eight or nine decades in Scotland were being undermined by the country's losing struggle to maintain its position as a credible political entity. This underlines the contention, first advanced in 1974, that by the early eighteenth century an independent Scotland was 'not financially viable'.[17] The country's trading balance was in deficit and deteriorating, even though invisible earnings are almost certain to have been greater than has been suspected until recently.[18] According to one contemporary estimate, by 1706 only one-sixth of the coin minted in Scotland since 1686 remained in the country.[19] By 1707 there was a shortfall on government expenditure of some £14,000 sterling, or around 12 per cent of total revenues. Payments of government officers were in several cases years overdue. And although state formation in Scotland had been taking place along European lines, the yield on

[12] NAS PA7. 15, f. 64, Parliamentary Papers, Supplementary Volumes, XV, 1695–7, Lord Belhaven, 'Reasons for Securing the Trade of the Nation by a Naval Force', n.d.
[13] Although some did; see R. Mitchison and L. Leneman, *Girls in Trouble: Sexuality and Social Control in Rural Scotland, 1660–1789* (Edinburgh, 1998), p. 16.
[14] For a study of daily life in élite society in the period, see H. and K. Kelsall, *Scottish Lifestyle 300 Years Ago* (Edinburgh, 1986).
[15] It included patriots such as Fletcher of Saltoun; see D. Daiches (ed.), *Andrew Fletcher of Saltoun: Selected Writings* (Edinburgh, 1979), pp. 27–66.
[16] J. Hoppit, *A Land of Liberty? England 1689–1727* (Oxford, 2000), pp. 1–9; B. Lenman, *Britain's Colonial Wars, 1688–1783* (London, 2001), p. 24.
[17] A. L. Murray, 'Administration and Law', in T. I. Rae (ed.), *The Union of 1707: Its Impact on Scotland* (Glasgow, 1974), p. 34.
[18] R. Saville, *Bank of Scotland: A History, 1695–1995* (Edinburgh, 1996), pp. 64–7.
[19] NAS GD 18/3129, J. Clerk, *Circumstances of Scotland Considered*, pp. 2–3.

customs and excise dues in Scotland was a small fraction of the English figure, and after around 1683 the collection system bore little comparison,
either in organisation or effectiveness.[20] In both real and relative terms the situation was worsening: Scottish public revenue in 1706 was less than it had
been in the 1650s and in the same time-span the ratio between the tax yields
in the two countries widened from 10.5:1 to 36:1.[21] Given the limitations of
central government in Scotland, about which more will be said below—and
the deteriorating economic base—it was highly unlikely that this could be
improved in the short term.[22]

The crisis—for that is what it was—that confronted Scotland as the seventeenth century drew to a close was complex and inter-related. At its heart
was impoverishment. But it was more than an economic crisis. The crisis had
a psychological dimension too.[23] On the national level this point is evidenced
by the concentration of anguished calls by the General Assembly of the
Church of Scotland for days of fasting, humiliation, and prayer from 1699
(after an apparent gap from 1692, others were held in 1700, 1701, 1704, 1705,
and 1706).[24] The calls were inspired by misery-inducing events such as dearth,
unseasonable spring weather, ailing trade, the failure at Darien, and even the
'stupendous wasting fire at Edinburgh' in 1700. If God's wrath upon the
Scots was to be curbed, the nation's sinfulness had to be eliminated and a
return to presbyterian piety effected. Each additional setback, no matter how
far its cause was self-evidently secular to modern eyes, was another sign of
Scottish iniquity: in December 1704, as news that the Bank of Scotland had
curtailed business broke, Sir John Clerk invited God to 'pitie' the Scots and
begged for forgiveness for the nation's 'crying sins & provocations the bitter
foundations of all our plagues & miseries'.[25] There are signs of a heightening
religious fervour in the 1690s, with greater activity than usual on the part of
the kirk sessions in their efforts to stamp out immoral behaviour, although as
this had its counterpart in England, with the formation of the societies for

---

[20] J. Brewer, *The Sinews of Power: War, Money and the English State, 1688–1783* (New York, 1989), pp. 91–5; E. J. Graham, *A Maritime History of Scotland 1650–1790* (East Linton, 2002), pp. 100–2.

[21] J. Goodare, *State and Society in Early Modern Scotland* (Oxford, 1999), p. 321.

[22] British Library (hereafter BL), Portland Papers, Add. 70047, Appendix 1, 'Concerning the revenue & charge of Scotland before the Union' (1712).

[23] The concept was used initially, although not developed, by Bruce Lenman, *An Economic History of Modern Scotland, 1660–1977* (London, 1978), p. 44.

[24] *Acts of the General Assembly of the Church of Scotland* (Edinburgh, 1893).

[25] NAS GD 18/2092/2, Sir John Clerk, Journals, 1699–1709, 18 December 1704.

the reformation of manners from 1691, care has to be taken not to exaggerate the distinctiveness of Scottish social phenomena.[26]

The notion of psychological trauma is supported by the slight but visible resurgence in accusations of witchcraft and enchanting from the end of the seventeenth century. This was in spite of growing scepticism on the part of Scottish lawyers, advocates, and judges about the rationality of such charges and the disappearance from much of the rest of Europe of the conditions in which witch-hunting flourished.[27] There are only vestigial traces of similar actions south of the Border. Albeit indirectly, in a number of Scottish cases, links can be established between deteriorating living standards, economic stress, and guilt associated with the inadequacy and extent of poor relief and a compulsion to eliminate the perceived causes of localised suffering.[28] It is striking that almost the last major witch-hunt in the English-speaking world, in Renfrewshire in the south-west of Scotland, occurred in the three years between 1697 and 1700, the first two of which were the most difficult of the 1690s famine.

The *inter-relatedness* of the crisis conditions with which the Scottish nation was faced through the greatest part of the reigns of King William and Queen Anne is difficult to convey. An attempt can be made, however, by focusing on the famine of the 1690s. Perhaps as part of the historiographical shift away from the profound pessimism which had permeated an earlier generation of historians' views of seventeenth-century Scotland, current portrayals of the impact of the famine are somewhat more benign. Certainly there has been a reaction to and rejection of the concept of 'King William's Seven Ill Years'. Quite legitimately, historians have sought to measure more precisely the demographic effects of the harvest failures, and concluded that the period of greatest hardship 'only' lasted for four years or even less (beginning in 1695) rather than seven.[29] The Europe-wide nature of the phenomenon has been emphasised too, thereby ensuring that Scotland's suffering is

[26] R. Mitchison and L. Leneman, *Sin in the City: Sexuality and Social Control in Urban Scotland* (Edinburgh, 1998), p. 41; R. A. Houston, *Social Change in the Age of the Enlightenment: Edinburgh, 1660–1760* (Oxford, 1994), pp. 193–4; C. Rose, *England in the 1690s: Revolution, Religion and War* (Oxford, 1999), pp. 205–9.

[27] E. J. Cowan and L. Henderson, 'The last of the witches? The survival of Scottish witch belief', in J. Goodare (ed.), *The Scottish Witch Hunt in Context* (Manchester, 2002), pp. 201–5; B. P. Levack, *The Witch-Hunt in Early Modern Europe* (Harlow, 1987), pp. 233–50.

[28] M. Wasser, 'The western witch-hunt of 1697–1700: the last major witch-hunt in Scotland', in Goodare (ed.), *Scottish Witch Hunt*, pp. 147–52; S. Macdonald, *The Witches of Fife* (East Linton, 2002), pp. 67–8.

[29] M. W. Flinn (ed.), *Scottish Population History from the Seventeenth Century to the 1930s* (Cambridge, 1977), pp. 164–86; N. Davidson, *Discovering the Scottish Revolution 1692–1746* (London, 2003), p. 94.

not mistaken as something unique.[30] Even so, new, comprehensive and systematic research is confirming that the effects of the crop failures were variable across the country but also that in several places these spanned the full seven years. It suggests too that there is much substance in the more vivid surviving descriptions of contemporary wretchedness and suffering, large-scale dislocation and population movement in search of sustenance in parts of the Lowlands (as the poor sought refuge from upland districts to better-placed burghs on low-lying land), as well as the North and North-East.[31] Total losses—from famine-related deaths and emigration—may have amounted to something under 200,000, that is, between one-fifth and one-sixth of the population.[32]

It should be borne in mind that the period c.1680 to c.1730 was the coldest cycle during what has been termed the Little Ice Age. It is important too to appreciate how devastating the effect of cold and wet and otherwise freakish weather conditions, which included excessive heat and drought, could be on a country like Scotland and others like it, where peasant-based subsistence agriculture was still the norm.[33] Indeed, investigation into long-term changes in food consumption has produced strong evidence to suggest that the reign of William and Mary had been preceded by two centuries of stagnant or reducing living standards, and a shift in dietary habits where flesh-eating was commonplace to a diet where the greatest part of the calorific requirements of most Scottish people was derived from oats and oatmeal.[34] Further, notwithstanding the evidence there is of change and innovation in Scottish agriculture in the early modern period, Professor Smout has argued that by the later seventeenth century, Scotland may have been suffering from long-term ecological degradation, specifically low nitrogen levels brought about by long-term woodland decline, leaching of the mineral content of soils, and

[30] D. Kirby, *Northern Europe in the Early Modern Period: the Baltic World, 1492–1772* (London, edn 1998), pp. 352–3.
[31] This comment is based on the doctoral work currently being carried out on the 1690s by Ms Karen Cullen at the University of Dundee; see too K. J. Cullen, 'King William's Ill Years: the Economic, Demographic and Social Effects of the 1695–1700 Dearth in the County of Angus' (unpublished M.A. dissertation, Department of History, University of Dundee, 2001); Flinn (ed.), *Scottish Population History*; R. E. Tyson, 'Famine in Aberdeenshire, 1695–1699: anatomy of a crisis', in D. Stevenson (ed.), *From Lairds to Louns* (Aberdeen, 1986), pp. 32–52.
[32] R. E. Tyson. 'Contrasting regimes: population growth in Ireland and Scotland during the eighteenth century', in S. J. Connolly, R. A. Houston, and R. J. Morris (eds), *Conflict, Identity and Economic Development: Ireland and Scotland, 1600–1939* (Preston, 1995), p. 67.
[33] B. Fagan, *The Little Ice Age* (New York, 2000), pp. 101–2, 113; T. M. Devine, *The Transformation of Rural Scotland: Social Change and the Agrarian Economy, 1660–1815* (Edinburgh, 1994), pp. 1–18.
[34] A. Gibson and T. C. Smout, 'Scottish food and Scottish history, 1500–1800', in R. A. Houston and I. D. Whyte (eds), *Scottish Society 1500–1800* (Cambridge, 1989), pp. 60–73, 75.

their further exhaustion by cultivation without adequate fertilisation. Seventeenth-century estate reorganisation, mainly by consolidating tenancy, provided limited benefits but was unable to stem this loss of fertility. Early modern methods of soil improvement, such as adding large quantities of turf to the infield or paring and burning mosslands provided only a temporary solution and had their own economic and environmental costs.[35] Large-scale liming, the addition of organic fertilisers through the cultivation of clover, and attempts at reafforestation, lay mainly in the future. There are signs that progress had slowed by the end of the century and even suggestions of retardation in some districts along with the abandonment of long leys and continuing problems of low crop yields.[36]

   With grain prices more or less static since the mid-century, the position of rural Scotland was surely more precarious than is implied by the judgement that improving trends were merely being concealed by short-term problems at the end of the century.[37] Aristocratic and landed debts acquired earlier in the century[38] were hard to throw off and bankrupt estates frequently changed hands (one in four between 1660 and 1710). Estate papers through the 1690s and into the first decade of the eighteenth century are riddled with reports of unpaid rents, and the dire consequences that could and did follow, both for poverty-stricken tenants (even the better-off had only minimal reserves with which to cope for more than a single bad year)[39] and proprietors. The idea that the famine was 'over' by 1700 would have surprised many contemporaries, although in terms of their ability to purchase grain and meal, consumers in the South-West fared better.[40] Economically the effects were cumulative, as the burden of 'rests' or unpaid rents grew and as tenants and cottars, who disposed of crucial assets such as livestock and working animals they could no longer afford to feed, sought assistance in order to buy seed to replace what they had had to eat or sell—and thus added to landed indebt-

[35] T. C. Smout, 'The improvers and the Scottish environment: soils, bogs and woods', in T. M. Devine and J. R. Young (eds), *Eighteenth Century Scotland: New Perspectives* (East Linton, 1999), pp. 210–11.

[36] H. Blair-Imrie, 'The Relationship between Land Ownership and the Commercialisation of Agriculture in Angus, 1740–1820' (unpublished Ph.D. thesis, University of Edinburgh, 2001), p. 4; NAS GD 112/39/174/2, James Stewart and Donald Sutherland to Glenorchy, 5 June 1696; GD 112/39/192/4, Duncan Toschach to Earl of Breadalbane, 28 January 1704; I am grateful to Mary Young, Ph.D. student at the University of Dundee, for information on crop yields in Perthshire.

[37] Stevenson, 'Twilight before night or darkness before dawn?', p. 40.

[38] K. M. Brown, *Noble Society in Scotland* (Edinburgh, 2000), ch. 4.

[39] I. D. Whyte and K. Whyte, 'Debt and credit, poverty and prosperity in a seventeenth-century Scottish rural community', in R. Mitchison and P. Roebuck (eds), *Economy and Society in Scotland and Ireland 1500–1939* (Edinburgh, 1988), p. 78.

[40] A. J. S. Gibson and T. C. Smout, 'Regional prices and market regions: the evolution of the early Scottish grain market', *Economic History Review* 48, 2 (1995), pp. 264, 269.

edness. Animal stocks took longer to rebuild.[41] Recovery was rapid in some places, less so in others: in Lanarkshire for example the harvest of 1703 was described as 'the worst . . . of any that has been yet' and conditions remained difficult at least until 1705.[42] (The demographic losses were not recovered until the 1720s, beyond that in some places.[43])

The other main elements of estate-related income were far from stable. The black cattle trade to England for instance, the country's fourth most important export earner in 1704, had expanded less than might have been anticipated in the second half of the seventeenth century, and was subject to marked fluctuations.[44] The famine too left its mark. Owing to the difficulties of finding sufficient grain during the years of 'Dearth & Scarcity', it was reported that 'the highlanders who breed them, eat them [sheep as well as cattle]', although whether this practice afflicted the South-West is not known.[45] Intriguingly, customs records, the reliability of which historians for almost the past thirty years have been inclined to doubt, do point to a marked fall in exports to England after 1687–98 (apart from 1700).[46] This is a pattern which, although improbably extreme (it is doubtful if Scottish cattle exports ceased altogether), finds support from the circumstantial evidence of the agrarian crisis of the 1690s, especially its impact on breeding stocks.[47]

Increasingly, and to a degree that may have been underestimated by historians of rural Scotland, the viability of the Lowland countryside came to depend on the linen trade, which had expanded dramatically since the reign of James VI.[48] This was in the form of the rents paid by the thousands of subtenants and cottars who were employed in the countryside as part-time lint spinners and linen weavers.[49] By the end of the century those parts of the country where the manufacture was extensive—Perthshire, Scotland's most populous county, and Renfrewshire—had become acutely vulnerable to the vicissitudes of a trade which in international terms was highly competitive

---

[41] See, for example, I. D. and K. Whyte, 'Continuity and change in a seventeenth-century Scottish farming community', *Agricultural History Review* 32, 2 (1984), pp. 166–7.

[42] NAS Hamilton MSS, GD 406/1/6747, Duchess of Hamilton to Duke of Hamilton, 27 February 1703.

[43] Flinn (ed.), *Scottish Population History*, p. 182.

[44] Whatley, *Scottish Society, 1707–1830*, pp. 35–6.

[45] For Perthshire, see Perth and Kinross Council Archives (PKCA), Perth Burgh Records, B59/26/4/1, Bundle 9, Petition of the Candlemakers and Fleshers to the Town Council, 1699.

[46] D. Woodward, 'A comparative study of the Irish and Scottish livestock trades in the seventeenth century', in L. M. Cullen and T. C. Smout (eds), *Comparative Aspects of Scottish and Irish Economic and Social History 1600–1900* (Edinburgh, 1977), pp. 150–3.

[47] Smout, *Scottish Trade*, pp. 213–14.

[48] Ibid., p. 233.

[49] L. Leneman, *Living in Atholl 1685–1785* (Edinburgh, 1986), pp. 30, 206; in parts of Lowland Perthshire, half of the rentals on some estates included a payment for linen cloth.

and subject to state intervention through the erection of tariff barriers. The consequences of an additional rise in the tariff on Scottish linen entering England, the major market, in 1698, had almost immediate—and deleterious—effects on both rural and urban Scotland.[50]

Where landowners in appropriate locations (mainly along the banks of the Forth) had diversified and tried to exploit estate assets through, for example, the opening of new coal pits or expansion of existing coal mining or salt making concerns, they had discovered that both costs and risks were high and, generally, income was small, even from the best-run colliery enterprises.[51] There were a handful of larger collieries, but national output and exports were less than half what historians once supposed.[52] Some feared that the nation's coal supplies were close to exhaustion. What all this reveals is that not only were the fortunes of the Scottish rural economy, trade, and manufacturing inextricably linked; around 1700 they were sinking, together.

With this background it is little wonder that the system of poor relief was unable to cope with the additional burden imposed upon it from 1695. More than three-quarters of the parishes in Scotland failed to assess the landholders within their domain and thereby increase the resources they had to distribute to those in need. That is assuming significant landed support could have been prised from emptying estate coffers, whose owners had from 1690 been faced with demands for a 'swingeing' increase in land tax.[53]

Only in parts of the Lothians, possibly Perthshire and thereafter in isolated parishes, was the system of poor relief effective.[54] The scale of the suffering was immense, however, and could not be ignored. Massive sums were spent nationally to feed the starving. Around £100,000 sterling was thought to have gone from the Scottish purse in 1696 alone to buy victual from England;[55] as the impact of the famine intensified, so the cost of alleviating it grew (perhaps to as much as £400,000), even though in 1698 and 1699 the Privy Council tried, with a modest degree of success, to shift some of the burden back to the localities. Some did nothing, exposing thereby the inadequa-

[50] Smout, *Scottish Trade*, p. 234.

[51] B. F. Duckham, *A History of the Scottish Coal Industry* (Newton Abbot, 1970), pp. 152, 159; C. A. Whatley, 'Salt, coal and the Union of 1707: a revision article', *Scottish Historical Review* 66 (1987), pp. 32–7; NAS Hamilton MSS, GD 406/1/5191, [?] to Duke of Hamilton, 2 November 1704.

[52] C. A. Whatley, 'New light on Nef's numbers: coal mining and the first phase of Scottish industrialisation, c.1700–1830', in A. J. G. Cummings and T. M. Devine (eds), *Industry, Business and Society in Scotland Since 1700* (Edinburgh, 1994), pp. 4–7.

[53] Goodare, *State and Society*, p. 320.

[54] R. Mitchison, *The Old Poor Law in Scotland* (Edinburgh, 2000), pp. 35–43.

[55] J. H. McMaster and M. Wood (eds), *Historical Manuscripts Commission Supplementary Report on the Manuscripts of His Grace the Duke of Hamilton* (London, 1932), p. 137.

cies of the fledgling system of county government.[56] However, with the sub-scription lists for the Company of Scotland having opened in February 1696, and pledges—along with £34,000 sterling in coin—pouring in through March and April, the country had already drawn heavily on its overstretched financial resources. The Bank of Scotland had earlier managed to raise another £60,000 (plus £6,000 in coin). Thus the cost of coping with the famine further sharply restricted the limited quantity of money within Scotland but also necessitated the accumulation of sizeable debts. Unfortu-nately no figures for these are available but what is clear is that even as late as 1705 contemporaries reckoned they were still paying heavily for the cost of famine relief.[57] Attempts to generate new sources of state revenue—a hearth tax and three poll taxes (in 1690, 1693, 1695, and 1698 respectively)—were not only resented but had also disappointed.[58]

As well as raising mortality levels, the dearth acted to spur further migra-tion out of Scotland. A matter of concern was that at least some of the emi-grants—'some few thousands'—were young, healthy, and economically active, tempted overseas by offers of employment as indentured servants in the plantations.[59] In an era when a nation's most valuable asset was deemed to be the number of its inhabitants, Scotland was at risk of becoming 'the only Christian Nation in the universe', that 'suffers it self to run the hazard of being dispeopled'. The outward flow of human beings from Scotland was nothing new: for decades (mainly) cash-strapped but often ambitious Scots had scoured Europe (often in disproportionate numbers)[60] and the Americas in search of economic and career opportunities that had been lacking at home—in the former mainly as pedlars and merchants, soldiers, and seamen, but also as scholars. Others were religious refugees, some of whom fled to East New Jersey in 1683, to settle Scotland's first American colony.[61] Frequently, 'undesirables' had been compelled or encouraged to go. Labour was a Scottish commodity in ample supply and for which there was a strong

---

[56] Mitchison, *Old Poor Law*, pp. 42–3; see too A. Whetstone, *Scottish County Government in the Eighteenth and Nineteenth Centuries* (Edinburgh, 1981).

[57] NAS GD 18/3129, Clerk, *Circumstances of Scotland Considered*, p. 5.

[58] Goodare, *State and Society*, p. 320.

[59] *An Essay Against the Transportation and Selling of Men to the Plantations of Foreigners With Special regard to the Manufacturies, and other Domestick Improvements of the Kingdom of Scotland* (Edinburgh, 1699), pp. 6–7. I am grateful to Professor E. J. Cowan for this source.

[60] S. Murdoch, 'The database in early modern Scottish history: Scandinavia and Northern Europe, 1580–1707', *Northern Studies* 32 (1997), pp. 98–100; A. Grosjean, 'Scottish-Scandinavian seventeenth century naval links: a case study for the SSNE database', *Northern Studies* 32 (1997), pp. 105–23; G. C. Simpson (ed.), *The Scottish Soldier Abroad, 1247–1967* (Edinburgh and Maryland, 1992); see too T. C. Smout (ed.), *Scotland and Europe 1200–1850* (Edinburgh, 1986).

[61] N. Landsman, *Scotland and its First American Colony, 1683–1765* (Princeton, 1985).

overseas demand, notably in the English West Indian colonies, where hardy, white, English-speaking, Protestant Scots who could bear arms were particularly welcome.[62] Ulster, which offered better prospects than Scotland at the end of the seventeenth century, was the main destination for those who were able to travel in the 1690s, with an estimated outflow of between 40,000 and 70,000 during the course of the decade. These included unknown numbers of desperately poor family groups and individuals, whose passages had to be paid for either by kirk sessions or by burgh councils.[63]

The severity of the reverberations of the famine for the urban population may not have been fully appreciated. Tallow, for candles, was in short supply, as were butter and cheese, which were consumed rather than sold, while brewing too had to be curtailed. Burgh revenues from petty customs fell as inland trade stagnated, with country spinners and weavers, for example, unable to afford to buy raw materials for their respective trades.[64] However, as has just been suggested, it was the cost of supporting the poor who flocked into the burghs that was the greatest problem, despite efforts being made, where appropriate in alliance with the kirk sessions, to reduce the volume of destitution, by restricting the allocation of beggars' badges, for example.[65] Even so, the expense incurred in dealing with the victims of the famine constituted an additional—and lasting—charge on precarious burgh finances as well as those of their inhabitants.[66]

Other than Glasgow and Edinburgh, the established towns—the royal burghs—of Scotland had seen little growth from the mid-seventeenth century. Some had declined.[67] By the end of the century most burghs were in debt, some severely, with heavy burdens accruing to a number from the effects of post-1688 warring, civil and external. In 1694, for example, Perth was still owed £772 sterling, the cost of stationing military forces in the burgh in 1689

---

[62] D. Dobson, *Scottish Emigration to Colonial America, 1607–1785* (Athens, Georgia, 1994), pp. 39, 69; Macinnes, Harper, and Fryer, *Scotland and the Americas*, pp. 12, 15–16.

[63] T. C. Smout, N. C. Landsman, and T. M. Devine, 'Scottish emigration in the seventeenth and eighteenth centuries', in N. Canny (ed.), *Europeans on the Move: Studies on European Migration, 1500–1800* (Oxford, 1994), p. 88. I am grateful to Karen Cullen for material in this section.

[64] Highland Council Archives, Inverness, PA/1B/M/66/6, Answer to the Chancellor's Letter to the Magistrates of Inverness, 1696; PA/1B/M/66/7, The Magistrates' Answer to the Chancellor's Letter, 1 June 1697; PKCA, Perth Burgh Records, B59/26/4/1, Bundle 9, Petition of David Taylor, 1699.

[65] Stirling Archives, Stirling Burgh Records, B 66/20/6, Council Minutes 1680–1703, 17 May, 2, 5 December 1699; see too Houston, *Social Change*, p. 273; H. M. Dingwall, *Late Seventeenth Century Edinburgh: a Demographic Study* (Aldershot, 1994), p. 261; NAS CH2/569/1, Kiltearn Kirk Session Minutes, 2 August 1697.

[66] R. A. Houston, 'The economy of Edinburgh 1694–1763: the evidence of the Common Good', in Connolly, Houston, and Morris (eds), *Conflict, Identity and Economic Development*, p. 53.

[67] M. Lynch, 'Continuity and change in urban society, 1500–1700', in Houston and Whyte (eds), *Scottish Society 1500–1800*, p. 105.

and 1690.[68] The burden of quartering soldiers on their townspeople continued to be both commonly and loudly complained of by the burghs through to and beyond 1707, and although in this respect Scotland was not unique the cost may have been felt more acutely, not least because of the disruption caused by soldiers from under-funded and ill-disciplined regiments.[69] A military force was essential, however, particularly in the Highlands but also in the Lowlands, to quell disturbances and maintain order when the stresses generated by want threatened to get out of control.[70] 'Where there are many Poor', wrote a concerned Sir Robert Sibbald in 1699, 'the Rich cannot be secure in the Possession of what they have.'[71]

Conflict abroad made its mark on burgh fortunes too. Scotland was drawn in 1689 into England's war with France (although inasmuch as the war was fought in the defence of Protestantism, it had many Scots supporters), the so-called Nine Years War. The War of the Spanish Succession followed in 1702. Few if any coastal burghs were able to preserve their full complements of either ships or men. The Burgh Register of 1692, which may be more reliable than has sometimes been thought, reveals that the Scottish merchant fleet was already in a parlous condition, with the Scottish marine amounting to one ton for every 100 for England, although this is likely to be an underestimate of Scottish capacity. War overseas did provide openings which sharp-eared Scottish merchants could exploit. But war was a fickle friend and Scotland's ability to win rich pickings during periods of conflict were costly, necessarily opportunist, and usually short-lived.

On the high seas—and even in Scottish waters—attempts to counter the actions of French privateers as they began to make an appearance in 1693 were largely futile.[72] It was in recognition of this (as well as other advantages that might result), that around 1695 Lord Belhaven called for the creation of a Scottish navy: without one and the protection it could offer to convoys of merchant ships, he feared 'the utter ruin of the nation'.[73] A navy was established, but with the nation's financial resources already stretched, it had to be

---

[68] PKCA, Perth Burgh Records, B 59/32/20, 'Abbreviat of the Accompts Losses Sustained be the Town of Perth by Ther Majesties Forces 1689–90 and preceding the first day of February 1691' (1694).

[69] Drumlanrig Castle, Buccleuch and Queensberry MSS, Remarks upon the State of ye Armie in Scotland, 16 October 1691.

[70] A. Bil, *The Shieling 1600–1840: the Case of the Scottish Central Highlands* (Edinburgh, 1990), pp. 284–5; P. Simpson, *The Independent Highland Companies 1603–1760* (Edinburgh, 1996), pp. 91–5.

[71] NAS Hamilton MSS, GD 406/1/6368, Earl of Ruglen to Duke of Hamilton, 23, 25 March 1699.

[72] Graham, *Maritime History*, pp. 77–80.

[73] NAS PA7.15, Supplementary Volume XV, 64, 'Reasons for Securing the Trade of the Nation by a Naval Force', c.1695.

limited to three vessels, with hulls borrowed from England and fitted out in
London at the expense of the Scottish treasury.[74] The English navy had been
supplemented by sixty-one newly launched capital ships between 1689 and
1698.[75] That shipping losses at the hands of French privateers declined in the
immediate pre-union period owes less to the strength of the Scottish navy
than to the temporary disappearance of the French to richer hunting
grounds. Instead Anglo-Scottish tensions over shipping intensified as
England declared what was in effect a maritime war against Scots shipping,
which was deemed to threaten the interests of the English monopolies. It
was only in 1706, with negotiations for a union under way, that English
men-of-war were instructed to protect convoys of Scottish ships.[76]

Suffering was not only felt in the royal burghs, although generally speaking the new burghs of barony and regality appear to have been more buoy-
ant—certainly the royal burghs thought so.[77] Yet while they were numerous
they were also small.[78] Enemy privateers attacked Scottish vessels, whatever
the legal status of their home port. Thus Bo'ness, a barony of regality which
had initially prospered after its foundation in 1669, not least through its role
as Glasgow's east coast port, had by 1705 lost as much as two-thirds of the
shipping it had had in 1698 and complained of the high level of taxation
imposed upon it. Glasgow itself claimed that it lost seventeen ships in the
year to June 1707, fourteen to seizures.[79]

These were savage blows for urban economies which were already
strained. Domestic purchasing power was weak, partly as a consequence of
relatively low and stagnant wage levels in the second half of the seventeenth
century.[80] Consumption levels were lower in the Scottish towns than those in
England.[81] As the situation deteriorated after 1700, loud complaints about
the continuing shortage of money with which to conduct business were
voiced right up to 1707. Examination of taxation data from Edinburgh's
Common Good accounts confirms the picture of urban adversity, with sharp
falls in revenue from key areas of economic activity from the end of the seventeenth century. These included timber imports—a telling indicator of

[74] Graham, *Maritime History of Scotland*, pp. 80–1.
[75] J. Black, *Britain as a Military Power, 1698–1815* (London, 1999), p. 79.
[76] NAS Privy Council Records, PC1/53, 6 June 1706; *Edinburgh Courant*, 26 August, 11 September 1706.
[77] J. D. Marwick (ed.), *Extracts From the Convention of the Royal Burghs 1677–1711* (Edinburgh, 1880), Appendix III, pp. 563–667.
[78] I. D. Whyte, 'Urbanisation in early-modern Scotland: a preliminary analysis, *Scottish Economic and Social History* 9 (1989), pp. 29–32.
[79] Whatley, *Scottish Society, 1707–1830*, pp. 39–40.
[80] L. M. Cullen, T. C. Smout, and A. Gibson, 'Wages and comparative development in Ireland and Scotland, 1565–1780', in Mitchison and Roebuck (eds), *Economy and Society*, p. 110.
[81] L. Weatherill, *Consumer Behaviour and Material Culture in Britain* (London, 1988), pp. 59–60.

building activity, and income from taxes on woollens, linen, and butter.[82] It
would be misleading, however, to give the impression that urban Scotland
had entered a period of terminal decline.[83] Building activity, for example, was
ongoing, although the scale of this varied from place to place, with the most
substantial developments occurring in Glasgow.[84] The crumbling condition
of many townhouses, other public buildings, and harbours is also indicative
of municipal financial struggle, and further undermined the hopes of an
aspiring civil, commercial society.[85]

Material accumulation was much more noticeable amongst the ranks of
the landed classes and leading merchants than those below them on the
social scale. But in the straitened circumstances of late seventeenth- and
early eighteenth-century Scotland, the proclivity of the fashion-conscious,
primarily but by no means only in and around Edinburgh (but also far into
the Highlands) to purchase luxury goods from abroad, served to exacerbate
the nation's economic difficulties by intensifying the imbalance in trade.[86]
Conspicuous consumption of this sort was productive of many grand as well
as more modest but fashionable houses, stocked with sumptuous furnishings
and modish artworks.[87] They were commissioned, however, by socially aspirant proprietors for whom indebtedness had become a way of life, and served
to create an illusion of Scottish wealth which contrasted with the penurious
conditions which surrounded many of these beacons of civility and taste.[88]

[82] Houston, 'Economy of Edinburgh', pp. 52–63; there are similarities between the patterns in
Edinburgh and Dundee, see C. A. Whatley, 'Economic causes and consequences of the Union of
1707: a survey', *Scottish Historical Review* 68 (1989), p. 168.

[83] I. D. Whyte, 'Urbanisation in eighteenth-century Scotland', in Devine and Young (eds),
Eighteenth Century Scotland, p. 189.

[84] Considerably more was done after 1707 than before. But for progress beforehand see
M. Glendinning, R. MacInnes, and A. MacKechnie, *A History of Scottish Architecture*
(Edinburgh, 1996), pp. 131–46; T. A. Markus, P. Robinson, and F. A. Walker, 'The shape of the
city in space and stone', in T. M. Devine and G. Jackson (eds), *Glasgow, I: Beginnings to 1830*
(Manchester, 1995), pp. 112–14; PKCA, Perth Burgh Records, B59/27/12, Double Report, 'The
Commissioners of Dundee, Stirling and Forfar Anent the Condition of the Burgh of Perth'
(1700) shows that building work was taking place, but that more than a quarter of the town was
'ruined and not Inhabited'.

[85] Whatley, *Scottish Society, 1707–1830*, pp. 39–40; but also documents such as Highland
Council Archive, PA/IB/CRB 20/84, Report, 'Visitation of the Burgh of Inverness' (1700).

[86] Saville, *Bank of Scotland*, p. 60; NAS PA.7.16, f. 88, Committee For Trade, 1698, 'Reasons,
General for a Sumptuary Law in Scotland' (1698); A. I. Macinnes, *Clanship, Commerce and the
House of Stuart, 1603–1788* (East Linton, 1996), pp. 127–8.

[87] C. McKean, *The Scottish Chateau: the Country House of Renaissance Scotland* (London,
2001), pp. 235–58; for an accomplished case study, see M. Clough, *Two Houses: New Tarbat,
Easter Ross, Royston House, Edinburgh* (Aberdeen, 1990), chs 2 and 3.

[88] For a contemporary critique, see *The Occasion of Scotland's Decay in Trade with a Proper
Expedient For Recovery Thereof And The Increase in our Wealth* (1705); see too comments of
John Clerk on Scottish pretensions, NAS GD 18/5218/23, Sir John Clerk to Henry Clerk, 2 April
1700. Dr Andrew Mackillop kindly provided this reference.

Moralising tirades against luxuries, and attempts by parliament and the Privy Council to ban the importation and use of certain manufactured goods highlight the poor condition of the country's emergent manufacturing sector. Improvement was crucial if Scotland was to free itself of its dependence on expensive imports and obtain the 'value added' which would accrue to an economy which made goods rather than exported raw materials. Yet Scotland's record was weak. Even though linen had become the main manufactured commodity, that the value of imported linen, muslin, and cotton was greater than the value of linen exports hints at the poor quality of most of the Scottish product. Between them, woollens and stockings earned an estimated £41,000, but this represents a fall, in volume terms, of perhaps as much as three-quarters since the 1670s in the case of plaids. By 1707 woollen cloth exports were 'moribund'.[89] Neither does the performance of the smaller industries provide much reason for optimism. The glass industry, for example, had been strongly supported by parliament, but comprised a single glass house in 1695, compared to England's eighty-eight. Fourteen of these were in the north of England.[90] Comparative data for paper making, soap production, starch manufacturing, and calico printing also point to Scottish underperformance.[91] When time series are available, as they have recently become for book printing and book selling, they show (after two impressive waves of Scottish pamphlet publishing, in the 1640s and the 1680s), that activity slowed and remained in something of a trough at least until 1707.[92]

Concerted efforts to establish new economic activities in Scotland demonstrate that at governmental level there was interest in and enthusiasm for national economic development and a determination to improve the collective fortunes of Scots on Scottish soil.[93] The revival in 1681 of the Council of Trade under James, Duke of York, and the Act of the Privy Council of the same date, 'For Encouraging Trade and Manufactures', signalled a shift in priorities, and offered generous incentives to prospective business leaders. The appointment of men like Sir Robert Sibbald to systematically record geographic knowledge and of others later to map Scotland's coastline reveals

---

[89] R. E. Tyson, 'The rise and fall of manufacturing in rural Aberdeenshire', in J. S. Smith and D. Stevenson (eds), *Fermfolk and Fisherfolk* (Aberdeen, 1989), pp. 64–5.

[90] J. Turnbull, *The Scottish Glass Industry 1610–1750* (Edinburgh, 2001), p. 283.

[91] A. G. Thomson, *The Paper Industry in Scotland 1590–1861* (Edinburgh, 1974), p. 4.

[92] A. J. Mann, 'The anatomy of the printed book in early modern Scotland', *Scottish Historical Review* 80 (2001), pp. 198–9; see too J. Redmond, *Pamphlets and Pamphleteering in Early Modern Britain* (Cambridge, 2003), pp. 181–7.

[93] M. Fry, 'A commercial empire: Scotland and British expansion in the eighteenth century', in Devine and Young (eds), *Eighteenth Century Scotland*, p. 55.

an impressive degree of modernity and pragmatism.[94] The appointments in the 1690s were part of a more intensive effort to regenerate Scotland's lagging economy with the emergence of what has been termed 'economic politics' after 1689.[95] But of forty-seven joint-stock companies formed between 1690 and 1695 only twelve appear to have survived until 1700, although in this the government in Scotland was not alone. Direct intervention rarely worked.[96] Even those concerns that kept going did so only by the skin of their teeth.[97] Both a symptom and cause of Scotland's relative backwardness as well as its poverty was a chronic and debilitating shortage of skills, certainly in those areas that would make a difference in the international marketplace. Skilled labour, however, was hard to recruit and retain.

Underdevelopment at the turn of the eighteenth century was a trap from which it was almost impossible to escape. Scotland's position had become particularly difficult following the end of the Cromwellian union and the subsequent Restoration of King Charles I. Excluded from the revised English Navigation Acts of 1660, 1662, 1663, and 1664, which created privileges that English merchants and manufacturers thereafter vigorously defended,[98] the Scots were painfully exposed as international trading rivalries intensified.

It has been argued in the context of Scottish development that the failure of parliamentary legislation to spark improvements in Scottish economic performance was of little consequence.[99] This, however, is precisely the wrong conclusion to draw. This was certainly recognised at the time: good and 'wholesome' laws had been passed, it was observed, but the problem was that these were ineffective, rendered 'Illusorie' by, for example, 'the fraud of Farmers, Collectors and others concerned in the Customs', who ignored legislation that had been designed to defend and support Scottish enterprises. Smuggling was rife.[100] Widespread disdain for the law and endemic tax evasion simply compounded the problem by further starving the state of essential revenue. Feudal privileges and powers and the status that went with these

[94] C. W. J. Withers, *Geography, Science and National Identity: Scotland Since 1520* (Cambridge, 2001), pp. 82–97; R. C. Cant, 'Origins of the Enlightenment in Scotland: the universities', in Campbell and Skinner (eds), *Origins and Nature of the Scottish Enlightenment*, pp. 42–64.

[95] R. Saville, 'Scottish modernisation prior to the Industrial Revolution, 1688–1763', in Devine and Young (eds), *Eighteenth Century Scotland*, pp. 7–14.

[96] S. C. Ogilvie, 'Social institutions and proto-industrialisation', in S. C. Ogilvie and M. Cerman (eds), *European Proto-industrialisation* (Cambridge, 1996), pp. 33–7.

[97] *Essay Against the Transportation and Selling of Men to the Plantations*, p. 12.

[98] Graham, *Maritime History of Scotland*, pp. 14–18.

[99] Devine, 'Union and Scottish development', p. 27.

[100] L. E. Cochran, *Scottish Trade with Ireland in the Eighteenth Century* (Edinburgh, 1985), p. 9.

were jealously guarded both by the royal burghs and the landed classes, with demonstrably harmful effects, on trade and agriculture respectively.[101]

That the Scottish state was insufficiently strong to support its legislative goals with the authority or legal, fiscal, military, or naval force available to others is of crucial importance in understanding the causes of Scottish economic weaknesses—and consequent political responses and actions—in this period of single-minded economy-led state building, seen for instance in Sweden, Russia, France—and England.[102] Unable to exploit a unique raw material or manufactured commodity and with little else to offer either in terms of quantity or quality (there were some successful artisan trades, but their scale was small), the Scots were in no position to bargain, as one after another the countries of northern Europe erected—deaf to the cries of Scots traders—imposing walls of tariff barriers.

Altogether the greatest disappointment however—the most politically significant in modern Scottish history—was the Darien venture. Although it was not the first attempt by the Scots to settle a colony across the Atlantic, launched in the depths of the economic and social mire of the mid-1690s Darien seemed to offer a means of catapulting Scotland into the world's premier league of opulent and powerful nations.[103] Yet as was sensed even by some of the Company's subscribers, and recognised by some of those who sailed to Darien, there were serious weaknesses in the vision, planning, and implementation of the project.[104] There was a culpable failure to recognise that whatever legal rights the Scots might claim to settle there, their presence was much more than a minor irritation to continuing Spanish interests in South America. They could reasonably have expected more of a monarch of the two kingdoms, and English interventions designed to blunt the Darien enterprise were distinctly unhelpful.[105] Nevertheless, the Scots had been

[101] For the alleged adverse effects of royal burgh impositions on the fishing industry of the Fife and Lothian coasts, see NAS Hamilton MSS, GD 406/1/5435, T. S. to Duke of Hamilton, 9 July 1705.
[102] M. Roberts, 'Introduction', in M. Roberts (ed.), *Sweden's Age of Greatness, 1632–1718* (London, 1973), p. 4; E. V. Anisimov, *The Reforms of Peter the Great: Progress Through Coercion in Russia* (New York, 1973), p. 77; on the launch of English economic aggression see C. Wilson, *Profit and Power: a study of England and the Dutch Wars* (London, 1957), pp. 94–103, and J. Scott, '"Good Night Amsterdam." Sir George Downing and Anglo-Dutch statebuilding', *English Historical Review* 118 (2003), pp. 334–56.
[103] Whatley, *Scottish Society, 1707–1830*, p. 38; D. Armitage, 'Making the empire British: Scotland in the Atlantic world, 1542–1717', *Past and Present* 140 (1997), p. 58; M. Fry, *The Scottish Empire* (East Linton and Edinburgh, 2001), pp. 19–30.
[104] Drawn from University of Glasgow Special Collections, MS Gen 1685, no. 6, Robert Turnbull to Col John Erskine, 11 April 1699; no. 9, A Short Account of our Voyage to Darien and wt happened after we came to the place, 1699; no. 11, Thomas Drummond to [?], 1 February 1700; no. 14, Alexander Stobo to [?], 1 February 1700; no. 17, Alexander Shields to [?], 25 December 1699; Mu16-h.19, F. Borland, *Memoirs of Darien* (Glasgow, 1724).
[105] G. P. Insh, *The Company of Scotland Trading to Africa and the Indies* (London, 1932), pp. 53–60.

warned that if they located at Darien this would also interfere with King William's foreign policy in the war against Louis XIV. Neither was their aggressive commitment to the presbyterian cause something that could be ignored by the Pope, Innocent XII.[106] The nationwide enthusiasm, even frenzy, which greeted the proposal to establish the Company for Scotland is understandable; investing in the Company also cocked a patriotic snook at the English who had withdrawn their investment to protect English East Indian interests.[107] But in 1699, so scarce was grain at an affordable price, that the provisioning of the second voyage to Darien was inadequate.[108] In other respects too, disappointment was self-induced. In 1700, after the remnants of the second expedition to Darien had surrendered to Spanish forces and tried to scuttle home, less attention might have been paid to the shrill voices of national resentment and rather more to the less common conclusion that it was not King William alone who had sealed the Scots' fate.[109]

As a nation Scotland alone or within the regal union as it was currently constituted, had severely limited options in an age of muscular mercantilism. Individual Scots could—and did—succeed, sometimes spectacularly, but this was more likely to happen abroad, mainly in commerce but also in military or naval service, where opportunities arose within the sheltered environments provided by aggressive and expansionary regimes. It has been demonstrated, persuasively, that in terms of its economic and social structure, Scotland had much in common with England.[110] But historians have to bear in mind what contemporaries knew, that the Scots were a long way behind, even allowing for the gains Scots made by exploiting loopholes in the Navigation Acts and through downright illegal trading.[111] Also, within the context of the British regal union, in key areas of economic life, Scotland was vulnerable to English political decisions, whether these were consciously designed to hurt the Scots or unintended side-effects. All the rhetoric, passion, and new-found assertiveness of the Scottish Estates after 1689—even the threat Scotland carried as a conduit for Jacobitism into England's back yard—could not conceal the underlying precariousness of Scotland's

---

[106] C. D. Storrs, 'Disaster at Darien (1698–1700)? The persistence of Spanish imperial power on the eve of the demise of the Spanish Habsburgs', *European History Quarterly* 29, 1 (1999), pp. 22–3, 27.

[107] J. S. Barbour, *A History of William Paterson and the Darien Company* (Edinburgh and London, 1907), pp. 22–3.

[108] NAS Hamilton MSS, GD 406/1/4383, Earl of Panmure to Duke of Hamilton, 2 May 1699.

[109] Borland, *Memoirs*, p. 19; Whatley, *Scottish Society, 1707–1830*, p. 38.

[110] K. E. Wrightson, 'Kindred adjoining kingdoms: an English perspective on the social and economic history of early modern Scotland', in Houston and Whyte (eds), *Scottish Society 1500–1800*, pp. 253–60.

[111] See Dobson, *Scottish Emigration*, ch. 2.

economic position.[112] Late to the game of wealth generation that was being played by the major powers, Scotland could either try to join in, but don British colours, or watch enviously from the sidelines, snatching an illicit kick at the ball when no one was looking.

The consequences of the deeply troubled circumstances in which the Scots found themselves at the start of the reign of Queen Anne were profound. Relative poverty and the economic weaknesses of the nation caused some rotting of the political fabric, and created a pungent venal mentality amongst the kinsmen and potential supporters of the four leading Scottish magnates, long familiar to political historians of the period.[113] The symptoms were unpredictable shifts in political allegiances and government instability, although as recent research is demonstrating, not a lack of engagement with the political issues of the day.[114] The result, from the English perspective, according to one recent commentator, was 'an ungovernable kingdom with an unmanageable parliament and a paralysed and useless privy council'.[115] When this was understood by King William and incorporating union fixed upon by Queen Anne as the only way to govern Scotland and ensure that she had a Protestant successor, the tools of court management were relatively easy to apply, thereby smoothing the passage of the Articles of Union through the Scottish Estates in 1706.[116] That a significant number of noble MPs also held posts in the British army, and might hope to advance further in this profession, almost certainly helped too.[117] The military threat in 1706, secret at the time, was real enough,[118] but the much-resented Aliens Act of 1705—which, by crippling the linen trade in particular, would probably have sent Scotland crashing to an insupportably low level of activity—had been sufficiently persuasive to get formal discussions started.

Contrary, however, to the views of those historians who have asserted that economic concerns had no impact when votes on the incorporating union were cast,[119] or who choose simply to ignore economic factors in their analy-

---

[112] See *Scotland's Interest: Or, The Great Benefit and Necessity of a Communication of Trade With England* (1704).
[113] P. W. J. Riley, *King William and the Scottish Politicians* (Edinburgh, 1979), pp. 1–4.
[114] See, for example, D. J. Patrick, 'People and Parliament in Scotland, 1689–1702' (unpublished Ph.D. thesis, University of St Andrews, 2002).
[115] M. Lee, *The 'Inevitable' Union and Other Essays on Early Modern Scotland* (East Linton, 2003), p. 21.
[116] W. Ferguson, *Scotland's Relations With England: a Survey to 1707* (Edinburgh, 1977, edn 1994), pp. 246–50.
[117] Davidson, *Scottish Revolution*, p. 163.
[118] J. R. Young, 'The Parliamentary Incorporating Union of 1707: political management, anti-unionism and foreign policy', in Devine and Young (eds), *Eighteenth Century Scotland*, pp. 43–4.
[119] P. W. J. Riley, *The Union of England and Scotland: a study in Anglo-Scottish Politics of the Eighteenth Century* (Manchester, 1978), pp. 205, 215.

ses of the politics of union, firm lines can be drawn from *economic* crisis (and not just the crisis in Anglo-Scottish relations) to the transition from regal union to incorporating union. In this sense, depictions of the negotiations which led to the Act of Union as melancholy and sordid, the politics of the closet,[120] are overly pessimistic and fail to acknowledge the patriotism of early eighteenth-century unionism.

Links include individuals like William Paterson, often overlooked in discussions of the politics of the making of the Union of 1707, but who was clearly highly respected in both London and Edinburgh, and also influential.[121] Paterson was convinced that the combined costs of the famine and the Darien scheme were the principal cause of Scotland's low condition by 1705, and that a 'complete union', the case for which he marshalled in considerable detail, offered the most likely means of recovery. A similar route to incorporating union was taken by the vociferous if politically duplicitous George Mackenzie, 1st Earl of Cromartie, Queen Anne's Secretary of State. Mackenzie, however, had experienced at first hand the economic and social trials and tribulations and dashed hopes of the pre-union period.[122] Although John Clerk of Penicuik, one of the Commissioners appointed by Queen Anne in 1705, was a reluctant unionist, he and his father, Sir John Clerk, were more knowledgeable about economic matters than many of their contemporaries, and acutely conscious of Scotland's financial difficulties. Those many Scots who resisted union on the grounds that Scottish liberties and independence would be lost or who favoured some sort of federal arrangement were urged to 'lay aside airy Schemes of Government, lest like the Dog in the Fable, we catch at the Shadow, and lose the Substance'.[123]

The motivations of the Squadrone Volante, whose votes were crucial to the passing of the Articles of Union in the Scottish parliament, have been viewed by some historians as somewhat contemptible. Lacking principle, it is alleged that the grouping was satisfied only by the payment of salary arrears, promotions and appointments, and the promise that they would do well by the arrangements made to compensate those who had made losses by investing in the Company of Scotland.[124] But bigger issues were at stake and the

[120] Lee, *'Inevitable' Union*, p. 23; C. Kidd, *Subverting Scotland's Past: Scottish Whig Historians and the Creation of Anglo-British Identity, 1689–c.1830* (Cambridge, 1993), pp. 33–50; for a fuller list see C. A. Whatley, *Bought and Sold for English Gold? Explaining the Union of 1707* (East Linton, 2001).

[121] S. Bannister (ed.), *The Writings of William Paterson*, 3 vols (New York, 1968), I, pp. ix–cxliv.

[122] Clough, *Two Houses*, pp. 99–102, 131.

[123] NAS Clerk of Penicuik MSS, GD 18/3129, Clerk, *Circumstances of Scotland Considered*, p. 1; see too Sir J. Clerk, *Letter to a Friend*, p. 6; also *A Sermon Preach'd to the People, At the Mercat Cross of Edinburgh On the Subject of the Union* (1706), p. 5.

[124] Riley, *Union of England and Scotland*, pp. 260–8.

picture of party political mendacity is relieved by, for example, the private
correspondence of one of the Squadrone adherents, William Bennet of
Grubbet. This provides compelling testimony that weightier considerations
mattered and had done so since the later 1690s; 'full union', Bennett was
persuaded, was the 'fair bargain' that would restore 'this sinking nation'.[125]

With the exception of the pamphleteers such as George Ridpath and
James Hodges, contemporaries were strangely reticent about coming forward
with better alternatives.[126] Andrew Fletcher's proposals for a federal union
attracted little support.[127] Others who might have advanced more construc-
tive schemes of government failed to do so. Anne, Duchess of Hamilton and
her son James, nominal leader of the opposition Country party, bemoaned
Scotland's dismal condition, shed crocodile tears, but contributed not a help-
ful word or deed. On the contrary and despite the Duke's admission in 1704
that only freedom of trade would save Scotland, his mother expressed her
relief that James had estates in England and was thereby sheltered from 'all
the straits of this nation [Scotland]'.[128] Thousands were confused and uncertain, and many sought advice about the best way forward through prayer.
Economic privation did not necessarily lead to support for incorporation.
The views of the royal burghs varied, with a large number for, though in some
cases reluctantly, while others, Selkirk for example, which conducted no foreign trade, saw no advantages, and feared (understandably) that union would
lead to yet higher taxes.[129] With recent experience having dented national
confidence, it is not surprising that some feared that free trade could further
damage Scottish interests. The Caribbean route was perhaps the most prom-
ising alternative but it was unlikely to realise its full potential as long as the
Scots were formally excluded by the Navigation Acts. It is striking not only
that Glasgow merchants were drawn to union by the prospect of the 'vast
wealth' the West Indian trade would bring in its wake, but also that a proposal for a new venture at Darien, which involved the export of linen, was
proposed after the terms of the incorporating union had been settled.[130]

For all the undoubted endeavour and accomplishments of the Scots in the
seventeenth century, if they were to flourish as members of polite society in

[125] NAS Bennet of Grubbet MSS, GD 205/38, William Bennet to William Nisbet, 10 March, 13
April 1706.
[126] J. Robertson, 'Sovereignty and the Act of Union', in H. T. Dickinson and M. Lynch (eds),
The Challenge to Westminster (East Linton, 2000), pp. 36–7.
[127] J. Robertson (ed.), *Andrew Fletcher: Political Works* (Cambridge, 1997), p. xvii.
[128] NAS Hamilton MSS, GD 406/1/6955, Duchess of Hamilton to Duke of Hamilton,
3 September 1705.
[129] Borders Council, Selkirk, Selkirk Council Book, 1/1/2, 1704–1717, 2 November 1706.
[130] NAS Hamilton MSS, GD 406/1/9747, R. Wylie to Duke of Hamilton, 1 July 1706, GD
406/1/5437, Richard Long to Duke of Hamilton, 7 March 1707.

Britain, or as equal cultural partners in the capitals of Europe and, collectively as a nation to act (as many wished) as a bulwark against Catholic France, Scotland required the support of a powerful state, and the protection and prospect of prosperity this would provide in an age of closed and competing empires. Regal union had run its course. The Scots, with bitter regret and considerable reluctance, had to surrender their parliamentary independence, but not all that they valued as distinctively Scottish institutions and culture, and accede to the British incorporating union.

Note.   The author is grateful to Dr Derek Patrick for his research assistance with this chapter.

7

The Law of the Sea and the Two Unions

JOHN FORD

IN NOVEMBER 1893 THREE SHIPS LAY SIDE BY SIDE AT A PIER IN ISLAY.[1] A
heavy gale blew up and the master of the middle ship, fearing that she would
be damaged if he left her where she lay, cut the ropes binding the vessels
together and put out to sea. Not surprisingly, the ship he had cut adrift suffered damage and litigation ensued, first in a local sheriff court, then on
appeal before the Court of Session in Edinburgh, and then on further appeal
before the judicial committee of the House of Lords at Westminster. Of the five
members of the committee three were, as usual, lawyers trained in England,
and they faced the not uncommon task of having to determine whether a
decision delivered by a Scottish court should be upheld when it clearly would
not have been delivered by an English court. In this case even the two Scottish
judges helpfully agreed that maritime issues should be governed by the same
law on either side of the Border. One of them declared that the court must
apply a body of law 'which, in my opinion, is neither English nor Scottish,
but British law'. One of the English judges similarly declared that 'on such
questions it is the law of Great Britain that prevails'. The law of the sea was
British law, which is no doubt what any innocent visitor to these islands
would have expected and might even now expect. With a unified monarchy, a
unified parliament, and a supreme court sitting as part of the unified parliament, how could Scotland and England have been governed by anything
other than British law? Of course, the short answer is that it was agreed three
hundred years ago that despite any monarchical or parliamentary union the
two nations should preserve their separate systems of private law. How, when,
and why this was agreed are questions that have been discussed at length and
would merit further discussion. The purpose of this brief essay, however, is
not to address these questions directly but to approach them from an oblique

---

[1] M. Rettie et al., *Cases Decided in the Court of Session, Court of Justiciary, and House of Lords,
from 1896 to 1897* (Edinburgh, 1897), pt 1, pp. 1–8.

Proceedings of the British Academy, **127**, 127–141. © The British Academy 2005.

angle by asking why in one area it did become possible to speak with some plausibility of a body of British law. In particular, the aim is to consider why lawyers in Scotland began to accept between the Unions of 1603 and 1707 that their sea law might need to be exposed to influence from south of the Border.

At the time of the Union of the Crowns, it has been suggested, Scots lawyers had a more advanced understanding of maritime law than English lawyers.[2] How far this was true is difficult to tell, for the surviving records of the Court of Admiralty in Scotland shed little light on the way in which questions of law were debated and determined.[3] Registers of the court's decisions before the 1670s survive only from the late 1550s and early 1560s and from the late 1620s and early 1630s.[4] In the early 1670s an anonymous lawyer read through the then surviving registers and made an abridgement which fills in some of the gaps, but neither this abridgement nor the registers themselves provide much information about the legal arguments advanced at the bar or accepted on the bench.[5] The suggestion that Scots lawyers had a particularly advanced understanding of the law of the sea rests largely on the fact that the first treatise on the subject to be printed in Britain was written by one of several Scots who had worked in the area. William Welwod was a professor of the civil law at the University of St Andrews when he published *The Sea Law of Scotland* in 1590.[6] He claimed in a preface to have written for the benefit of Scottish mariners and merchants, who appeared to him to be less well acquainted with the law regulating their trade than they ought to be, and he certainly tried to make his book accessible to laymen by writing in the vernacular and presenting the law in the form of rules. An earlier book had apparently been written in a similar style by David Kintor, a judge in the

[2] A. R. G. McMillan, 'Admiralty and Maritime Law', in H. McKechnie (ed.), *An Introductory Survey of the Sources and Literature of Scots Law* (Edinburgh, 1936), p. 325, at p. 329.
[3] For the history of the Scottish court see further A. R. G. McMillan, 'The Scottish Court of Admiralty: a retrospect', *Juridical Review* 34 (1922), p. 38. On the more extensive records of the English court and some of the documents that can be used to supplement them, see R. G. Marsden (ed.), *Select Pleas in the Court of Admiralty* (London, 1897), pp. lxxix–lxxxviii, and A. Wijffels, 'Civil Law in the Practice of the High Court of Admiralty at the time of Alberico Gentili' (Ph.D. thesis, University of Cambridge, 1993), pp. 1–10.
[4] The volume covering the late 1550s and early 1560s has been published by the Stair Society as T. C. Wade (ed.), *Acta curiae admirallatus Scotiae* (Edinburgh, 1937). The volumes covering the late 1620s and early 1630s are preserved in the National Archives of Scotland as AC. 7/1–2, followed by six more volumes covering (with some gaps) 1672 to 1692. I am grateful to the archivists and librarians of the National Archives of Scotland (NAS), the National Library of Scotland (NLS), Edinburgh University Library (EUL), and the British Library (BL) for permitting me to make use of manuscript materials in their collections.
[5] NLS Adv. MS 6.2.1, ff. 20–104.
[6] 'The Sea Law of Scotland', ed. T. C. Wade, in a Scottish Text Society *Miscellany Volume* (Edinburgh, 1933), p. 23.

Court of Admiralty at the end of the 1550s. His book has not survived, but extracts from it appear in other works, including a treatise on sea law attached to the well known 'practicks' of Sir James Balfour of Pittendreich, which was written at about the same time as Welwod was gathering his materials together.[7] Towards the end of the sixteenth century another treatise was written by Alexander King, who had studied and taught law on the Continent before returning to Scotland to become an advocate in 1581 and a judge in the Admiralty Court in 1587.[8] By the time King produced his treatise— written in Latin and in a style suited to professional readers, who regarded the law less as a collection of rules than as a body of learning—Welwod was running into personal difficulty at St Andrews.[9] In 1611 he resigned his chair and moved to England, where he tried to reach a wider audience by publishing an expanded version of his treatise under the title *An Abridgement of All Sea-Lawes*, and a further expanded version of one of the additional chapters under the title *De dominio maris*.[10] Another Scots lawyer, Habakkuk Bisset, immediately began to collect material on sea law which he formed into a new compendium in 1622.[11] His was the last sustained effort to produce a survey of maritime law in Scotland before the Union of the Parliaments.[12]

The writers of these books drew material from three main sources, usually starting with the statutes passed by the Scottish parliaments. In fact there had not been a great deal of legislative activity in this area, but some statutes were considered to be important, above all an act passed in 1429 to provide that 'strangers incurring schipwracke in Scotland suld haif the samin favour

[7] P. G. B. McNeill (ed.), *The Practicks of Sir James Balfour of Pittendreich* (Edinburgh, 1962–3), II, pp. 614–44. Welwod, 'Sea Law', pp. 42–5, claimed to have started work on his book in the late 1570s in response to the same demands for law reform that are believed to have inspired Balfour's work.

[8] NLS Adv. MS 28.4.7 and MS 1948, and EUL La. III. 741. The first copy has attached to it a vernacular treatise on court procedure which can also be found in NLS Adv. MS 81.4.12, pp. 29–56.

[9] In a preface (NLS Adv. MS 28.4.7, f. 2) King wrote of the need to combine the theory and practice of law, a standard motif in the emerging *usus modernus pandectarum*, as is explained in K. Luig, 'The Institutes of National Law in the seventeenth and eighteenth centuries', *Juridical Review* n.s. 17 (1972), pp. 193–226, at pp. 196–7. For an account of the difficulty Welwod was facing, see J. W. Cairns, 'Academic feud, bloodfeud, and William Welwood: legal education in St Andrews, 1560–1611', *Edinburgh Law Review* 2 (1998), pp. 158 and 255.

[10] *An Abridgement of All Sea-Lawes* (London, 1613), and *De dominio maris* (London, 1615). On the publication of the latter, see J. D. Alsop, 'William Welwood, Anne of Denmark, and the sovereignty of the sea', *Scottish Historical Review* 59 (1980), p. 171.

[11] P. J. Hamilton-Grierson (ed.), *Habakkuk Bisset's Rolment of Courtis* (Edinburgh, 1920–6), I, p. 13, and II, pp. 198–266.

[12] J. A. Clyde (ed.), *Hope's Major Practicks* (Edinburgh, 1937–8), II, pp. 312–13, contains no more than a tentative beginning of a collection. For another tentative effort made at the end of the 1650s, see J. D. Marwick (ed.), *Extracts from the Records of the Convention of the Royal Burghs of Scotland, 1615–76* (Edinburgh, 1878), pp. 486–7 and pp. 519–20.

and grace of us that our people in like caise use to receave on thair coast'.[13]
Quite apart from its obvious relevance in cases of shipwreck, this act was
taken to justify the general recourse of Scots lawyers to the example of foreign laws.[14] Where one of the parties to an action was from abroad, the judges
of the Admiralty Court were sometimes urged to consider the law of his
nation, and often their attention was drawn to 'the ressaivid and observid
custome of other nationnes in materis of the lyke kynd', or to 'the constant
custome of all our nighbour nations', especially if it was expected that Scots
would receive 'the lyke favour frae them'.[15] When advocates referred in their
arguments to 'the marine law', 'the sea lawes and customes' or 'the custome
of the sea', they usually had in mind the standard practices that mariners
believed they were obliged to follow.[16] Often these practices had been prescribed in written statements of maritime law produced in other countries, for
instance in the Laws of Oleron, which were taken to regulate trade on the
Atlantic coast, or in the Laws of Wisby, which were taken to regulate trade
in the Baltic.[17] The Scottish writers on maritime law made extensive use of
these foreign codes, but on the clear understanding that they could be binding only to the extent that they had been 'authorizit be our natioun' or that
the provisions they contained had been 'ressavit in this realme'.[18] When Bisset
included translations of large parts of the foreign codes in his compendium
he explained that his aim was to facilitate their reading in Scotland, 'nocht
that we suld be subject therto, bot as the lawes and practik of this realme per-
mittis to be considderred'.[19] Like any customary practices, the customs of the
sea required to be both proved and approved in the courts before they could
be given effect, though unlike most customs they could be proved by the tes-

---

[13] *Acts of the Parliaments of Scotland*, T. Thomson and C. Innes (eds) (Edinburgh, 1814–75), II,
p. 19; Welwod, 'Sea Law', pp. 74–5; McNeill (ed.), *Practicks of Sir James Balfour*, II, p. 624;
Hamilton-Grierson (ed.), *Bisset's Rolment of Courtis*, II, p. 206 (and see too p. 201 and pp. 212–15,
where Bisset claimed that the Scottish legislation on shipwreck dated back to the thirteenth
century and had been copied in England).

[14] NLS Adv. MS 6.2.1, ff. 57r–58r; Hamilton-Grierson (ed.), *Bisset's Rolment of Courtis*, II,
p. 263.

[15] NAS AC. 7/1, pp. 9–10, 14–15, 36–7, 42–3, 56–7, 78–9, 85–6, 103, 120, 127, 148, 163–4, 186,
217, and 230; NLS Adv. MS 6.2.1, ff. 51r–58r.

[16] NAS AC. 7/1, pp. 229 and 276, and AC. 7/2, pp. 221 and 373; NLS Adv. MS 6.2.1, ff. 43v–44r,
46, 47r, and 54v.

[17] Welwod, *Abridgement*, p. 22, noted that charter parties often provided that disputes should be
regulated by the Laws of Oleron, which meant that these rules would have bound the parties even
when they were not generally believed to be binding.

[18] Welwod, 'Sea Law', pp. 44–5; Wade (ed.), *Acta curiae admirallatus Scotiae*, pp. 164–5.

[19] Hamilton-Grierson (ed.), *Bisset's Rolment of Courtis*, II, p. 264. Many copies of the foreign
codes can still be found in Scottish libraries, for example in NLS Adv. MSS 6.2.2, 24.6.3, 28.4.6,
and 28.6.7, and EUL La. III. 740.

timony of witnesses from overseas.[20] Once they were approved in the courts they came to be regarded as part of the 'common custome' or 'common lawe' of Scotland.[21]

The customary law approved in the courts of Scotland had been called the common law since the thirteenth century, but in relation to maritime law this usage was especially apt to confuse.[22] In the records of the Admiralty Court and the books written about maritime law the expression 'common law' (or *ius commune*) was often used with reference to the civil law, meaning the law of ancient Rome as commented on in the university faculties devoted to its study.[23] After the legislation of the Scottish parliaments and the customs of mariners, the civil law was the third main source drawn on by the writers on sea law. As Alexander King explained, where a dispute could not be resolved by reference to the laws and customs of a particular nation, sentence was expected to be given by admiralty judges *ex iuris civilis dispositione*, the assumption being that the civil law had common authority throughout Europe.[24] Although explanations of its authority varied, the vital point is that the civil law was taken to be legally binding for some reason in most European countries. In this it differed from *ius naturale et gentium*, which is what the Roman jurists had been thinking of when they originally contrasted the common law with their own civil law.[25] University scholars had also studied the law of nature and nations, but as a form of ethical enquiry and in faculties of arts and theology rather than of law. In the sixteenth century moral theologians had started to attend more closely to the teaching of civil lawyers, and civil lawyers had then started to take more account of the teaching of theologians, but a distinction had still been drawn by lawyers between studying what the law should be and what it actually was.[26] Where this distinction began to break down was in relation to the law regulating the relations between nations. The Roman jurists had used the expression *ius gentium*

---

[20] Wade (ed.), *Acta curiae admirallatus Scotiae*, p. 86.

[21] Welwod, 'Sea Law', pp. 44–5 and pp. 76–7.

[22] W. D. H. Sellar, 'The common law of Scotland and the common law of England', in R. R. Davies (ed.), *The British Isles, 1100–1500* (Edinburgh, 1988), p. 82. Few errors cause greater confusion in the study of early modern legal history than the careless assumption that all lawyers who referred to the common law meant the same or even roughly the same thing. The key to a proper understanding is to ask what the common law was being contrasted with as proper law.

[23] NAS AC. 7/1, pp. 9, 14–15, 36–7, 42–3, 56–7, and 78–9; NLS Adv. MSS 6.2.1, ff. 58v–59r, and 28.4.7, ff. 10r, 17v, 18r, and 49v; Welwod, 'Sea Law', pp. 64–5; Hamilton-Grierson (ed.), *Bisset's Rolment of Courtis*, II, pp. 255 and 260.

[24] NLS Adv. MS 28.4.7, f. 8v.

[25] A. Watson (ed.), *The Digest of Justinian* (Philadelphia, 1985), 1.1.1–6; *Justinian's Institutes*, trans. P. Birks and G. McLeod (London, 1987), 1.2.*pr*.–2 and 11.

[26] For an exemplary study of these developments, see J. Gordley, *The Philosophical Origins of Modern Contract Doctrine* (Oxford, 1991).

in a less theoretical sense to designate the parts of their law that they assumed all nations would share, either because they were straightforward applications of natural law or because they were so expedient that no nation could survive without them. In this sense *ius gentium* was a branch of *ius civile* (broadly taken), and when Scottish writers on sea law used the expression they were usually drawing attention to provisions of the civil law that were not peculiarly Roman.[27] But in the sixteenth and seventeenth centuries a new usage was starting to develop.[28] With the emergence of the conception of the nations of Europe as sovereign states, subject to no superior, there arose the assumption that the relations between nations could be governed only by the law of nature or by the practices customarily observed among nations. Although the regulation of affairs between nations was quite different from the regulation of affairs within them, the expression *ius gentium* also came to be used with reference to the regulation of international relations.[29] A new body of international law began to take shape, based on study of the literature on natural law and of the treaties and practices of states. The development of this body of law was influenced by civilian doctrine, but in the sense of international law *ius gentium* was not directly dependent on the learning of the law schools.

In some respects the law of the sea was affected by the development of the new law of nations. In 1609, for example, a treatise asserting the freedom of navigation on the high seas was published under the title *Mare liberum* by Hugo Grotius, often glibly described as 'the father of international law'.[30] It was in response to the appearance of this treatise that Welwod added to his *Abridgement of All Sea-Lawes* the chapter later expanded into his own treatise *De dominio maris*. Welwod was the only critic to elicit a response from Grotius, but the response consisted largely of the justifiable complaint that he had failed to understand the nature of Grotius' enquiry. The author of the *Mare liberum*, as Welwod rightly observed, had based his argument on 'the authority and wordes of such old writers as have beene esteemed most mighty in the understanding and judging upon the naturall condition of things here belowe'.[31] Welwod tried to respond to Grotius in his own terms,

---

[27] Welwod, *Abridgement*, p. 57 and pp. 65–6; NLS Adv. MS 28.4.7, ff. 19r, 25v, and 29r.

[28] For an unusual but illuminating discussion of these developments, see C. R. Rossi, *Great Chain of Being: James Brown Scott and the Origins of Modern International Law* (The Hague, 1998).

[29] The nearest Roman equivalent to international law was not *ius gentium* but *ius fetiale*, on which see A. Watson, *International Law in Archaic Rome* (Baltimore, 1993).

[30] See, for instance, C. S. Edwards, *Hugo Grotius: the Miracle of Holland* (Chicago, 1981), pp. 9–25.

[31] Welwod, *Abridgement*, pp. 61–72. It was this version of Welwod's argument that Grotius answered.

and he started by using biblical texts to elucidate 'the first verity of the nature of things'. But he denied the relevance of the opinions of the poets, orators, and philosophers cited by Grotius, he complained that Grotius had 'wrested' the legal texts he cited away from their proper meaning, and he generally accused Grotius of losing touch with his 'profession of the lawes'. Welwod himself claimed to have written on the strength of his 'profession of the civill lawe', and he based his own argument on the authority of civilian commentators who had drawn support from Roman law for the dominion claimed by Genoa and Venice over stretches of the Mediterranean adjacent to their coasts.[32] It was the dominion nations claimed over adjacent waters that Welwod sought to defend, for he believed that Grotius' ostensible concern with freedom of navigation on the high seas was a red herring and that what he was really concerned with was the freedom to trade in soused herring drawn from the North Sea.[33] In response Grotius explained that freedom of navigation had become an issue in international law and that in handling such issues 'we should have regard not so much for the commentators, who lived a few centuries back and who often disagreed with others and with each other, as for the ancient authorities and the very principles and rules of the law themselves'.[34] Grotius defended his reading of the legal texts he had cited and also his use of other classical sources, claiming that they provided instructive guidance on *ius gentium*, which arose partly from 'divine providence' and partly from 'the common consent of nations'. Welwod, he complained, had failed to understand the meaning of the expression.

Although Welwod was inconsistent in writing about *ius gentium*, he specifically denied that the expression could be taken to mean 'any law set downe by common consent of all nations', and he was more interested in what could be learned from the 'common consent of lawyers' than in the treaties of states or the treatises on natural law.[35] Alexander King made a passing reference to the treatises on natural law when he wrote about reprisals—the practice of seeking redress for wrongs committed by foreigners

[32] Welwod, *Abridgement*, p. 6. On the views of the commentators, see D. M. Johnston, *The International Law of Fisheries* (New Haven, 1987), pp. 160–3.

[33] For general background to the debate, see T. W. Fulton, *The Sovereignty of the Sea* (Edinburgh, 1911). It has often been said, and with some justification, that Welwod's discussion prepared the way for but was eclipsed by John Selden's *Mare clausum*, which was first written shortly afterwards but not published until 1636: see, for example, D. Armitage, *The Ideological Origins of the British Empire* (Cambridge, 2000), pp. 110–11. However, it is important to bear in mind that Selden succeeded in replying to Grotius in his own terms in a way that Welwod did not. Selden made no attempt to write as a civilian but engaged fully in the new discourse of natural and international law.

[34] *Bibliotheca Visseriana*, VII (1928), pp. 154–205 (translation adjusted from the edition in S. Muller, *Mare clausum* (Amsterdam, 1872), pp. 331–61).

[35] Welwod, *Abridgement*, pp. 4–5, 10, 18, 29, 48, and 66.

through the seizure of ships or cargoes belonging to their compatriots.[36] King
acknowledged that there had been no such practice in Roman times and that
it had been introduced in medieval Europe *iure gentium ex maxima aequitate*,
but just as Welwod based his treatment of the dominion of the seas on the
novel use the Italian commentators had made of Roman law texts, so King
based his account of reprisals on the novel use the same commentators had
made of other Roman law texts.[37] King came closer than any other Scottish
author on sea law to writing about the emerging law of nations, but like
Welwod he continued to work within the civil law tradition and to rely on the
learned authority of the schools for solutions to any issues left unresolved by
the local sources. The same appears to have been true of the advocates who
practised in the Scottish Court of Admiralty, for there is no evidence in the
surviving records that they began in the first half of the seventeenth century
to take account of the new international law in the way that their English
counterparts are known to have done.[38] It appears to have been in the late
1660s, at the time of the second Dutch war, that Scots lawyers began to
appreciate the relevance of the changing conception of *ius gentium* for some
aspects of maritime law.[39] John Lauder, an advocate recently admitted to
practice at the bar, wrote a brief review of the prize cases resulting from that
war around 1670.[40] He began by noting that old grievances had been dredged
up in 1664 because 'it was thought England's interest to have war with Holland
on any termes', and that the Scots had been drawn into the war 'contrare to
our interest'. Excluded from their familiar markets in the Netherlands and
France, many mariners had taken to privateering and had become adept at 'the

---

[36] NLS Adv. MS 28.4.7, ff. 22–4.

[37] On the use made of the Roman concept of *pigneratio*, see G. Butler and S. MacCoby, *The
Development of International Law* (London, 1928), pp. 173–7. King referred quite often to the
works of humanist jurists, particularly in discussing the origin and meaning of terms, but like
most practising lawyers he continued to rely heavily on the doctrine of the Italian commentators.

[38] Compare A. Wijffels, *Alberico Gentili and Thomas Crompton* (Leiden, 1992) and *Consilium
facultatis iuridicae Tubingensis* (Leiden, 1993), with A. Wijffels and I. van Loo, 'Zealand privateering and the Anglo-Spanish peace treaty of 1630', in B. C. M. Jacobs and E. C. Coppens (eds),
Een rijk gerecht (Nijmegen, 1998), p. 635.

[39] Of course, the deficiency may be in the record more than the reality of admiralty practice. In
NLS Adv. MS 6.2.1, ff. 51–2r, there is an account of a case decided in 1648 which hints at a
movement towards the concerns of the late 1660s. Even here, however, the argument turned on
the application of a text from Justinian's *Digest*.

[40] Sir John Lauder of Fountainhall, *Historical Observes of Memorable Occurrents in Church and
State*, ed. D. Laing (Edinburgh, 1840), pp. 253–63. The review ends with a brief discussion of
cases arising from the third war, but it is clear both from the tenor of the earlier discussion and
from the change of ink in NLS Adv. MS 24.4.1, f. 13, that the earlier part was written before the
third war began. Lauder had intended to develop his review into a treatise on prize law but never
did so, perhaps because he felt that the task had been accomplished in a passage added to Stair's
Institutions of the Law of Scotland in 1681, to which reference is made below.

Hollander's way of trading and warring togither'. The Court of Admiralty had sat almost constantly to adjudicate on the ownership of the ships and cargoes they captured, many of the court's rulings had been reviewed by the lords of session sitting in Scotland's highest civil court, and in three years Scots lawyers had 'learned more marittime law and cases arising theirfrom, nor ever our praedecessors'.[41]

The turning point had come with the intervention of the lords of session. At the start of 1667 they had received a letter from the king complaining that prize cases involving ships from neutral countries were being mishandled in the Court of Admiralty, reminding them that they had authority to review that court's decisions, and urging them to exercise their authority with due regard to the treaties entered into with nations like Sweden and Spain, 'whose ships and goods are to pass free'.[42] The lords of session had promised to comply with the king's request, but in fact no prize case was reviewed before July 1667, when the judges were impressed with arguments that passes issued to foreign ships by the English admiral must be irrelevant, '*Scotland* being a free Kingdom', and that acts of the English Privy Council 'could not be effectual as to *Scotland*, and much lesse to Strangers'.[43] The judges decided rather vaguely that these cases must be governed *communi iure gentium*, yet they also recognised that the king 'alone *dat leges bello*', and as complaints about the mishandling of cases continued they took further advice from his secretary in London, as they did again at the start of 1668.[44] Evidence was received of 'the Custom of *England*', and while the judges accepted the argument that Scotland, 'being a distinct Kingdom, is not Ruled by the Custom of *England*', they also accepted that English admiralty practice provided valuable evidence of 'the Custom of Nations'. It was 'the Law and Custom of Nations', they believed, that must govern these disputes, particularly as adumbrated in the king's declaration of war, from which his treaties were understood to make exceptions.[45] In the spring of 1668 the lords of session again sought guidance from the king's secretary, who told them that 'the Admirall Courts in all

---

[41] For details of some of the privateers and their captures see S. Mowat, *The Port of Leith* (Edinburgh, 1994), pp. 214–16, and E. J. Graham, *A Maritime History of Scotland* (East Linton, 2002), pp. 20–5.

[42] *The Acts of Sederunt of the Lords of Council and Session* (Edinburgh, 1790), p. 102; NAS CS. 1/6/1, pp. 226–7; BL Add. MS 23126, f. 3r.

[43] EUL La. III. 354(1), f. 45; BL Add. MS 23127, f. 107; Sir James Dalrymple of Stair, *The Decisions of the Lords of Council and Session* (Edinburgh, 1683–7), I, p. 480.

[44] BL Add. MS 23128, f. 142; Stair, *Decisions of the Lords of Council and Session*, I, pp. 482–4, 502–5, and 529–31; Sir John Nisbet of Dirleton, *The Decisions of the Lords of Council and Session* (Edinburgh, 1698), pp. 55–6; Sir George Mackenzie of Rosehaugh, *Pleadings, in Some Remarkable Cases* (Edinburgh, 1672), pp. 120–30; Historical Manuscripts Commission, *Report on the Laing Manuscripts* (London, 1914), I, p. 365. See too EUL La. III. 354(2), f. 85.

[45] Stair, *Decisions of the Lords of Council and Session*, I, pp. 534–5.

nations walk by the Rule of the Maritime Laws', subject to 'their particular Customs' and with advice from 'Civill Lawyers', and that 'as to this war, the King's Declarations are the Rule of the Admirality here, together with the particular Treaties which the King hath made with Sweden and Flanders, which are to be punctually observed'.[46] In the following summer the lords of session accepted in a series of cases that 'the Kings Proclamation of the War, behoved to be the Rule to the Kings Judges', that 'the Law of Nations must take place, or the Custom of *Scotland*, in cases not exprest in the Kings Declaration', and that 'the Kings Proclamation being the Rule of War, the Treaties with Allies do only explain or restrain the same'.[47] In response to pleas that 'these cases with Strangers are to be Ruled by the Law of Nations, and not by peculiar Statutes and Customs', it was argued that the king's declaration of war 'was most consonant to the Law of Nations', which was otherwise to be clarified by reference to the practice of admiralty courts abroad, especially in England. Some judges had even come to believe that acts of the English Privy Council could be relevant in Scottish cases.

Notwithstanding their willingness to follow the example of English admiralty practice, however, the lords of session often declared ships to be prizes in the face of evidence that English judges would have reached a different decision. Scottish politicians believed that the number of ships added to their merchant fleet would strengthen the argument they had been advancing since the beginning of the war for a commercial alliance with England.[48] Deprived of access to their traditional markets yet also excluded by a series of Navigation Acts from trade with England and her colonies, the Scots complained that they were being expected to suffer the privations of war without much prospect of benefit.[49] They recalled that during the first Dutch war they had been able to trade with both France and England, and since this was partly a consequence of the parliamentary union imposed in the 1650s, the prospect of a closer political union was naturally revived as an alternative to a merely commercial arrangement.[50] In 1670 commissioners were appointed to represent Scotland in negotiations for a closer union, among them several lords of session and other lawyers, some of whom were opposed to any form of

---

[46] *Report on the Laing Manuscripts*, I, p. 367; 'Lauderdale Correspondence', in the *Fifth Miscellany of the Scottish History Society* (Edinburgh, 1933), pp. 193–4.

[47] Stair, *Decisions of the Lords of Council and Session*, I, pp. 544–5, 550–2, 617–20, and 626.

[48] BL Add. MS 23129, f. 41; NLS MSS 7023, f. 210, and 7033, f. 137.

[49] J. Bruce, *Report on the Events and Circumstances which Produced the Union of England and Scotland* (London, 1799), I, pp. 185–230; G. W. T. Omond, *The Early History of the Scottish Union Question* (Edinburgh, 1897), pp. 122–46; E. Hughes, 'Negotiations for a commercial union between England and Scotland in 1668', *Scottish Historical Review* 24 (1927), p. 34.

[50] BL Add. MSS 23127, f. 107, 23128, ff. 56 and 76, 23130, ff. 18 and 70, and 23132, ff. 147–8; NLS MS 7023, ff. 206 and 210.

parliamentary union but most of whom were prepared to countenance union so long as it was agreed that the two nations would retain their separate systems of law.[51] The same circumstances thus gave rise on the one hand to a determination to preserve a separate legal system in Scotland and on the other hand to a willingness to expose the handling of admiralty cases to English influence, a willingness that continued into the early 1670s. During the third Dutch war the same directions were issued to the admiralty courts of the two nations, an English judge was appointed to sit in the Scottish court, and the lords of session continued to review the court's decisions in the light of the king's declarations and treaties and of English admiralty practice.[52] This combination of an insistence on the preservation of Scots law with an acceptance of the need for assimilation in admiralty practice was to emerge again in the terms of the union eventually agreed in 1707.[53] The eighteenth article of the Treaty of Union provided that no change could be made to those 'Laws which concern private Right, except for evident utility of the subjects within Scotland', and the nineteenth article that no change could be made to the constitution or jurisdiction of the Courts of Session, Justiciary, and Admiralty except 'for the better Administration of Justice'. But the nineteenth article also spelled out that there should be an admiralty court in Scotland 'as in England', placed both courts under the control of 'the Admiralty of Great Britain', and allowed that the new parliament could 'make such Regulations and Alterations, as shall be judged expedient for the whole United Kingdom'.

So why was the handling of maritime matters excepted from the general insistence on the preservation of a separate legal system in Scotland? The explanation provided in the 1890s for the emergence of a body of British sea law was that the admiralty courts in both Scotland and England had tended to base their decisions on 'the same source', on 'the law and customs of the sea generally prevailing among maritime states', or more specifically on 'the laws of Oleron, supplemented by the civil law'.[54] No doubt there was an element of truth in this, for the admiralty courts of both nations had taken account of the customs observed by seamen, and the lawyers who practised

---

[51] BL Add. MS 23132, ff. 135–6; NLS MSS 7004, ff. 161–2, and 7023, f. 246; Sir George Mackenzie of Rosehaugh, *Memoirs of the Affairs of Scotland from the Restoration of King Charles II*, ed. T. Thomson (Edinburgh, 1821), pp. 149–55 and 193–212; Daniel Defoe, *The History of the Union between England and Scotland* (London, 1786), pp. 21–31.

[52] NLS Adv. MS 6.2.1, ff. 93–104; *Register of the Privy Council of Scotland*, 3rd series, eds P. H. Brown, H. Paton, and E. W. M. Balfour-Melville (Edinburgh, 1908–70), IV, pp. 69–71; *Acts of Sederunt*, pp. 110–11; Stair, *Decisions of the Lords of Council and Session*, II, pp. 142–4, 154–7, 173–5, 177–94, 212–21, and 229–30.

[53] *Acts of the Parliaments of Scotland*, XI, pp. 410–11. These provisions of the 1707 treaty appear to have been based on the terms discussed in 1670. See C. A. Whatley, *Bought and Sold for English Gold? Explaining the Union of 1707* (East Linton, 2001), p. 20.

[54] *Cases Decided in the Court of Session, Court of Justiciary, and House of Lords*, pt 1, pp. 2–3.

in the English court had been trained in the same civilian tradition as most Scottish advocates.[55] William Welwod's attempt to repackage his treatise on sea law for a British audience in 1613 was evidently successful, for the revised version of his book was reprinted in 1636 and was later incorporated into a compendium designed for use by English merchants and mariners without any mention of its Scottish origin.[56] As Welwod himself had acknowledged, and as the lords of session had been reminded in 1668, all nations had sea laws of their own, yet these laws were at least drawn from a common source, whereas most English law was believed to have been developed indigenously in common law courts that paid little attention to foreign laws.[57] It could therefore have been believed in Scotland that sea law was an exceptional area in which lessons could be learned from England without the essential character of Scots law being endangered. It could have been believed that sea law was an area in which a more British approach could be taken to the resolution of disputes without incurring any risk of the alien law of England simply being imposed on Scotland. Yet it is far from clear that Scots lawyers appreciated in the late 1660s that English sea law was exceptionally similar to their own. Those who had written about the relationship between the laws of Scotland and England in the first half of the seventeenth century had come to the conclusion that the two systems had a great deal in common, not least in areas of central importance like land law and succession.[58] It was on this understanding that English judges had been sent into Scotland during the 1650s to administer justice in place of the lords of session.[59] At the same time English judges had also been sent north to sit in a new admiralty court, but they had not been civilian practitioners in the English court and their approach to dealing with cases had surprised the local advocates.[60] 'In the

---

[55] B. P. Levack, *The Civil Lawyers in England, 1603–41* (Oxford, 1973), pp. 16–21; D. R. Coquillette, *The Civilian Writers of Doctors' Commons, London* (Berlin, 1988), pp. 22–32; W. R. Cornish and G. de N. Clark, *Law and Society in England, 1750–1950* (London, 1989), pp. 28–9.

[56] Gerard Malynes, *Consuetudo, vel, lex mercatoria* (London, 1685), pt 2, pp. 43–78.

[57] Sir Edward Coke, *Second Part of the Institutes of the Laws of England* (London, 1642), p. 98, and *Third Part of the Institutes of the Laws of England* (London, 1648), p. 100; Sir John Davies, *Le primer reports des cases et matters en ley resolves et adjudges en les courts del roy en Ireland* (Dublin, 1615), ff. 1–11; John Selden, *Ad Fletam dissertatio*, trans. D. Ogg (Cambridge, 1925), pp. 164–7.

[58] Thomas Craig of Riccarton, *De unione regnorum Britanniae tractatus*, trans. C. S. Terry (Edinburgh, 1909), pp. 327–8, and *Ius feudale*, trans. J. A. Clyde (Edinburgh, 1934), I, p. ix; Sir John Skene of Curriehill, *Regiam maiestatem Scotiae veteres leges et constitutiones* (Edinburgh, 1609), sigg. A3v and A5r; *The Workes of the Most High and Mighty Prince, James* (London, 1616), pp. 520–1.

[59] C. S. Terry (ed.), *The Cromwellian Union* (Edinburgh, 1902), p. 180.

[60] NLS MS 7032, f. 61, and Adv. MS 6.2.1, ff. 52–4; Terry (ed.), *Cromwellian Union*, pp. 67–8; *Decisions of the English Judges, during the Usurpation* (Edinburgh, 1762), pp. 30–2. The diet book of the court has been preserved as NAS AC. 2.

usurpers time', it was observed by the lawyer who reviewed the admiralty records in the early 1670s, 'ther was little or noe forme, but only what they pleased was both law and forme.' If lawyers were encouraged by the later Dutch wars to cast their minds back to the handling of prize cases during the first war, this cannot have led them to believe that they could learn how to deal with cases in a civilian way from lawyers in England. There is no evidence that the lords of session tried to learn in the late 1660s about the English understanding of the Laws of Oleron or the civil law.

What the lords of session tried to learn about was the English understanding of the new law of nations. What they recognised for the first time was that many maritime disputes needed to be determined in accordance with the emerging principles of international law, for it was in the prize cases arising from the later Dutch wars that they appear for the first time to have examined the treaties and practices of nations as evidence of customary law, based on their common consent, along with extracts from the works of Grotius and others on *ius naturale et gentium*. When Sir James Dalrymple of Stair, a member of the session in the 1660s and president of the court in the 1670s, wrote a survey of the prize cases in 1681, he took them to be governed by 'the law and custom of nations', consisting partly of 'equity, and that common justice which is acknowledged by all nations as the rule of right and wrong', and partly of 'the custom of all nations, by their common consent'.[61] In these cases, he explained, the lords of session had been dealing with 'the peculiar right of private persons', yet in relation to ships and cargoes seized during war their fundamental enquiry had been into 'appropriation by public right'. *Ius gentium* in the modern sense of the law regulating the relations between nations was a kind of public law, which suggests another explanation for the exceptional treatment of sea law. In 1707 it was agreed that while the private law of Scotland had to be preserved, the law concerning 'publick Right' could be 'made the same throughout the whole United Kingdom', and it was perhaps with this in mind that particular provision was made for the regulation of admiralty practice in any way that was found 'expedient for the whole United Kingdom'. Since the admiralty courts were concerned in at least some cases with the law regulating the relations between states, they had to be concerned with the law regulating the affairs of the United Kingdom of Great Britain, created by the first article of the Treaty of Union. The law of the sea had therefore to be excepted from the insistence that changes could be made to the private law of Scotland only for the evident utility of subjects in the

---

[61] D. M. Walker (ed.), *Institutions of the Law of Scotland* (Edinburgh, 1981), 2.2. On Stair's survey, see A. J. Carty, 'The law of nature and nations as a source', in D. M. Walker (ed.), *Stair Tercentenary Studies* (Edinburgh, 1981), p. 127, and also E. J. Graham, 'The Scottish marine during the Dutch wars', *Scottish Historical Review* 61 (1982), pp. 67–74, at pp. 71–4.

northern kingdom, even though it related largely to the private rights of individuals. Indeed, even in cases relating solely to the private rights of individuals
it was a short if illogical step from recognising that the customs of mariners
were common to different nations to regarding them as international laws.
Thus in a case decided as early as 1672, involving an argument over the carriage
of a cargo from Leith to Montrose, the lords of session were urged to follow
the example of the Dutch, 'who best know the advantage of Navigation', on
the assumption that the rule they applied represented the 'common custom
of Nations'.[62] The rule was in fact derived from the Roman *ius gentium* and
had been modified by the later practice of mariners, but whether the court
was being invited to approve the custom of the maritime community or to
accept the binding force of the common consent of nations was unclear.

That there was a theoretical difference between approving the customs of
mariners and identifying the requirements of international law is important,
for it shows that the move towards developing a British law of the sea cannot
simply have resulted from recognition that many maritime disputes had to be
determined in accordance with international law. While it had made sense for
Welwod as a conventional civil lawyer to publish a book on *The Sea Law of
Scotland*, it would not have made sense a hundred years later for anyone to
write about the international law of Scotland. By definition international law
could not have been peculiar to any nation, yet the move that began between
the Unions of 1603 and 1707 was from Scottish to British sea law. The impetus was a request from Charles II to the lords of session that they try to make
sure that prize cases were dealt with in Scotland in accordance with directions
issued in England. Confronted with the obvious objection that directions
issued in England could have no relevance in Scotland, the lords of session
treated the king's pronouncements and English admiralty practice as evidence of the law of nations, provoking the further objection that they were
not genuinely following the law of nations. What they were following was a
British interpretation of the international law of the sea, built up through
their critical appraisal of English practice. Charles I's attempt to develop a
common fishing policy in the 1630s had run aground on the insistence that
there could be no dominion over the British seas when there was no British
state.[63] After the experience of the 1650s and the first Dutch war, a more

---

[62] Stair, *Decisions of the Lords of Council and Session*, II, p. 131. In the same year Stair reported,
for the first time, several cases in which the customs of merchants were referred to as 'the
Common Law of Nations' (II, pp. 42–3, 50–1, and 79–80). On the varying conceptions of the
customs of merchants, see J. H. Baker, 'The law merchant and the common law before 1700',
Cambridge Law Journal 38 (1979), pp. 295–322, at pp. 295–6.

[63] Fulton, *Sovereignty of the Sea*, pp. 209–45; T. G. Snoddy, *Sir John Scot, Lord Scotstarvit*
(Edinburgh, 1968), pp. 179–204; A. I. Macinnes, *Charles I and the Making of the Covenanting
Movement, 1625–41* (Edinburgh, 1991), pp. 108–13.

accommodating approach had been adopted in response to Charles II's foreign policies and the later Dutch wars, but by the end of the century attitudes had again hardened. With English ships openly violating the sovereignty of the Scottish seas in search of Jacobite insurgents, with the parliaments of the two nations legislating in defence of their trade, and with vessels from each nation being declared prizes on the other side of the Border, the need to move towards a British understanding of maritime law became pressing.[64] To secure the coasts against invasion and to promote mutual trade there had to be a British admiralty regulating the exercise of jurisdiction over British ships in the British seas. To these ends the law of Scotland was to be exposed to influence from England and the British parliament was to legislate in the interests of the whole United Kingdom, which may well have seemed, given the Union of the Crowns, an unavoidable consequence of the conjunction of trade and war. Otherwise, however, it was not intended that the law of Scotland would be altered or that legislation affecting Scotland would be passed in anything other than the Scottish national interest. If the legal provisions of the Treaty of Union are any guide, seventeenth-century Scots did not intend to become North Britons.

[64] D. Aldridge, 'Jacobites and the Scottish seas, 1689–1719', in T. C. Smout (ed.), *Scotland and the Sea* (Edinburgh, 1992), p. 76; Armitage, *Ideological Origins of the British Empire*, pp. 157–63; Graham, *Maritime History of Scotland*, pp. 63–99.

8

South Britons' Reception of North Britons, 1707–1820

PAUL LANGFORD

EMIGRATING SCOTS HAVE BEEN MANY THINGS, victors in war, innovators in peace, victims of processes that can be blamed on class oppressors or the auld enemy. But a Scot in search of a living was not required to seek it overseas. The alternative was Dr Johnson's noblest prospect, the high road to England. From a Scottish standpoint, this was potentially problematic. To seek fame and fortune in England itself might imply disloyalty, even subjection. When the nationalist J. H. McCulloch proposed a book on the Scot in England he was told it might do but only 'if ye can manage tae keep the damned English oot o't!'[1]

Scots acquired no new rights of residence by the Act of Union in 1707; Calvin's Case a century earlier had given those born after the Union of the Crowns in 1603 the rights of Englishmen in England, and needed no amendment. No court or courtiers moved south, as they had in 1603. There were, of course, the forty-five MPs and sixteen elected peers with their followers. But these were élite Anglo-Scots for whom the union merely extended existing opportunities. Investment in England was in any case expensive. Only the richest took it in their stride. One of earliest of the elected peers, the Earl of Home, was persuaded to make the journey to London in 1711 only with difficulty and a loan of £100 for the journey.[2] At that time the Duke of Roxburgh was ordering £100 in cash per month for transport by wagon from Scotland to spend in the metropolis.[3] A major British event such as a coronation caused agonies of aspiration for the Scottish peerage and evoked pity from English and Irish counterparts. Emily, Duchess of Leinster asked in

---

[1] John Herries McCulloch, *The Scotsman in England* (London, 1934), p. 128.
[2] G. S. Holmes, *British Politics in the Age of Anne* (London, 1967), p. 394.
[3] Thomas Somerville, *My Own Life and Times, 1741–1814* (Edinburgh, 1861), p. 353.

Proceedings of the British Academy, **127**, 143–169. © The British Academy 2005.

1761, 'How can the poor Scotch peeresses afford to walk, such as Lady Halkerton, for example, who has wrote to my sister to provide everything for her?'[4]

At less exalted levels there was certainly movement southwards, though neither the volume nor the extent to which it increased after the union can be derived from eighteenth-century statistics. Contemporary comment emphasised males on their own, somewhat in contrast with Irish and Welsh migrants. In dialects along the Great North Road, 'Scotchman' allegedly displaced the word 'pedlar'. Personal service, trade, or a profession were the main objectives. There is no suggestion of large-scale migration to work in English manufactures. Individuals depended on winning favour with masters, customers, congregations, or patrons. In education and vocational training they were often superior. This made the perceptible impact of Scottish immigration distinctive. Even in rural Norfolk, Parson Woodforde was approached by an unknown young Scotsman who offered his services as parish schoolmaster.[5]

London was, and long remained, the prime destination. Where it is possible to find reliable statistics they suggest that the London Scot was well established by the reign of George III. Six per cent of all married patients and eight per cent of all single men treated by the Westminster General Dispensary between 1774 and 1781 had been born in Scotland, compared with nine and ten per cent respectively of Irish patients. Considering the larger population of Ireland this seems rather surprising. It is possible that the Irish were more prominent in the poorer parts of the City within and without the walls.[6] Even so, the incidence of Scottish employees, especially servants whose employers might seek insurance of the Dispensary kind, must have been relatively high and would fit with some English perceptions that deserve examination in depth.

The English view of such immigrants appeared in potent visual forms, the most influential probably stage Scotsmen. Sauny the Scot was the eponymous hero of a doctored version of *The Taming of the Shrew* that placed Shakespeare's comedy in polite London society.[7] It lasted from the 1660s to the 1750s, when Garrick superseded it with a more refined and sentimental

[4] B. Fitzgerald (ed.), *Correspondence of Emily, Duchess of Leinster (1731–1814)*, I: *Letters of Emily, Duchess of Leinster, James, First Duke of Leinster, Caroline Fox, Lady Holland* (Dublin, 1949), p. 103.
[5] John Beresford (ed.), *The Diary of a Country Parson, the Reverend James Woodforde*, 5 vols (Oxford, 1968), V, p. 317.
[6] M. D. George, *London Life in the Eighteenth Century* (London, 1966), p. 118.
[7] *Sauny the Scot: or, the Taming of the Shrew. A Comedy*. Written Originally by Mr. Shakespeare. Alter'd and Improv'd by Mr. [John] Lacey, Servant to His Majesty (London, 1731).

piece.[8] Sauny's function was to protect the gentility and refinement of his master Petruchio, by taking over the more objectionable of the indignities he inflicted on Katherina (Margaret in the new version). It also involved adding wholly invented episodes, principally a bedroom scene in which Sauny was instructed to disrobe her before bed, resulting in some coarse observations on his experience with Scottish maids. This was the Scot as barbarian, a being beyond the pale of English civilisation, and incidentally the epitome of that devotion to Stuart popery and despotism which permitted eighteenth-century Scots to be treated as presumptive Jacobites.

Sauny had successors created by Charles Macklin, Irish playwright and actor. One, Sir Archy Macsarcasm, was a North British knight, obsessed with his noble ancestry and connections, and absurdly boastful of Scottish superiority in all situations. He figured in a two-act comedy in which four rivals, Macsarcasm himself, a Jew, a Yorkshireman, and an Irishman seek the hand of a wealthy City heiress.[9] The Irishman emerges triumphant when the heiress's guardian pretends that she has lost her money, thereby exposing the other three as mere fortune-hunters. Macsarcasm remained for long a favourite minor role for comedians playing to the prejudices of English audiences, and no more than mildly offensive by the standards of the London stage. More virulent was Sir Pertinax Macsycophant, central character of *The True-Born Scotchman*, first presented in Dublin in 1764. In England the play, diplomatically renamed *The Man of the World*, was nonetheless prohibited by authority until 1781.[10]

As a stage Scotsman Macsycophant was no lovable buffoon but a cynical, sinister careerist whose political life and social manners neatly combined the most unpleasant perceptions of allegedly North British characteristics. He rose from lowly origins in Scotland, became a beggarly clerk in a Scottish counting house in the City of London, identified a target for profitable marriage in a mad Methodist old maid whom he married in a fortnight and buried in a month, abducted a second wealthy bride from a boarding school, obtained a place at the Treasury from his new relations, and embarked on a long career as a Member of Parliament. His philosophy was explicit in its reliance on the doctrine of systematic subservience to the great men who dominated Westminster and Whitehall. Every bow carried Sir Pertinax higher and made him wealthier until even his own parliamentary patron, the bluff but feckless Lord Lumbercourt became his dependant.

---

[8] William Shakespeare, *The Taming of the Shrew*, Arden edition, ed. Brian Morris (London, 1981), pp. 89–97.

[9] Charles Macklin, *Love-a-la-mode. A Comedy in Two Acts* ([London], 1784).

[10] Charles Macklin, *The Man of the World* (1792), introduction by Dougald MacMillan (Augustan Reprint Society 26, 1951).

Figure 8.1. 'Progress of a Scotsman', Richard Newton, 1794 (BMC 8550). Graphic portrayal of the methods of a Scot on the make, rising from beggary to a seat in the Lords.

He met his match in his own family. His wife took no pleasure in his politics or his behaviour. One of his sons joined the opposition, for which he was
dismissed from the paternal presence and cut off from his patrimony. The
other, the hero of the piece, gave up the name of Macsycophant to take advantage of the inheritance of an English godfather. His tutor, significantly named
Sidney, taught him ancient Roman principles of patriotism, which Sir Pertinax
pronounced 'damned unfit for modern Britons' and which led him to declare
his aversion to English university-bred fellows and their saucy notions of
English liberty. When the son pleads conscience to defy his father's instructions on how to vote in parliament, he is told that conscience is an unparlia-
mentary word. When he speaks of patriotic principle he is made a figure of
fun. 'A fine time of day for a blockhead to turn patriot; —when the character
is exploded —marked —proscribed; —why the common people —the very
vulgar —have found the jest, and laugh at a patriot now-a-days, —just as they
do at a conjurer, —a magician, —or any other impostor in society.'[11]

In the end Scottish hypocrisy and cynicism are defeated. The action of the
play turns on the father's attempt to force his son to make a Highland marriage as part of a corrupt bargain with a Scottish boroughmonger. The son
rebels, secures the English woman of his dreams, and preserves his political
virtue. In the era of the theatre of sensibility all might have been expected to
end in joy rather than tears, with the father reformed and the family at one.
Nothing of the kind happens. Sir Pertinax secures his corrupt bargain by
other means, rejects his wife and family, and adjusts neither his behaviour nor
his belief.

Much of the comic xenophobia that packs the play, the mockery of
unmodish Scottish customs and manners, the barbarity of the Scots dialect,
might be dismissed as so much froth. But *The Man of the World* is ultimately
a more serious story of a vicious and unprincipled Scotsman on the make.
Macklin had made his name as Shylock and also attracted notoriety by playing Macbeth in Scottish dress. Sir Pertinax certainly has tragic potential. But
the Scottishness is not incidental, any more than the Jewishness of Shylock.
Unsurprisingly, in defending himself against the censor, Macklin emphasised
the redemption of the son rather than the irredeemability of the father. He
'fancied that the Character of an amiable Scotch Son, who from his Manners
and principles might be justly deemed an Honour to his Country and stand
a fair Example of the highest public and private Esteem, —such a Character
he thought might win the Affections of Englishmen and by that, —cure or at
least abate their national Prejudices against their fellow Subjects.'[12]

---

[11] Ibid., p. 18.
[12] Dougald MacMillan, 'The censorship in the case of Macklin's *The Man of the World*',
Huntington Library Bulletin 10 (1936), pp. 84-5.

The play was hugely successful, and not only south of the Border. Harry Johnston, the 'Scotch Roscius', acted both Macsarcasm and Macsycophant, and *The Man of the World* was staged frequently in Edinburgh, leading a Swiss visitor in 1811 to compliment its citizens on their tolerance.[13] The heavily political tone of Macklin's creation no doubt made it easier for a self-respecting Scot to treat Macsycophant as a grotesque and despicable relic of a bygone age. It was thus that many Englishmen sought to write off the politics of their eighteenth-century forebears as part of a corrupt world in process of being reformed. Even so one might have expected the gratuitous offensiveness of Macklin's association of sycophancy with Scottishness to be difficult to stomach. The stereotypes retained their currency for a considerable time. As late as 1833 the former US President John Quincy Adams was expressing relief that while Macsarcasm and Macsycophants plainly still flourished elsewhere they had never succeeded in establishing themselves in New England.[14]

Scots in the South also had to endure a continual battering in the public prints. With the sole exception of the French, no other nationality was so despised and derided in the vast array of caricatures turned out by the London press. Sauny himself figured frequently as the plebeian, bare-arsed Scot delighted but baffled by the luxuries of London life. He outlived the anti-Jacobite scares of George II's reign to remain a familiar exhibit of print-shop windows well into the nineteenth century. Political controversies involving North Britons accounted for a predictably high proportion of satires that were venomous even by the standards of England's notorious press. The high point of anti-Scottish feeling was undoubtedly the 1760s, in the furore created by Lord Bute's Prime Ministership and continued by his supposedly malign influence. But perhaps most striking is the consistency of the hostility throughout the eighteenth century and into the early nineteenth. It is very rare to come across more favourable depictions. Scotland's resistance to Catholic relief legislation in 1779 yielded a brief respite, quickly forgotten in the hysteria that identified the principal opponents of the Gordon rioters with Lord Bute's followers. Invocations of patriotic Britishness during the Revolutionary and Napoleonic Wars included an appeal to Scots as well as the other nationalities of the British Isles but even these had to jostle with highly critical characterisations of a more traditional kind.

Political antagonisms naturally changed with the times. But the most common complaint concerned the exploitative nature of the Scottish presence. When Dr Johnson was told by Alderman William Lee during the

[13] Louis Simond, *Journal of a Tour and Residence in Great Britain, during the Years 1810 and 1811, by a French Traveller*, 2 vols (Edinburgh, 1815), II, p. 375.
[14] Alan Nevins (ed.), *The Diary of John Quincy Adams, 1794–1845* (New York, 1951), p. 441.

Figure 8.2. 'Sawney in the Boghouse', George Bickham, 1745 (BMC 2678). A barbarous High-lander enjoying the luxuries of London life. This was a response to the Forty-five, but proved such a popular image that it was revived in cartoons of 1762 and 1779.

American War of Independence that Old England was lost, he replied 'It is not so much to be lamented that old England is lost, as that the Scotch have found it.'[15] Throughout the period the widely held belief was that Scots were parasites for whom England was a guaranteed source of communal relief and

[15] Charles Ryskamp and Frederick A. Pottle (eds), *Boswell: the Ominous Years, 1774–1776* (London, 1963), p. 350.

Figure 8.3. 'Sawney's Defence against the Beast, Whore, Pope, and Devil', 1778 (BMC 5534). A rare example in praise of Scots, inspired by Scottish resistance to the Catholic Relief Act of 1778.

Figure 8.4. 'The Caledonians Arrival in Moneyland', 1762 (BMC 3857). Ragged Scots arrive in England and pay tribute to Bute and the Dowager Princess of Wales (mother of George III and Bute's supposed mistress).

personal enrichment. A high proportion of the published satires, graphic and otherwise, centred on this belief and many others related it to more specific complaints about individual Scots. For at least a century after the parliamentary union the obvious conclusion was that the benefits operated overwhelmingly in favour of North Britain at the cost of South. If this were not the case, why did so few natives of the latter not take the road northwards?

How does the testimony of resident Scots about their treatment in England fit with the evidence of their publicised unpopularity? Perhaps surprisingly, there is little suggestion of marked anti-Scottish feeling to greet Scots who found themselves south of the Border (excluding Jacobites in 1715 and 1745, of course). It was a period of intense xenophobia. Successive waves of carpet-baggers arrived in the wake of William of Orange after 1689 and George, Elector of Hanover, after 1714. Even during the intervening reign of Anne Stuart agitation against poor Protestant immigrants fleeing the Catholic armies of Louis XIV in the Palatine gave rise to controversy and popular turbulence. Such anxieties probably made Scots considerably less noticeable or objectionable than they might have been. Or perhaps the union generated sufficient eirenic enthusiasm to lessen national animosities. Certainly, in parliament, the most visible of all new immigrants, Scottish representative peers and MPs, were received with notable good humour and amity.[16] The House of Commons in particular was notoriously club-like, its ambience determined by the English landed gentry. It apparently incorporated the newcomers with little difficulty, as institutions of government did. Even during the Fifteen and the Forty-five, there seems to have been no attempt to victimise resident Scots.

Successive generations of Scots who tested the temperature in England declared their satisfaction in print. The secret agent John Macky remarked that 'altho' the English give no great Encouragement to Strangers to settle among them for Life; yet there is no Nation under Heaven, when a Gentleman-Traveller meets with so much Humanity, Civility, and good Entertainment.' As a Whig who could recall the Revolution of 1688, he paid particular tribute to 'this glorious Country of Liberty'.[17] He toured it in every direction from London and offered little that was critical of the manners or morals of his hosts. A later tourist and countryman William Macritchie, in 1795, found the English unexpectedly gracious and gregarious. 'We may boast of our Scotch hospitality as we please, but I have repeatedly found

---

[16] D. W. Hayton (ed.), *The History of Parliament: the House of Commons 1690–1715*, 5 vols (Cambridge, 2002), I, p. 511.

[17] John Macky, *A Journey through England, In Familiar Letters*, 3rd edn (London, 1723), I, p. iv.

hospitality in England too.'[18] James Mackintosh, not known in print or person for his sycophancy, was described by his fellow author Thomas Green as extolling what he called 'the characteristic *bon naturel*—the good temper and sound sense of the English people; qualities, in which he deliberately thought us without a rival in any other nation on the globe'. To leave no doubt he added that he spoke as a foreigner and did not include his own countrymen in the praise.[19] And half a century further on again, the geologist Hugh Miller thought the English an exceedingly civil and also much franker yet less prying people than the Scotch.[20] Sampling public statements of this kind is not a scientific process; yet it is hard to find counter-examples of visiting or resident Scots publishing their resentment of the way they were received.

What does one make of this generally favourable cast of comment? Was it the desire of Scots to demonstrate their own integration in a British community which included a nation they had traditionally been taught to regard as the enemy? Or were they merely seeking to maximise approval for their reporting? If so this can only be true of those who intended to publish their views. A number had to wait until long after their death before they were published.

One such was George Macaulay, native of Lewis, who set foot in London at the age of fifteen in 1765, and worked his way up to become an Alderman, Warden of the Bowyers Company, and eventually Sheriff of London in 1790. His diary was thus of one who had lived through a period of intense political controversy in which Scots found themselves the repeated butt of ridicule and worse. Yet there is no hint of resentment on Macaulay's part. A compatriot of Bute, he wholeheartedly detested the court of George III, reviled John Wilkes not for his anti-Scottishness but for reneging on his radical patriotism, revelled in the political and social culture of London, relished his country weekends with his wife in Bedford, took pride in Britain's victories over the French, and recorded nothing that suggested alienation in a life that was remote indeed from his native Hebrides. Macaulay regarded himself as an Englishman by personal choice if not birth. Only when given an opportunity to consider temperamental failings did he resort even to mild criticism, notably when war losses suggested that the bravery of an Englishman was more in evidence than his brain.[21]

---

[18] William Macritchie, *Diary of a Tour through Great Britain in 1795*, ed. David MacRitchie (London, 1897), p. 147.

[19] *Memoirs of the Life of Sir James Mackintosh*, ed. Robert James Mackintosh, 2 vols (London), I, p. 93.

[20] Hugh Miller, *First impressions of England and its People* (London, 1847), p. 70.

[21] W. C. Mackenzie (ed.), *The War Diary of a London Scot (Alderman G. M. Macaulay) 1796–7* (Paisley, 1916).

Men like Macaulay might be considered sufficiently integrated in the English community to have lost their sensitivity on the score of their Scottish origins. But integration, after all, is what acceptance was about. Take a higher level and the other sex. Lady Louisa Stuart was the daughter of the Marquess of Bute, an active member of Society with a capital S, and accustomed to mixing with English, Scottish, and Irish men and women of the landed aristocracy. She had no sympathy with those in Scotland who looked back to the days of national independence, considering that 'The Union troubled the Scotch no more now than the Norman conquest did the English.'[22] Yet she accounted herself a Scotswoman, and conventionally referred to other Scots she met as her countrymen.

Lady Louise disliked the dirt and disarray that she found in Scottish settings below those enjoyed by the very highest aristocratic echelons, was discomforted by Scottish accent and dialect, and resented fashionably romantic perceptions of Scotland in the later part of her long lifetime. When the 5th Duke of Buccleuch proposed taking his bride, of the house of Longleat, on honeymoon to Dalkeith, she voiced her scepticism:

> It will be a test of her character, I think, to see how she is struck with a strange country. If she finds all barbarous and odious, shrinks from the twang of broad Scotch, and wonders what people can admire in rocks and rivers . . ., she may turn out a very good sort of woman, but Walter Scott must shut up shop.[23]

Not all impressions come from the highly placed. The seaman John Nicol told a heart-warming tale of his childhood at the height of anti-Scottish fever in the 1760s. He recalled the rare sight of a dead monkey in the Thames near the Tower and his desire to possess it:

> An English boy, who wished it like-wise, but who either would or could not swim, seized it when I landed, saying, 'He would fight me for it.' A crowd gathered, and formed a ring. Stranger as I was, I got fair play. After a severe contest, I came off victor. The English boy shook hands, and said, 'Scotchman, you have won it.'[24]

English fair play was not generally claimed for Scots at this time, even by Scots.

For their part the English were certainly not slow to criticise their neighbours. North Britons were accused of overreacting to satire. It was an unfair accusation and depends on literary anecdotes like Smollett's irritation at the

---

[22] Hon. James A. Home (ed.), *Letters of Lady Louisa Stuart to Miss Louisa Clinton*, 2nd series (Edinburgh, 1903), p.10.
[23] Ibid., p. 165.
[24] Gordon Grant (ed.), *The Life and Adventures of John Nicol, Mariner* ([1822] London, 1937), pp. 37–8.

graffiti in coaching inns north of Doncaster.[25] There were other accusations, the most common relating to what Dr Johnson called 'extreme nationality'.[26] Scots were frequently criticised for 'sticking together like bricks' or 'swarming like bees'.[27] Yet settlement patterns do not suggest it. The London Irish and Jews constituted colonies, lower-class Scots did not. Nor did their betters, though other well-off immigrants, for example French and Dutch merchants and even American loyalists, did.

A fair sample should be the home addresses of the governors of the Scottish Hospital, a self-identified cohort of Scottish residents who were scattered all over London, in the City, in the West End and the parishes between, and in the areas of Middlesex beyond. In 1775 there were some 300 of them, in 1794, 800. The Hospital had been founded under James I, refounded under Charles II, and again under George III, to provide relief for poor Scots not entitled to relief under the English Poor Law. Originally it was situated at Blackfriars in the City. By the time of Dr Johnson it was located in Crane Court, Fleet Street, a stone's throw from his residence. Like many such charitable organisations in England it probably operated as a kind of insurance company for employers who reckoned to unload their responsibility for sick or unsatisfactory employees. In any event, as an index of respectable London Scots it clearly suggests a degree of residential dispersion that paid no regard to the need for ethnic solidarity.[28]

The metropolitan clubs and associations which provided a focus for inhabitants of individual English counties throughout the eighteenth century seem not to have had matching Scottish equivalents until well into the nineteenth century. County societies played a crucial role in relieving social needs neglected by the machinery of poor relief. In the case of Scots, further from home than most, the need must have been even more pressing. Yet apart from the Scottish Hospital and a similar society in Norwich, the societies seem to have been missing. (It may be significant that the Scots Society in Norwich renamed itself the Society of Universal Goodwill in 1787.)[29] In Glasgow there were a number of such associations to assist Scots far from home.[30] South of the Border they are much less in evidence.

[25] Tobias Smollett, *The Expedition of Humphry Clinker*, ed. A. Ross (London, 1967), p. 232.
[26] William K. Wimsatt, Jr. and Frederick A. Pottle (eds), *Boswell: For the Defence, 1769–1774* (London, 1960), p. 193.
[27] Christopher Pemberton Hodgson, *Reminiscences of Australia, with Hints on the Squatter's Life* (London, 1846), p. 118; *Complete Works of William Hazlitt*, ed. Percival Presland Howe, 21 vols (London, 1930–4), XVII, p. 100.
[28] Bodleian Library, Gough London 42: published lists of officers and governors.
[29] *An Account of the Scots Society in Norwich*, 2nd edn (Norwich, 1787), p. 48.
[30] Peter Clark, *British Clubs and Societies 1580–1800* (Oxford, 2000), pp. 294–5.

Coffee houses were natural centres of association and, like inns and lodging houses, must have generated Scottish associations. But only one was particularly well known for its Scottishness, the British Coffee House in Cockspur Street, newly built after the union and a going concern well into the nineteenth century. Defoe noted its Scottish gatherings, news of Culloden was received by assembled Scots there, and when the house was rebuilt in 1770 Robert Adam was appropriately the architect. But it was never exclusively a Scottish asylum. The opposition Whig Lord Egmont dined there with friends in the 1730s, John Wilkes did so thirty years later, and at the turn of the century its principal associations seem to have been those of aristocratic Whigs.[31]

There were also three Scotch churches in the City at Lothbury, London Wall, in Covent Garden, and in Swallow Street, Piccadilly. They waxed and waned with the popularity of their (not invariably Scottish) preachers but it seems doubtful that they did much to reinforce identity. Eighteenth-century presbyterianism, whether Scottish or English, was not a very cohesive substance.

If there were no other source, Boswell's journals would confirm that Scots of the higher class did form social groupings. Why should they not? In this they resembled the cousinages that kept English politicians in touch with their roots. That patronage acquired a national complexion when dispensed by Scots to Scots was inevitable. Equally natural would be a liking for the company of compatriots. Perhaps it was the English who were warped. According to the American William Austin in 1804, 'a Scot is partial to his fellow-Scotchmen, with very little fondness for Scotland: an Englishman is still more partial to England, with very little fondness for Englishmen.'[32]

A metropolis attracts men and women on the make, but Scots were considered more successful and less scrupulous than most. One can think of reasons why. The union added to parliament a constituency that was liable to manipulation. Scotland as represented in the House of Commons could be likened to Cornwall, with its tiny electorates and its readiness to vote to order. In the House of Lords it resembled the bench of English bishops, being effectively chosen by the government of the day. The images thus presented were highly unattractive, but recriminations were delayed. While Highland Jacobitism threatened the English polity, the corruptibility of Scottish Whigs was a minor issue. Anglo-Scottish clashes under George I and George II were not uncommon and, in cases that gave rise to controversy in Scotland itself, sometimes bitter. But so far as the wider political community

---

[31] Brian Lillywhite, *London Coffee Houses* (London, 1963), p. 133.
[32] William Austin, *Letters from London: Written during the years 1802 and 1803* (Boston, 1804), p. 46.

Figure 8.5.   'The Scotch Victory', 1768 (BMC 4197). The death of a rioter in 1768 presented as Scottish assassination of an English Wilkesite.

in England was concerned, none generated animosity to compare with that unleashed by the patriotic project of George III and Bute in the 1760s.

That project supposedly combined two nightmare scenarios, subverting simultaneously the independence of Crown and parliament. It did not help that Scotland's first Prime Minister displayed less judgement than any of his successors. Radical Whig followers of John Wilkes and less radical but not less malicious aristocratic Whigs ousted by Bute extracted every ounce of political advantage from Bute's Scottishness, including his supposed inheritance of treasonable Jacobite and divine right tendencies. In any event, the resulting outcry made possible Sir Pertinax Macsycophant. It also made government hysterically fearful of employing Scottish ministers. When Dundas did emerge in that role, he became the last politician to be impeached for corruption, in 1805. The resulting anti-Scottish cry recalled the 1760s.

Politics aside, London was an arena in which ambitious Scots battled for money and status. Some of them had Bute and his circle as patrons. But this was largely incidental. It was rather the earned success and prominence of his successful countrymen that reinforced English anxieties. In the publishing industry and the Grub Street culture that it sustained, Scots were well established by the 1750s and grew ever more visible in the following decades. The success of the universities at Edinburgh, Glasgow, and Aberdeen in medical studies at the expense of Oxford and Cambridge gave Scottish physicians a much commented-on advantage in catering to the needs of polite society. Perhaps more important still was the participation of Scottish businessmen in the financial life of the metropolis.

Professional and personal rivalries had a way of translating themselves into national animosities, a process that once under way was naturally self-reinforcing. Choosing Adam or Chambers in the 1760s and 1770s was not just a matter of taste. The clash between the copyright interests of Edinburgh and London publishers, which occupied much parliamentary time and many newspaper columns in the early 1770s, was by no means a narrow legal issue. And worst of all, in 1772–3 when overheated financial markets brought a major crisis to the City, the worst since the South Sea Bubble, it was the Ayr Bank that precipitated the disaster, and the alleged corruption of a prominent Scotsman, Sir Alexander Fordyce, that was blamed. The fact that Fordyce had two brothers in London, a Society sermoniser and a Society doctor, reinforced the search for a Scot in every scandal. The demonisation of Bute's North Britons worked because there was usable evidence of an incubus to underpin more bizarre kinds of guilt by association. A Wilkesite speciality was enrolling Bute supporters as honorary Scotsmen, in the case of Warwickshire's Lord Denbigh because an aunt several generations removed had married a Hamilton.

Generous-minded Scots attributed their unpopularity to plebeian xenophobia and even excused the shameless Wilkes on that account.[33] But they underrated genteel prejudices. The more the Scot impressed as a servant, the less he seemed a gentleman. As in other respects it only required a well-known figure to reinforce stereotypes. The founder of the most famous of assembly rooms, Almack's in Pall Mall, was an obvious target. Almack was a transposition of its founder's natal name MacCaul; trying to pass as a Yorkshireman convinced no one. The man-about-town Gilly Williams relished describing him at work: 'Almack's Scotch face, in a bag-wig, waiting at

---

[33] *Caledonian Mercury*, 6 April 1776.

Figure 8.6. 'The Hungry Mob of Scriblers and Etchers', 1762 (BMC 3844). Bute's hireling supporters in the press. Scots were notoriously well represented among journalists and publishers.

supper, would divert you, as would his lady in a sac, making tea and curtseying to the duchesses.'[34]

This was English snobbery. But it could draw on real differences. One had to do with what constituted good behaviour, especially in Edinburgh, the centre of Scottish civility. Foreigners found its manners urbane and accessible, and fair-minded.[35] Englishmen, including Dr Johnson's friend Edward Topham, who published an admired book on the subject, did not disagree.[36] Edinburgh society had old associations with the Continent, and lacked the back-biting alliance of aristocracy and plutocracy that ruled England. But *Kleinstädterei* put it at a disadvantage. As Lockhart observed, London's papers took three days to reach Edinburgh but its fashions took two years.[37] Reverse traffic was unlikely. According to Boswell the best breakfasts were a true union of Scotland and England, apparently a result of the introduction of marmalade from the North.[38] Another rare export to England was dance. Whether the result was Scottish is debatable. Elizabeth Grant thought it had more of Hertfordshire than the Highlands about it.[39]

Social survival in Birmingham or Norwich was one thing, but Scots seeking acceptance in London faced Society at its most exclusive. Ironically, Bute, who provoked so much xenophobic hysteria, was himself a striking instance of integration. He was born in Edinburgh to a family that opposed the union and appears today in the Museum of Scotland in Stuart glory. But his mother was a Campbell, he was educated at Eton, and he married into an English family. He and his wife abandoned the Isle of Bute for amateur dramatics in Twickenham. Destiny took the form of a rain shower which stopped play during a cricket match at Cliveden, or according to an alternative version, interrupted racing at Egham. In any event, Bute was near enough to the Prince of Wales's party to be called to the card table. His subsequent rise to favour not only with the prince, but with his widow and their son George III, no doubt infuriated many potential rivals, yet there was nothing about it that could be traced to his Scottish origins, except in the English stereotyping that made every Scot a natural courtier.

[34] J. H. Jesse (ed.), *George Selwyn and his Contemporaries*, 4 vols (London, 1882), I, p. 369.

[35] Guido di Pino (ed.), *Luigi Angiolini, Lettere sull'Inghilterra* (Milan, 1944), p. 361; Adolphe Blanqui, *Voyage d'un jeune français en Angleterre et en Écosse pendant l'automne de 1823* (Paris, 1824), ch. 17; Charles Le Mercher de Longpré, Baron d'Haussez, *Great Britain in 1833*, 2 vols (London, 1833), II, p. 192.

[36] Edward Topham, *Letters from Edinburgh: Written in the Years 1774 and 1775* (London, 1776), p. 82.

[37] John Gibson Lockhart, *Peter's Letters to his Kinsfolk*, 2nd edn, 3 vols (London, 1819), III, p. 115.

[38] Wimsatt and Pottle (eds), *Boswell: For the Defence*, p. 103.

[39] Elizabeth Grant, *Memoirs of a Highland Lady*, ed. Andrew Tod, 2 vols (Edinburgh, 1990), I, p. 261.

In his prosperity, Bute built a country seat in Bedfordshire, and a mansion in Berkeley Square. Eventually his painful martyrdom by the press altered his view of his adopted land. 'I regret every day I live more and more ever having a permanent settlement in a country that of all Europe is the most improper for a gentleman,' he told his son in 1778.[40] Bute House was sold, and Luton neglected for a home almost as far south as he could go, near Bournemouth. Here he spent his time botanising and walking by moonlight on his Dorset beach. A portrait would have made an interesting contrast with his Highland image of forty years earlier. But there was no stopping the process. His own and his son's marriage ensured that the Victorian Butes joined the super-rich of Britain.

Anglo-Scottish personal unions multiplied after the parliamentary union. The percentage of daughters of Scottish peers marrying Englishmen rose from 16 per cent in the first half of the eighteenth century, to 36 per cent in the second, and 42 per cent in the first half of the nineteenth century.[41] Intermarriage could be seen as diluting Scottish identity or alternatively as border-raiding on English wealth. There was certainly English resentment of the process. When the Dowager Countess Gower heard in 1772 of the intended marriage of Lady Bell Grey and Lord Polwarth, which brought into the latter's hands the lands of the last Duke of Kent, she confessed, 'I'm such an English Joan Trot as to lament *the three greatest fortunes* this age has produc'd being transplanted into Scotland!' Ironically, thirteen years later the head of her own family married the heiress to the vast property of the Sutherlands, in due course becoming the first Duke of Sutherland. Presumably she would have considered this as the triumph of South Britain over North.[42]

The great Anglo-Irish dynasts of Whiggery were particularly reluctant to share their blood lines with North Britons. The 6th Duke of Bedford's decision to break ranks by marrying a Gordon in 1793 provoked a diatribe from the Duchess of Devonshire, a Friend of the People but not of the Scots. 'What a futurity to be surrounded with plotting, shabby Scotts men. The very amabilité that some time arises from the grotesque originality of Scotch people is ... very different from what one should have thought would be [his choice] for the Mistress of Wooburn.'[43] However, the Russells having weakened, other Whigs followed suit, leaving the Cavendishes in isolation.

[40] E. Stuart Wortley (ed.), *A Prime Minister and his Son* (London, 1925), p. 141.
[41] J. Cannon, *Aristocratic Century: the Peerage of Eighteenth Century England* (Cambridge, 1984), p. 88.
[42] Lady Llanover (ed.), *The Autobiography and Correspondence of Mary Granville, Mrs. Delany*, 2nd series, 3 vols (London, 1862), I, p. 436.
[43] Mabell, Countess of Airlie, *In Whig Society 1775–1818* (London, 1921), pp. 33–4.

Chatsworth has still to receive a Scottish chatelaine, though one wonders what the duchess would have made of Harold Macmillan, who combined descent from a crofter with a Cavendish wife and was not without a certain Whiggery of manner and thought.

Perhaps the most sensitive arena in aristocratic life was the military. The early evolution of parliamentary union coincided with the establishment of a standing army that offered career opportunities in peace as well as war. In most business and professional activities aristocratic young men were unlikely to engage at all, let alone find themselves in competition with Scots. The army was the major exception. By the mid-eighteenth century the Scots constituted a quarter of the officer class, a proportion that remained steady but grew in absolute numbers with the expansion of the armed forces. Fashionable regiments resisted the incursion longer than others, but the tensions were perceptible for much of the period. It was the Whig 3rd Duke of Richmond who warned his brother against mixing with Scottish officers: 'Do not choose among them your friends. It can never do you honour and may be of disservice to you.'[44] The lingering taint of Jacobitism partly accounted for such suspicion but social snobbery was also a consideration, and one which diminished only very gradually as the Scottish élite itself integrated by degrees with polite English, and more particularly metropolitan society.

The irony of integration was that it tended to heighten the walls that excluded Scots who failed to behave like their hosts. Integrated Scots were embarrassed by their less adaptable countrymen. High-born Scots dutifully welcomed their compatriots to the metropolis, all too aware that it involved mixing in 'not the genteelest set in London'.[45] Two daughters of the 5th Earl of Balcarres who married English money and blue blood respectively, blotted their copybook by furnishing London houses for profit. A so-called friend 'wished to God those two very agreeable women would leave off being upholsterers and begin to be women of fashion'. The elder also spoke what was described as a 'vulgar sort of half-Scotch'.[46]

Language was perhaps increasingly the prime criterion of full acceptability. Following the union, dialect and accent seem not to have been disturbing. Regional English was as outlandish as Scottish to an educated Englishmen. But by mid-century, with the evolution of a received standard accent dictated by the mores of London, deviant accents were becoming a disadvantage. The

---

[44] James Hayes, 'Scottish officers in the British Army 1714–63', *Scottish Historical Review* 37 (1958), pp. 23–33, 30.

[45] Mrs. Godfrey Clark (ed.), *Gleanings from an Old Portfolio containing some Correspondence between Lady Louisa Stuart and her Sister Caroline, Countess of Portarlington, and other Friends and Relations*, 3 vols (Edinburgh, 1895), II, p. 22.

[46] Francis Bickley (ed.), *The Diaries of Sylvester Douglas (Lord Glenbervie)*, 2 vols (London, 1928), I, pp. 68–9.

Figure 8.7. 'Sawney Scot and John Bull', 1792 (BMC 8188). Continuing Anglo-Scottish animosity recalling old conflicts: the Forty-five Rebellion and Number 45 of John Wilkes' anti-Bute *North Briton*.

young and ambitious Alexander Wedderburn took lessons from Sheridan senior in 1757 on this account. It was even alleged that George III's accession speech in 1760 revealed traces of a Scottish accent, attributable to Bute.[47]

Solving this problem was difficult. Few Scottish parents could afford an English school. Eton school lists show an infinitesimal corps of Scottish gentry in the mid-eighteenth century, and only a smattering in the late eighteenth century, reflecting more the presence of the Anglo-Scottish class in England than the export of Scots-based young men to English schools.[48] Oxbridge was recognised as bestowing desirable refinement for Scots as part of a two-way traffic that for fashionable Whigs made Edinburgh the place for 'a better coating of education'.[49] But the formula did not always work. Francis Jeffrey lost his accent at Oxford only to acquire what was described as 'a mixture of provincial English, with undignified Scotch'.[50]

Some formidable parliamentarians, Dundas, Brougham, and the Peelite Duke of Argyll, succeeded despite their accents, according to the foremost parliamentary reporter of early Victorian Westminster.[51] A clear case of career damage was the formidably coarse and indecent parliamentary bruiser, Lord Lauderdale, unlikely ancestor of Arthur Balfour. He was humiliated at Queen Caroline's trial when he accused her of consorting with a Tuscan Countess whose language revealed her low birth, leading an opponent to ask whether she 'spoke Italian with as broad an accent as the noble Earl who has just sat down speaks with in his native tongue'.[52]

Some orators certainly concealed their Scottishness. Francis Horner was one. After an Edinburgh education, a spell in the care of a Middlesex clergyman was prescribed to free him 'from the disadvantages of a provincial dialect to a public speaker'. He left an interesting, unregretful account of his de-Scottification.[53] So did James Stephen, who initially escaped an accent thanks to his birth in England. When his father fell on hard times and the family were sent north, instructions were given that they must avoid school

---

[47] Countess of Ilchester and Lord Stavordale, *Life and Letters of Lady Sarah Lennox, 1745–1826* (London, 1904), p. 14.

[48] R. A. Austen Leigh (ed.), *Eton College Lists, 1678–1790* (Eton College, 1907), July 1735, 19 May 1790.

[49] Violet Dickinson (ed.), *Miss Eden's Letters* (London, 1919), p. 73.

[50] Lockhart, *Peter's Letters to his Kinsfolk*, II, p. 60.

[51] Edward Michael Whitty, *St Stephen's in the Fifties. The Session 1852–3: a Parliamentary Retrospect*, introduction by Justin M'Carthy (London, 1906), p. 43.

[52] K. Garlick, A. Macintyre, and K. Cave (eds), *The Diary of Joseph Farington*, 16 vols (New Haven, 1978–84), VI, p. 2359; Henry Reeve (ed.), *The Greville Memoirs: a Journal of the Reigns of King George IV and King William IV. By the late C. F. Greville., Esq.*, 3rd edn, 3 vols (London, 1875), I, p. 38.

[53] Leonard Horner (ed.), *Memoirs and Correspondence of Francis Horner, M.P.*, 2 vols (London, 1843), pp. 6, 7, 17, 41.

there to preserve their English pronunciation. But alas, they returned to London with Buchan tones. The story supposedly had a happy ending, none the less. Learning to read at a day school at South Lambeth completely wiped away all trace of Buchan.[54] Such remedial action was not always possible. Foreigners from northern Europe often learned their English from Scottish *émigrés*. The Russian visitor Oloff Napea was mortified to find that he had been 'taught a provincial English; ... improper, and only used by the northern English and Scotch'.[55]

Growing awareness of Scotland as a country and a culture did not necessarily lessen prejudice. In the wake of George IV, Walter Scott, and the Edinburgh literati, Hazlitt expressed a common irritation: 'Scotch magazines, Scotch airs, Scotch bravery, Scotch hospitality, Scotch novels, Scotch logic. What a blessing that the Duke of Wellington was not a Scotchman, or we should never have heard the last of him!'[56]

War and imperial expansion plainly gave Scots a larger share in Britishness and a stronger sense of their own contribution to the joint enterprise it implied.[57] English and more particularly metropolitan opinion sometimes responded positively but not altogether ungrudgingly. In polished circles came a new superiority, less contemptuous but not less discriminating. Scots still complained that they were all the recipients of any criticism, regardless of regional, social, or political distinctions. Byron's Scotophobia (notwithstanding Scottish blood in his veins) is not evidence for wider perceptions but did employ a new kind of sneer. Was it really necessary, for instance, to blame Caledonia's 'meanness, sophistry, and mist' for Elgin's alleged theft of the marbles?[58]

Perhaps the most interesting by-product of this period of increased attention and sensitivity to Scottishness was the refinement, indeed redefinition of national characterisation that took place. The two central charges of the eighteenth century, beggarliness and sycophancy, gradually receded in the early nineteenth century. Economic change and so-called improvement in Scotland made poverty less visible, albeit in some cases by removing it to distant parts of empire. Sycophancy had derived much of its plausibility from the supposed subserviency of Scottish politicians. Their behaviour in the second century of the union and the manners that went with it made the charge less compelling.

---

[54] Merle M. Bevington (ed.), *The Memoirs of James Stephen Written by Himself for the Use of His Children* (London, 1954), pp. 54–5.
[55] Oloff Napea, *Letters from London: Observations of a Russian, during a Residence in England of ten Months* (London, 1816), p. 17.
[56] Hazlitt, *Complete Works*, XVII, p. 100.
[57] Linda Colley, *Britons: Forging the Nation 1707–1837* (New Haven, 1992), ch. 3.
[58] Leslie A. Marchand, *Byron: a Portrait* (London, 1971), p. 95.

Figure 8.8. 'A Flight of Scotchmen', Richard Newton, 1796, published by William Holland (Lewis Walpole Library, Yale University, 796.9.3.1.). Hordes of Scottish adventurers making their way from barren Scotland to London, still a sensitive issue at the end of the eighteenth century.

Changes in migration patterns may have had the most important consequences of all. There is evidence of a marked increase in the flow of Scots
into England in the last quarter of the eighteenth century and the first of the
nineteenth, as the pace of economic growth south of the Border intensified
and its extent broadened. As late as 1823 vagrancy statistics continued to
show Scots heavily outnumbering the Irish throughout the eastern counties
of England and into counties south and west of London. Thereafter the pattern was reversed radically, as the influx of poor Irish multiplied. Within ten
years of the 1823 survey, the Irish were outnumbering Scots massively, even
in the counties most accessible from the north, such as Northumberland. The
effect was surely to render the Scots in comparative terms less visible and
objectionable. If they had been the most noticeable of 'foreigners' throughout much of England including London for many decades, they ceased to be
so by the 1830s. Whether their presence in the class most liable to criticism
and recrimination, that of servants, diminished in absolute terms is not
known. But their relative diminution was plainly very marked.[59]

In any event, a new element was added to complete the developing trip-
tych, eventually displacing the earlier components: the Scot as uncivilised
barbarian and the Scot as plausible sycophant giving way to the Scot as mer-
cenary calculator. Of the modern characterisation of Scots as excessively
careful with money and unpleasantly canny in their use of it, there seems
little evidence in the eighteenth century. Boswell, usually prone to criticise his
countrymen, specifically contrasted an instance of English penny-pinching
with what he took to be Scottish attitudes. 'The Scots may be greedy, but they
have something of a gentlemanly spirit that keeps them from giving attention
to the difference between a halfpenny and a farthing.'[60] They were indeed
depicted as a miserably poor nation with the habits and manners of peasants.
But this was the patronising English assumption about a poorer nation, and
had no particularly Scottish component. Significantly, when Irish or French
poverty were being discussed, the English were much readier to link it to the
alleged national character of those involved.

By the early nineteenth century, there seems to have been more of a readiness to recognise niggardliness as a Scottish characteristic. It is possible that
this arose in part from the readiness of Scots themselves to claim prudent
economy as something to be boasted of, at a time when emergent discourses
of political and moral economy favoured the notion. A Scottish physician,

[59] Arthur Redford, *Labour Migration in England 1800–1850*, ed. W. H. Chaloner, 3rd edn
(revised, Manchester, 1976), pp. 135ff.
[60] Ryskamp and Pottle (eds), *Boswell: the Ominous Years*, p. 81.

himself an immigrant to England, remarked in 1816 that of every ten men
who possessed the disposition to Oeconomy, one would be Irish, two English
and seven Scottish.[61]

Other explanations have been proposed. Wallace Notestein, whose *Scot in
History* cheerfully acknowledged ethnic and racial influences, put it down to
the appearance of the English sportsman in the Highlands and his discovery
that his hosts were not so much beggarly as grasping and stingy.[62] This is
plausible enough. One of the earliest sporting tours published, that of
Yorkshire's Thomas Thornton, certainly emphasised the Highlander's notion
of an Englishman as a walking mint, and his belief that only he understood
the value of money.[63]

Be that as it may, this could be something that Scots might acknowledge
to themselves, and even take pride in, while it simultaneously permitted a
degree of friendly ridicule. The latter figured largely, of course, but it did not
have about it the venomous contempt that went with much anti-Scottish sentiment in the age of Bute. It took the form of what passed for innocent
humour. Here was a new game for the self-consciously tolerant but gently
mocking English gentleman. An archdeacon of Calcutta could observe that
St Andrew must have been selected as patron saint of Scotland because 'he
discovered the lad who had the loaves and fishes!'[64] The Duke of Wellington
could, when asked a leading political question, respond in his own language,
'I came the Scotchman over him, for I said, Why, I should like to know in the
first place what *you* think of it.'[65]

This was small beer, of course. Foreigners took it for such. Scots in
England were likened to Tyroleans in Austria, or Gascons in France, or
Savoyards in Italy. It was not a bad comparison. Such attitudes were characteristic of metropolitan opinion in a phase of cultural self-assertion. Scotland
was a province and its inhabitants provincial, to use the term newly employed
for people from anywhere else in Britain and even from other parts of the
English-speaking world. Scots as provincials could be accommodated. They
were no longer an alien presence. Nor, on the other hand, were they yet as
North Britons fully equals of South Britons, in the terminology recom-

[61] Garlick, Macintyre, and Cave (eds), *Diary of Joseph Farington*, XIV, p. 4917.
[62] Wallace Notestein, *The Scot in History: a Study of the Interplay of Character and History* (London, 1946), p. 332.
[63] Thomas Thornton, *A Sporting Tour through the northern Parts of England and Great Part of the Highlands of Scotland* (London, 1896), p. 64.
[64] [Samuel Reynolds Hole], *The Memories of Dean Hole* (London, 1892), p. 166.
[65] Elizabeth Longford (ed.), *Notes of Conversations with the Duke of Wellington 1831–1851* (London, 1998), p. 180.

mended by the makers of the union. Scots were free to think of themselves as far more than provincials, of course, and some, like Robert Burns, raged against the word and the idea. But on English terms in England that was what was on offer.

9

Eighteenth-Century Scotland
and the Three Unions

COLIN KIDD

EIGHTEENTH-CENTURY SCOTS THOUGHT ABOUT UNIONS MORE THAN THEY DID ABOUT IDENTITY. In fact, despite what some scholars have suggested, Scots did not experience a 'crisis of identity' during the eighteenth century,[1] nor did they spend the first century of Anglo-Scottish incorporation worrying over the effects which the Union of 1707 would have on Scotland's culture or self-esteem. Although self-consciously provincial, eighteenth-century North Britain was far from introverted. Its intellectuals were cosmopolitan and outward-looking, and tended, therefore, to consider issues of union and state formation in terms of the broad perspective of European history. More remarkably, during the high Enlightenment of the mid-eighteenth century, historians, jurists, and social commentators felt able to contemplate the union with a degree of philosophical detachment from the immediate hurly-burly of Anglo-Scottish politics in the raw. Yet this theoretical sophistication was married to practicality. The concerns which surface in eighteenth-century Scottish political argument were very practical: the attainment of civil free-doms, the acquisition of political and economic privileges, and the winning and maintenance of prosperity. These issues—not an anxiety to preserve Scotland's national identity—prompted an ongoing discussion of union.

From the debates which preceded the parliamentary union of 1707 to the discussions which accompanied the British union with Ireland in 1800, the topic of union was a staple feature of pamphlets, speeches, treatises, and histories. Scots pondered not only the merits and drawbacks of the Union of 1707, but also those which had followed in the wake of the earlier Union of

---

[1] e.g. D. Daiches, *The Paradox of Scottish Culture: the Eighteenth-Century Experience* (London, 1964); K. Simpson, *The Protean Scot: the Crisis of Identity in Eighteenth-Century Scottish Literature* (Aberdeen, 1988).

Proceedings of the British Academy, **127**, 171–187. © The British Academy 2005.

1603. However, eighteenth-century Scots also looked beyond the canonical sequence of unions — 1603, 1707 (and, later, 1800) — which constitute the core narrative of British state formation. In particular, they also displayed a keen awareness of the Cromwellian union of the 1650s when Scotland and Ireland had sent representatives to the parliament of the Commonwealth of England, Scotland, and Ireland. Furthermore, Scots held the view that the Union of 1707 had been a stepping stone towards rather than a culmination of British integration: that the Union of 1707 needed to be completed with a set of further measures conferring fuller civil liberties on Scots, a process only properly accomplished in the post-1745 reforms abolishing wardholding feudal vassalage and heritable jurisdictions, the feudal franchise courts held by nobles and landowners.[2] Any convincing rendering of eighteenth-century discussions of union needs to engage with an unexpected consensus on the short-lived union of the 1650s and the widespread view that the union was not completed until 1747–8, which became a standard terminus for histories of Scotland throughout the late eighteenth and nineteenth centuries.

Indeed, the eighteenth-century view of the Unions of 1603 and of 1707 concentrated not on the ways in which these shaped relations *between* Scotland and England, but on the ways in which the unions altered social relations *within* Scotland. The focus of the Scottish Enlightenment was on the deeper social and economic underpinnings of political systems, not on the epiphenomenal superficialities of national status. In particular, the enlightened historians of eighteenth-century Scotland believed that the progress of civil liberty marched in step with the wider history of civilisation. Eighteenth-century Scots tended not to apply the rhetoric of freedom and slavery to their predicament as a nation, but towards the experience of the Scots as a people oppressed by their own domestic superiors. As a result, the litmus test applied by the Scottish Enlightenment to past Anglo-Scottish unions was primarily sociological. How had the Union of 1603 or the Cromwellian union or the Union of 1707 impacted upon the common people of Scotland? The cosmopolitan sociological outlook which characterised the Scottish Enlightenment's view of union did not appear suddenly in the middle of the eighteenth century, but had been foreshadowed during the first decade of the eighteenth century in the union debates.

While hindsight tends to lump 1603 and 1707 together as part of a sequence, on the assumption that the Union of the Crowns was a staging post on the road to full incorporation, this was decidedly not the view of any Scot writing during the union debates of 1700–7.[3] Instead there was, amidst much

---

[2] The standard account of the reforms remains B. F. Jewell, 'The Legislation relating to Scotland after the Forty-five' (Ph.D. thesis, University of North Carolina, 1975).

[3] For the union debates, see J. Robertson, 'An elusive sovereignty: the course of the Union debate in Scotland 1698–1707', in J. Robertson (ed.), *A Union for Empire: Political Thought and*

wrangling on other major issues and a rich variety of options for Scotland's constitutional future, a unanimous verdict among political commentators that the Union of the Crowns had been a disaster for Scotland and that something new had to be ventured, whether incorporation, separation, or some form of regular federation. During the union debates nobody argued that the Union of the Crowns was a stepping stone to a more complete union. A consensus reigned that the Union of the Crowns had been bad for Scotland, producing serious irregularities in Scotland's governance and leading to a decline in Scottish trade. A pamphlet written in support of the Act of Security (1704) claimed that under the Union of the Crowns Scottish government had been 'clogged with many inconveniences'.[4] Incorporating union, it seemed, could hardly be worse. The Scots episcopalian unionist and royal physician, Dr John Arbuthnot, produced the startling claim that 'England has oppressed Scotland ten times more, since the Union of the Two Crowns, than ever they will be able to do after the Union of the Two Parliaments.'[5] Even those Scots who contended for a continuation of a loose Anglo-Scottish relationship with separate parliaments — most volubly the presbyterian federalists, James Hodges and George Ridpath — nevertheless argued that the Union of the Crowns had worked for a century against the interests of Scotland.[6] Another federalist, Andrew Brown, argued that the 'long, unequal and irregular conjunction' experienced during the Union of the Crowns had brought Scotland to such a low ebb that the remedy lay either in total separation or in a new framework of association with England.[7] There was a universal consensus that the status of the Scots parliament had declined during the Union of the Crowns. Unionists and anti-incorporationists disagreed only about the solution — strengthening safeguards for the Scots legislature within a confederal union, or writing the parliament off as a loss of little account to Scotland. Commentators traced not only the unfortunate political and economic consequences of the Union of 1603, but also the impact of the Union of the

---

the Union of 1707 (Cambridge, 1995), pp. 198–227; W. R. and V. B. McLeod, Anglo-Scottish Tracts 1701–14, University of Kansas Library Series 44 (1979).

[4] The Act of Security is the only rational method of procuring Scotland a happy constitution, free from the illegal invasion of its liberties and laws, and the base usurpation of its ancient sovereignty (1704), p. 3.

[5] John Arbuthnot, A Sermon Preached to the People at the Mercat Cross of Edinburgh on the Subject of the Union (London, 1707), p. 7.

[6] George Ridpath, The Reducing of Scotland by arms, and annexing it to England as a province considered (London, 1705?); James Hodges, The Rights and Interests of the Two British Monarchies . . . Treatise I (London, 1703); Hodges, The Rights and Interests . . . Treatise III (London, 1706).

[7] [Andrew Brown], Some Very Weighty and Seasonable Considerations tending to dispose, excite and qualify the Nation for the more effectual treating with England in relation to an Union of Confederacy (1703), p. 5.

Crowns in consolidating some of the most oppressive aspects of Scottish feudal society, an argument which provided a persuasive accompaniment to Sir William Seton of Pitmedden's case for incorporating union.[8] The feudal consequences of the Union of the Crowns would later become a leading refrain within the Scottish Enlightenment's analysis of the Scottish past.

The Union of the Crowns was not the only union under investigation. During the union debates Scottish pamphleteers did not confine their discussions of union to an Anglo-Scottish context. Andrew Fletcher of Saltoun's utopian, albeit pessimistic, *Account of a Conversation* (1704) considered Europe as a whole and the general problem of core–periphery relationships, arguing that the security of a small state such as Scotland could not be guaranteed under the existing states system in Europe; the only hope for small entities was a complete reordering of Europe into leagues of city-states.[9] In addition, many pamphlets discussed the Union of Kalmar (1397–1523), which had combined Denmark, Sweden, and Norway under the primacy of Denmark; the Union of Lublin (1569), which created the Polish-Lithuanian commonwealth; the United Provinces of the Netherlands; the Helvetic League of the Swiss Cantons; and the composition of the imperial monarchies of France and Spain. However, Scots did not agree upon the lessons which might be drawn from European history. *A Short Account of the Union betwixt Sweden, Denmark and Norway which commenced about the year 1396 and was broke about the year 1523 . . . Fit to be perus'd by Scotsmen at this juncture . . .* (Edinburgh, 1706) took the form of an anti-unionist warning, which emphasised the Danish oppression of Sweden and Norway within the Union of Kalmar. More positively, Ridapth pointed to the equal authority enjoyed by the various cantonal assemblies in the Swiss confederal association as a model for the Anglo-Scottish relationship. He also argued that the Polish-Lithuanian commonwealth, the Spanish union, and the United Provinces of the Netherlands all preserved important constitutional privileges within their component parts.[10] Rigid centralisation, Ridpath argued, was not necessary for effective association. Europe provided a set of models of successful federal relationships.

Unionists saw the same European polities in a quite different light. When is a nation not a nation, asked the most penetrating spokesmen for incorporating union? Where anti-unionists saw nations, Seton and Cromartie saw

---

[8] William Seton, *A Speech in Parliament the Second Day of November 1706* (1706), p. 11.

[9] Andrew Fletcher, *An Account of a Conversation concerning the Right Regulation of Governments for the Common Good of Mankind* (1704), in J. Robertson (ed.), *Andrew Fletcher: Political Works* (Cambridge, 1997).

[10] George Ridpath, *A Discourse upon the Union of Scotland and England* (1702), p. 90; Ridpath, *Considerations upon the Union of the Two Kingdoms* (1706), pp. 37–8, 68–9.

successful incorporating unions. Seton cited several examples of successful incorporating unions, such as the ten kingdoms of Spain, the twelve states of France and — closer to home — the English heptarchy. On the other hand, noted Seton, within looser non-incorporating unions, the weaker partner tends to lose out and eventually separates, as Portugal had from the Spain of Philip IV, or Sweden from Denmark.[11] Cromartie claimed that the most successful power in the history of Europe — ancient Rome — was built upon an incorporating union within the Italian peninsula of Romans, Sabines, Volsci, and Samnites. Cromartie also exploded the distinction between support for nationhood and support for union. What was viable nationhood in the Europe of 1700, suggested Cromartie, but the result of a series of successful unions and amalgamations? French, Spanish, and English nationhood rested on such unions. Would Aragon, say, or Brittany, Cromartie wondered, be better off as independent units? England too, he argued, was not so much a nation as a union, the historic merger of the Anglo-Saxon heptarchy into a single, indivisible national unit.[12]

According to both Seton and Cromartie, the history of Scotland itself involved a history of successful incorporation, though they differed in their accounts of this history. Whereas Seton claimed that 'Scotland itself was formerly divided into two kingdoms, which at present are incorporated into the one kingdom of Scotland',[13] Cromartie maintained that Scottish nationhood was the outcome of a series of amalgamations of ancient tribes and ethnic groups such as the Catti, Horesti, Brigantes, and Picts. Indeed, Cromartie insisted that Scottish nationality was a construct, like those of other European kingdoms. The direction of history, Cromartie seemed to be suggesting, was towards the amalgamation of larger entities. Quite explicitly, he ridiculed the sentimentality of shedding tears for smaller entities which had outlived their sovereign capacities. What mattered to Cromartie—who mocked the 'sophisms' of pretend patriots—were practical interests, not names or identities.[14]

Needless to say, the unemotional sophistication of this unionist case did little to win over public opinion to the union. Techniques of political management rather than compelling advocacy enabled the passage of the union through the Scottish parliament.[15] The Union of 1707 — which had been conceived under pressure of events largely as an anti-Jacobite measure to win

[11] Seton, *Speech*, pp. 9–10.
[12] Earl of Cromartie, *Paraneisis Pacifica* (London, 1702), pp. 4–5; Cromartie, *Trialogus* (1706), pp. 6, 9; Cromartie, *A Letter from E. C. to E. W. concerning the Union* (Edinburgh, 1706), p. 3.
[13] Seton, *Speech*, p. 10.
[14] Cromartie, *Paraneisis*, p. 4; Cromartie, *Trialogus*, pp. 9–15; Cromartie, *Letter from E. C. to E. W.*, pp. 5–7; Cromartie, *A Second Letter on the British Union* (1706), pp. 2–3, 18.
[15] P. W. J. Riley, *The Union of England and Scotland* (Manchester, 1978).

over Scotland to the Hanoverian succession[16]—remained unpopular for some years, and there was a motion to repeal the union in 1713, which failed by only four votes in the House of Lords.[17] Until the middle of the eighteenth century the Jacobite movement presented a viable alternative to union in the form of a Stuart restoration and a return to some form of Scottish autonomy,[18] and on the margins of presbyterian culture there were loud complaints that the Union of 1707 involved a breach of an earlier scheme of union, the Solemn League and Covenant of 1643.[19] Nevertheless, the mainstream of Scottish public opinion came by the middle of the eighteenth century to welcome the union as a liberation of the Scottish people from the dead hand of feudal society. This notion was coined during the union debates, refined during the Scottish Enlightenment, and popularised—certainly at the level of the professions, the articulate leaders of eighteenth-century Scottish provincial society—in histories, pamphlets, university lectures, and the agenda of student clubs and agricultural improvement societies.[20]

Several myths have grown up about the Scottish response to union. In particular, there has been a widespread assumption that, because the Treaty of Union preserved a distinctive Scots legal system and the accompanying acts for securing the privileges of the Churches of Scotland and England guaranteed the independence of the established Scots presbyterian kirk,[21] Scots law and presbyterianism became mainstays of Scottish identity in the supposed vacuum created by the loss of Scotland's parliament. These assumptions are questionable, at least in so far as they describe the eighteenth-century Scottish response to union. In spite of the constitutional provisions regarding the status of the kirk, its position was perceived by contemporaries to be highly precarious and, as a result, this tended to inhibit the shrill assertion of Scots presbyterian differences from the Church of England. At the time of the union, the presbyterian establishment had only been in existence since 1690. The kirk was less than twenty years old, and was under sustained challenge from supporters of the previous episcopalian establishment, who, wisely, targeted their propaganda efforts on their Anglican co-religionists. The broad thrust of the episcopalian critique of the current kirk establishment was to taint mainstream Scots presbyterianism with the radical extremism and uncompromising religious enthusiasm of the Cameronians, the undiluted remnant of the Covenanting movement. Relying on the turbulent recent his-

[16] W. Ferguson, *Scotland's Relations with England* (Edinburgh, 1977), chs 10–14.
[17] W. Ferguson, *Scotland 1689 to the Present* (Edinburgh, 1987 edn), p. 61.
[18] B. Lenman, *The Jacobite Risings in Britain, 1689–1746* (London, 1980).
[19] C. Kidd, 'Conditional Britons: the Scots Covenanting tradition and the eighteenth-century British state', *English Historical Review* 117 (2002), pp. 1147–76.
[20] C. Kidd, *Subverting Scotland's Past* (Cambridge, 1993).
[21] B. Levack, *The Formation of the British State* (Oxford, 1987), p. 102n.

tory of these islands under the Stuart multiple monarchy, episcopalian pamphleteers reminded their readers of presbyterian atrocities, such as the assassination of Archbishop Sharp in 1679, blamed 'king-killing' presbyterians for the circumstances which had led Charles I to the block, and smeared presbyterians as deluded fanatics who subscribed to resistance theory at its most demotic.[22] In effect, episcopalians asked the Anglican political nation whether or not they could trust presbyterians to control the Scottish establishment. As well as responding directly to episcopalian smears, Scots presbyterians of a pragmatic cast tried to stabilise the position of the kirk by projecting a more apologetic, less embattled profile.[23] The kirk appeared to be engaged in a treacherous campaign of self-censorship and doctrinal dilution which outraged some traditionalists within its ranks. However, the loss of the Seceders, who broke with the kirk over its willingness to comply — however reluctantly — with British legislation of 1712 restoring lay patronage in Scotland, further marginalised hardline elements within the kirk.[24] This process culminated in the emergence of the Moderate party in the kirk during the 1750s, a clerical faction which embodied, extended, and clearly articulated the values of pragmatism and compromise.[25] Without openly sacrificing any points of Calvinist doctrine or betraying any fundamental aspect of the presbyterian system of church government, the Moderates promoted a religion of civility and moral and social responsibility, and made clear their distaste for some of the more controversial dimensions of the Scots presbyterian tradition between the Reformation and the union. The leader of the Moderates, William Robertson, published a *History of Scotland* (1759), which, although focused largely on the events of the Reformation, amounted to a lukewarm and oddly detached celebration of Scottish Reformation principles.[26]

A different kind of ambivalence surrounded eighteenth-century Scottish attitudes to the law. Although the Scottish legal system had been preserved in Articles Eighteen, Nineteen, and Twenty of the Treaty of Union, the distinctiveness and semi-autonomy enjoyed by Scots law did not constitute bulwarks of Scottish nationhood within the new British state. Scots lawyers had no sense that the laws of Scotland were a peculiar embodiment of the values

---

[22] Kidd, *Subverting Scotland's Past*, pp. 54–9.

[23] C. Kidd, 'Constructing a civil religion: Scots presbyterians and the eighteenth-century British state', in J. Kirk (ed.), *The Scottish Churches and the Union Parliament 1707–1999* (Scottish Church History Society, Edinburgh, 2001).

[24] A. L. Drummond and J. Bulloch, *The Scottish Church 1688–1843* (Edinburgh, 1973), pp. 37–44.

[25] I. D. L. Clark, 'From protest to reaction: the moderate regime in the Church of Scotland, 1752–1805', in N. T. Phillipson and R. Mitchison (eds), *Scotland in the Age of Improvement* (Edinburgh, 1970).

[26] S. J. Brown (ed.), *William Robertson and the Expansion of Empire* (Cambridge, 1997).

of the people. Legal nationalism is a much more recent coinage and was quite absent throughout the eighteenth century. Nor did the union foster among Scots lawyers a closed culture of defensiveness predicated upon the need to maintain the integrity of Scots law from the meddling of an English-dominated legislature whose members had little familiarity with Scots law. Rather, eighteenth-century Scots legal circles exhibited a remarkable openness and keen receptivity to outside influences. The Scots did not think of their legal system as impeccably Scottish in pedigree and character; rather they acknowledged that they participated—by way of their share in the pan-European inheritance of civil, canon, and feudal law—in a supra-national *ius commune*, which was gradually becoming differentiated into distinct bodies of national law.[27]

Scots lawyers—many of whom were trained in Leiden and Utrecht in the civil law—did not treat the status of Scots law in a narrow positivist or nationalist idiom, but in terms of the law of nature and nations. The authority of Scots law rested not on any sense that it reflected the will of the Scottish nation, but in the recognition that it manifested, under local conditions, the universal truths of the law of nature. This outlook is epitomised by the claim of the Scottish judge Lord Cullen that anyone 'who has the Common and Scotch law, may soon acquire that of any disciplined country. Reason (whence it proceeds) is every where the same; though uttered and applied by different signs, of words and forms.'[28] Scots jurists also acknowledged that other legal systems bore the imprint of natural law; as such they were worthy of imitation in areas where Scots law was found wanting. As John Cairns has argued, in the Scotland of 1707 natural law enjoyed 'primacy' over theories of sovereignty.[29] Contemporary projections of Scots law as a national system of law were set within the context of the wider law of nature and nations from which national laws derived their ultimate authority. For example, the jurisprudence of Lord Stair had involved an attempt to systematise the various components of Scots law—customs, decisions, and statutes; feudal, canon, and civil law—and to relate the whole to the law of God as revealed to man in scripture and a universal law of nature which was made manifest to man through the faculty of reason.[30]

---

[27] K. Luig, 'The Institutes of National Law in the seventeenth and eighteenth centuries', *Juridical Review* n.s. 17 (1972), p. 193–226; J. Cairns, 'Institutional writings in Scotland reconsidered', in A. Kiralfy and H. MacQueen (eds), *New Perspectives in Scottish Legal History* (London, 1984), pp. 76–117; O. F. Robinson, T. D. Fergus, and W. M. Gordon, *An Introduction to European Legal History* (Abingdon, 1985), pp. 179–80, 202–6.

[28] Francis Grant, Lord Cullen, *Law, Religion and Education Considered* (1715), I, 'Law', p. 97.

[29] J. Cairns, 'Scottish law, Scottish lawyers and the status of the Union', in Robertson (ed.), *Union for Empire*, p. 268.

[30] James Dalrymple of Stair, *The Institutions of the Law of Scotland Deduced from its Originals, and Collated with the Civil, Canon and Feudal-Laws; and with the Customs of Neighbouring Nations* (Edinburgh, 1681), Part I, Title 1, 'Common Principles of Law'.

The eighteenth century witnessed only a gradual domestication of legal education. Many Scots continued to study law at the Dutch universities until about the middle of the eighteenth century.[31] Indeed, the development of legal education within Scotland was carried out in a cosmopolitan spirit. In 1707, for example, Edinburgh University established a Professorship of Public Law and the Law of Nature and Nations. Further chairs followed at Edinburgh: a chair of Civil Law, by which was meant Roman law, in 1709, and only in 1722 a chair of Scots Law. The order in which these professorships were established accurately reflected contemporary priorities. Indeed, not until 1750 did Scots law become a necessary element in the training of a Scottish lawyer. Scots law played only a very minor role in determining entry to the legal profession. Entrance to the legal profession was by way of the civil law, that is Roman law, a subject to which aspirant Scots advocates were exposed in the Dutch universities. Only in 1692 did an alternative method of entry to the Faculty of Advocates present itself, by way of an examination in Scots law. In 1724 the Dean of Faculty recommended that entry should depend on an examination in Scots law. After some discussion, the proposal fell by the wayside, and only after a further effort did an examination in Scots law become a formal requirement for advocates in 1750.[32]

Unlike twentieth-century legal nationalists, eighteenth-century Scots jurists—intellectually programmed to conceive of national legal traditions as variants of the law of nature and nations—had no anxieties about a British appellate jurisdiction contaminating the jurisprudential integrity of Scots law. Eighteenth-century Scots jurists complacently accepted the appellate jurisdiction of the House of Lords, despite the fact that the Treaty of Union was silent on the subject of such appeals. From the outset of the new united state, the British House of Lords responded to appeals from the Scottish courts by bringing them within its jurisdiction, beginning with 'Rosebery v. Inglis' in 1708. The question of appellate jurisdiction only became a controversial issue when it became entangled with religion in the Greenshields case of 1710–11. Here it was the religious dimension of the issue which was controversial, not the juridical role of the House of Lords in overturning a Scottish decision. For much of the eighteenth century the British House of Lords exercised appellate jurisdiction over both civil and criminal causes from the Court of Session and the High Court of Justiciary

[31] J. Cairns, 'Legal theory', in A. Broadie (ed.), *The Cambridge Companion to the Scottish Enlightenment* (Cambridge, 2003), p. 235.
[32] *Minute Book of the Faculty of Advocates*, I: *1661–1712*, ed. J. A. Pinkerton (Stair Society, Edinburgh, 1976), pp. 115–16; *Minute Book of the Faculty of Advocates*, II: *1713–1750*, ed. Pinkerton (Stair Society, Edinburgh, 1980), pp. 72–5, 77, 79, 85, 115–16, 232, 239, 241.

in the absence of any significant disquiet on the part of Scottish lawyers and judges.[33]

Lawyers and judges displayed little concern about preserving law unchanged as a totem of Scottish semi-autonomy within the union. Indeed, works such as Lord Kames's *Essays on British Antiquities* (1747) and Sir John Dalrymple's *Essay towards a History of Feudal Property in Great Britain* (1757) constituted exercises in a kind of ecumenical legal history which traced the common Anglo-Norman origins of legal institutions on both sides of the Border and their subsequent divergence. Some form of reassimilation remained possible, and inspired champions of the campaign from the mid-1780s for a civil jury in Scotland.[34] At any rate, the primary focus of Enlightenment jurisprudence was not on national differences, but on the sensitivity of legal systems, such as Scots law, to underlying patterns of social and economic change. Given this agenda, it is unsurprising that jurists worried less about the gradual Anglicisation of the Scots law, than about the law's responsiveness to the transition between agrarian and commercial society. Progress—rather than nationhood—provided the most compelling benchmark for determining the effectiveness of Scots law.[35]

Received opinion about the importance of law and religion to eighteenth-century Scots depends logically on the further assumption that the kirk and the legal system acted as surrogates for a lost parliament. However, contemporaries did not hold the old Scots parliament in high esteem. In 1747 a letter to *The British Magazine, or London and Edinburgh Intelligencer* conceded that 'we have surely no reason to complain from the loss of our parliament'. The Union of 1707, the correspondent remarked, had 'delivered' Scotland from a weak, unicameral parliament which throughout the seventeenth century had displayed a marked lack of dignity or responsibility. The Union of 1707 had admitted Scots to a share in the direction of a vigorous British parliament which was 'better formed to redress grievances, than ever our own had been'.[36] Eighteenth-century Scots considered it more important for Scots to be governed by an effective parliament in London than for Scotland to have an ineffective parliament of its own. By the same token, Robertson deemed the seventeenth-century Scots legislature a mere simulacrum of a parliament:

---

[33] A. J. MacLean, 'The 1707 Union: Scots law and the House of Lords', in Kiralfy and MacQueen (eds), *New Perspectives*, pp. 50–75; MacLean, 'The House of Lords and appeals from the High Court of Justiciary, 1707–1887', *Juridical Review* n.s. 30 (1985), pp. 192–226.

[34] N. Phillipson, *The Scottish Whigs and the Reform of the Court of Session 1785–1830* (Stair Society, Edinburgh, 1990).

[35] P. Stein, *Legal Evolution* (Cambridge, 1980), ch. 2; D. Lieberman, 'The legal needs of a commercial society: the jurisprudence of Lord Kames', in I. Hont and M. Ignatieff (eds), *Wealth and Virtue* (Cambridge, 1983).

[36] *The British Magazine, or London and Edinburgh Intelligencer* (April, 1747), pp. 192–3.

'All business was transacted there by the Lords of Articles, and they were so servilely devoted to the court, that few debates arose, and, prior to the Revolution, none were conducted with the spirit and vigour natural to a popular assembly.'[37] At the radical extreme of the Scottish Enlightenment, Gilbert Stuart, otherwise a critic of Robertson's historical politics, concurred with this analysis. Stuart noted that between the Union of 1603 and the Union of 1707 'the commons of Scotland' — as he termed them — 'never assembled by themselves', but always met in the same house with the nobility. As a result, the commons of Scotland, Stuart claimed, 'never attained that elevation and grandeur which have distinguished and immortalised the commons of England'.[38] The old Scots parliament passed unlamented.

Indeed, there was very little scope for national sentiment in political analysis. The subject of union attracted theoretical detachment rather than national chauvinism. Adam Ferguson's pragmatic outlook on state formation betrayed little sign of nostalgia for a lost sovereignty. Ferguson, who was otherwise a keen proponent of the close-knit solidarity associated with the small republics of antiquity, recognised that effective sovereignty in the early modern states system required more extensive — and hence viable — national units:

> The measure of enlargement to be wished for any particular state, is often to be taken from the condition of its neighbours. Where a number of states are contiguous, they should be near an equality, in order that they may be mutually objects of respect and consideration, and in order that they may possess that independence in which the political life of a nation consists. When the kingdoms of Spain were united, when the great fiefs in France were annexed to the crown, it was no longer expedient for the nations of Great Britain to continue disunited.[39]

What had Scotland really lost by the Union of 1707? The Reverend Thomas Somerville, who wrote histories of seventeenth-century Britain, contended that by 1707 'national sovereignty of which the Scots so proudly vaunted' had become 'nothing more than an empty phantom'.[40]

Nevertheless, eighteenth-century Scottish historians made no attempt to align the Union of 1603 and the Union of 1707 in a benignly unfolding story of ever-closer British integration. Despite the unionist outlook of the Scottish Enlightenment, the two unions — of 1603 and 1707 — enjoyed quite different

---

[37] William Robertson, *History of Scotland* (1759) in Robertson, *Works* (London, 1831), p. 260.
[38] Gilbert Stuart, *Observations concerning the Public Law and the Constitutional History of Scotland* (Edinburgh, 1779), pp. 129–30.
[39] Adam Ferguson, *An Essay on the History of Civil Society*, ed. D. Forbes (Edinburgh, 1966), p. 60.
[40] Thomas Somerville, *The History of Great Britain during the Reign of Queen Anne* (London, 1798), p. 148.

reputations. 1603 was not regarded as a welcome staging post on the road to 1707. Whereas eighteenth-century Scots celebrated their good fortune in the incorporation with England in 1707, the Union of the Crowns was universally lamented as one of the worst things that had ever happened to Scotland. In particular, a chorus of commentators agreed that the Union of the Crowns had disfigured the development of Scottish institutions. Attention focused on the feudal consequences of 1603. A number of commentators pointed to the way in which the Union of the Crowns had fastened more tightly on the people of Scotland the chains of feudal vassalage. The Union of 1603, so the argument ran, had elevated the king so far above the reach of Scotland's magnates that the monarchy could comfortably leave its politically weakened baronage unmolested in the petty tyranny of their bailiwicks. Kames outlined the unwelcome social consequences of the Union of the Crowns:

> The union of the two crowns of England and Scotland was a fatal event for the latter. The great increase of power which our kings thereby acquired, reduced the Scotch nobility to a state of humble dependence. From being petty monarchs, they became slaves to the crown, and had nothing left to support their accustomed dignity, but, under protection of the crown, to enslave their inferiors.[41]

As a consequence, commercial and agrarian energies were stifled. Somerville claimed that the history of seventeenth-century Scotland 'exhibits a gradual tendency to national depression'.[42]

The fullest analyses of the Union of the Crowns came from the Moderate cleric William Robertson and from John Millar, Professor of Civil Law at Glasgow University. In his influential *History of Scotland* Robertson claimed that the Union of the Crowns enabled the Stuart monarchy to tame its over-mighty subjects: 'by his accession to throne of England, James acquired such an immense accession of wealth, of power, and of splendour, that the nobles, astonished and intimidated, thought it vain to struggle for privileges which they were now unable to defend.' Henceforth , 'the will of the prince became the supreme law in Scotland'. Nevertheless, the nobles did not lose out entirely under the new dispensation. 'Satisfied with having subjected the nobles to the crown,' Robertson noted, 'the king left them in full possession of their ancient jurisdiction over their own vassals.' The result was an oppressive aristocratic tyranny, not least as the Scottish nobles, according to Robertson, needed to find ways of financing the expenditure of attendance at a distant English court as well as their attempts to emulate the luxurious ways of their southern peers. As a result, Scotland's feudal élite 'multiplied exactions upon the people, who durst hardly utter complaints which they knew would never

---

[41] Henry Home, Lord Kames, *Progress of Flax-Husbandry in Scotland* (Edinburgh, 1766), p. 5.
[42] Somerville, *History of Great Britain*, p. 147.

reach the ear of the sovereign, nor move him to grant any redress'. Robertson's verdict on the domestic consequences of 1603 was unambiguously negative:

> From the union of the Crowns to the revolution in 1688, Scotland was placed in a political situation, of all others the most singular and the most unhappy; subjected at once to the absolute will of a monarch, and to the oppressive juris-diction of an aristocracy, it suffered all the miseries peculiar to both these forms of government. Its kings were despotic; its nobles were slaves and tyrants; and the people groaned under the rigorous domination of both.[43]

Millar painted a very similar picture, though he framed it in a wider European context of general trends in state formation and political develop-ment, in respect of which Scotland, as a direct result of the Union of the Crowns, was a sad and unduly oppressed anomaly. Millar argued that through the Union of the Crowns the authority of the Scottish monarch had been elevated to such an extent relative to the nobility of Scotland that this meant there was no imperative to make alliances, as happened elsewhere in Europe between monarchy and commons to tame the feudal nobility:

> In England, as well as in many other European governments, where the preroga-tive advanced gradually and slowly, in consequence of the gradual advancement of society, the king was under the necessity of courting the lower orders of the community, and of promoting their freedom, from the view of undermining the power of the nobility, his immediate rivals. But in Scotland, after James VI had mounted the English throne, neither he nor his immediate successors, had any occasion to employ so disagreeable an expedient. They were above the level of rivalship or opposition from the Scottish vassals of the crown; and had therefore no temptation to free the vassals of the nobility from their ancient bondage. A great part of the old feudal institutions, in that country, were accordingly permitted to remain, without undergoing any considerable alteration.

As a result of the Union of the Crowns, claimed Millar, the commons of Scotland had sunk under the petty feudal depotism of their lairds.[44]

Given the horrors of the Union of the Crowns, as related by the socio-logical historians of the Scottish Enlightenment, it becomes easier to explain why these same historians put a positive gloss on the enforced Cromwellian union of the 1650s. The events of the Cromwellian union complemented the Scottish Enlightenment's equation of Anglicisation with modernisation, par-ticularly in the sphere of feudal law. Under the Cromwellian union the Court of Session had been replaced by seven Commissioners for the Administration of Justice, three Scots outnumbered by four English judges (an imbalance which later Scottish commentators generally welcomed). The Ordinance of

---

[43] Robertson, *Works*, p. 257.
[44] John Millar, *An Historical View of the English Government*, 4 vols ([1787] London, 1803), III, pp. 73–5.

Union had abolished oppressive feudal jurisdictions, such as regality and
barony courts, transforming them into 'courts baron' similar in their limited
powers to English manor courts, while vassalage was also abolished in
Scotland.[45] As a result, eighteenth-century Scots tended to depict Cromwell
and his Scottish satrap, General Monck, in a very favourable light, welcom-
ing the Cromwellian union as an era of peace and plenty which had also
included an all-too-brief liberation of the common people from feudal
oppression. Scots during the 1650s, it was argued, had enjoyed a measure of
civil liberty which, after the Restoration of Charles II and the old forms of
government, they would not taste again until the anti-feudal reforms accomplished in the aftermath of the 1745 rebellion. While making no attempt to
conceal the naked power politics underlying Cromwellian rule in Scotland,
David Hume listed a number of sensible improvements in the administration
of Scotland, and claimed that 'in the main, the Scots were obliged to
acknowledge, that never before, while they enjoyed their irregular factious
liberty, had they attained so much happiness as at present, when reduced to
subjection under a foreign nation.'[46] James Macpherson, best known for his
'discovery' of Ossian, took a similar line, extolling the administration of justice in Scotland under General Monck's regime.[47] Hugo Arnot in his *History
of Edinburgh* noted that although under the Cromwellian occupation 'government was founded in manifest usurpation, peace and order were maintained, and justice distributed with a more steady and impartial hand, than
when Scotland was under the government of her native monarchs; or, indeed,
to speak more properly, under the influence of her tyrannical nobles.' In particular, Arnot praised the 'sagacity' of Cromwell 'in wrenching the exorbitant
power from the Scottish chieftains, by the abolition of their vassalage, in
which they held their dependants enslaved, and which has been found so
incompatible with liberty'.[48] Similarly, Robert Heron lauded Cromwell's rule
in Scotland for introducing a measure of peace and civilisation into what had
hitherto been an unruly and anarchic society.[49]

In the eyes of the Scottish Enlightenment the Union of 1707 marked a
crucial transition in the internal social affairs of the Scottish nation. The
significance of the union lay not only in the reconfiguration of the Anglo-
Scottish relationship, but in the realignment of social and political forces
within Scotland. The Revolution of 1688–90 had, of course, marked an

---

[45] F. Dow, *Cromwellian Scotland 1651–1660* (Edinburgh, 1979), pp. 53–5, 121.
[46] David Hume, *History of England*, 6 vols (Indianapolis, 1983), VI, p. 91.
[47] James Macpherson, *History of Great Britain from the Restoration to the Accession of the
House of Hanover*, 2 vols (London, 1775), I, pp. 21–2.
[48] Hugo Arnot, *The History of Edinburgh* (Edinburgh, 1779), pp. 136–7.
[49] Robert Heron, *A New General History of Scotland*, 5 vols (Perth and Edinburgh, 1794–9), V,
pt. 1, pp. 549–50.

important step forward, but it had done nothing to remedy the main source of Scottish dysfunction, the Union of the Crowns. Despite his loyal whiggery, Robertson gave only two cheers for the Revolution: 'Another great event [the union] completed what the Revolution had begun.'[50] Incorporation with an advanced commercial society had, it seemed, inaugurated the liberation of the Scottish people from a feudal aristocracy. For Scots of the Enlightenment, this was the real significance of 1707. Thus, although Scots readily resorted to the vocabulary of liberty and slavery with respect to the Unions of 1603 and 1707, they tended not to think in terms of the freedom of Scotland from England or in terms of a union which subjected Scots to Englishmen. Rather they were concerned about the ways in which the Union of 1603 had fastened tighter the subjection of Scot to Scot, commoner to noble, and how the Union of 1707 — and the further measures taken to complete the union in 1747–8 — had lifted the yoke of feudal bondage imposed by Scots on their fellow Scots. Kames proclaimed that the common people had been 'restored to liberty and independence' by the Union of 1707.[51] 'At the Union of the two kingdoms,' claimed Robertson, 'the feudal aristocracy, which had subsisted so many ages, and with power so exorbitant, was overturned, and the Scottish nobles, having surrendered rights and pre-eminences peculiar to their order, reduced themselves to a condition which is no longer the terror and envy of other subjects.'[52] The Union of 1707, most commentators agreed, had initiated a process of liberation from the shackles of feudalism.

Yet the Union of 1707 was, in this vital respect, incomplete. However glorious, most Scottish commentators agreed, the Union of 1707 had been imperfect and had needed completion. Many historians, jurists, and political commentators agreed that only with the anti-feudal reforms which followed the defeat of the Jacobite rebellion of 1745–6 had Scotland been fully integrated within the union. Lord Bankton, a judge and author of an important synthesis of Scots law, argued that the abolition of heritable jurisdictions had put Scots 'upon the same foot of liberty and independency with the other people of Britain'.[53] Similarly, the jurist George Wallace depicted relief from heritable jurisdictions and wardholding vassalage as the rescue of the Scottish commons from slavery: 'oppressive jurisdictions, which subjects had possessed, were resumed to the crown; servile tenures were abolished; and tyrannical principles were banished from the law.'[54] Reflecting at the very end of the

[50] Robertson, *Works*, p. 258.
[51] Kames, *Progress of Flax-Husbandry*, p. 5.
[52] Robertson, *Works*, p. 258.
[53] Andrew McDouall, Lord Bankton, *An Institute of the Laws of Scotland in Civil Rights*, 3 vols (Edinburgh, 1751–3), II, p. 446.
[54] George Wallace, *A System of the Principles of the Law of Scotland* (Edinburgh, 1760), I, p. xix.

eighteenth century on the Union of 1707, the Reverend Ebenezer Marshal in his *History of the Union* (1799) was in no doubt about the liberal potential which inhered in the incorporating Union of 1707: 'The Union furnished the means of taking the rod of terror from the hands in which the feudal system had placed it, and of removing the shackles of servitude which checked the genius of enterprise.' Nevertheless, Marshal pointed out that economic improvement had been slow until the post-1745 reforms which brought 'deliverance from that feudal bondage, which the Union had left to subsist in all its slavish and degrading rigour'.[55]

Eighteenth-century Scots were obsessed with equality within the union. However, by equality they tended not to mean the association of Scotland and England as equal partners; rather they focused upon the equality of individual Scots and English subjects in the enjoyment of liberty and property. As a result, Scots aspired not to distinctiveness within the union, but to sameness, to the same rights and privileges of their fellow Englishmen. Emulation and imitation of English ways, rather than a guarded defence of Scottish pluralism, marked the Scottish response to union. Even during the 1760s the shrill Wilkesite Scotophobia of the English metropolis[56] did little to disturb the assimiliationist anti-feudalist ethos of North Britain, which at this point was fixated upon the question of reforming Scots entails.[57] Although Tobias Smollett's measured response to the Wilkesite threat in his epistolary novel, *Humphry Clinker* (1771), includes a powerful condemnation of the Union of 1707 out of the mouth of Lieutenant Lismahago, this reported outburst was more than counterbalanced by the observations of various characters on the subject of Scottish improvement.[58] Famously the poet Robert Burns denounced the *means* used to accomplish the Union of 1707: 'Bought and sold for English gold'; yet nobody—apart from the fictional and intentionally comic Lismahago—seems to have questioned the practical *benefits* which it brought the people of North Britain.[59]

[55] Ebenezer Marshal, *The History of the Union of Scotland and England* (Edinburgh, 1799), pp. iii, 208.
[56] J. Brewer, 'The misfortunes of Lord Bute', *Historical Journal* 16 (1973), pp. 3–43; Brewer, *Party Ideology and Popular Politics at the Accession of George III* (Cambridge, 1976).
[57] See e.g. John Dalrymple, *Considerations upon the Policy of Entails in Great Britain* (Edinburgh, 1764); John Swinton, *A Free Disquisition Concerning the Law of Entails in Scotland* (Edinburgh, 1765); Swinton, *Proposals for Amending the Law concerning Tailzies in Scotland* (Edinburgh, 1765) etc.
[58] Tobias Smollett, *The Expedition of Humphry Clinker*, ed. A. Ross ([1771] London, 1967), pp. 269, 274, 283–5, 292, 315–18.
[59] Robert Burns, 'Such a Parcel of Rogues in a Nation', in *Burns Poems and Songs*, ed. J. Kinsley (1969, Oxford, pbk edn 1971), pp. 511–12; C. Whatley, 'Burns and the Union of 1707', in K. Simpson (ed.), *Love and Liberty: Robert Burns, A Bicentenary Celebration* (East Linton, 1997), pp. 183–97.

By the final quarter of the eighteenth century, other potential unions tended to displace attention from the Anglo-Scottish connection, whose security and stability was now unquestioned. Indeed, the Anglo-American crisis and problems in the Anglo-Irish relationship brought into sharp focus the solid loyalty of North Britons. The attention of Scottish political commentators was also drawn to these other troubled parts of the Hanoverian world. Adam Smith's celebrated *Wealth of Nations* (1776) famously concludes with a call either for a proper union of Britain with her North American colonies or a retreat from this costly empire of the imagination. Less poignantly, Smith also raises the prospect of a union with Ireland, which, following the precedent of 1707, would involve freeing the common people from an even more 'oppressive aristocracy', in the case of the Irish one founded on religious prejudice.[60] By the end of the century Scotland's liberating experience of union with England became a propaganda tool of those keen to further a union of Britain with Ireland. The principal Scottish politician of the day, Henry Dundas — an unrecognised heir of Enlightenment values who championed Smith and was a consistent supporter of Catholic Emancipation — had no need to exaggerate Scottish happiness with the Union of 1707 when he put forward the case for British–Irish Union in the House of Commons in February 1799. Rather Dundas's celebrated setpiece speech revisited some of the main themes which had been the common currency of the Scottish Enlightenment, including the assumption that union had brought about the demise of Scottish feudalism: 'If the union has had a tendency to break asunder the bands of feudal vassalage, which prevailed to too great an excess in that country, wise and virtuous men will not be disposed to consider this as one of the evil consequences to be lamented in the formation of a legislative union of the two kingdoms.'[61] Dundas perceived that the union with Ireland, like the Union of 1707, needed to be a vehicle for social transformation. However, in this instance, hopes that union would lead immediately to a similarly welcome liberation in the shape of Catholic Emancipation were dashed on the intransigence of George III,[62] and it failed — in an unexpected departure from the successful precedent of 1707 — to win over hearts and minds on the same scale.

[60] Adam Smith, *An Inquiry into the Nature and Causes of the Wealth of Nations*, ed. R. H. Campbell et al., 2 vols (Oxford, 1976), V.iii.89–92.
[61] *Cobbett's Parliamentary History of England*, 36 vols (London, 1806–20), XXXIV, col. 354.
[62] M. Fry, *The Dundas Despotism* (Edinburgh, 1992), p. 238.

10

Scottish–English Connections in British Radicalism in the 1790s

BOB HARRIS

THE PAN-BRITISH DIMENSION TO RADICAL POLITICS IN BRITAIN AND IRELAND in the 1790s is well established, although historians continue to debate its relative importance in different national radical traditions.[1] It was symptomatic of a shared real Whig ideological and Enlightenment intellectual inheritance, as well as a presumption on the part of reformers that they were actors in a common European, if not global, struggle for liberty. Real Whig patriotism encouraged less a nationalistic than a cosmopolitan political outlook,[2] and this, together with an emphasis on reason as the ultimate arbiter in political debate, fostered a 'radical imaginary' that looked beyond nation. Looking further back, the reformers of the 1760s and '70s had perceived and portrayed the cause of liberty in terms of the inter-linked fortunes of freedom in the different parts of the British state and empire.[3] The radicals of the 1790s were the direct inheritors of this tradition.

From a Scottish perspective, however, our understanding of the British elements of the radical experience is a partial one. Two areas that have been reasonably well covered in the existing literature are ideology and connections to Ireland. With regard to the former, several historians have commented on the readiness with which Scots reformers exploited Whig

---

[1] In an Irish context, see the comments in Jim Smyth, *The Men of No Property: Irish Radicals and Popular Politics in the Late Eighteenth Century* (Dublin, 1992), pp. 80–91.

[2] See the comments in J. T. Leerson, 'Anglo-Irish patriotism and its European context: notes towards a reassessment', *Eighteenth-Century Ireland* 3 (1988), pp. 7–24.

[3] See e.g. Peter N. Miller, *Defining the Common Good: Empire, Religion and Philosophy in Eighteenth Century Britain* (Cambridge, 1994), esp. ch. 6.

Proceedings of the British Academy, **127**, 189–212. © The British Academy 2005.

narratives of English liberty to support their cause.[4] Thomas Muir was unusual, although not unique, in arguing that liberty in Scotland had a history as least as long as in England.[5] More typical were those who asserted that for political purposes the Scots and the English should be considered as one 'people'. Links with Irish radicalism have also received substantial attention in recent years.[6] By contrast, and partly as a consequence, the connections to radicalism south of the Border have tended to be relegated to the margins of historical debate.

The recent emphasis on relationships forged between Scottish radicals and their counterparts in Ireland is not hard to explain. In part, it is a by-product of the great profusion of scholarship in the last two decades on the dramatic political developments in Ireland in the 1790s, which culminated in rebellion and union.[7] It also undoubtedly reflects an important dimension to Scottish radical experience in this period. Firstly, through the agency of Thomas Muir, links with the leading Irish radical society, the United Irishmen, were established at a relatively early stage (probably by the summer of 1792), although the precise nature of these remains obscure.[8] The early radical career of Muir, indeed, neatly encapsulates the pan-British and internationalist cast of radicalism in the early 1790s. In 1793, following his indictment for sedition, Muir travelled, as a self-styled martyr in the cause of liberty, to London and then to Paris, before returning via Belfast to Scotland to face the sneering Lord Braxfield at the High Court.[9] In January 1793, the balloonist and printer-journalist James Tytler, faced with the prospect of

---

[4] See esp. John Brims, 'The Scottish "Jacobins", Scottish Nationalism and the British Union', in Roger A. Mason (ed.), *Scotland and England 1286–1815* (Edinburgh, 1987); Brims, 'The Covenanting tradition and Scottish Radicalism in the 1790's', in Terry Brotherstone (ed.), *Covenant, Charter and Party: Traditions of Revolt and Protest in Modern Scottish History* (Aberdeen, 1989).

[5] Muir made his claim in interventions in debates at the first national convention of the Scottish Friends of the People. See Henry W. Meikle, *Scotland and the French Revolution* (Glasgow, 1912), esp. pp. 250–1, where the minutes of this convention are reproduced in an appendix.

[6] See esp. John Brims, 'Scottish Radicalism and the United Irishmen', in David Dickson, Daire Keogh, and Kevin Whelan (eds), *The United Irishmen: Republicanism, Radicalism and Revolution* (Dublin, 1993); E. W. McFarland, *Ireland and Scotland in the Age of the French Revolution* (Edinburgh, 1994); McFarland, 'Scottish Radicalism in the later eighteenth century: "The Social Thistle and Shamrock" ', in T. M. Devine and J. R. Young (eds), *Eighteenth Century Scotland: New Perspectives* (East Linton, 1999).

[7] This scholarship is too extensive to list here, but, for a strong representation of recent work, see the essays in the recent volume: Thomas Bartlett, David Dickson, Daire Keogh, and Kevin Whelan (eds), *1798: A Bicentenary Perspective* (Dublin, 2003).

[8] Unfortunately, the correspondence between Muir and Hamilton Rowan, which began in 1792, has been lost. But see W. H. Drummond, *Autobiography of Archibald Hamilton Rowan, Esq. with Additions by William Hamilton Drummond, D.D., M.R.I.A.* (Dublin, 1840), p. 170.

[9] Christina Bewley, *Muir of Huntershill* (Oxford, 1981).

going up before the High Court for authorship of an allegedly seditious handbill, fled Edinburgh for Belfast. Pan-Celtic solidarity was a significant theme in Tytler's thinking; in 1795 he talked of the Scots and Irish uniting to bring down the 'proud and tyrannical' English.[10] Towards the end of 1793, Archibald Hamilton Rowan and Simon Butler, both leading members of the Dublin United Irishmen, were admitted as members of the British Convention of Radicals which met in Edinburgh, although they had not come to Edinburgh as delegates.[11] Such links grew in importance in the later 1790s, when the United Irishmen played a major role in the formation of the United Scotsmen in 1797. Delegates from the United Irishmen travelled from Belfast to Scotland in 1796 and 1797, while persecuted United Irishmen from Ulster readily found their way to Scotland following the campaign of terror unleashed on the province by General Lake.[12] While the nature of the Irish influence on the United Scotsmen is a matter of debate, that the society was, in its organisation and forms (if not perhaps ideology), modelled on the United Irishmen is not.[13]

Secondly, the emphasis on the Scots–Irish connection reflects the formative influence on Irish presbyterian radicals of an education provided by the Scottish universities.[14] This relationship was not without its ironies. While in the case of some of the Irish, a Scottish education may have helped catalyse a radical outlook and disposition, Scottish historians tend to view the Enlightenment as a conservative, stabilising force in Scottish society, although this may reflect too uniform a view of what was, in reality, a quite diverse series of intellectual and cultural developments.[15] The contribution, meanwhile, of presbyterian theology and experience to Irish radicalism has been traced by, amongst others, Ian McBride.[16] Such an impact is harder to discern in Scotland, however, which is not to say that it did not exist, as Liam McIlvanney has recently emphasised in the case of Robert Burns or Colin

---

[10] See James Quinn, *Soul on Fire: a Life of Thomas Russell* (Dublin, 2002), pp. 126–8.

[11] Hamilton Rowan's mission was to challenge the Lord Advocate, Robert Dundas, for having characterised the United Irishmen as 'wretches' in his speech at the trial of Thomas Muir. He left Edinburgh without attending the British Convention, although Butler did attend briefly. See Meikle, *Scotland and the French Revolution*, p. 140, n. 1.

[12] See Meikle, *Scotland and the French Revolution*, pp. 190–1, n. 4; J. D. Brims, 'The Scottish Democratic Movement in the age of the French Revolution' (unpublished Ph.D. thesis, University of Edinburgh, 1983), p. 163.

[13] See esp. the discussion in McFarland, *Ireland and Scotland*, ch. 6.

[14] See Ian McBride, 'William Drennan and the Dissenting tradition', in Dickson et al. (eds), *The United Irishmen*, pp. 49–61.

[15] See esp. Richard B. Sher, *Church and University in the Scottish Enlightenment* (Edinburgh, 1985).

[16] Ian McBride, *Scripture Politics: Ulster Presbyterians and Irish Radicalism in the Later Eighteenth Century* (Oxford, 1998).

Kidd in the case of the Covenanting tradition.[17] We might also note in passing here, in a similar context, the links that existed between Scottish presbyterianism and the English dissenting reform tradition. Two figures who stand
out here are the schoolmaster and radical ideologue, James Burgh and the
Newcastle radical and independent presbyterian minister, James Murray.
Murray, a graduate of Edinburgh University, maintained close links in his
early years to several popular evangelical ministers back in Scotland. A member of Murray's High Bridge Street congregation in Newcastle was the land
reformer Thomas Spence, whose parents had come to Newcastle from,
respectively, Orkney and Aberdeen.[18] Thomas Hardy seems to represent
another, similarly overlooked link here, and his apocalyptic understanding of
events in the 1790s may well be traceable to his presbyterian education and
roots.[19]

   Political preoccupations and developments — the establishment of the
Scottish parliament in 1999 and the peace process in Ireland — have also,
however, played a role in influencing the direction of scholarship on this
topic. To some, Ireland's recent experience has appeared to constitute a
model for Scotland, and this has deepened preoccupation with the shared histories of the two 'Celtic' countries.[20] This paper is partly a counter-reaction
to these developments. Its modest ambitions are, more importantly, to begin to
map Scots–English connections in the reform politics of the decade; and,
secondly, to re-focus attention on the importance of English developments in
the history of Scottish radicalism in this period. If we wish fully to compre-
hend the British dimension to Scottish radical history in the 1790s, we need
to devote similar attention to the role of England and the English to that
which has been given in recent years to Ireland and the Irish.

   The influence of the English reform movement on the emergence of an
organised campaign for parliamentary reform in Scotland in the 1790s has
not always been fully appreciated, although it appears to have been a significant one. It signalled, firstly, the close linkages between the two countries in
reform politics in this period and, secondly, the fact that the revival of reform
south of the Border was closely watched by Scots. The minute book of the

---

[17] Liam McIlvanney, *Burns the Radical: Poetry and Politics in Later Eighteenth Century Scotland*
(East Linton, 2002). See also Colin Kidd, 'Conditional Britons: the Scots Covenanting tradition
and the eighteenth-century British state', *English Historical Review* 117 (2002), pp. 1147–76.
[18] See James Bradley, *Religion, Revolution and English Radicalism: Non Conformity in Eighteenth
Century Politics and Society* (Cambridge, 1990). For Murray's early links with evangelical ministers, see National Library of Scotland (NLS) MS 1954, Minutes of the Edinburgh Reformation of Manners Society, 1740–5.
[19] For evidence for this view, see British Library (BL) Add MS 27,811, ff. 19v–19r; The National
Archives (TNA) Kew, TS 11/953/3497.
[20] See e.g. Murray G. H. Pittock, *Celtic Identity and the British Image* (Manchester, 1999).

Edinburgh Friends of the People refers briefly and opaquely to the society's origins in 'sundry private, ad hoc meetings' and to 'an opportunity' occurring for the formation of a permanent body.[21] It was not simple coincidence, however, that this 'opportunity' followed on closely from the formation of the Whig Association of the Friends of the People in London, which is not to overlook the importance of purely Scottish factors, most notably the latest parliamentary defeat (on 18 April 1792) for the cause of burgh reform. The formation of the English body of moderate reformers formed, nevertheless, a crucial part of the immediate political context in which Scottish burgh reformers responded to this latest setback. The initial declaration and address of the Whig Friends of the People, agreed at its first meetings of 11 and 26 April, were widely reprinted in the Scottish press.[22] On 17 June, the leading burgh reformer Archibald Fletcher wrote to Robert Graham of Gartmore: 'The association of the Friends of the People is the only Party, who at present, points to any which so far as I can see, merits the attention of the people at large.' Fletcher talked of a similar association being planned for Scotland by a group of Edinburgh lawyers.[23] Another individual who commented at around the same time on the stimulus to Scotland's reformers provided by the Friends of the People in London was Colonel Norman Macleod. The Opposition Whig MP for Inverness-shire and a keen supporter of county and burgh reform, Macleod was also a member of the Whig Friends of the People, along with a considerable number of other Scottish advanced Whigs and reformers.[24] In a letter written from Edinburgh to Charles Grey, one of the leading figures behind the Whig Friends of the People, Macleod observed: 'Many of the most reputable people here have assured me that to the Association they owe the exertion of spirit which is now going on.'[25] The title chosen for the new Scottish reform body, the 'Associated Friends of the

[21] National Archives of Scotland (NAS) Justiciary Papers, JC 26/280, minute book of Society of the Friends of the People, 9 August – 25 September 1792.
[22] See e.g. *Glasgow Advertiser*, 11–14 and 14–18 May 1792; *Glasgow Mercury*, 1–8 May 1792.
[23] NAS Cunninghame Graham Muniments, GD 22/1/315: Fletcher to Graham of Gartmore, 17 June 1792. The only names which Fletcher mentioned were Erskine of Mar; Col. Fullarton; Col. Dalrymple; Robertson of Lude. He also called on Graham to add his name to the initiative.
[24] A list of the initial signatories of the declaration of the London Friends of the People can be found in *Political Papers, Chiefly Respecting the Attempt of the County of York, and other Considerable Districts . . . to Effect a Reformation of the Parliament of Great-Britain: collected by the Rev. Christopher Wyvill*, 4 vols (York, 1794–1802), III, pp. 129–31. The Scots included, as well as Macleod: Thomas Maitland; William Cunninghame; the Earl of Lauderdale; James Mackintosh; Thomas Christie; Malcolm Laing; Lord Kinnaird; Thomas Erskine; William Fullarton; Lord Daer; John Douglas; John Wilson; Andrew Stirling; James Perry; William Maxwell. There were also several Scottish non-resident members: the Earl of Buchan; John Millar; Robert Montieth and J. Richardson, both of Glasgow.
[25] Edward Hughes, 'The Scottish Reform Movement and Charles Grey 1792–94: some fresh correspondence', *Scottish Historical Review* 35 (1956), pp. 27–9: Macleod to Grey, 4 July 1792.

People', was symptomatic of the strong influence on Scottish reformers of the London body. The Edinburgh reformers were also quick to open a correspondence with the Whig Friends of the People.[26]

The pattern of events in Glasgow was broadly similar, and reinforces this picture of influence at a distance. In the same month that the Edinburgh Friends of the People was established, a much more shadowy group of reformers in Glasgow, the Glasgow Society for Effecting Constitutional and Parliamentary Reform, briefly flickered into life. Its members expressed their 'warmest sentiments of veneration and regard' for the Friends of the People in London, also resolving to be 'ready to correspond and act in conjunction with the other Associations formed in Great Britain' provided that these groups remained committed to moderate reform.[27] The beginning of October saw the establishment of the better-known Glasgow Associated Friends of the Constitution and of the People, which was the society of which Muir was a leading member. The society's published resolutions included one calling for co-operation with the Whig Friends of the People on parliamentary reform. On 17 October, it issued a vote of thanks to Charles Grey, while on 7 November the chairman and secretary wrote to the Friends of the People in London informing them of the establishment of the Glasgow society. Their society was, the letter declared, 'associated for the purpose of cooperating with the Friends of the People in London'.[28]

The alliance between Scotland's reformers and the Whig Friends of the People was based on ideology as well as strategy. The Scottish reformers, or at least their leaders, were moderates and included a significant advanced Whig element. They were keen to distance themselves from any suspicion of disloyalty or extremism. This was a key theme during the deliberations of the first national convention of Scottish Friends of the People, which met in Edinburgh between 11 and 13 December 1792. At this convention, the desire for continued co-operation with the London Friends was also clearly evident. The plan of petitioning parliament for reform in support of Charles Grey's expected reform motion received strong support from most delegates.[29] Perhaps more important in the present context, on 12 December, William Skirving made a series of far-reaching proposals for co-ordination of activ-

---

[26] NAS JC 26/80, letter from the Edinburgh Association to the General Association, 28 August 1792.

[27] The initial resolutions of the Society are the only evidence we possess of its existence. These are reproduced in Wyvill, *Political Papers*, III, p. 45. They were also published in the *Glasgow Courier*, 24 July 1792.

[28] Hughes, 'Scottish Reform Movement', pp. 29–30.

[29] See the detailed discussion of the convention in Brims, 'Scottish Democratic Movement', pp. 307–10.

ity with the London and English Friends of the People.[30] These proposals included sending several deputies to London to consult with the London Friends of the People. The deputies would consult with committees appointed in Scotland, which would meet on a weekly basis. Skirving also proposed a convention to meet to agree 'a common plan of operation' and to co-ordinate the presentation of reform petitions to parliament. These proposals have tended to be overlooked by historians, perhaps because nothing substantial came of them, although the convention did add a resolution on 13 December to its published resolutions, agreed to on the previous day, which included the commitment that 'this Convention will, as far as their principles and objects will allow them, co-operate with the Society of the FRIENDS of the PEOPLE in LONDON.' There was strong appreciation in Edinburgh of the advantages to be gained from establishing close links to English reformers. Skirving's proposals also have added significance in the light of his role from May 1793 in the planning of what became the British Convention of Radicals.

Links between the Whig and Scottish Friends of the People continued during 1793, but they were never to be as significant or smooth as they were in the final months of 1792. In January 1793, the Scottish reformers agreed a text for their petition for reform closely modelled on that of the Friends of the People in London. In May, following the failure of Grey's reform motion, the Whig Friends of the People voted a resolution of thanks to corresponding reform societies, including the Scottish Friends of the People. Copies of this were sent to the chairmen of the Edinburgh and Glasgow Friends of the People for circulation to reform societies throughout Scotland.[31] This represented, however, the end of something rather than its continuation. Following their parliamentary defeat, and in the face of mounting difficulties, the enthusiasm of the Friends of the People in London subsided sharply, and between June 1793 and January 1794, they failed even to meet.[32] Correspondence between Skirving and Daniel Stuart, secretary to the Whig

[30] Meikle, *Scotland and the French Revolution*, p. 255.
[31] 'The Second Report of the Commons Committee of Secrecy (1794)', Daniel Stuart to Charles Grey, 11 June 1794, in Michael T. Davis (ed.), *The London Corresponding Society, 1792–1799*, 6 vols (London, 2002), VI, p. 106. NAS JC 26/280, item 10, Vote of thanks of the Society of the Friends of the People to the Convention of Delegates at Edinburgh, 10 May 1793 (on the back of this document is a reference to several other communications, not identified, from various societies in England expressing approbation of the proceedings in Edinburgh and the resolutions reached at the Convention); item 13 (1), Daniel Stuart to Skirving, 28 May 1793. In his response to this letter of 5 June, Skirving informed Stuart that he had used the 'channel of newspapers' to communicate with the societies. He also noted the Edinburgh reformers' communications with Sheffield, Leeds, and 'some other places both in England and Irland [*sic*] Scotland': item 13 (2).
[32] P. J. Brunsdon, 'The Association of the Friends of the People 1792–1796' (M.A. thesis, University of Manchester, 1961), p. 243, cited in Brims, 'Scottish Democratic Movement', p. 424.

Friends of the People, persisted during the summer and autumn, but it increasingly reflected the distance which was opening up between the Scottish Friends of the People and Whig reformers.[33]

The Scottish reformers also, at an early stage, began to correspond with the more popular radical societies in England, including, most importantly, the London Corresponding Society. Significantly, in the light of later developments, the initiative behind the latter correspondence appears to have come from Thomas Hardy, the Scottish-born first secretary of the Society, often credited with being its founder. In June and July 1792, Hardy sent letters to several correspondents in Scotland informing them of the establishment of the London Corresponding Society and asking for information about reform activity in Scotland. One of these letters was sent to Lord Daer, eldest son of the Earl of Selkirk.[34] Daer, who had well-established connections to English reformist circles, was a member of the Whig Friends of the People and the Friends of the Liberty of the Press, and may have been a member of the Society for Constitutional Information.[35] He also joined the London Corresponding Society in May 1792 and was present at the first and third national conventions of the Scottish Friends of the People. In a postscript to his letter, Hardy requested Daer to keep him informed of the 'progress of liberty in Scotland'. On 17 January 1793, Daer wrote a lengthy letter to Charles Grey reflecting on the reform cause and on the need for close co-operation between reform societies in London and those whom he called 'the supporters of freedom at a distance'. Daer also floated the idea of holding a convention of radicals in England similar to that which had taken place in Edinburgh, which delegates from Scotland would attend as representatives of their individual societies. Daer held notably critical views of the union, but in his case, as with Muir, nationalist feelings were no impediment to thinking and acting as a British radical.[36]

Hardy wrote a further two letters to Daer in 1792, both dated 8 September, one in a private capacity and one in his 'official' role of secretary

---

[33] 'Second Report of the Commons Committee of Secrecy (1794)', pp. 104–6. See also the debate on the occasion of Pitt's presentation of the supplement to the second report of the committee of secrecy to the Commons: Davis (ed.), *London Corresponding Society*, VI, pp. 111–14.

[34] BL Add MS 27,811, f. 15, Hardy to Daer, 14 July 1792. See also ff. 12–13, Hardy to John Walker (Hardy's uncle), 4 June 1792. See also T. B. Howell and T. J. Howell (eds), *A Complete Collection of State Trials*, XXIV (1818), p. 375, copy of a letter to Mr Buchanan at Edinburgh, 20 August 1792.

[35] He was certainly present at two meetings of the society in April 1793: Howell and Howell (eds), *State Trials*, vol. 24, 549, 551. For further evidence of Daer's reform activities in London in 1792, see BL Add MS 27, 817, ff. 23–5. This concerns Daer's admission to a body called 'The London Society of the Friends of the People'. Unlike the Whig Friends of the People, this body committed itself to universal male suffrage. John Thelwall was another member.

[36] Hughes, 'Scottish Reform Movement', p. 33.

to the London Corresponding Society. In the former he mentioned that the Edinburgh bookseller Walter Berry had been introduced to the London Corresponding Society by fellow Scot Thomas Christie, a member of the Society.[37] Hardy wrote that the Society had been 'highly pleased with the informations' that Berry had 'communicated' from Scotland. He went on:

> If you now judge it proper and have opportunity to promote a correspondence between any of the societies in Scotland and the London Corresponding Society it will tend to cement us together for by uniting we shall become stronger and a threefold cord is not easily broken — It appears absolutely necessary by communicating with each other we shall know one another's mind and act with one heart in the same important cause.[38]

Such activity was symptomatic of the London Corresponding Society's goal of opening communications with radicals throughout Britain. In the autumn of 1792, reflecting this same impetus, Edinburgh radicals were invited to join the Society's address to the French Constituent Assembly. This was a step too far for the Scottish Friends of the People, and in a letter written on 31 October on their behalf Captain William Johnston declined the invitation.[39] Further letters to the Society were forthcoming from Paisley, Edinburgh, Glasgow, Dundee, and Banff during the winter of 1792–3.[40] This correspondence took place before 17 May 1793, when Hardy wrote to Skirving in Edinburgh soliciting his views about how to proceed following the defeat (on 7 May) of Grey's reform motion. It was this letter which led Skirving to resurrect his plans for organised links between the radical societies in Scotland and England, and which led, in turn, to the British Convention of Radicals.

The London Corresponding Society, which during 1793–4 took over from the Society for Constitutional Information as the pre-eminent reform society in London and which increasingly assumed a co-ordinating role in radical politics in Britain, was, from its inception, a genuinely British initiative.[41] This may have reflected Hardy's Scottishness, and indeed the extent of Scottish

---

[37] T. Christie, *Letters on the Revolution of France and on the New Constitution established by the National Assembly occasioned by the Writings of the Rt. Hon. Edmund Burke, M.P. and Alex. De Calonne, late Minister of State* (1791).

[38] BL Add MS 27,814, f. 184, copy of a private letter from Hardy to Lord Daer, 8 Sept. 1792; Add MS 27,811, f. 17, Hardy to Daer, 8 Sept. 1792.

[39] Mary Thale (ed.), *Selections from the Papers of the London Corresponding Society 1792–1799* (Cambridge, 1983), pp. 20–22, 26; TNA TS 11/965/3510A, Johnston to Hardy, 31 October 1792.

[40] Thale (ed.), *Selections*, pp. 31, 35, 44, 54.

[41] See the original proposals for the society: Howell and Howell (eds), *State Trials*, vol. 24, pp. 373–5. In a letter of 27 October 1791, Hardy included amongst some proposals for regulations for the society, 'That a society be instituted and called by the name of The Corresponding Society of the Unrepresented Part of the *People of Great Briton*' (my emphasis, BL Add MS, 27,811, f. 3).

influence in the early stages of the Society. This is a topic which has received scant comment in the existing literature. Scottish influence in the London Corresponding Society was, nevertheless, quite extensive, and there is no doubt that this facilitated the creation of connections between radicals across national boundaries. One early spy, a Captain Munro, who was himself Scottish, after visiting several divisions of the society, reported on 15 November 1792: 'I beg leave to remark that all the Divisions I have seen are attended by the very lowest tradesmen, and the most of them seem Scotch shoemakers.'[42] Several of the most active early members of the Society, in addition to Hardy, were Scots. They included Dr Robert Watson, erstwhile secretary to Lord George Gordon. Watson's radicalism was to lead him to confinement in Newgate for two years from November 1794. In 1797, he was present at Portsmouth during the naval mutinies, but not as an agent of the London Corresponding Society. After this, he went to Paris, where he joined Muir in urging a French invasion of Scotland.[43] Hardy later admitted to having been impressed by Gordon, and the activities of the Protestant Association may have formed an important bridge for Scots in London to the London Corresponding Society. We know that there was a significant Scottish contingent in the procession which accompanied Gordon to the House of Commons in 1780. One division of the London Corresponding Society left the society over the issue of the non-admission of a former attorney to Gordon. This division reconstituted under the title the 'British Citizens'.[44] Hardy's first assistant secretary was a Robert Littlejohn, who returned to Scotland in late 1792 under the threat of persecution from the authorities. Littlejohn was a delegate of a division which met at the 'Scotch Arms'.[45] Another Scot who was active in the society in its early stages was a Robert Thompson. An auctioneer by trade and a poet, he was responsible for the radical anthem 'God Save the Rights of Man'. He again fled under threat of official harassment, but to France where he set up as a bookseller, apparently successfully. Thompson was later to be identified by Hardy as one of three individuals, including himself, who had been the moving forces behind the establishment of the London Corresponding Society.[46]

These individuals almost certainly represent the tip of an iceberg; behind them are those who can only be glimpsed in the historical record and for

---

[42] Thale (ed.), *Selections*, pp. 27–8.
[43] For Watson's political career, see Graham Bain, *The Thunderbolt of Reason* (Elgin, 1996).
[44] Thale (ed.), *Selections*, pp. 50–1, 52, 54, 55–6.
[45] Thale (ed.), *Selections*, p. 29 n. 126, p. 35. Littlejohn was one of the members of the LCS who was elected as an associate member of the SCI in 1792. He objected strongly to his discharge from the society on his return to Scotland protesting his undimished commitment to the cause: Howell and Howell (eds), *State Trials*, vol. 24, p. 792.
[46] Thale (ed.), *Selections*, p. 42, n. 7.

whom we lack further information. A loose coterie of Scottish radicals may
have persisted in London into the early 1800s. In 1802, Thomas Hardy was
involved in the establishment of a society in London dedicated to the memory of the 'Great Scottish Patriot', William Wallace, which met for a com-
memorative dinner in that year. The toasts given on that occasion made clear
the radical or reformist character of the initiative. Significantly, in the context
of the theme of this paper, they included one to the 'Great Alfred', viewed in
radical circles as the founder of English, or perhaps more usually by this date
British, liberty.[47]

Connections between the Scottish Friends of the People and the London
Corresponding Society do not represent the totality of cross-border contacts
with the popular radical societies in this early phase of open radical cam-
paigning, although there is only limited evidence about this. In July 1792,
Walter Miller from Perth wrote to John Horne Tooke of the Society for Constitutional Information regarding the popularity and influence of Paine's
Rights of Man in the Perth area.[48] Whether this was the first or last contact
between the two is not known. In March 1793, the same society received a letter from Edinburgh regarding recent trials of radicals in the Edinburgh High
Court.[49] Communications were opened with several English provincial radical societies. In October 1792, Matthew Campbell Browne, the editor of the
Sheffield radical periodical, the *Patriot*, wrote to the London Corresponding
Society informing them of the recent upsurge in radical activity in
Edinburgh. The letter also declared that the Sheffield radicals had been
impressed by 'some most spirited communications' from Edinburgh, which
led to the observation:

> We clearly foresee that Scotland will soon take the lead of this country, and
> conceive it will be necessary to take the greatest care that an universal commu-
> nication should be constantly kept up between the several societies, however
> distant, and that all should determine to act upon the same principle, and move
> together, as near as may be, in regular and active unison.[50]

Early issues of the *Edinburgh Gazetteer*, the main Scottish radical newspaper of the period, included news of events in Sheffield, which were

[47] BL Add MS 27,818, f. 38, Hardy to A. Grant, 23 April 1802; f. 39, Grant to Hardy, 27 April
1802; f. 43, description of meeting held on 22 November 1802. Other toasts were to 'William
Tell', 'Carracticus', 'General Washington', and to 'The good men of all nations'.
[48] TNA TS 11/3495.
[49] *Morning Chronicle*, 15 March 1793.
[50] 'Second Report of the Commons Committee of Secrecy (1794)', copy of a Letter from the
Editors of the *Patriot* to the secretary of the London Corresponding Society, Sheffield, 15
October 1792, in Davis (ed.), *London Corresponding Society*, VI, pp. 69–70.

probably communicated through the same channels.[51] In April 1793, the Sheffield Constitutional Society sent two letters to Skirving enclosing, respectively, printed copies of its petition on parliamentary reform and its resolutions on peace. With respect to the latter, the Sheffield reformers urged the desirability of radicals in Britain forming a common front and united campaign.[52] On 10 May, Skirving wrote back to the Sheffield Constitutional Society enclosing a copy of the *Caledonian Chronicle* which contained the resolutions of the Scottish Friends of the People agreed to at their second national convention in Edinburgh. The Sheffield society, like the London Corresponding Society, was, as referred to above, actively promoting correspondence between radical societies throughout Britain, and later in May, in response to this, a letter was sent by the Leeds Constitutional Society to Skirving as President of the Scottish Friends of the People.[53] In July, a radical society in Nottingham made contact with Skirving. The Leeds society had links in the same period with Glasgow reformers.[54]

The story of the British Convention has been carefully told elsewhere, most recently by Albert Goodwin and John Barrell, and there is no need to rehearse it in detail here.[55] Several points, however, do deserve special emphasis. The first is Skirving's role in driving forward his vision of Anglo-Scots radical co-operation, a vision which culminated in the visit of the four English delegates to Scotland in late 1793.[56] Secondly, in London it was Hardy who seems to have been crucially responsible for imparting energy to the London radicals' response to Skirving's initiative. Hardy pressed for English delegates to be sent to Edinburgh, and was instrumental in organis-

---

[51] See *Edinburgh Gazetteer*, 7 December 1792; 22 January 1793.

[52] NAS JC 26/280, Bundle 1, item 2, letter from William Camage to Skirving, 17 April 1793; item 3, letter from Camage to Skirving, 24 April 1793.

[53] 'Second Report of the Commons Committee of Secrecy (1794)', Delegate Meeting of the Constitutional Society, Leeds, 29 May 1793, in Davis (ed.), *London Corresponding Society*, VI, p. 92.

[54] For Nottingham, see NAS JC 26/280, Bundle 1, item 14, letter from Nottingham society to Skirving, 6 July 1793 (the actual letter is at the time of writing missing from the bundle). For Leeds, see copy of a letter from the Secretary of the Constitutional Society at Leeds to the Secretary of the Society for Constitutional Information, 21 July 1793: 'Second Report of the Commons Committee of Secrecy (1794)', in Davis (ed.), *London Corresponding Society*, VI, p. 83.

[55] John Barrell, *Imagining the King's Death: Figurative Treason, Fantasies of Regicide 1793–1796* (Oxford, 2000), ch. 4; Albert Goodwin, *The Friends of Liberty: the English Democratic Movement in the Age of the French Revolution* (London, 1979), ch. 8.

[56] See esp. Skirving's letter of 25 May to Hardy, contained in the Second Report of the Commons Committee of Secrecy, Davis (ed.), *London Corresponding Society*, vol. VI, pp. 79–80. See NAS JC 26/280, bundle 1, item 30, Hardy to Skirving, 5 October 1793, where Hardy informed Skirving that the notion of a convention was supported by him and Margarot but now needed to be communicated officially to the London Corresponding Society.

ing the outdoor meeting held on 24 October 1793 at which the two delegates from the London Corresponding Society were elected.[57] Thirdly, the plans for a union of radicals met a generally strongly positive response from Scottish radicals looking for a new sense of direction following the cumulative set-backs of 1793. Plans for closer co-operation between radicals in different parts of Britain appear to have been widely discussed in the autumn of 1793. In mid-October, a meeting of the Fife radical societies advocated the estab-lishment of committees of correspondence in different parts of Britain.[58] Around a month earlier, one radical wrote from Cromarty of the advantages which union promised to their cause. 'This union betwixt the two nations', he enthused, 'shall not, like the former [i.e. the Union of 1707] be effected by the distribution of sordid gold; but result from the genuine impulses of Patriotism, uniformly tending to one centre.'[59] Skirving's plans for union were, therefore, working closely with the grain of radical opinion in Scotland.[60] During the Convention itself, the proposals for a union met with unanimous support, albeit there were divisions about the precise mechanisms for calling further British radical conventions. One of the divisions, or 'sec-tions', in which delegates met in the mornings, drew up a document entitled 'Hints on the Question of Union'. The first of these hints read:

> That the people of Great Britain, (disclaiming every distinction of Scots & English,) from this Period, & forever; doe unite themselves into one Mass, & in an Indissoluble Union, Boldly appeal to this Island & to the Universe; that they demand the restoration of the Rights, from which demand they shall never depart.

In order to achieve this end, the division recommended that delegates from national conventions in England and Scotland meet twice yearly on the banks of the River Tweed. This would be a symbolic meeting place 'where the Ashes of their Ancestors now Lye', ancestors who had been condemned to die because of the 'caprice of the few in the Paltry Feuds of Court Etiquette'. It was also suggested that a weekly communication be opened up between 'South' and 'North' either by letter or in person so that 'Occurrences maybe known from one end of the Kingdom to the other' in order to 'strengthen & Instruct every individual of this great but one indivisible Mass'.[61]

---

[57] Another historian who has emphasised these points is Alexander Murdoch, 'Scotland and the Idea of Britain', in T. M. Devine and J. R. Young (eds), *Eighteenth Century Scotland: New Perspectives* (East Linton, 1999), p. 108.

[58] NAS JC 26/280, bundle 2, item 16.

[59] NAS JC 26/280, Bundle 1, item 22, letter from [?] Calder, Cromarty to Skirving, 4 Sept. 1793.

[60] The language of 'union' did cause some concern amongst Dundee radicals, but this was focused on the terms of union which was proposed. See NAS JC 26/280, bundle 2, item 31, letter from Dundee, 14 November 1793.

[61] NAS JC 26/280, loose papers, 'Hints on the Question of Union Suggested by Class No. 3'.

Fourthly, the months between the Convention and the arrest of Hardy and other radicals in London and other parts of Britain in May 1794 represented the apogee of links, real and planned, between radical groups throughout the British Isles during the open phase of radical agitation. Against the background of common threats of official repression and harassment, radicals quickly recognised the necessity for association and correspondence over and above the desirability of union which had been identified from the outset of the radical campaign, and which had its roots in the reform politics of the early 1780s. It was official harassment which imparted the impetus behind the plans for a further British convention in the spring of 1794, plans which got as far as the election of delegates in Scotland and England, and which have their immediate roots in the idea of the emergency convention put in motion at Edinburgh.[62]

Official harassment drew radicals and reformers from different countries together in other ways. During the winter of 1793–4, the opposition Whigs in London, along with several radical and reform societies, took up the cause of Thomas Fyshe Palmer and Thomas Muir, the first two Scottish martyrs for the cause of liberty.[63] London, with its vastness and potential for anonymity, and its guarantee of radical fellowship, also served as a refuge to a number of Scots fleeing repression in Edinburgh. Daniel Isaac Eaton's bookshop in London acted as a magnet to advanced radicals from throughout the British Isles, and we know that several Scottish radicals found their way there in 1794.[64] One of these was James Kennedy, assistant secretary to the British Convention, who fled Edinburgh following the exposure of the so-called Watt Plot.[65] Kennedy may have been the 'very violent Democrat' from Scotland referred to in a spy report on a division of the London Corresponding

---

[62] A printed letter from Hardy calling for elections of delegates to a new convention was distributed in Scotland via Edinburgh. It was certainly sent to Perth, Paisley, and Strathaven, and may have been sent to Dundee: Howell and Howell (eds), *State Trials*, vol. 24, pp. 116–17, 118–19, 841. James Wilson of Strathaven was elected a delegate by the united societies of Strathaven, Kilmarnock, Galston, Newmills, and Derwall. Provincial conventions to elect delegates were held in Glasgow, Perth, and Fife. See also NLS Melville Papers, MS 351, f. 15.

[63] See Thale (ed.), *Selections*, p. 124. For an address of thanks to the martyrs by the SCI on 28 March 1794, see Howell and Howell (eds), *State Trials*, vol. 24, pp. 561–2. Some popular radicals were evidently suspicious of the closeness of the relationship between Muir and Palmer and the opposition Whigs. On this, see esp. John Martin to Maurice Margarot, 22 January 1794, where Martin wrote: 'Between us, Muir and Palmer have put themselves into the hands of the opposition who, I fear, will use their case no farther than as an argument to help themselves into administration': Howell and Howell (eds), *State Trials*, vol. 24, pp. 478–9.

[64] Michael T. Davis, ' "That Odious Class of Men called Democrats": Daniel Isaac Eaton and the Romantics, 1794–1795', *History* 84 (1999), pp. 74–92.

[65] James Kennedy, *TREASON!!! OR, NOT TREASON!!! Alias the Weaver's Budget. By James Kennedy, Scotch Exile* (1794?). For Kennedy, see Barrell, *Imagining the King's Death*, pp. 116–18, 254.

Society from early June 1794. This individual talked, apparently, of 'the Scotch to be in great force, and resolved on obtaining a reform and redress of their Grievances, that they would long ago have proceeded to violent measures but that they had been induced to wait from the favourable Reports they had heard of the London Corresponding Society . . .'.[66] Alexander Scott, charged with seditious libel for reports on the British Convention printed in the *Edinburgh Gazetteer*, fled to London and to Eaton's shop. Arrested in London, he was subsequently released on agreeing to act as an informer.[67] Other Scottish radicals who fled to the relative safety of the British capital in the same period included Thomas Muir's solicitor, William Moffatt, who became a member of the London Corresponding Society, and George Ross, who had been a clerk working on the *Edinburgh Gazetteer*. Moffatt had been secretary of the Portsburgh Society of the Scottish Friends of the People and was a delegate at the second and third national and British conventions. Ross was arrested in London in 1794, but appears to have been released without trial. Like Moffatt, he became a member of the London Corresponding Society and later publisher of several radical London newspapers, including the *Albion* (1799–1801), owned and edited by another Scot, Allan Macleod.[68] Another radical who may have found refuge in London later in the decade was Angus Cameron, the suspected United Scotsman and a key figure in stirring up opposition to the Militia Act in Perthshire in 1797.[69]

Government repression and the trials of 1794 delivered a severe check to radicalism throughout Britain, and to the plans for a national (meaning British) union of reformers. Tracing connections between radicals in Scotland and England from this point onwards becomes more difficult, not least because radical activity tended to become less coherent, but also because it became less open and more elusive in significance as physical force activists gained greater prominence. A good starting point, however, is a letter sent by Robert Sands to the secretary of the London Corresponding Society in mid-October 1795.[70]

Sands, a Perth weaver, had come to the fore in local and national radical circles in 1793–4. He was present at the second and third national

[66] Thale (ed), *Selections*, p. 177.
[67] TNA HO 42/33, Paul Le Mesurier to John King, 26, 27 August 1794.
[68] On 9 January 1794, Moffatt, present at a General Committee of the London Corresponding Society, was described as the 'Delegate of the Scotch Convention': Thale (ed.), *Selections*, p. 105. For Ross, see Thale (ed.), *Selections*, pp. 188, 212. Macleod was editor of another London paper, the *Gazetteer*, in 1797. As owner and editor of the *Albion*, he was repeatedly prosecuted, spending three and a half years in Newgate. He was pardoned in 1804 and died in Edinburgh in 1805.
[69] See BL Add MS 27,818, f. 169: Hardy to [?], March 1814.
[70] BL Add MS 27,815, ff. 5–6, Sands to John Ashley, 19 October 1795.

conventions and the British convention, and was detained as part of the wave of arrests of radicals which followed the revelation of the Watt Plot. He was an important figure in the Scottish radical circles which survived, albeit in largely unorganised form, the repression of the mid-1790s. What provided the immediate stimulus to his sending the letter in 1795 is unclear. During 1795–6, however, the London Corresponding Society, as part of its effort to recover from the setback of the Treason trials of late 1794, was seeking to re-open communications with radicals in other parts of Britain. In May 1795, an address was sent by the society to the 'Scotch Patriotic Societies'. This spoke of 'the renewal of a correspondence which has been so long inter-rupted'.[71] On 3 September, the Dundee radical George Mealmaker sent a let-ter to the Society via an individual named Gilchrist. The response to this letter evidently failed to reach Mealmaker, and he wrote again to the society on 21 November.[72]

Sands's intervention should be seen, therefore, against the background of this re-opening of communications and renewed reform activity. Like Mealmaker, his letter was sent via Gilchrist, which suggests a degree of co-ordination between Sands and Mealmaker. Sands and Mealmaker had a sig-nificant record of co-operation in radical activity. In June 1794, both had been arrested in Arbroath, where they had fled to the safety, or so they hoped, of Sands's father's house following the renewed round of official repression of radicalism which followed the discovery of the Watt Plot. Some time in 1796–7, Mealmaker became a leading member of the United Scotsmen, a move which Sands resisted; in 1798 Sands was to give evidence against Mealmaker in the latter's trial for treason.[73] In November 1795, another let-ter was sent to the London Corresponding Society from Perth from a group calling itself the 'Friends of Liberty, Peace, and Humanity', but internal evi-dence suggests that this was an independent initiative which had no link to Sands's communication.[74] This may, in turn, be an indication of the fragmented and ill-coordinated condition of Scottish radicalism at this time.

In his letter Sands described the condition of the reformers in and around Perth — still committed but cowed by 'a banditti of armed ruffians', probably a reference to troops who, against the background of unrest over rising meal prices, were a source of great tension in the town in the second half of 1795.[75]

---

[71] Thale (ed.), *Selections*, p. 242; Davis (ed.), *London Corresponding Society*, II, pp. 132–3. Where in Scotland this address was received is unknown.

[72] Davis (ed.), *London Corresponding Society*, II, pp. 165–7; III, pp. 125–6; Thale (ed.), *Selections*, pp. 308, 333.

[73] Howell and Howell (eds), *State Trials*, vol. 26, p. 1154.

[74] Davis (ed.), *London Corresponding Society*, III, pp. 127–8.

[75] See C. A. Whatley, *Scottish Society 1707–1830: Beyond Jacobitism, Towards Industrialisation* (Manchester, 2000), p. 303.

He also referred to the failure by the Perth reformers to respond to an earlier letter from the London Corresponding Society — which does not survive — calling for financial contributions to help with defence costs at the Treason trials of 1794. It was, however, Sands's appreciation of the importance of the London Corresponding Society and developments in London that was the most striking element of what he wrote, and this section of the letter merits quotation in full:

> We look up with anxiety to the London Corresponding Society, and the Others who have affiliated with them. We know the whole depends on their exertions, and that without them nothing can be done. It is an old doctrine of mine that the Metropolis is the same to a Nation as the heart is to the body. It is the seat of life. If it is pure the whole body must be so, and vice versa. If the Channel of corruption is not stopt [sic] in London, you cannot expect it so in Perth or any where else. The heavy part of the burthen must lye on your shoulders, but you may be sure we will not be the last to help to take the load.

Sands also mentioned a manuscript of a small pamphlet which he had sent in the previous year to the radical publisher in London, John Smith. To date, he had received no response about this. It had been sent in a cask directed to a Mr Grant's in Charing Cross Road. Sands urged the secretary of the society to make use of it as he saw fit, but that if he was to have it printed to ensure that at least a hundred copies were sent to him.

Efforts at communication between the London Corresponding Society and the Scottish radicals continued into 1796. In April of that year, the society issued a further address to the people of Scotland, this one in response to a letter from Edinburgh reporting on the decline of reform societies in Scotland. Money was collected from Edinburgh, Perth, Stirling, and Paisley to help defray the costs of the defence of John Binns and John Gales Jones, who were facing trials for sedition following their arrest on embassies from the London Corresponding Society to reform societies in Birmingham. *The Moral and Political Magazine of the London Corresponding Society*, which began publication in July, was also circulated in Scotland.[76] In the following year, the society sent an agent to Edinburgh and Glasgow, where he was closely watched by the authorities, only escaping arrest by turning informer in Glasgow.[77]

The above details furnish several important pieces of information about the nature of the contacts between the London Corresponding Society and Scottish radicals in the mid-1790s. On the one hand, they suggest something of their tenuous nature. Correspondence was intermittent, and on occasion interrupted. Certainly, there was no faith in the post office, reasonably so

---

[76] Thale (ed.), *Selections*, pp. 360, 371.
[77] Meikle, *Scotland and the French Revolution*, p. 186.

since it was systematically intercepted by the authorities.[78] Communication depended, as a result, on personal contacts, and Scots present in the metropolis facilitated such connections. 'Citizen Gilchrist' was just such an individual, and was very likely to have been a member of the London Corresponding Society. There was, however, also a continuing commitment in Scottish radical circles to the desirability (and necessity) of maintaining links with the London and English radical societies.

A further perspective on Scottish–English connections in radical politics at this time is provided by the career of Alexander Leslie, a bookseller from Edinburgh who was arrested for treasonable activities in late 1797 as part of a wider clampdown on radical activity triggered by the anti-militia riots of that year and anxiety about the activities of the United Scotsmen. Bailed to appear in court, he fled Edinburgh, and a verdict of outlawry was passed in his absence in May 1798.[79]

Surviving details about Leslie are scanty, although we know from his own testimony that he was a native of Jedburgh and that he had arrived in the Scottish capital some time in the early 1790s to take up a position as an apprentice shoemaker.[80] There is no independent record of his involvement in the earlier phase of radical politics, although he claimed to have been forced to quit his apprenticeship because of political harassment, a claim which suggests that he was involved in radicalism in the early 1790s. By 1796 he was established in Nicolson Street as a bookseller. In that year, he wrote to the London Corresponding Society offering to act as their agent, boasting of his contacts throughout much of Lowland Scotland.[81] It was a role which the London Corresponding Society was happy for him to adopt, at least initially.[82] In 1797, as referred to above, the London Corresponding Society sent an agent to Scotland, and he found his way to Leslie's bookshop, a bookshop which was described by one radical as a haunt of 'democrats'.[83]

What stands out about Leslie in the present context is the range of his contacts with radicals both south and north of the Border. Leslie dealt closely with several important radical printers and booksellers from London, notably Eaton, but also John Smith, referred to above, J. S. Jordan, John

[78] As early as 1793, radicals were not entrusting their correspondence to the post office.

[79] NAS JC 26/293, Petition of Alexander Leslie to the Lord Justice Clerk and Lords Commissioners of Justiciary for Scotland, 2 April 1798; Minute Book of the High Court of Justiciary, 30 October 1797–25 July 1799.

[80] BL Add MS 27,815, ff. 74–5.

[81] See n. 84, below.

[82] Thale (ed.), *Selections*, pp. 370, 381.

[83] For the agent's presence in Leslie's shop, see NAS JC 26/293, 'Excerpts of Sales taken from the Day Book of Alexander Leslie'. NAS JC 26/281, Thomas McCleish to George Mealmaker, Edinburgh, 20 July 1797.

Bone, and Thomas Evans, all members of the London Corresponding Society.[84] He also had links with Thomas Spence. At several times during this period, he dispatched large orders of pamphlets to Eaton, Smith, Jordan, Bones, and Evans, as well as to John Ashley, the then secretary of the London Corresponding Society. His customers in Scotland included leading radicals throughout Lowland Scotland, including Sands and James Wilson of Strathaven, the radical martyr of 1820.

Leslie was joint publisher of several pamphlets with London's radical printing fraternity, further emphasising the closeness of the connections between them. John Martin's *A Letter to the Hon. Thomas Erskine, with a Postscript to the Right Hon Lord Kenyon, upon their Conduct at the Trial of Thomas Williams for Publishing Paine's Age of Reason* (1796) was published by Leslie in collaboration with Smith, Bone, Evans, and T. G. Ballard. He also published several works on his own account, including Edinburgh editions of Paine's *Agrarian Justice* and *A Letter to George Washington, on the Subject of the late Treaty Concluded between Great Britain and the United States of America*; a translation of Helvetius' *Catechism*; a number of radical poems; and a song book published in parts, the title of which was *Patriot Songs; or Patriotic Musical Companion*. All of these works were sent south to London's radical booksellers, as well as to booksellers and radicals in different parts of Scotland.

Leslie was a republican and a deist. It is also highly probable that he was a member of the United Scotsmen. In August 1797, a fellow radical wrote to him from Linlithgow: 'I think the Soceity [*sic*] in London is doing well. I hope they give Arastockrats [*sic*] a Sweet very Soone . . .'.[85] This may indicate links to the United Englishmen. He was frequent visitor to Glasgow — on one trip there he got married — visiting radical groups in various places *en route*. Among the pamphlets seized from his shop were two in the name of the British Union Society, a breakaway group from the London Corresponding Society of impatient extremists formed in August 1797. Both pamphlets were signed by the society's president and secretary.[86]

Leslie's short career as radical bookseller underlines several of the points already emphasised, notably the efforts by Scottish radicals to renew links to the London Corresponding Society following the demoralising blow of the suppression of the British Convention. In the case of Leslie, there are hints of links to ultra-radical circles in London. The scope and nature of his

---

[84] These connections are revealed in NAS JC 26/293, 'Excerpts of Sales taken from the Day Book of Alexander Leslie'.
[85] NAS JC 26/293, William Hinselwood, Linlithgow, to Alexander Leslie, August 1797.
[86] *Constitution of the British United Society 1797*; *An Address to the Nation from the British Union Society*. Leslie claimed that they had been left in his shop on one of his visits to Glasgow.

publishing interests also emphasise, however, the importance of a further facet of Scottish–English relations in the reform and radical politics of the decade — the role of print in creating bridges across national boundaries. It is this latter area which provides the focus for the final section of this chapter.

Correspondence and personal contacts across national boundaries were intermittent; the flow of print, in both ways, was continual. This gave print added importance in facilitating and rendering visible — to radicals as well as others — a radical struggle conducted throughout the Britain and Ireland, and indeed further afield. Radical and other newspapers, periodicals, and pamphlets published in England (and in Ireland, although to a lesser extent) were very widely circulated and read in Scotland. As indicated by the scope of Leslie's business and political contacts, radical pamphlets published in London continued to be available in Edinburgh and other Scottish towns and cities even after the repression of 1793–4. How far this was the case at the very end of the decade, when, as elsewhere in the British Isles, booksellers became much more wary about handling such material, the current state of research makes it impossible to say, although there are indications that some booksellers could still be encouraged to do so.[87] Meanwhile, radical newspapers from London and the English provinces found an eager readership in Scotland. They included the extreme London radical papers, the *Courier*, and, later in the decade, *Albion*, and, from provincial printers, the *Sheffield Register*, the *Manchester Herald*, and the *Newcastle Chronicle*.[88] In the mid-1790s, James Montgomery's *Sheffield Iris* was read in Glasgow and other parts of the country.[89] In 1797, a correspondent from Glasgow wrote of the 'very extensive circulation' of the *Chester Chronicle* 'among the friends of humanity'.[90] The opposition Whig reformist *Morning Chronicle* was very widely read north of the Border and regularly contained correspondence and news from Scotland. In 1793, the Reverend Thomas Fyshe Palmer wrote several letters to the paper complaining of his treatment by the Scottish legal system, a cause which, as mentioned above, was enthusiastically embraced by the opposition Whigs in London.[91] Letters from other Scottish radical sup-

---

[87] See the correspondence between John Millar and the Reverend Christopher Wyvill about arrangements for the dissemination of a pamphlet by the latter in Scotland in 1800. The booksellers had to be offered full profit from the venture to encourage their participation: Wyvill, *Political Papers*, VI, pp. 95–105.
[88] M. J. Smith, 'English Radical Newspapers in the French Revolutionary Era, 1790–1803' (Unpublished Ph.D. thesis, University of London, 1979), ch. 4.
[89] *Sheffield Iris*, 6 February, 3 July 1795; 1 January, 1 July, 30 December 1796; 30 June 1797.
[90] *Chester Chronicle*, 17 February 1797, quoted in Smith, 'English Radical Newspapers', p. 177.
[91] Fyshe Palmer to Chairman of the Society for Constitutional Information, 16 April 1794, Davis (ed.), *London Corresponding Society*, V, pp. 112–13.

porters appeared in this paper.[92] The *Edinburgh Gazetteer* and *Caledonian Mercury*, the two Scottish radical newspapers, were, meanwhile, circulated in radical circles south of the Border.[93]

Facts such as these actually underestimate the extent to which, through the press, Scottish radicals (and indeed non-radicals) were joined to circuits of communication which were British, if not European-wide, in scope. This reality can be traced in several ways. Scottish radical resolutions were commonly sent to newspapers south as well as north of the Border, while some English resolutions appeared in Scottish papers.[94] Items first printed in Scottish newspapers quite regularly appeared in English ones, and vice versa. In 1797, a 'citizen of Glasgow' wrote to the *Scots Chronicle* with rules for establishing working-class reading societies. This letter was subsequently reprinted in the *Manchester Gazette*, the *Chester Chronicle*, the *Telegraph*, the *Courier*, the *Monthly Magazine*, and the London Corresponding Society's *Moral and Political Magazine*.[95] Items in Scottish newspapers appear to have been quite regularly responded to in English ones. In 1793, for example, a vigorous controversy over the peace petition organised in Glasgow spread from the Glasgow press on to the pages of the *Morning Chronicle*.[96]

The full extent of cross-Border collaboration in the area of radical printing and publishing remains to be uncovered. A good example, however, of this practice from the open phase of Scottish and British radicalism was the production of printed accounts of the Scottish trials of radicals from 1793 to 1794, starting with Fyshe Palmer and Muir. Within radical circles, there was an understandable anxiety to ensure that accurate and fair versions of these trials found their way into print. This was also prompted by the rush to publish similar accounts, some from hostile sources. To counteract these, and to ensure that 'truthful' versions of the trials were available, the radicals organised their own printed accounts. The London Corresponding Society sent a member with shorthand skills to Scotland, William Ramsay, to record the events in court. The account of Fyshe Palmer's trial appears to have been organised by his fellow radical Skirving, and included the defence that

---

[92] See e.g. *Morning Chronicle*, 9 August; 16 August; 7 September; 11 October; 15 November 1793.

[93] For circulation of the *Gazetteer* in English radical circles, see, respectively, NAS JC 26/280, bundle 1, item 62, William Camage to Skirving, 14 November 1793; Howell and Howell (eds), *State Trials*, vol. 24, pp. 428–9, 435–6, 483–4, 487–8, 1354.

[94] See my 'Representing Revolution: Scotland's newspapers and the French Revolution' (unpublished paper).

[95] Smith, 'English Radical Newspapers', p. 162.

[96] *Morning Chronicle*, 16 August 1793; *Glasgow Courier*, 13, 16, 18, 20, 27 July, 17 August 1793.

Palmer would have given in court had he not employed a counsel.[97] The printer of the resulting trial narratives was James Robertson, who, along with Walter Berry, had been tried for seditious libel in early 1793 and who, again with Berry, had been responsible for the publication of the short-lived radical paper, the *Caledonian Chronicle*. Produced in Edinburgh, they were sold through a series of booksellers with radical sympathies in Scotland and London and Sheffield.[98]

The Border between Scotland and England was, therefore, one which was frequently crossed in the radical and reform politics of the 1790s, in the imagination as well as in reality. This chapter has mapped some of the resulting connections, but by no means all of them. In the 1800s, Hardy continued to maintain links, through correspondence, to radical friends in different parts of Scotland, many of whom shared, with Hardy, a background in the struggles of the French Revolutionary era.[99] The Reverend Christopher Wyvill was corresponding in the later 1790s and early 1800s with Professor John Millar and the Earl of Buchan as he sought to renew the cause of moderate reform after a decade of disappointments and frustration.[100] Little has been said about the connections which may have existed in the later 1790s and early 1800s in the context of insurrectionary ambitions amongst radicals, although it was touched on very briefly in the case of Alexander Leslie. Evidence of such links is, of course, patchy and usually elusive in significance. On the other hand, most insurrectionary conspiracy from this period was conceived of as British-wide in scope, even if in practice the linkages between conspirators in different parts of the British Isles seem to have been notably tenuous, a pattern which was to be repeated in the later 1810s.[101]

The tendency to forge links across national boundaries stemmed in part from the very close links between Scottish and English political life, and the growing integration of Scotland into English (or in some contexts British) political life in the later eighteenth century, a trend exemplified by the mem-

---

[97] *The Trial of the Rev. Thomas Fyshe Palmer, Before the Circuit Court of Justiciary, Held at Perth, on the 12th and 13th of September, 1793, on an Indictment for Seditious Practices* (Edinburgh, 1793).

[98] See the advertisements for Muir's trial in the *Morning Chronicle*, 9 September 1793. Agents for Fyshe Palmer's trial were James Robertson and Walter Berry in Edinburgh; Robert Galloway in Glasgow; Edward Leslie in Dundee; George McFarlane in Perth; and H. D. Symonds, James Ridgway and Marson and Ramsay in London.

[99] Correspondents included the Paisley radical Archibald Hastie, and the Glasgow radical John Richardson.

[100] Wyvill, *Political Papers*, VI. Other Scottish correspondents of Wyvill were Colin Maclaurin, son of the famous mathematician; and Anderson, the biographer of Smollett.

[101] See W. M. Roach, 'Alexander Richmond and the radical reform movement in Glasgow in 1816–17', *Scottish Historical Review* 51 (1972), pp. 2–19; F. K. Donnelly, 'The Scottish rising of 1820: a re-interpretation', *Scottish Tradition* 6 (1976) pp. 27–37.

bership of the Whig Association of the Friends of the People. A factor which may have reinforced this tendency was the sense on the part of some Scots of their relative lack of experience in reform politics. As Lord Daer wrote in early 1793: 'One of the greatest Bonds of Union betwixt the two nations at present is that the Reformers here feel they have need to lean upon you. If it be possible once to teach them that they can take the lead many may be for bidding you farewell.'[102] In the late 1770s and early 1780s, Scottish reformers had not been indifferent to reform politics in England, and connections had begun to be made between burgh and county reformers, but these were limited in scope. Indeed, it was only in the later stages of the Association Movement that Scottish grievances began to be incorporated in Wyvill's reform campaign.[103] For tactical reasons, after 1785 the Scottish county and burgh reformers also quickly distanced themselves from this connection. If we are looking for precedents in Scotland for this tendency, we may be better looking elsewhere, to, for example, parliamentary lobbying, which from an early stage was often organised on a British scale, or to philanthropic campaigns, which were often British-wide, or even more significantly in the context of the emerging radical movement to the abolitionists from 1787.

Whatever its causes, Scottish radicals were, like their counterparts in other parts of the British Isles, quick to recognise the advantages of co-operation and co-ordination. It would perhaps be pushing the point a little far to say that Scotland's contribution to the radical politics of the decade was the notion of the convention, although the first main articulation of the idea in reform propaganda was by a Scot, James Burgh (in 1775). Scots were, nevertheless, very active in promoting the idea in the early 1790s, as we have seen, notably Lord Daer and William Skirving and, in London, Thomas Hardy. Thomas Muir was another Scottish advocate of a national (meaning British) convention.[104] It is tempting to suggest that here was another case of the Scots being better Britons than the English. Against this, however, English reformers were discussing the idea of a convention before the spring of 1793, although it is not clear that they were thinking of including Scots; they also tended to discuss it as an ultimate rather than immediate objective. As we saw earlier, the Sheffield Constitutional Society were also firm

[102] Hughes, 'Scottish Reform Movement', p. 37.
[103] See esp. Wyvill to Professor Dunbar, 16 May 1792, in Wyvill, *Political Papers*, III, pp. 62–6. It is clear from other correspondence in this volume that it was only in 1783 that Scottish concerns were taken up by the Yorkshire reformers and that correspondence between the burgh reformers and Wyvill commenced.
[104] For Muir's advocacy of a convention, see Brims, 'Scottish Democratic Movement', p. 296.

supporters of a common British radical front long before the British Convention met in Edinburgh.[105]

During the 1790s, union was, in sum, a crucial element of radical strategy and tactics in Britain. This conviction took deep root amongst Scottish (and indeed English and Irish) radicals in this period and connections forged across national borders need to be viewed in this light. Ireland certainly featured significantly in this context, but it was London and England which, certainly before 1796–7 and the formation of the United Scotsmen, represented the more significant influence on the course of Scottish radicalism. It should be no surprise, therefore, to see a similar pattern re-emerge in the rather better known radical agitations of the first two decades of the nineteenth century.[106]

[105] See esp. the United Societies of Norwich to the Society for Constitutional Information, 5 March 1793, where they wrote of the notion of a convention: 'this is the object we pursue, and esteem any other means only in subordination to, and as having a tendency to accomplish that desirable end': Howell and Howell (eds), *State Trials* vol. 24, pp. 548–9. Many English radicals appear to have believed that public opinion was not yet ready for the calling of a convention which would represent the unanimous views of the English or British people.
[106] See n. 101, above.

11

Scottish Élites and the Indian Empire, 1700–1815

T. M. DEVINE

I

THE SECOND HALF OF THE EIGHTEENTH CENTURY saw the power and function of the East India Company (EIC) transformed. The success of the Company's forces against the Nawab of Bengal at Plassey in 1757 coincided with victory over the French in the same area and in Madras during the Seven Years War. After these triumphs the EIC was no longer simply a great trading organisation. Instead, it had become an expansionist territorial body which in these years laid down the military and political foundations for the British Empire in India. By 1815, around 40 million Indians were living under the authority of the EIC, which extended over virtually the whole of the eastern subcontinent and a large part of the Ganges valley.[1]

This massive increase in territorial and commercial power inevitably demanded more personnel in the EIC service, whether in the Company's civil administration, armed forces, shipping fleets, or professional cadres, such as physicians and surveyors. By 1800, for instance, the EIC army had grown into one of the largest military formations in the world, with numbers multiplying from 8,000 men in 1783 to over 154,000 by 1805. Most of the rank and file were native Indians (sepoys) but the officers were European and the Company also employed 10,000 white soldiers in the 1770s. Royal forces also expanded in the same period, as the age-old struggle with France also took on an Indian dimension during the American War of Independence and the world-wide struggle for naval and

---

[1] Rajat Kanta Ray, 'Indian society and the establishment of British supremacy, 1763–1818', in P. J. Marshall (ed.), *The Oxford History of the British Empire*, II: *The Eighteenth Century* (Oxford, 1998), pp. 508–29.

Proceedings of the British Academy, **127**, 213–229. © The British Academy 2005.

military supremacy between the British and the French which then followed during the Napoleonic Wars.[2]

Ironically, however, as the empire expanded, it steadily became less English and more British. Even the East India Company, which had jealously guarded its status against all interlopers in the later seventeenth century from elsewhere in Britain, had been transformed a mere few decades later. In the words of one scholar, by the mid-eighteenth century, 'the English empire had become a fiction . . . [S]lowly, almost imperceptibly the empire emerged into a multinational business and military enterprise.'[3] Nowhere was this more true than in the bureaucracies of the EIC. There the Scots were to the fore in exploiting the huge expansion in career opportunities after *c.* 1760. Sir Walter Scott once famously remarked that 'India is the corn chest for Scotland where we poor gentry must send our younger sons as we send our black cattle to the south.'[4] Such was the scale of the Caledonian invasion of the Indian empire that jealous reaction to it in London helped to fuel the Scottophobia of those years and the fiery campaigns of John Wilkes against the supposed political incursion of the despised North Britons.[5] Indeed, an additional factor in the opposition to *arriviste* wealthy nabobs, returning from the subcontinent with plundered fortunes, was that many of the most prominent were Scots. One correspondent to the *Public Advertiser* argued passionately that the EIC had to be reformed because the 'Scotch' were 'so deeply interested in our commerce and great trading concerns'.[6]

In broad terms, the fears of English contemporaries about a growing Scottish presence in the Company and the royal forces in India have been fully supported by modern research. In Bengal, the richest of the EIC's provinces, 47 per cent of writers appointed between 1774 and 1785 were Scots. Earlier, in 1750, the Caledonian influx was already noted, with three out of every eight writers in the province young men from Scotland. It was a similar pattern in the commercial sphere. By 1813, 37 per cent of the greatest private merchant houses in Calcutta were Scottish concerns. Nowhere was the Scot more prominent than in the officer class of both the royal and Company armies. Fourteen royal regiments helped to garrison the Indian provinces of the EIC between 1754 and 1784. Of these, seven had been raised in Scotland and were led by Scottish officers. Scottish physicians were not only to be found throughout the Indian empire but were also prominent in

---

[2] T. M. Devine, *Scotland's Empire, 1600–1815* (London, 2003), p. 203.

[3] H. V. Bowen, *Elites, Enterprise and the Making of the British Overseas Empire, 1688–1775* (Basingstoke, 1996), p. 150.

[4] Quoted in Alex M. Cain, *The Cornchest for Scotland: Scots in India* (Edinburgh, 1986), p. 7.

[5] Philip Lawson and Jim Phillips, '"Our Execrable Banditti": perceptions of nabobs in mid-eighteenth century Britain', *Albion* 16 (1984), p. 230.

[6] *Public Advertiser*, 6 December 1767.

the great shipping fleets of the Company. As early as 1731, John Drummond of Quarrell, a major patron of Scots in the EIC, complained to one of his kinsmen not to recommend any more surgeons to him: 'all the East India Company ships have either Scots Surgeons or Surgeon's mates, and till some of them die I can, nor will look out for no more, for I am made the jest of mankind, plaguing all the Societys [sic] of England with Scots Surgeons . . .'.[7] From 1720 to 1757, all the Principal Medical Officers in Madras were Scots, while by 1800 they made up nearly 40 per cent of the province's total medical establishment. A strong Scottish presence was also noted in the 1740s and 1750s in the élite ranks of the captains of the East Indiamen which plied the lucrative trade between Britain and Asia.[8]

Several conclusions emerge from this evidence. First, Scots achieved a much higher recruitment to Indian posts than might have been expected from the Scottish share of the population of the British Isles, which stood at around 10 per cent of the total in the middle decades of the eighteenth century. Second, the Scottish penetration of the Indian empire was all pervasive, encompassing the civil service, merchanting, army, the professions, and the shipping services. Third, while some accounts suggest that the Scottish role only became decisive after c.1760, there are clear indications of a major Scottish presence in the EIC from the 1720s, several decades before the era of massive territorial expansion of empire in India. Fourth, Scottish success in the higher echelons of the Company was not mirrored by any comparable achievements by the Welsh or the Irish. The presence of the former on the subcontinent was hardly noticed, while the Irish, although very significant in the rank and file of the army — by 1815 over 50 per cent of the Crown forces in India were Irishmen, were notable by their virtual absence in the EIC civil service and the commercial sphere.[9] Even in the military, the Scots had a much

---

[7] J. Drummond of Quarrell to William Drummond, 18 March 1731, quoted in G. K. McGilvary, 'East India Patronage and the Political Management of Scotland, 1720–1774' (unpublished Ph.D. thesis, The Open University, 1989), p. 207.

[8] The figures for Scottish recruitment in this paragraph come from: John Riddy, 'Warren Hastings: Scotland's benefactor?', in Geoffrey Carnall and Colin Nicholson (eds), The Impeachment of Warren Hastings (Edinburgh, 1989), p. 42; Cain, Cornchest for Scotland, p. 13; G. J. Bryant, 'Scots in India in the eighteenth century', Scottish Historical Review 64 (1985), pp. 23–4; G. K. McGilvray, 'Post-Union Scotland and the Indian connection', Cencrastus 37 (1990), pp. 30–4; James G. Parker, 'Scottish enterprise in India, 1750–1914', in R. A. Cage (ed.), The Scots Abroad (London, 1985), pp. 197–8; A. Mackillop, '"The Hard Men of the Peripheries", Scotland's military élite and the Imperial crisis, 1754–1784', unpublished paper given at the Eighteenth Century Scottish Studies Conference, University of Edinburgh, July 2002 (I am grateful to Dr Mackillop for allowing me to use his interesting paper).

[9] Devine, Scotland's Empire, p. 260; Thomas Bartlett, '"This famous island set in a Virginian sea": Ireland in the British Empire, 1690–1801', in Marshall (ed.), Oxford History of the British Empire, p. 212.

better record in achieving officer commissions both in royal and Company service. Fifth, the surge of Scottish migrants to India was not unique but was reflected everywhere in the British Empire from the frozen wastes of northern Canada (then British North America) to the tropical islands of the Caribbean and beyond.

The Caledonian role in empire has attracted considerable scholarly interest in recent years.[10] However, there is as yet no entirely convincing explanation of the remarkable Scottish success rate in gaining access to imperial positions. Each of the two most familiar theories leaves something to be desired. Traditionally, Scottish hegemony has been interpreted as a consequence of the influence of Henry Dundas, later Viscount Melville, in his key office as a commissioner of the Board of Control of the East India Company in 1784 and later as President of the EIC's Board between 1793 and 1801. 'King Harry the Ninth', as he was dubbed in Scotland, was by any standard a highly effective political operator. By 1790, such was his personal authority, he delivered no less than thirty-four of the forty-one contested Scottish constituencies in support of the Westminster government. Equally, there is little doubt that access to patronage, the promise of places, appointments, and sinecures, was crucial to his overwhelming control of the political scene north of the Border. In particular, his role in securing imperial posts for relatives, friends, and political allies is very well documented. The Earl of Rosebery, for instance, a century later memorably remarked that because of his close friendship with William Pitt, Dundas had 'Scotticised India and Orientalised Scotland'.[11] That assessment, however, does not fit the facts. No significant increase in the number of Scots gaining Indian positions has been recorded during his time at the Board of Control. Indeed, Dundas was very conscious of the suspicion that he was bent on advancing his fellow countrymen. The evidence demonstrates that appointments of Scotsmen actually declined somewhat during his Presidency of the Board of Control compared to earlier years. Time and time again Dundas tried to disabuse those who sought his patronage by stressing that it was the Directors of the Board of Control rather than the President who, in the final analysis, controlled the appointments system of the EIC. Whatever the precise nature of Dundas's influence, the essential truth was that several decades before he came to political and administrative prominence, Scottish hegemony in the Company's service was already established.[12]

---

[10] See, for example, John M. Mackenzie, 'Essay and reflection: on Scotland and the Empire', *International History Review* 15 (1993), pp. 714–39; Michael Fry, *The Scottish Empire* (Edinburgh, 2001); S. Murdoch and A. Mackillop (eds), *Military Governors and Imperial Frontiers, c.1600–1800: a Study of Scotland and Empires* (Leiden, 2003).

[11] Quoted in Michael Fry, *The Dundas Despotism* (Edinburgh, 1992), p. 111.

[12] Parker, 'Scottish enterprise in India', pp. 197–8; Riddy, 'Warren Hastings: Scotland's Benefactor?', p. 42.

Linda Colley's argument is more subtle and, at first, more persuasive. In her analysis, 'well-born and/or well-educated Englishmen usually had the pick of jobs back home' and hence were less willing to risk life and limb at the frontier of empire. Thus, in her view, it was the 'outsiders' who were most willing to abandon the comforts of home for overseas adventures. From England, 'the less affluent, the less fortunate, the less reputable and the less able' were attracted to the other end of the world. But the Scots excelled because even the most talented among them had fewer prospects on the British mainland and so were more likely to try to make good in the colonies: 'Having more to win and less to lose, Celtic adventurers were more willing to venture themselves in primitive conditions.'[13]

The seductive power of the thesis is undeniable. No one can deny that the opportunities available in both Scotland and through Crown appointments in the metropolis were more limited in the early eighteenth century for Scots from landed families than for the male progeny of English élites. In addition, Colley's stress on the risks of the imperial enterprise has a special resonance in the case of India. With the Caribbean, the subcontinent was notoriously the white man's grave.

Mortality rates among the Company's men were often horrendous. Even on the outward bound voyage to India disaster could occur. Highland regiments, usually famed for their sense of discipline and *esprit de corps*, were sometimes liable to mutiny when the dread news came through that they were to be posted to India. Episodes such as the fate of the Highlanders of the 78th Foot were long remembered. During the long voyage to the East, the regiment lost 247 men, including its commander, the Earl of Seaforth, from fever and scurvy. While a single human catastrophe on this scale may have been unusual, more typical was the lethal impact of disease on Europeans in India itself. Over the period 1707 to 1775, 57 per cent of the EIC's civil servants died there. Before the 1760s about two-thirds of all the writers, who had competed so eagerly to go to India and make their fortunes, never returned:

> Grisly as an average mortality of 57 per cent for the whole period 1707 to 1775 undoubtedly is, the averages per decade tell an even more macabre story: 66 per cent of those who joined the civil service between 1707 and 1716 died in India; between 1717 and 1726 the rate was 60 per cent; it was 66 per cent between 1727 and 1736; 62 per cent from 1737 to 1746; and 74 per cent from 1747 to 1756. Thereafter the figures begin to improve . . .[14]

---

[13] L. Colley, *Britons: Forging the Nation 1707–1837* (London, 1996 edn), p. 135.

[14] P. J. Marshall, *East India Fortunes: the British in Bengal in the Eighteenth Century* (Oxford, 1976), pp. 218–19.

Ironically, this grim harvest took place at a time when mortality among the British upper classes at home was falling. Hollingsworth's study of the British peerage shows that nearly 45 per cent of male peers died between fifteen and fifty, which was roughly the age of service in India.[15] Before the 1770s, however, around two-thirds of the civil service aged from seventeen to forty would die in Bengal: 'a man aged twenty in the sample who stayed in Britain could expect another forty years of life; a young man who went to Bengal could expect to die there'.[16] It has to be remembered also that the civil servants were the salaried élite of the EIC, who lived in much more comfortable circumstances than the Company's servants as a body. The rate of culling was even worse in the army. In the 1760s such was the death rate among the European regiments that annual renewal of men of at least a quarter was necessary. One return of casualties among the officers and cadets of the Bengal army between 1770 and 1776 crystallises the enormity of the problem. A mere six fell in action, nine died by drowning, but 208 were killed by disease.[17] Manifestly, even if some did make their fortunes, the riches would often only be enjoyed by widows, fatherless children, and other family members back in Britain.

Yet the Colley thesis does not entirely convince. The risks may have been very great but, especially in the 1760s and 1770s, the temptation of making massive fortunes in India far outweighed the threat of succumbing to an early death. Historians of the period have demonstrated that the key British victories at Plassey (1757) and Buxar (1764) triggered a veritable bonanza of pillage.[18] Gifts from Indian princes, protection money, bribes, and the acquisition of booty from victorious wars and successful sieges made some servants of the EIC very wealthy. At home, India came to be seen for a time as the route to easy riches. Even the bad publicity which the few outrageously successful nabobs attracted helped to put India on the map. Samuel Foote's satire, *The Nabob*, was first performed on the London stage in 1773.[19] In the same year, Horace Walpole fumed: 'What is England now? A sink of Indian wealth, filled with nabobs and emptied by Macaronis! A senate sold and defused! A country overrun by horse-races! A gaming, robbing, wrangling, railing nation without principles, genius, character or allies.'[20] Walpole may have exaggerated somewhat but the oxygen of publicity which his heated

[15] T. H. Hollingsworth, 'A demographic study of the British ducal families', in D. V. Glass and D. E. C. Eversley (eds), *Population in History* (London, 1965), pp. 354–378.

[16] Marshall, *East India Fortunes*, p. 255.

[17] Ibid., p. 253.

[18] Summarised in Devine, *Scotland's Empire*, pp. 257–9.

[19] Lawson and Phillips, '"Our Execrable Banditti"', pp. 230–2.

[20] Quoted in Lawrence James, *Raj: the Making and Unmaking of British India* (London, 1998 edn), pp. 47–8.

remarks and those of many others generated helps to explain the new and intense clamour for India jobs which was such a marked feature of the period.

The assumption behind Colley's thesis that India posts were not attractive to the sons of the metropolitan élites is therefore unfounded for the post-1770 period. The two to three hundred nabobs who returned to Britain from the Company's presidential and trading posts made a deep social impression, even if most of them had achieved little more than modest wealth.[21] The sub-continent had come to be regarded as a fabled land of 'limitless gold and lacs of rupees'. The demand for posts in the service of the EIC reached unprecedented levels. By the mid-1770s, it was alleged that Company Directors could ask for as much as £4,000 for their patronage in the appointment of writers, the most senior grade in the service. Competition for places in all other ranks became much more acute.[22] Only powerful connections could now deliver the glittering prizes. To some extent, then, the popularity of Indian careers further deepens the puzzle of Scottish success from the 1720s. In that earlier period at least Scottish owners of India stock and Scottish Directors on the Board of the EIC were few and far between.[23] But it was only men of this status who really possessed the necessary clout and influence to guarantee success in the competition for appointments.

II

Analysis of the system of Indian patronage is obviously vital to a full understanding of Scottish achievements. But we need to begin by seeing the scramble for positions in the subcontinent and elsewhere in the empire within a much broader historical context. A key social group in this respect were the non-inheriting sons of the lairds or petty gentry class in Scotland. It was these small landed families who produced disproportionate numbers of 'the stream of Caledonians' found throughout the empire by the end of the eighteenth century. For instance, of the 114 applications which survive from Scotsmen to join the civil service of the EIC between 1750 and 1795, a little over one-third listed their father's occupation. Over half were from gentry or the tacksman class of the Highlands, with the rest split between commerce, the professions, and a sprinkling of noble families.[24] A more impressionistic trawl through memoirs, local histories, and government files would also

---

[21] Lawson and Phillips, '"Our Execrable Banditti"', pp. 230–2.
[22] McGilvray, 'Post-Union Scotland and the Indian connection', p. 31.
[23] McGilvray, 'East India Patronage', p. 84.
[24] Bryant, 'Scots in India', pp. 23–4.

strongly suggest that sons of the medium and small landowners (with valued rentals c.1770 ranging from £2,000 to £100 Scots) were a prime source of imperial recruits.

A core objective of this class was the maintenance of the economic position and social status of non-inheriting younger sons. A number of influences over the century between the Reformation and the outbreak of the Wars of the Covenanters in the 1630s helped to secure this:

> In the later sixteenth century the secularisation of church lands, the growing business potential of the legal profession, and after 1603 the increased patronage of the crown, all helped to maintain noble kindreds with the minimum of economic and social debasement among their junior ranks. However, by the third decade of union of the Crowns there was no more church land to go around, and the crown was soon to initiate moves to recover some of those lands already distributed; royal patronage was drying up due to economics and the fact that the Scots were increasingly unpopular in London; the legal profession was consolidating around established legal dynasties able to freeze out new-comers; merchant wealth was such that penurious younger sons could not possibly compete with the urban élite; and with the decline in feuding, noblemen were less inclined to support large retinues. In addition, noble finances in general were less secure than they had been for centuries.[25]

At this time of emerging crisis the huge military demands of the Thirty Years War provided vast new opportunities for members of the laird class and their male offspring. In Scandinavia and the Baltic states alone there were over 3,500 Scottish officers fighting against the House of Habsburg, of whom several were ennobled for their services and became members of the landed aristocracies of Sweden and Denmark. Entire military dynasties were established around an occupation which was honourable, remunerative, and a potential route to worldly success.[26] But this élite employment, though massive and lucrative, was transitory. When the Thirty Years War ended with the Peace of Westphalia in 1648 the huge continental demand for Scottish soldiers, which had boomed since the 1620s, virtually collapsed. The major database of élite migrations to Scandinavia and northern Europe, consisting of the biographies of nearly 7,000 Scottish officers, merchants, students, and diplomats (compiled within the AHRB Centre for Irish and Scottish Studies at Aberdeen University) plots the decline in detail. The last significant movement to Sweden and Denmark occurred in the 1650s as many royalists fled from the Cromwellian government. Small numbers of merchants and others

---

[25] Keith M. Brown, 'From Scottish lords to British officers: state building, elite integration and the army in the seventeenth century', in N. Macdougall (ed.), *Scotland and War AD 79–1918* (Edinburgh, 1991), p. 143.

[26] Steve Murdoch, *Britain, Denmark-Norway and the House of Stuart, 1603–1660* (East Linton, 2000), pp. 208–13.

continued to arrive but this was a mere trickle compared to the enormous flood of young men in earlier decades.[27]

The social anxieties which were stoked up as a result can only be guessed at. An underdeveloped Scottish economy, despite expanded activity in the 1660s and 1670s, was ill prepared to take up the slack. Ulster, Scotland's 'first colony' was by now only attractive to farmers, servants, and cottars, rather than landed gentlemen. One illustration of the concerns was the new popularity of colonial schemes, which culminated in the ill-fated Darien adventure. The plans for a Scottish colony in East New Jersey in the 1680s was dominated by laird families of the north-east region, significantly a major source of Scottish officers during the European conflict of a few decades before. The projectors envisaged a colony of landed estates and among those who eventually emigrated to the New World were a very high proportion of younger sons of the north-east gentry. Thus, three members of the Gordons of Straloch purchased proprietary shares, but only the two younger brothers actually travelled to the colony. Several other emigrants can be identified as sons of minor, cadet branches of landed families. Robert Gordon of Cluny probably spoke for many of his fellow proprietors when he stated that his own reason for being attracted to the project of colonisation was to provide land for his young son, 'since I had not estate whereby to make him a Scotch laird'.[28] The Darien adventure and the new role of the Scottish military in both the colonial militias of the Caribbean, the American empire and in the royal army during the War of the Spanish Succession is suggestive of the same pressures.[29]

But it is unlikely that either of these emerging opportunities solved the potential social crisis because, increasingly, there were many more younger sons than ever before to be found suitable employment. Scottish landed families were simply having more surviving adult children as infant mortality levels started to fall rapidly at that time. No exact figures exist to prove the point conclusively from a specifically Scottish perspective. However, research on the demography of British ducal families for the period can provide a useful surrogate source of information on changing patterns of population growth among the nation's governing classes.[30] Family size among this élite was relatively stable until the later seventeenth century (see Table 11.1). But then, a few decades later, rapid growth started among the ducal families at a

[27] In a project led by Drs S. Murdoch and A. Grosjean, 'Scotland, Scandinavia and Northern Europe, 1580–1707', www.abdn.ac.uk/ssne

[28] Quoted in Ned C. Landsman, *Scotland and its First American Colony, 1683–1765* (Princeton, 1985), p. 107.

[29] Devine, *Scotland's Empire*, pp. 32–48.

[30] Hollingsworth, 'British ducal families', pp. 354–78.

Table 11.1. Mean number of ducal sons and daughters surviving to adulthood, 1330–1939.

Cohort born	Dukes' sons	Dukes' daughters
1330–1479	3.7	4.6
1480–1679	3.9	4.6
1680–1729	4.3	4.5
1730–1779	5.6	5.4
1780–1829	4.3	5.6
1830–1879	3.0	4.6
1880–1939	2.4	2.9

Source: T. H. Hollingsworth, 'A demographic study of the British ducal families', in D. V. Glass and D. E. C. Eversley (eds), *Population in History* (London, 1965), p. 370.

rate which was considerably higher than in the general population increase in the country as a whole. The percentage of children of dukes dying under the age of sixteen was 31.1 between 1480 and 1679; from 1680 to 1779, the figure fell to 25.9, and declined further to 21.1 between 1780 and 1829.

There were now many more sons surviving into adulthood. If this pattern was replicated across the Scottish landed classes, the concerns for placing younger sons in employment which was both gainful and socially acceptable must have become even more acute.

But this was not all. Changes in the composition of the Scottish landed structure added to the challenge. In 1700 there were around 9,500 landowners in Scotland, only about half of whom had the right to inherit or sell the land they possessed. The structure was dominated by the great aristocratic land-lords and their associated kinship groups. This élite was remorselessly expanding its territorial control at the expense of the lesser lairds between the later seventeenth century and the 1770s. Thus, the number of proprietors in Aberdeenshire fell by a third between *c.*1670 and *c.*1770 (621 to 250) and the steepest decline occurred among the smallest group of landowners. In Argyll the erosion was even more dramatic with a 42 per cent fall between 1688 and 1802. The trend was repeated all over Scotland. The total of 9,500 landown-ers at the beginning of the eighteenth century dropped to 8,500 by the 1750s and fell further to around 8,000 at the start of the nineteenth century.[31] The growth of the aristocratic territorial empires at the expense of the minor lairds was a sure sign of the latter's relative economic malaise. As the number of estates possessed by this class was squeezed, one favoured option some-

[31] L. Timperley, 'The pattern of landholding in eighteenth century Scotland', in M. L. Parry and T. R. Slater (eds), *The Making of the Scottish Countryside* (London, 1980), pp. 137–54; R. F. Callander, *A Pattern of Landownership in Scotland* (Finzean, 1987), pp. 45–8; Allan I. Macinnes, 'Landownership, land use and elite enterprise in Scottish Gaeldom: from clanship to clearance in Argyllshire, 1688–1858', in T. M. Devine (ed.), *Scottish Elites* (Edinburgh, 1994), p. 4.

times adopted to solve the chronic problem of younger sons, namely the acquisition of small properties in their names, became much more difficult. The problem was hardly helped by the years of European peace after 1715, which lasted until the 1740s (and so limited military employment), or by the continued stagnation in rental income and the stubbornly low levels of productivity on Scottish landed estates, which only eased in the period of agrarian transformation after c.1760, and this during an era when élite expenditure was rising because of the social costs of competitive display.[32] In an important sense, therefore, Indian posts came not simply as an opportunity but more urgently as a crucial lifeline for many landed families. It is this which helps to explain the note of desperation in much of the correspondence which deluged potential patrons among the important and influential figures of the time and also accounts for the hunger for posts even when located in some of the more lethal, dangerous, and distant parts of the world.[33] After all, there was nothing new in this. For centuries, the Scots élite had been accustomed to sending their sons abroad and many never returned because they died of disease or fell in battle. For many generations the axis of that migration had leaned towards Europe. Now it shifted towards the Atlantic and Asia, the new imperial frontiers in the historic diaspora of the Scots.

III

There can be little doubt of the demand for Indian careers. Achieving access to appointments, however, was a quite different matter. Only the power of patronage could easily unlock them. As one senior army officer put it, though the Company was 'resolved to employ such as appears to have the most merit, at the same time there is no doubt but *interest will in the end prevail . . .*'.[34] Only in recent years has the story emerged in full detail of how Scottish outsiders colonised the jealously guarded citadels of India patronage. From modern researches a powerful link can be established between British politics in the post-union period and the increasing preferment of Scots to posts at the periphery of empire.

The crux of the matter was the volatility of the union relationship in the first few decades after 1707. The treaty had been born out of a marriage of convenience between the governing classes in Edinburgh and London, and its

---

[32] T. M. Devine, *The Transformation of Rural Scotland: Social Change and the Agrarian Economy 1660–1815* (Edinburgh, 1994), pp. 19–35.

[33] Devine, *Scotland's Empire*, p. 255.

[34] My italics. General S. Fraser to William Campbell of Succoth, 25 November 1769, quoted in Bryant, 'Scots in India', pp. 29–30.

successful passage through the Scottish parliament was a close-run thing, delivered in the teeth of a good deal of popular hostility outside the House. This was hardly the context for the stable and harmonious development of 'Great Britain'. Then again there was the continuing Jacobite threat, which was always more menacing in Scotland than in England, not least because the exiled House of Stuart could usually count on the military support of several of the strongest Highland clans. Jacobites were implacably opposed to the union since they viewed it—correctly—as a means of buttressing the Revolution of 1688-9 and so ensuring that the Stuarts would never return to their rightful inheritance. Until Jacobitism was finally crushed (and this did not happen until after the Forty-five), the union was always likely to be threatened to a greater or lesser extent. This was especially the case if France, with its enormous military and naval resources, chose to intervene on the Stuart side.

At first, the London strategy seems to have been to do as little as possible and so keep the Scots quiet.[35] On the whole the policy succeeded at first, apart, however, from the abolition of the Scottish Privy Council, the chief executive organ of government in Scotland, in 1708. The end of the Privy Council was a key development because it gravely weakened the ability of government to respond vigorously and decisively in crisis situations. The vacuum which it left at the centre of power could only give further comfort to the Jacobites. More provocative and serious were the inflammatory acts of the Tory government which replaced the Whig coalition at the elections of 1710. The High Church Tories seemed bent on a policy of cutting down the privileges of the Church of Scotland enshrined in the Treaty of Union. This was not so much hostility towards the Scots as such, as a general campaign against presbyterians in both England and Scotland by high Anglicans in the Tory Party. The initiative was enthusiastically supported by Scottish Tories, who were also noted for their episcopalian loyalties. In 1711 James Greenshields, an episcopalian minister, appealed to the House of Lords against his imprisonment by the magistrates of Edinburgh for defying the presbytery of the city and using the English liturgy. Recourse to the Lords was possible within the terms of the Treaty of 1707, but the subsequent decision to allow the Anglican prayer book to be used for worship in an episcopalian meeting house enraged the capital's presbyterians. This was then followed in 1712 by two more offensive measures, the Toleration Act and the Patronage Act. The former granted freedom of worship to Scottish episcopalians as long as they agreed to pray for the reigning monarch, while the latter re-established the primary right of patrons, who were usually local landowners, to appoint to vacant parishes and church offices. Patronage had been abolished as part of

[35] J. S. Shaw, *The Political History of Eighteenth Century Scotland* (Basingstoke, 1999), pp. 38–62; P. W. J. Riley, *The English Ministers and Scotland, 1707–1727* (London, 1964), *passim.*

the presbyterian revolution of 1690 because it conflicted with the rights of the community itself to decide on a candidate to fill a parish vacancy.

All this outraged the kirk and seemed to undermine the act guaranteeing the security of presbyterian rights in the event of union, an enactment central to the acceptance of the treaty itself. But, in addition, the legislation of 1712 raised the issue of the nature of 1707 and the extent to which the treaty was an inviolate, fundamental law or subject to change at the whim of the sovereign legislature in Westminster. Perhaps of more direct impact, however, on the Scottish people was the new taxation regime within the union.[36] In the first few decades after 1707 there was a huge increase in customs and excise duties together with a significant extension in the range of commodities on which tax was paid. Partly, this was because the existing levels of taxation were simply not sufficient to cover the cost of Scottish civil government and administration, and London ministers were also soon appalled at the scale of smuggling and customs evasion. In addition, after the War of the Spanish Succession ended in 1713, the tax burden in Britain started to shift from the land tax to customs dues and excise payments on a whole range of commodities, including beer, salt, linen, soap, and malt. These were all vital necessities of life for most people in Scotland. Salt, for instance, was the universal food preservative of the day and linen the most widely produced cloth. Equally, tax increases were likely to bite deeply because the Scottish economy was still in the doldrums in the first decade after union, and those pamphleteers who had optimistically predicted an economic miracle were now proven hopelessly wrong. Home salt, which had not been taxed before 1707, doubled in price when duties were imposed in 1713. That same year, the House of Commons voted to apply the malt tax to Scotland in direct defiance of the provisions of the treaty itself, a decision which would have significantly pushed up the price of ale, the most popular drink in Scotland at the time. The fury was such that the tax was never properly enforced.

To the Scots this was the climax of a whole stream of provocative actions which threatened to break the union. Scottish peers and members of the Commons came together in a series of meetings and agreed that the only solution was repeal of the treaty. What was remarkable was the unanimity of all parties on such a fundamental issue, a very rare occurrence indeed in the faction-ridden world of Scottish politics. The motion was put by the Earl of Findlater in the House of Lords in June 1713 and was only narrowly defeated by four proxy votes. The outcome demonstrated not only the disillusionment of the Scottish nobility but also the fact that there was little enthusiasm in

---

[36] Christopher A. Whatley, *Scottish Society, 1707–1830: Beyond Jacobitism, Towards Industrialisation* (Manchester, 2000), pp. 171–4; T. M. Devine, *The Scottish Nation, 1700–2000* (London, 1999), pp. 18–22.

England for the union either. This alienation helped to feed the next great Jacobite rising, led by the Earl of Mar in 1715. Mar himself had been a crucial figure in helping the court manage the votes for the treaty in 1706–7 and had then sat in the United Kingdom parliament. But he was out of favour with the new Hanoverian monarch, George I, and changed sides to the Stuarts, thus living up to his nickname, 'Bobbing John'. In 1715 Mar was able to assemble an army of 10,000 men, which was more than double the force that the government levies under the Duke of Argyll were able to muster. After the collapse of the Fifteen, the Earl of Stair, an ultra-loyal Whig and British ambassador to France, noted that there was a real danger of another rebellion unless the ruinous consequences of the union were addressed. This was an admission by a high-ranking friend of the court that the survival of the union was not yet assured.

However, Stair's hopes for an improvement in Anglo-Scottish relationships were premature, since there was a fundamental cause of friction which would not easily or quickly disappear. The view from Westminster was that the Scots were not paying their way through taxation because of the enormous scale of smuggling and systematic revenue fraud said to be endemic in Scottish society. On the other hand, Scotland had been accustomed to low taxes and relaxed methods of gathering revenue before the union, so that the new impositions after 1707 were bitterly resented both on economic grounds and because they were seen as an attempt by London to force Scotland to contribute to the English National Debt, which had swollen hugely to finance the Spanish Succession War. Popular retribution both against revenue increases and against more rigorous methods of collection was exacted through violence against the hated customs officers. These local incidents were nothing, however, compared to the national outrage after the decision in 1724 by Sir Robert Walpole's government to apply the malt tax to Scotland with effect from June 1725. The earlier attempt in 1713 had brought about a vote in the House of Lords which nearly dissolved the union, and this latest initiative unleashed a wave of popular anger in the summer of 1725, with riots breaking out in Stirling, Dundee, Ayr, Elgin, Paisley, and Glasgow. The disturbances in Glasgow were by far the most serious. The local Member of Parliament, Daniel Campbell of Shawfield, was suspected of supporting the hated Malt Tax Act. The mob took its revenge by burning and looting his impressive town house, engaged in a pitched battle with the local garrison, which resulted in eight fatalities, and then drove the retreating troops out of the city towards Dumbarton. It took the intervention of General Wade with a force of 400 dragoons and accompanying foot to restore order finally and bring to an end a dangerous challenge to the union state.[37]

[37] Whatley, *Scottish Society, 1707–1830*, pp. 171–4.

Certainly the riots of 1725 concentrated the minds of Walpole's government on the Scottish problem. The insurrection itself was a serious matter, but of equal concern was the apparent impotence of the Scottish administration when confronted with such a major challenge to law and order. The Lord Advocate of Scotland, the country's senior law officer, Robert Dundas, had in fact opposed the Malt Tax and was dismissed as a result. The Secretary for Scotland, the Duke of Roxburgh, did little; and the vacuum in executive authority left by the abolition of the Privy Council was now very obvious for all to see. The Earl of Islay, younger brother of the Duke of Argyll, who was sent to investigate the situation, reported to Walpole that there had been 'a long series of no administration' in Scotland and the 'mere letter of the law had little or no effect with the people'.[38] This was tantamount to saying that Scotland was ungovernable within the union. It was not a situation which could be allowed to continue.

Walpole's solution was to sack the incompetent Roxburgh and appoint Islay to manage Scottish affairs. The decision was a turning point, not only in Anglo-Scottish relationships, but in the development of the Scottish connection with India. Islay, later 3rd Duke of Argyll from 1743, became the dominant political figure in Scotland between the 1720s and his death in 1761, excepting the brief few years 1742–6. Such was his power that he became known as the 'King of Scotland'. His influence rested on a solemn contract with Walpole: Islay would deliver political stability in Scotland and the votes of most Scottish MPs in return for the lion's share of patronage and the authority to govern north of the Border. The Walpole connection soon gave Islay immense sources of patronage, which he deployed with great skill in alliance with his two principal agents, Andrew Fletcher, Lord Milton, and Duncan Forbes of Culloden, 'King Duncan' as he was dubbed in the Highlands. The civil administration, law courts, army, church, and universities were all penetrated as Islay relentlessly built up a formidable empire of clients and dependants. It was reckoned that two-thirds of the judges promoted to the Court of Session owed their position to his influence, and the Campbell interest was also paramount in the appointment of sheriffs who, it was alleged, were 'little more than a list of the sons, sons-in-law, and alliances' of Islay's clients.[39] By the 1730s his power was such that even the monarch could describe him as 'Vice Roy in Scotland'. Fundamental to the operation of this new patronage machine was access to India posts.

There were never enough Scottish jobs available for use as sweeteners to the country's tiny electorate of around 4,000 individuals, their associates and dependents. Nor was it easy to surrender to the Scots the existing Crown

---

[38] Quoted in J. S. Shaw, *The Management of Scottish Society 1707–1764* (Edinburgh, 1983), p. 86.
[39] Ibid.

appointments in London which were claimed by English interests. The rich vein of East India posts promised an attractive alternative. The Company was an independent corporation but ministers could always lean on it to provide a source of patronage in return for periodic renewal of its Charter and the promise of commercial favours from the state in areas like government contracting for the army and navy. Thus it was that East India postings became the foundation for bringing more political stability to Scotland and forging a stronger union. For Walpole's government it was a more effective and less costly strategy than military coercion which could have been both very messy and probably counterproductive. Its impact was quickly apparent. By 1750 there was already a marked influx of Scots into the Company. By that date they had taken three out of every eight writers' posts in Bengal. A key figure in the deployment of this patronage between 1725 and 1742 was John Drummond of Quarrell, one of the few leading Directors in the Company of Scottish birth.[40] He linked the Argyll interest in the North with EIC contacts in London and the Walpole political connection, which increasingly depended on an amenable phalanx of Scottish votes in the Commons for support. Jacobite families who had been 'out' in the Fifteen were given special attention for favour and reward in order to integrate them into the Whig establishment in church and state. One reason for the steady haemorrhaging of Jacobite support between the two major rebellions of 1715 and 1745 may well have been this untold story of the impact of India patronage on traditional loyalties.

This early bedrock of Scottish success meant that when demand for India posts became insatiable after Plassey in 1757 Scottish interests and networks were already firmly established. By that date more Scots than ever before had now become members of the Company's Directorate and major holders of stock.[41] Some of the early eighteenth-century generation had also returned to Britain as rich men and maintained a strong interest in the Company's affairs.[42] These men were important conduits for the distribution of patronage in later decades. In India, as elsewhere in the empire, Scottish family, local, and personal networks provided the mechanism for advancing the next generation to posts and careers. It was the same kind of ethnic solidarity which had promoted Scottish interests in Europe since medieval times. Nevertheless, it was an Englishman, Warren Hastings, who really drove the Caledonian gravy train by the 1770s in the subcontinent. Hastings was Governor of Bengal from 1772 to 1774 and subsequently Governor-General

---

[40] McGilvray, 'East India Patronage', *passim*; J. G. Parker, 'The Directors of the East India Company, 1754–1790' (unpublished Ph.D. thesis, University of Edinburgh, 1977).
[41] Parker, 'Directors of the East India Company'.
[42] Devine, *Scotland's Empire*.

of India from 1774 to 1785. He was impeached by parliament for the alleged criminality of acts committed in these offices. His highly publicised trial lasted from 1788 to 1795. Less well known than this notoriety, however, was his role as 'Scotland's Benefactor'. It was he rather than Henry Dundas who unashamedly promoted Scots and ensured that they attained a greater representation in the civil and military services than ever before or since. Hastings' policy was based on pragmatism and expediency. Surrounded by enemies in both London and India, he came to rely on the Scottish stockholders in the Company to maintain his position. They were never a majority but they proved their loyalty on several occasions. In return, Hastings was prepared to favour their kin and friends if they demonstrated ability. His 'Scotch Guardians', as he called them, were always selected for the most important and challenging missions of his governorship. They included Major Alex Hannay of Kirkcudbright, who led the mission to the Moghul court in 1775, and Alexander Elliot, son of Sir Gilbert Elliot of Minto, Treasurer of the Navy, who was Hastings' emissary to the Bhonsla Raja of Berar (the Mahratta leader). The irony was that these Scots and others were fully implicated in Hastings' alleged crimes during his lengthy impeachment. But this was also confirmation of how close they had come to the very centre of power in the Indian Empire.[43]

[43] Riddy, 'Warren Hastings: Scotland's benefactor?', pp. 30–57.

12

Anglo-Scottish Relations:
the Carlyles in London

ROSEMARY ASHTON

IN AUGUST 1831 THOMAS CARLYLE, AGED THIRTY-FIVE, travelled to London
with the manuscript of *Sartor Resartus* under his arm, hoping to find a
publisher for that strange satirical rhapsody. His point of departure was
Craigenputtoch, the isolated farmhouse in Dumfriesshire—he liked to
describe it to correspondents such as Goethe and Emerson as a wilderness, a
'Patmos'—to which he had taken his reluctant wife Jane in search of health
and a cheap rent, and from which he had lately sent increasingly influential
articles on the 'signs of the times' to the *Edinburgh Review* and other
periodicals.[1]

The Carlyles had begun their married life in Edinburgh in the autumn of
1826, but, though Jane was relatively happy there, Carlyle could not get on
with his fellow men of letters and hated what he later called in his *Reminiscences* 'dead Edinburgh Whiggism, Scepticism, and Materialism'.[2] By 1827
he was desperate to find relief from the dyspepsia which had tormented him
since early adulthood and in need of either a regular income, or cheaper
accommodation than Edinburgh could offer, or both. With disconcerting
inconsistency, he swung between two possibilities: taking up the life of a
Dumfriesshire farmer on land at Craigenputtoch owned by his mother-in-
law, or applying for professorships in the new University of London (the god-
less institution of Gower Street, soon to be renamed University College
London after King's College was set up as a church-and-state rival). He tried
for a chair in rhetoric, and one in moral philosophy, but was unsuccessful, and
by May 1828 he and Jane had moved not to London but to Craigenputtoch,
which was to be farmed by Carlyle's brother Alick while Carlyle himself rode

[1] See Rosemary Ashton, *Thomas and Jane Carlyle: Portrait of a Marriage* (London, 2002), p. 105.
[2] Thomas Carlyle, *Reminiscences*, eds K. J. Fielding and Ian Campbell (Oxford, 1997), p. 362.

Proceedings of the British Academy, **127**, 231–246. © The British Academy 2005.

and walked for his health and pursued at a distance from the literary centres of London and Edinburgh his precarious career as essayist and reviewer. He also set about writing *Sartor Resartus*.³

This work, purporting to be the 'Thoughts on Clothes' of a German philosopher, Professor Diogenes Teufelsdröckh (asafoetida, or Devil's Dung, an emetic), mounted a sustained rhetorical attack on 'the condition of England', a phrase later to become famous when Carlyle used it to open his most influential work, *Past and Present*, in 1843. As for *Sartor*, Carlyle felt that, while he had *written* it during a self-imposed internal exile in his isolated Scottish farmhouse, he wanted to ensure its *publication* in the great metropolis itself. For this he could have relied on friends and acquaintances in London, of whom he had several willing to help, but a second motive was at work in him, closely connected with the completion of *Sartor*. London in 1831 was full of talk of reform, with successive attempts being made by radicals and Whigs to get a Reform Bill through parliament. Carlyle's own reformist social and political views had found timely dramatic expression in *Sartor*, and he now wished not only to find a publisher for it but also to see if he could add to the debate in other ways. He hoped, as he confided to his brother John, that once in London he might:

> Deliver a Dozen of Lectures, in my own Annandale accent, with my own God-created brain and heart, to such audience as will gather round me, on some section or aspect of this strange Life in this strange Era; on which my soul like Eliphaz the Temanite's is getting fuller and fuller [Job 4:2]. Does there seem to thee any propriety in a man that has organs of speech and even some semblance of understanding and Sincerity, sitting forever, mute as [a] milestone, while Quacks of every colour are quacking as with lungs of brass? True I have no Pulpit; but as I once said, cannot any man *make* him a pulpit, simply by inverting the nearest Tub? And what are your whigs and Lord Advocates, and Lord Chancellors, and the whole host of unspeakably gabbling Parliamenteers and Pulpiteers and Pamphleteers; — if a man suspect that 'there is fire enough in his belly to burn up' the entire creation of such!⁴

Rhetorically, this passage in a private letter to his brother closely resembles the language of *Sartor* and, indeed, of all Carlyle's subsequent published works; in it are to be found some of the clues to his extraordinary influence on his contemporaries. The combination of frequent references to the Bible, particularly the Old Testament, and a characteristically Scottish habit of vehemence and exaggeration — especially the insulting use of names and the

---

³ Ashton, *Thomas and Jane Carlyle*, pp. 86–93.
⁴ Carlyle to John Carlyle, 4 March 1831, *The Collected Letters of Thomas and Jane Welsh Carlyle*, eds C. R. Sanders, K. J. Fielding et al. (Durham, North Carolina), 30 vols so far (1970–), V, pp. 243–4. Henceforth referred to as *Collected Letters*.

pluralising of the enemy or intended victim of authorial scorn, here 'your whigs and Lord Advocates, and Lord Chancellors', along with the alliterative list of 'gabbling Parliamenteers and Pulpiteers and Pamphleteers' —proved immensely effective in attracting readers and imitators over the next twenty years. Dickens is only the best known of these; his own rhetoric of anger about the condition of England rings with a similar bold denunciatory tone, full of allusion and alliteration, and Dickens was quick to declare his admiration for Carlyle, his sense of the older man's having carved out the path down which he also strode.[5]

Carlyle says in his letter that he has no pulpit (he had given up studying for the ministry more than ten years earlier), and suggests he might invert a tub and speak from it, thinking, no doubt, of the sceptical Greek philosopher Diogenes, who was reputed to have lived in a tub and whose name Carlyle had given to his fictional German professor in *Sartor*. 'Providence', he continues in his letter to John, 'seems saying to me: Thou wilt never find Pulpit, were it but a Rhetoric chair, provided for thee: invert thy Tub, and speak, if thou have aught to say!' His *alter ego* Diogenes Teufelsdröckh does have a chair, if Carlyle does not, but in a characteristically broad yet private joke he is 'Professor der Allerley-Wissenschaft' (Professor of Things in General) at the University of Weissnichtwo (Know-Not-Where). The dyspeptic Scottish inventor of the rhapsodic-sceptical German professor hopes that the philosophy of Diogenes Teufelsdröckh will prove an emetic for an English reading public which sorely needs purging in this 'strange Era' of Establishment resistance to political and social reform: 'I sometimes think the Book *will* prove a kind of medicinal Assafoetida for the pudding Stomach of England', as he puts it to John.[6]

It is not the case that the Scottish Carlyle opposed all things English as somehow inferior to the institutions and doings in his native land. He was never inclined to support Scottish separatism, as he made clear in articles and letters attacking Irish agitation for repeal of the union, at its height in 1848 after nearly a decade of Irish starvation and emigration. A letter to an Edinburgh correspondent, John Steill, in May 1848 declared characteristically, 'If I thought that "native Parliaments", or indeed any kind of Parliaments, and Public Babblements, . . . could do us any good, . . . I too should vote strenuously for native Parliaments, Nationalities &c &c both in Scotland and Ireland; but I fear there lies no hope for us at all in that direction.'[7]

[5] Ashton, *Thomas and Jane Carlyle*, pp. 245–6.
[6] Carlyle to John Carlyle, 17 July 1831, *Collected Letters*, V, p. 305.
[7] Carlyle to John Steill, 10 May 1848, *Collected Letters*, XXIII, p. 28. See also Carlyle's two articles on the subject, 'Ireland and the British Chief Governor', *Spectator*, 13 May 1848, and 'Legislation for Ireland', *Examiner*, 13 May 1848. I am indebted to Professor K. J. Fielding for directing my attention to the letter to Steill.

In his personal life, he had found Edinburgh and his study for the ministry at university there not at all to his taste, partly because of philosophical and religious doubts but also because of the petty narrowmindedness and worldliness of the professors and students he met there. He and Jane subsequently agreed in preferring life in London, for all its fogs, filth, and faults, to the tight-lipped self-congratulation they had detected in middle-class Edinburgh during the first year of their marriage.

The point Carlyle wished to carry, and which he eventually succeeded in carrying, to England and the English related to a large extent to the life of the United Kingdom as a whole. The 'condition of England' meant for him the condition of Britain; the place to direct one's criticism, he felt, was at the centre of government and power, namely London and the great offices of state located there.[8] Therefore it is that the satire in *Sartor Resartus* is aimed mainly at abuses and absurdities in the institutions of parliament, the established Church of England, and the aristocracy, the class which still held most power in an as yet unreformed parliament.

By means of an allegory of clothes, the outer vestments through which the eyes of the philosopher Teufelsdröckh penetrate, Carlyle ridicules these institutions, showing them to be in desperate need of reform. The worldliness and loss of spiritual direction of the Church of England is criticised through the shovel hats and bishops' aprons of its clergy; against these signs and symbols of an outworn institution obsessed with wealth and material comforts Carlyle pits the founder of the Quaker faith, George Fox, the shoemaker whose break from the complacent church is symbolised by his making for himself a new vestment, a 'perennial suit of leather'. 'Stitch away, thou noble Fox', exclaims Teufelsdröckh, addressing a historical figure in the dramatic present tense (as Carlyle the historian was to do with the protagonists of 1789 in his most famous work, *The French Revolution*, 1837); 'every prick of that little instrument is pricking into the heart of Slavery, and World-worship, and the Mammon-god.'[9] This passage was read aloud a few years later by the atheist Utilitarian John Stuart Mill, who, like so many of his contemporaries, was surprised by the power of Carlyle's visionary rhetoric on him; the friend who recorded the occasion after hearing with Mill one of Carlyle's London lectures on heroes and hero-worship (1840) noted that Mill's voice 'trembled with excitement as he read, "Stitch away, thou noble Fox", &c.'.[10]

---

[8] For an interesting account of Carlyle's attitudes towards England, Scotland, and Britain, see Ian Campbell, 'The Scottishness of Carlyle', *Carlyle Studies Annual* Special Issue 17 (1997), pp. 73–82.

[9] *Sartor Resartus* (1833–4), eds Mark Engel and Rodger L. Tarr (London, 2000), p. 156 (Book III, ch. 1, 'Incident in Modern History').

[10] Caroline Fox's journal, 17 May 1849, *Journals of Caroline Fox 1835–1871*, selected and edited by Wendy Monk (London, 1972), pp. 90–2.

In attacking the class system, or at least in criticising the do-nothingism of those in power, Carlyle, like Dickens after him, concentrates his fire-power on a lazy, uncaring, disgraceful aristocracy. Borrowing from Swift a rhetorical trick of seeming approval, and alluding closely to a recently published 'fashionable' novel by Edward Lytton Bulwer — *Pelham* (1828) — Carlyle attacks the phenomenon of dandyism, again by resorting to an analysis of clothing. First he quotes the 'Articles of Faith' from the dandy's 'Bible', the equivalent of the Thirty-nine Articles of the Church of England. This is done with an apparently straight face. The first few articles read as follows:

1. Coats should have nothing of the triangle about them; at the same time, wrinkles behind should be carefully avoided.
2. The collar is a very important point: it should be low behind, and slightly rolled.
3. No licence of fashion can allow a man of delicate taste to adopt the posterial luxuriance of a Hottentot.
4. There is safety in a swallow-tail.
5. The good sense of a gentleman is nowhere more finely developed than in his rings.
6. It is permitted to mankind, under certain restrictions, to wear white waistcoats.
7. The trowsers must be exceedingly tight across the hips.

If we feel inclined to think this rather too broad a parody, we need only look at the equivalent passage in the original, Bulwer's *Pelham; or, the Adventures of a Gentleman*, where a scarcely less preposterous list of 'Maxims' is set down, including this one: 'There is an indifference to please in a stocking down at heel — but there may be a malevolence in a diamond ring.'[11]

Not content with ridiculing the dandy code, Carlyle shows his Swiftian sense of moral outrage in his apparently guileless comparison of the dandy's clothing with that of the poorest of the poor in England, Scotland, and Ireland. His own gift for naming and coining phrases joins happily with the many terms already in existence in different parts of the country to describe the most wretched members of society, and he pretends that, like the dandy, these are members of a religious community:

> In strange contrast with this Dandiacal Body stands another British Sect, originally, as I understand, of Ireland, where its chief seat still is; but known also in the main Island, and indeed every where rapidly spreading . . . in England they are generally called the *Drudge* Sect; also, unphilosophically enough, the *White Negroes*; and, chiefly in scorn by those of other communions, the *Ragged-Beggar* Sect. In Scotland, again, I find them entitled *Hallan-shakers*, or the

---

[11] [Edward Lytton Bulwer], *Pelham; or, the Adventures of a Gentleman*, 3 vols (1828), I, p. 69.

> *Stook-of-Duds* Sect; any individual communicant is named *Stook-of-Duds* (that
> is, Shock of Rags), in allusion, doubtless, to their professional Costume. While
> in Ireland, which, as mentioned, is their grand parent hive, they go by a
> perplexing multiplicity of designations, such as *Bogtrotters, Redshanks,
> Ribbonmen, Cottiers, Peep-of-day Boys, Babes of the Wood, Rockites, Poor-Slaves.*

The articles of faith of *this* sect appear to be 'the two Monastic Vows, of
Poverty and Obedience', especially Poverty, which, 'it is said, they observe
with great strictness'.[12]

Sartor Resartus would eventually claim the status of an iconic work;
George Eliot remembered her reading of it as an 'epoch' in her life and knew
that many others felt the same; to one young man who read it in 1841 it was
'the *Pilgrim's Progress* of the nineteenth century'; it was a success in America,
thanks to the proselytising of Emerson, who found a publisher for it before
one could be found in England; and Oscar Wilde included it in the list of
books he requested from his prison cell in 1896.[13] But when Carlyle took his
manuscript to London in August 1831 he was unable to get it published,
partly because of the book's strangeness, partly because everyone was
obsessed with party politics, and partly because Carlyle's dealings with the
famous London publishers John Murray and the Longmans were naïve and
lacking in tact.[14] In his *Reminiscences* he wrote sourly, 'The beggarly history
of poor *Sartor among the Blockheadisms* is not worth my recording.'[15]

Though Carlyle made some new friends in London during this visit —
among them Mill, Leigh Hunt, and assorted radicals — he was unsuccessful
in his two aims of publishing his manuscript and organising a lecture series.
The best he could do was submit to the cutting up of *Sartor* to appear in
serial parts in *Fraser's Magazine*, a middlebrow magazine of vaguely radical
or progressive views, which duly serialised the work during 1833–4. To his
embarrassment, Carlyle agreed to have his portrait sketched by the resident
artist at *Fraser's*, Daniel Maclise. He went down to the Regent Street offices
of the magazine in February 1832 to sit, or rather stand, for his likeness,
which was drawn 'in foolish attitude, leaning on elbow (it was his choosing),
at full length'.[16] The resulting sketch, humorously making something of a
dandy of the scourge of dandyism, appeared in *Fraser's* in June 1833. It is, as
it happens, the earliest surviving likeness of Carlyle, and therefore of interest,
foolish attitude or not.

---

[12] *Sartor Resartus*, pp. 204–6 (Book III, ch. 10, 'The Dandiacal Body').
[13] See Ashton, *Thomas and Jane Carlyle*, pp. 145, 164, 167, 178, 249.
[14] Ibid., pp. 118–19, 128.
[15] Carlyle, *Reminiscences*, p. 83.
[16] Carlyle to John Carlyle, 16 February 1832, *Collected Letters*, VI, p. 125.

Figure 12.1.   Thomas Carlyle, sketch by Daniel Maclise, *Fraser's Magazine*, June 1833 (Victoria and Albert Picture Library).

Meanwhile, in the spring of 1832 there was no immediate career prospect for Carlyle in London, so he and Jane (who had joined him for the winter months) returned to their Dumfriesshire wilderness. Two more years went by, years of financial struggle, of writing articles for periodicals, of corresponding with Emerson, who had been so struck by Carlyle's anonymous articles on German literature and on the state of England in the *Edinburgh Review* that he sought out the author in the summer of 1833 while on a tour of Europe, turning up at Craigenputtoch out of the blue to converse with the man he admired as much as he did the more famous Wordsworth and Coleridge, whom he also visited. Then in spring 1834 Carlyle and Jane took the opportunity of the surprise announcement by their servant Grace that she was leaving them to decide on a new and — as it proved — final move for themselves. As Carlyle represented it to John, it was a sudden decision:

> After meditating on it [Grace's announcement] for a few minutes, we said to one another: 'Why not *bolt*, out of all these rocky despicabilities, of . . . peat-moss, and isolation, and exasperation, and confusion, and go at once to London?' *Gedacht, gethan* [no sooner said than done]![17]

At thirty-eight, Carlyle was ready to try once more to take London by storm. Life at Craigenputtoch had been lonely and strained, especially for Jane, who had no books and articles to keep her busy, to whom no children had been born, and who found her dyspeptic husband a difficult companion. It is true that she had suffered during the winter of 1831–2 from the famous London fogs, telling a cousin in December 1831 of a fog 'so thick you might put it in your pocket' and of 'a dead sea of greencoloured filth under foot'.[18] And she had been critical of some of the London 'literary ladies' she met, with their 'fine en-thu-si-asm' and desire to 'swear everlasting friendship' with her. But she had also seen how Mill and his friends admired Carlyle, and she had hopes that he would at last find success in London, which to her, though no longer the destination of her youthful dreams, was a desirable alternative to the 'desert' of Craigenputtoch and the deadening narrowness of polite Edinburgh.[19]

Carlyle preceded Jane to London in search of a house. He sent back lively letters describing his adventures, including an incomparable verbal portrait of the Chelsea household of Leigh Hunt, literary survivor of the Romantic period, famous for having libelled the Prince Regent in his younger years, famous for having been the friend of Shelley and Byron, famous still for

---

[17] Carlyle to John Carlyle, 25 February 1834, ibid., VII, p. 103.
[18] Jane Carlyle to Mary Welsh, 27 December 1831, ibid., VI, p. 81.
[19] See Ashton, *Thomas and Jane Carlyle*, p. 130.

being an inveterate 'borrower of shillings', as the Carlyles soon found. Carlyle visited the Hunts in Upper Cheyne Row:

> O ask me not for a description till we meet! The Frau Hunt lay drowsing on cushions 'sick, sick' with thousand temporary ailments, the young imps all agog to see me jumped hither and thither, one strange goblin-looking fellow, about 16, ran ministering about tea-kettles for us; it was all a mingled lazaretto and tinkers camp, yet with a certain joy and nobleness at heart of it; faintly resembling some of the maddest scenes in *Wilhelm Meister*, only madder.[20]

Still, for all his 'poetic Tinkerdom', Hunt helped Carlyle to find the perfect house in nearby Cheyne Row at a rent of £35 a year. Jane came south with all the furniture and her canary Chico, and the pair settled in at number 5, Cheyne Row, which would become within a few years, thanks to them, the most famous address in Chelsea, if not in the whole of London. Dickens has famously been called a special correspondent for posterity; the phrase applies at least equally to both Carlyles, whose letters comment almost daily on the goings-on in London, great and small. Jane started straight away in a letter to her Edinburgh friend Eliza Stodart, who had known of her utter loneliness and desolation at Craigenputtoch:

> Well! is it not very strange that I am here? sitting in my own hired house by the side of the Thames as if nothing had happened; with fragments of Haddington [her home town in East Lothian], of Comely Bank [her first married home in Edinburgh], of Craigenputtoch interweaved with *co[c]kneycalities* into a very habitable whole? Is it not strange that I should have the everlasting sound in my ears, of men, women, children, omnibuses, carriages glass coaches, streetcoaches, waggons, carts, dog-carts, steeple bells, doorbells, Gentleman-raps, twopenny-post-raps, footmen-showers-of raps, of the whole devil to pay, as if plague pestilence, famine, battle, murder sudden death and wee Eppie Daidle [a child in Scott's *Heart of Midlothian*] were broken loose to make me diversion. — And where is the stillness, the eternal sameness, of the last six years.—? Echo answers at Craigenputtoch! There let them 'dwell with Melancholy' [Milton, 'Il Penseroso'] and old Nanny Macqueen, for this stirring life is more to my mind . . .[21]

Jane was soon rivalling Carlyle in her disapproving but not altogether hostile descriptions of the Hunt household round the corner. Writing to Carlyle's thrifty mother, she contrasts English and Scottish housekeeping (though it has to be admitted, even by Jane, that poor Mrs Hunt should not stand as a representative of the ordinary English housewife):

> Our little household has been set up again, at a quite moderate expence of money and trouble (wherein I cannot help thinking with a *chastened vanity*, that

---

[20] Carlyle to Jane Carlyle, 17 May 1834, *Collected Letters*, VII, pp. 152–3.
[21] Jane Carlyle to Eliza Stodart, *c*. August 1834, ibid., VII, p. 251.

the superior shiftiness and thriftiness of the Scotch character has strikingly manifested itself). The English women turn up the whites of their eyes and call on the 'good Heavens' at the bare idea of enterprises which seem to me in the most ordinary course of human affairs—I told Mrs Hunt one day I had been very busy *painting*: 'What?' she asked is it a portrait? 'O No', I told her 'something of more importance, a large wardrobe'—She could not imagine she said 'how I could have patience for such things'—And so having no patience for them herself what is the result? she is every other day reduced to borrow my tumblers, my teacups, even—a cupful of porridge, a few spoonfuls of tea are begged of me, because 'Missus has got company and happens to be out of the article'—in plain unadorned English because 'Missus is the most wretched of Managers and is often on the point of having not a copper in her purse'.

Getting into her stride and widening her observations beyond the hapless Mrs Hunt, Jane continues:

To see how they live and waste here it is a wonder the whole City does not bankrape and go out of sight—flinging platefuls of what they are pleased to denominate '*crusts*' (that is, what I consider all the best of the bread), into the ash-pits.—I often say with honest self congratulation in Scotland we have no such thing as '*crusts*'.[22]

Carlyle too regales his mother with details of the Londoner's daily diet. The beer and potatoes are fine, as are meat and bread; but the milk is adulterated and disgusting—a frequent complaint about London milk at this time—and Carlyle defends his one luxury in the food line. 'To give real money for imaginary milk', he tells his mother in July 1834, 'is a thing I will not consent to; so we have given it up, and get "two-penn'orth" of cream night and morning which (when the weather is not "thundery") really answers very well.' As for butter, meal for porridge, and ham, he will rely on a 'huge barrel' of these provisions being sent by his farmer brothers from Dumfriesshire every so often.[23] The Carlyles persisted in their habit of eating porridge in the evening, and Carlyle later remembered how Leigh Hunt, with his 'tricksy turns of intellect' and his 'pretty little laugh' (Carlyle and Jane privately called him a 'kind of talking nightingale'), would join in, accepting 'a tiny basin' and eating the porridge 'with a teaspoon, to sugar'.[24] An insight into one possible cause of the digestive problems from which Carlyle, and sometimes Jane too, suffered is afforded by a remark of Jane's, in another scornful letter about Mrs Hunt's housekeeping, on the English practice of eating fruit: 'When we dine out we see as much money expended on a dessert

---

[22] Jane Carlyle to Margaret Carlyle, 1 September 1834, ibid., VII, pp. 287–8.
[23] Carlyle to Margaret Carlyle, 6 July 1834, ibid., VII, pp. 235–6.
[24] Carlyle's notes (1866) to Jane's letters, ibid., VII, p. 290.

of fruit (for no use but to give people a cholic) as would keep us in necessaries for two or three weeks.'[25]

For all this self-stereotyping as frugal Scots aghast at London prodigality, the Carlyles settled down with gusto to their new London life. They needed to be penny-pinching; it would be several years before Carlyle made enough money from his published works to render them comfortably off. But in spite of English amusement at their evening bowl of porridge, they attracted increasing numbers of friends and acquaintances to their modest house in Chelsea. Carlyle's name was already known in some literary and political circles, as we have seen, and he became a powerful magnet to all sorts of groups and individuals, from foreign exiles and refugees, beginning with Mazzini, who sought out Carlyle in the early 1840s and became one of Jane's closest friends, to literary men and women, including both Brownings, Tennyson, A. H. Clough, Thackeray, and Dickens, and later the scientists Darwin and Huxley. The magnetism was due in about equal measure to his writings, his lecturing, which he began in the late 1830s with a course arranged by Harriet Martineau and other friends who knew of his relative poverty, and his conversation.

Indeed both Carlyles were famed for their spoken wit, which appears to have been as ready as their undeniable brilliance in letters. In the circle of aspiring writers who gathered round Leigh Hunt, Jane was known as 'a Scotch Madame de Staël', and Dickens wrote admiringly of her verbal 'flashing and shining' at a breakfast given by the ancient poet Samuel Rogers.[26] Not everyone liked Jane's wit; her brother-in-law John Carlyle disparaged it as 'Galloway Doric', and Carlyle's biographer J. A. Froude reported that she had a tongue 'like a *cat's*' which 'would take the skin off with a touch'.[27] All agreed that she was a witty, if cruel, conversationalist, notable, like Carlyle, for her exaggeration, especially when denouncing. Their younger Scottish friend Margaret Oliphant thought she understood this trait in both Carlyles; it was, she said:

> A mixture of Scotch shyness, and a good deal of that uncomprehended, unexplainable feeling which made Mrs Carlyle reply with a jibe, which meant only a whimsical impulse to take the side of the opposition, and the strong Scotch

[25] Jane Carlyle to Margaret Carlyle, 21 November 1834, ibid., VII, p. 338.

[26] See Charles Richard Sanders, *Carlyle's Friendships and Other Studies* (Durham, North Carolina, 1977), p. 158; Dickens to Washington Irving, 5 July 1856, *The Letters of Charles Dickens*, eds Madeleine House, Graham Storey, Kathleen Tillotson et al., 12 vols (Oxford, 1965–2002), VIII, p. 151.

[27] Sanders, *Carlyle's Friendships*, p. 158; Froude to Amely Bölte, 27 May [1882?], Manfred Eimer, 'Briefe an Amely Bölte aus Carlyles Freundeskreis', *Englische Studien* 49 (January 1916), p. 271.

sense of the absurdity of a chorus of praise, but which looks so often like detraction and bitterness.[28]

Carlyle's own vehemence in speech, so much of a piece with his writing, was a subject of great interest to scores of his contemporaries. Thackeray relished telling a story of Carlyle trouncing an opponent at the dinner table in 1850, the unfortunate diplomat and writer Henry Reeve:

> Who had a stiff white neckcloth, wh. probably offended the Seer. He tossed Reeve and gored yea as a bull he chased and horned him: for an hour or more he pitched about him ripping open his bowels and plunging his muzzle into Reeve's smoking entrails.[29]

A number of friends, especially female friends like Harriet Martineau and Elizabeth Barrett Browning, came to the conclusion that Carlyle's savageness and scorn were his way of expressing an acute sensitivity.[30] This was certainly the impression he made on his hearers when he took, with extreme nervousness, to the lecturing stage. Harriet Martineau noticed that at his first series in 1837 (on German literature) he stood 'yellow as a guinea, with downcast eyes, broken speech at the beginning, and fingers which nervously picked at the desk before him'.[31] His evident sincerity overcame these disadvantages, however, and his lectures were deemed a success with the literary and fashionable London audience they attracted. When he lectured again in 1839, now well and truly famous as the historian of the French Revolution, Leigh Hunt gave accounts of the lectures — on revolutions in modern Europe — in the *Examiner*, noticing 'a noble homeliness, a passionate simplicity and familiarity of speech', and continuing with mingled admiration and gentle teasing:

> Hearty convictions like these, uttered in such simple, truthful words, and with the flavour of a Scottish accent (as if some Puritan had come to life again, liberalised by German philosophy, and his own intense reflections and experience), can be duly appreciated only by those who see it. Every manly face among the audience seems to knit its lips, out of a severity of sympathy, whether it would or no; and all the pretty church-and-state bonnets seem to thrill through all their ribbons.[32]

[28] Mrs Harry Coghill (ed.), *Autobiography and Letters of Mrs Margaret Oliphant* (1899, repr. Leicester, 1974), p. 5.
[29] Thackeray to James Spedding, 5 January 1850, Gordon N. Ray (ed.), *The Letters and Private Papers of William Makepeace Thackeray*, 4 vols (Cambridge, Mass., 1945–6), II, p. 628.
[30] Harriet Martineau, *Autobiography*, 2 vols (London, 1877, repr. 1983), I, pp. 381–2; Elizabeth Barrett Browning to Miss Mitford, 22 October 1851, Frederick G. Kenyon (ed.), *The Letters of Elizabeth Barrett Browning*, 2 vols (London, 1897), II, p. 27.
[31] Harriet Martineau, *Autobiography*, I, p. 383.
[32] Leigh Hunt, quoted by Thomas Ballantyne, *Passages selected from the Writings of Thomas Carlyle. With a biographical memoir* (London, 1855), pp. 21–2.

Hunt here hits on an important reason for Carlyle's huge success as both writer and conversationalist. All those who recognised his importance for them and their generation were responding to a unique combination of Scottish presbyterian earnestness and high-mindedness (the gospel of work, the tendency to sharpness and denunciation, the readiness in quoting the grimmer parts of the Bible) and an openness, a freedom from dogma, a sense of the romance of life and the wonders of the natural world, which Carlyle nourished by immersing himself in German literature and philosophy of the late eighteenth century. Diogenes Teufelsdröckh is the chief embodiment of this heady compound, able to sound satirical like Swift or Sterne, earnest and puritanical like Luther or Bunyan, philosophically idealist like Schiller, and urbane, witty, and all-comprehending, like Goethe. At a time when reform of the national institutions was required, Carlyle steered an invigorating path between, on the one hand, the tired old privileged unjust world of parliament, the Church of England, and the entrenched class system, and, on the other, the main radical opposition, Benthamite and Millite, which he considered preferable to the moribund status quo but morally arid and inclined to throw out spiritual truths along with their discredited forms and doctrines. The following of this Scotto-Germanic path was what Carlyle urged in *Sartor* and in all his works. As Henry James senior put it in a letter of 1843 to Emerson, Carlyle was:

> The very best interpreter of spiritual philosophy . . . *for this age*, the age of transition and conflict. And what renders him so is his natural birth- and education-place. Just to think of a *Scotchman* with a heart widened to German spiritualities![33]

In *Sartor* itself Carlyle's German philosopher Teufelsdröckh states that he honours two kinds of men, 'and no third'. The first is 'the toilworn Craftsman that with earth-made Implement laboriously conquers the Earth, and makes her man's'. He venerates this man's 'rugged face, all weather-tanned, besoiled, with its rude intelligence; for it is the face of a Man living manlike'. The second is the man 'who is seen toiling for the spiritually indispensable; not daily bread, but the Bread of Life'. Complementing the other, he is the 'Artist; not earthly Craftsman only, but inspired Thinker, who with heaven-made Implement conquers Heaven for us!'[34]

These two types, the noble peasant and the hero as a man of letters, appear again and again, in different guises, in all Carlyle's writings. His own father, James Carlyle — farmer, stonemason, semi-literate speaker of great

---

[33] Henry James to R. W. Emerson, 11 May 1843, Alfred Habegger, *The Father: a Life of Henry James, Sr.* (New York, 1994), p. 202.

[34] *Sartor Resartus*, p. 168 (Book III, ch. 4, 'Helotage').

natural power (Carlyle said he spoke constantly in metaphors, 'though he knew not what a metaphor was'), choleric, a man whose children 'dreaded his wrath', and who believed in the literal truth of hell-fire for the majority of sinners after death, who was upright-downright honest and fearless —was the first and best type of the labouring craftsman. 'I have a sacred pride in my Peasant Father', Carlyle says in the reminiscence he wrote immediately after hearing of his father's death early in 1832.[35] He was still in London with the unpublished *Sartor* on his hands when he got the news, whereupon he shut himself up in his rented room in the reform-mad metropolis to write his homage to old James Carlyle, who had never been out of Dumfriesshire in his life. The chief example in *Sartor* of the second type of man, the artist-thinker, is Goethe, the writer whom Carlyle most revered as 'my Teacher and Benefactor', as he told Goethe himself in a letter of 1827.[36]

Carlyle had suffered as a young man in Edinburgh from doubts about his vocation, even about religion itself, and from a depression of spirits and of physical health which nearly drove him mad. He owed his recovery chiefly to a reading of Goethe's works, particularly *Faust*, in which he discovered that Goethe had suffered in the same way and had reached a level of serenity and resignation to which Carlyle also aspired. He later told Goethe that he was once 'an Unbeliever, not in Religion only, but in all the Mercy and Beauty of which it is a symbol, . . . storm-tossed in my own imaginations; a man divided from men; exasperated, wretched, driven almost to despair'. Goethe's acquisition of calm wisdom had encouraged him, even saved him from thoughts of suicide.[37] He gave dramatic and, it has to be said, rather un-Goethean expression to his spiritual travails in the biographical part of *Sartor Resartus*, where Teufelsdröckh goes through his famous phase of unbelief, the Everlasting No, which is followed by a sojourn in the Centre of Indifference, and culminates in the Everlasting Yea of a renewed spiritual belief shorn of sectarian dogma and best expressed by Carlyle's term 'natural supernaturalism' —in effect a kind of pantheism modelled on Goethe's.

Goethe and other German writers helped Carlyle out of his 'pit of Tophet', but as the phrase itself (a favourite of his) suggests, his rhetoric was largely homegrown, the offspring of his Scottish, Bible-inspired upbringing. The chief clue to his extraordinary influence on his contemporaries lies in the vividness of his language, and in particular its inventiveness, which in turn derives from a combination of eclectic reading in German and other literatures, inwardness with the language of the Bible, and local and family phrases from rural Dumfriesshire, all rolled into a glorious and sometimes outrageous whole.

[35] Carlyle, *Reminiscences*, pp. 6, 9, 10, 12.
[36] Carlyle to Goethe, 20 August 1827, *Collected Letters*, IV, p. 248.
[37] Carlyle to Goethe, ibid.

Here, to conclude, are a few of the words and phrases either invented or naturalised by Carlyle, and brought by him to the status of household words in English:

- Philistinism (from the German, first used in his *Edinburgh Review* article 'The State of German Literature', 1827).
- Gigmanity (meaning an outward show of respectability, after a famous murder trial of 1824, in which a witness attested to the respectability of one of the parties by referring to his owning a gig; first used in an essay on Jean Paul Friedrich Richter, *Foreign Review*, 1830).
- Environment (first used by Carlyle in its modern sense of that which surrounds, rather than the older meaning of the act of surrounding, in the *Foreign Review*, 1830).
- The unspeakable Turk (used during the Crimean War, but first in an article on the *Nibelungenlied* in the *Westminster Review*, 1831).
- Backwoodsman (*Sartor Resartus*).
- Industrialism (*Sartor Resartus*).
- National Palaver (for parliament, first used in *Chartism*, 1839).
- Morrison's Pill (would-be universal panacea, *Past and Present*, 1843).
- Captains of industry (*Past and Present*).
- Cash nexus (*Past and Present*, borrowed, along with 'captains of industry', by Marx and Engels in *The Communist Manifesto*, 1848).
- Dismal Science (for political economy, first used in 1849 in 'The Nigger Question').

There are many more, some outlandish, some witty, many insulting; they occur in Carlyle's works, his letters, and his conversation. Some of the expressions he shares with Jane. They picked up phrases from the conversation of others and adopted them for comic purposes, using this 'Coteriesprache' in letters to one another; Mazzini's peculiar semi-command of English comes alive in this way in the pages of their correspondence. The passion for naming and nicknaming was one which Carlyle identified as a Scottish characteristic.[38] He himself took the art to new heights.

The distinctive Carlylean voice of *Sartor Resartus* acted on its readers as a secular Bible, a *Pilgrim's Progress* for the age. The description of Teufelsdröckh's journey from doubt and despair to affirmation spoke to a whole generation of young men and women at mid-century who found themselves spiritually and professionally adrift, unable to cling to old certainties

---

[38] Notebook entry of September 1830, *Two Note Books of Thomas Carlyle*, ed. Charles Eliot Norton (New York, 1898), p. 168.

of belief in the face of the findings of geology, comparative history, and biology. Carlyle's admirer and biographer Froude describes his own experience as a student in Oxford in the 1840s, when 'all round us, the intellectual lightships had broken their moorings', the lights were 'all drifting, the compasses all awry', and there was 'nothing left to steer by except the stars'. To this generation, which included Arnold, Clough, Kingsley, and many more, Carlyle's voice rang 'like the sound of "ten thousand trumpets" in their ears, as the Knight of Grange said of John Knox'.[39]

By the 1840s Carlyle had become the single most admired writer of the day, the two Carlyles the most famous married couple of the day, and the little house in Chelsea a mecca for all sorts and conditions of men and women. Thackeray, trying to persuade his mother in 1848 that taking a modest house for rent would not compromise her respectability or dignity, reached for a salient example. 'Tom Carlyle', he wrote, 'lives in perfect dignity in a little [£]40 [actually £35] house at Chelsea with a snuffy Scotch maid to open the door, and the best company in England ringing at it.'[40] Carlyle had come to London nearly twenty years earlier with a desire to purge English philistinism by administering an emetic in the shape of *Sartor Resartus*. He had now reached a wide audience and, moreover, one which seemed happy to swallow the medicine and consider itself restored and reinvigorated by the Germano-Scottish Sage of Chelsea.

[39] J. A. Froude, *Thomas Carlyle: a History of his Life in London*, 2 vols (London, 1884), I, pp. 311–12.
[40] Thackeray to his mother, 4 August 1848, Ray (ed.), *Letters and Private Papers*, II, p. 418.

13

Anglo-Scottish Political Relations in the Nineteenth Century, *c*.1815–1914

I. G. C. HUTCHISON

I

FROM CERTAIN PERSPECTIVES, ENGLISH AND SCOTTISH POLITICS IN THE NINETEENTH CENTURY were pretty fully meshed together—certainly compared to Ireland. The tensions which had bedevilled relations between the two countries in the preceding couple of centuries, as outlined by earlier contributors to this volume, seemed to have evaporated. Lord Rosebery, one of the foremost Scottish beneficiaries of this process, reflected in 1871: 'Now indeed the jealousies and mistrust which once separated the two countries divide them no more than does the Roman wall.'[1] Scottish integration was highlighted by participation in government at the highest levels. There were four Scottish-born Prime Ministers in this period, against one in the eighteenth century and three since 1918. Scots occupied most of the other senior ministerial posts at some point. There was also the anomaly of four Scots, as Lord Chancellors, sitting at the head of the English legal system. This interchangeability perhaps reached its zenith in 1892, when Gladstone appointed the Englishman, Sir G. O. Trevelyan, albeit representing a Scottish constituency, as Scottish Secretary. The first chair—in 1889—of the London County Council was Rosebery, a very potent indicator of the metaphorical dismantling of Hadrian's wall.

The extent of this political relationship can be exemplified in three areas: policy, party system, and personnel. There were, naturally, certain general elections where specifically Scottish issues gained saliency north of the Border, such as the Church of Scotland crisis in 1841, and both Scottish disestablishment and the Highland land question in 1885. But as a general rule,

---

[1] Lord Rosebery, *Miscellanies, Literary and Historical* (London, 1921), II, pp. 101–2.

Proceedings of the British Academy, **127**, 247–266. © The British Academy 2005.

elections were fought on the same issues in both countries, especially when major issues were at stake, e.g., parliamentary reform (1830), Irish Home Rule (1886), free trade (1906), land reform and the House of Lords (both 1910 contests). This was underlined by English politicians regularly election-eering in Scotland, and vice versa. Gladstone's Midlothian campaign of 1879–80 is the best illustration of the former. Examples of the latter include the Edinburgh Radical Duncan MacLaren's support of John Bright at the 1857 Birmingham election hustings, while the Scottish Secretary, Lord Pentland, campaigned in more English than Scottish towns in the 1910 elections.

These cross-border fusions also operated below the level of high national issues. Middle-class political preoccupations were shared: opposition to the Orders in Council during the Napoleonic wars was as vociferous among Scottish as English commercial groups. Support for the Anti-Corn Law League was widespread in Scotland; indeed MacLaren chaired the first three days' proceedings at a huge conference held by the League in London in 1842. The Scottish-born MPs W. S. Lindsay, John Holms, Samuel Laing, W. E. Baxter, and R. A. MacFie were all leaders in the Financial Reform move-ment, a key middle-class pressure group of the mid-Victorian years.[2] The Montrose-born Joseph Hume was a prominent champion of British middle-class radicalism in the second quarter of the century. On winning Hume's old Scottish seat in 1896, John Morley, the embodiment of the next radical gen-eration, described him as: 'the leader who succeeded in the virtuous addition of retrenchment to peace and reform as the Radical watchwords'.[3] In the 1870s and 1880s, Joseph Chamberlain's radicalism found an eager army of followers in Scotland.

Likewise, working-class politics were firmly British in scope: the 1820 Rising in Scotland was intended to coincide with similar movements in the north of England, which never came off. The language of these Scottish rad-icals was saturated with British references, most notably the invocation of Magna Carta. John Bragshaw, a Dorset radical, conducted a speaking tour of Scotland in early 1820, and the subsequent unrest was ascribed in part to the influence of his rhetoric.[4] Alexander Campbell, the Scottish co-operative propagandist, spent eighteen years in England from 1838, and claimed to have played a crucial role in launching the Rochdale pioneers.[5] The trial in 1837 of the Glasgow Cotton Spinners acted as a major factor in the emer-

---

[2] G. Searle, *Entrepreneurial Politics in Mid-Victorian Britain* (London, 1993), pp. 6, 101–3, 106–7, 110, 185; H. Malchow, *Gentlemen Capitalists* (London, 1991), pp. 304–5.
[3] J. Morley, *Recollections* (London, 1917), II, p. 47.
[4] E. Royle and J. Walvin, *English Radicals and Reform, 1760–1848* (London, 1982), p. 127.
[5] W. H. Fraser, *Alexander Campbell and the Search for Socialism* (Manchester, 1996), pp. 76–140.

gence of Chartism: the Manchester Trades Council held five meetings in six months to discuss the implications, and the first great Chartist meeting, addressed by English leaders, was held in Glasgow.[6] Scots contributed in other ways to English Chartism: Samuel Kydd, from Arbroath, was a leading figure in the movement in Tyneside, while John Cluer, a Rutherglen weaver, was a popular orator in the west of England.[7]

The creation of a separate working-class political movement in the late nineteenth century was effectively kick-started by developments in Scotland, namely Keir Hardie's candidature in the 1888 Mid-Lanark by-election and the concomitant formation of the Scottish Labour Party. It is not surprising, therefore, that the Independent Labour Party and the pre-war Labour party were dominated by three Scots, Hardie, Glasier, and MacDonald, with Snowden the sole Englishman of equal prominence. The socialists ranged across the Border in both directions. The eccentric English socialist H. H. Champion was a dominant figure in the Aberdeen movement in the 1890s. Ramsay MacDonald built his political career almost exclusively in England. Katharine and Bruce Glasier propagandised for the ILP in Wales, northern England, and Lowland Scotland, and in 1898 they settled in Lancashire to promote the cause there.[8]

The party labels were the same, although there were nuanced differences and an element of organisational distinctiveness. The Liberals and the Conservatives had national organisations in Scotland separate from their English equivalents, but from 1908 Labour had a centralised British-wide structure. There was no party unique to either country, whereas in Ireland, the emergence of the Irish Nationalist Party from the later 1870s emphasised the distinctiveness of politics there. In contrast, no one seriously advocated the formation of a Scottish nationalist party before 1914. The land agitation played a central role in the formation of the Irish Nationalist Party, but in Scotland, the electoral triumphs in 1885-6 of the Crofters' Party, also derived from acute, and contemporaneous, agrarian unrest, did not change the party system. Within a couple of elections, virtually all of the party's six MPs had been absorbed into the two existing parties.

Many Scots sat for English seats (including two Lord Advocates and two Tory party leaders), and vice versa (including two Prime Ministers). While some Englishmen — and Scotsmen — were returned for Irish constituencies

---

[6] D. Thompson, *The Chartists* (London, 1984), pp. 21–3, cf. pp. 138–9; R. Sykes, 'Early Chartism and Trade Unionism in south-east Lancashire', in J. Epstein and D. Thompson, *The Chartist Experience* (London, 1982), pp. 153, 156–8, 166, 159.

[7] O. Ashton, R. Fyson, and S. Roberts, *The Chartist Legacy* (Rendlesham, 1999), pp. 58–9, 64, 66.

[8] L. Thompson, *The Enthusiasts* (London, 1971), pp. 91–5, 111–12.

until the early 1870s, thereafter virtually all Irish seats (certainly in nationalist areas) were occupied only by Irishmen. These movements between
Scotland and England were often highly emblematic of the British-wide
dimension. The return for Stirling in 1847 of the head of the Anti-Corn Law
League, the Manchester businessman J. B. Smith, stressed Scotland's whole-
hearted commitment to that cause. Gladstone chose to fight Midlothian in
1880 in order to emphasise that opposition to Tory foreign policy existed
across Britain. Churchill, rejected in 1908 by Manchester for his social reform
programme, won Dundee with insouciant ease. As a sort of compensation,
England acted as a host to prominent Scots. Bonar Law, rebuffed in Glasgow
in 1906, was granted political asylum within four months, when he was
elected MP for Dulwich.

     This cross-over process was particularly strong in working-class move-
ments. Two English Chartist leaders, Robert Lowery and Henry Vincent,
stood for Scottish seats in 1841. The Scottish miners' union leader, Alexander
MacDonald, became the first Scottish working man to sit in parliament.
MacDonald represented Stafford from 1874, having lost at Kilmarnock in
1868. Keir Hardie sat both for English and Welsh seats, but never a Scottish
one. The Glasgow-born Pete Curran was Labour's victor at the famous 1907
Jarrow by-election. Against this, Englishmen stood in Scotland as Labour or
socialist candidates; for example, Tom Mann at North Aberdeen, Joseph
Burgess at both Glasgow Camlachie and Montrose, and Fred Bramley at
South Aberdeen.

     Some men, having initially moved over the Border, remained there for the
rest of their parliamentary careers: Arthur and Gerald Balfour, although
Scottish, both sat always for English constituencies, while Asquith, Yorkshire
born and bred, represented only Scottish seats. Others, however, moved freely
back and forth between the two countries. The fluidity of national boundaries was nicely illustrated by two Scottish brothers, Sir James Fergusson and
Sir Charles Dalrymple (the latter changed his surname in order to inherit).
Both initially sat for Scottish constituencies — Fergusson held Ayrshire from
1859 to 1868, and Dalrymple, Buteshire from 1868 to 1885 — but subsequently held English seats; Fergusson representing Manchester North-east
from 1885 to 1906, and Dalrymple, Ipswich from 1886 to 1906. Moreover,
Ipswich's two MPs for a decade after 1886 were both Scots, and, as a counter-
balance, Kilmarnock elected Englishmen for all but seven of the years
between 1832 and 1880.

     If anything, the balance of movement between countries seems to have
altered appreciably over the period. The trend was highlighted by an incident
in the 1890s, when two rising Liberal party stars, Asquith and Augustine
Birrell, climbed a hill behind Kirkcaldy. As they looked over the Firth of
Forth and the surrounding land, one exclaimed: 'What a grateful thought

Table 13.1.   Numbers and percentages of Scots MPs in English and Welsh seats, and English and Welsh MPs in Scottish seats, between 1832 and 1914.

General election	Scots in English and Welsh seats		English and Welsh in Scottish seats	
	Number	%	Number	%
1832	12	2.4	0	0
1868	14	2.9	3	5.2
1885	9	2.0	5	7.1
[Aug. 1914]	19	3.9	12	17.1

that there is not an acre in this vast and varied landscape that is not represented at Westminster by a London barrister.'[9] This process intensified as the Liberals steadily lost ground in England, so that Scottish seats offered a safer prospect. In 1914, eleven of the twelve English-born MPs in Scotland were Liberals, but in England and Wales, only four of the nineteen Scots were. By 1911, complaints were being aired in Scotland about the influx of English carpet-baggers; after all, on strict proportionality, there should have been eighty-four Scots sitting for English constituencies. Interestingly, the target of the most vociferous objections was Gladstone's grandson, who stood for Kilmarnock.[10]

These exchanges were not confined to the electoral level: cross-border personal linkages occurred among all classes. Among the political élite, many were related by marriage to families from the other country: Lord John Russell married Lord Minto's daughter, while Arthur and Gerald Balfour were Salisbury's nephews. Middle-class connections were mainly through business and professional activities on both sides of the Border, but some had marriage links. John Bright's sister met Duncan MacLaren at an Anti-Corn Law League meeting, and from these improbable romantic beginnings, love flourished, so that she became his third wife. The ILP stalwart Bruce Glasier married an English fellow-socialist, Katharine Conway, while his sister married the secretary of the Hammersmith Socialist Society.

II

Nevertheless, there was a sense of grievance among Scots that their national interests and institutions were not being fairly or properly treated by the British state. There was, nonetheless, an inherent contradiction in their main

---

[9] Earl of Oxford and Asquith, *Memories and Reflections* (London, 1928), I, p. 105.
[10] I. G. C. Hutchison, *A Political History of Scotland, 1832–1924* (Edinburgh, 1986), pp. 239, 241.

complaints. On the one hand, it was asserted that Westminster, dominated by English MPs and peers, passed laws which aimed to Anglicise Scottish institutions. On the other hand, parliament was charged with neglecting Scottish legislation, assigning it to the end of the session's timetable, or else elbowing it aside for non-Scottish matters deemed more pressing, so that bills often fell from lack of time. A third grievance was that English ignorance of Scottish matters created serious problems.

Lord Rosebery summed up the feelings of those Scots who detected Anglicisation when he complained in 1882 that legislation was framed on the basic principle that: 'Every part of the United Kingdom must be English because it is a part of the United Kingdom.'[11] Scots law was one of the two main areas where Anglicisation has been most frequently discerned. As an instance of this, the House of Lords was the final court of appeal for Scottish cases, yet until 1876 there was no requirement that a Scottish judge should be on the panel. This resulted in many decisions being grounded in English legal precedents and jurisprudential theory, however contrary to Scots law, and, moreover, they were frequently accompanied by disparaging comments on the Scottish legal system.[12]

However, in addition to this back-door infiltration of Scots law, more direct offensives were asserted. Reforms of the Scottish judicial system and legal procedure were frequently introduced, especially in the first third of the century, with the English model being invoked as the ideal form. Thus trial by jury in civil cases, a breach with Scottish tradition, became law in 1814. The Home Secretary, Peel, justified further changes to Scottish procedure in the 1820s, on the grounds that the Scottish system was 'totally different from English practice, and rather repugnant to English feelings'.[13] In the second half of the century, commercial law seemed a new area of assimilation. Scottish laws were replaced by essentially English-based measures, for example, the Partnership and the Sale of Goods Acts, so that by about 1900 English commercial law applied across all of Britain.

Yet caveats must be entered. For one thing, Peel, the main proponent of change in the 1820s, stated that if Scottish practice could be demonstrated to be rational or effective, then government would not impose Anglicisation.[14] Perhaps more important, moves towards closer integration frequently came from within Scotland. For many Scottish reformers, the motives for change were modernisation and efficiency *per se*, not a slavish adulation of all things

---

[11] Rosebery, *Miscellanies*, II, p. 112.
[12] D. Walker, *A Legal History of Scotland*, VI: *The Nineteenth Century* (London, 2001), pp. 306–23.
[13] M. Fry, *The Dundas Despotism* (Edinburgh, 1992), pp. 358–9.
[14] N. Gash, *Mr Secretary Peel* (London, 1961), pp. 318–20.

English. The Scottish Whigs, who agitated ceaselessly to improve the delivery of justice, were prepared to apply the English model only if it appeared superior. They therefore backed English-style civil juries because they regarded Scottish judges as mere government placemen, so that juries would be more efficient and honest.[15] In the middle of the century, the campaign to assimilate commercial law originated among Scottish entrepreneurs, particularly the Aberdeen and Glasgow Chambers of Commerce, who claimed that the anomalies between the two sets of legislation were highly disruptive to business efficiency. When major measures were extended to Scotland, such as the 1890 Partnership Act and the 1893 Sale of Goods Act, the Faculty of Advocates added its express approval to that of the business lobbies. In some instances, indeed, English opinion was averse to the Scots' Anglicisation demands. The delays in achieving assimilation of commercial law were caused by the indifference of English legislators, who were more interested in the codification of British commercial law.[16] Moreover, recent commentaries point out that English law and practice were not applied blindly. The 1814 Civil Jury Act, far from being a blanket application of the English set-up, was much modified to meet Scottish circumstances. The most detailed history of nineteenth-century Scots law concludes that even in commercial law, full integration was never achieved, and indeed asserts that most of Scots law, in every branch, survived the century pretty much free of pervasive English influences.[17]

Education constituted the second field where the Scottish approach was depicted as being supplanted by English values and methods. For twenty-five years from 1846 the government's involvement in education policy towards Scottish schools was carried out through a committee of the Privy Council, which was headed by English politicians and staffed by English civil servants, and which was denounced for installing English schemes alien to Scottish norms. The introduction of pupil-teachers was highlighted as an instance of this pernicious trend, since Scotland had always relied on university-trained teachers in its parish schools. The changes arising from the 1872 Education Act, introduced by a Lord Advocate described by a biographer as generally too favourable to English law, have been criticised for intensifying the dilution of Scottishness. The timing of the act added to feelings of an English-inspired measure. A Scottish Education bill had failed in 1869, and it was only after an English Education Act was passed in 1870 that Scotland was

---

[15] N. T. Philipson, *The Scottish Whigs and the Reform of the Court of Session* (Edinburgh, 1990), pp. 30, 135–7, 148–56, 165–6.
[16] A. Rodger, 'The codification of commercial law in Victorian Scotland', *Proceedings of the British Academy* 80 (1991), pp. 149–70; Hutchison, *Political History of Scotland*, pp. 93–5.
[17] Walker, *Legal History of Scotland*, VI, pp. 714, 1052–4.

legislated for. But this act had been substantially altered from its earlier, unsuccessful version, and seemed influenced by the intervening English act. The abolition of the old Scottish parochial school system was a central point in this critique. More important, the central body charged with overseeing Scottish schooling, the Scotch Education Board, was located in London, and so perpetuated the pattern of English influence laid down by the Privy Council committee. The civil servants could operate untrammelled by any democratic Scottish control.[18]

But some historians have contended that, far from the 1872 act representing the infiltration of English approaches, it was in reality decidedly different from, and superior to, the 1870 act. It was more forward-looking: schooling was made compulsory, direct religious control was eliminated, school boards were given appreciably greater powers than in England and were more democratic, since, unlike England, they had no seats reserved for landowners only. The failure to locate the Education Board in Edinburgh was, on balance, beneficial: landowners were denied control of Scottish education, so that forward-looking technocrats were freer to innovate. The doughty watchdog against slights to Scottish interests, Duncan MacLaren, rejected the case for an Edinburgh board, as it would prove a waste of taxpayers' money.[19]

It has also been claimed that the unique qualities of the historic Scottish university system were undermined by the imposition of the English model. The most notable success for the Anglicisers was the introduction of Honours degrees. These, with their focus on the in-depth study of a single subject over four years, are alleged to have rapidly ousted the Scottish traditional three-year Ordinary degree, which emphasised breadth of subjects taken. In particular, Philosophy, a compulsory core of the Ordinary degree curriculum, was downgraded to a mere optional subject. So, Oxbridge values won over native traditions.[20]

However, the most authoritative account of Scottish education in the Victorian era argues that this interpretation is overstated. The initiators of change, that is, those sitting on the parliamentary commissions which advocated Scottish university reform, were overwhelmingly Scottish and Scottish-educated, with the English component very much in the minority. Moreover,

[18] J. D. Myers, 'Scottish Nationalism and the antecedents of the 1872 Education Act', *Scottish Education Studies* 4 (1972), pp. 73–92; B. Lenman and J. Stocks, 'The beginnings of state education in Scotland', *Scottish Education Studies* 4 (1972), pp. 93–106.

[19] D. J. Withrington, 'Towards a national system, 1867–1872: the last years in the struggle for a Scottish Education Act', *Scottish Education Studies* 4 (1972), esp. pp. 118–22.

[20] G. Davie, *The Democratic Intellect* (Edinburgh, 1961), esp. Part I.

the pressure for innovation, notably the Honours degree programmes, largely arose within Scotland, not from outside. Scottish students — and their parents — became alarmed at the obstacles which they faced as candidates in competitive public examinations, because these, dovetailed to the levels of English university degrees, called for more advanced knowledge than the Scottish system provided. Moreover, until 1914 it remained the case that the majority of graduates from Scottish universities took the traditional Scottish Ordinary degree.[21]

The complaint that Scottish business was neglected by parliament was a repeated refrain across the period, but seemed to grow increasingly loud and frequent in the thirty years before the World War. Rosebery, again, articulated this viewpoint in 1906, when he objected: 'Scotland, if she asks for ever so little, is always stinted and always starved.'[22]

There were, broadly speaking, two streams to this discontent. The first was that legislation affecting Scotland was not given priority, and indeed was normally the prime casualty if any bills had to be discarded during a parliamentary session. Only twenty-two of the forty-five Scottish bills introduced by J. A. Murray, the Lord Advocate in Melbourne's 1837–41 government, got on to the statute book, and a decade later, in 1848, Scottish MPs were objecting to the lack of fair treatment of Scottish legislation, compared to English and Irish bills.[23] A prominent item in the catalogue of insults to Scotland expounded by the National Association for the Vindication of Scottish Rights in the mid-1850s was inadequate parliamentary time allocated for Scottish issues.[24] The Liberal Lord Advocate of the time seemed to confirm this when he objected to the Cabinet that Scotland was treated unfairly:

> In bills affecting Scotland, in which none but Scottish members take an interest, the business may generally be conducted satisfactorily without any serious encroachment on the Government of the House. But whenever a Scottish measure occurs which the Opposition as a body treat as a party question, its defeat is all but certain, unless it be brought in on proper Government nights, and with the same precautions to secure success which are adopted in regard to English measures.[25]

Gladstone's 1868–74 ministry saw these allegations continued. In the interests of securing the passage of the disestablishment of the Church of

---

[21] R. D. Anderson, *Education and Opportunity in Victorian Scotland* (Edinburgh, 1983), pp. 351–61.

[22] Marquess of Crewe, *Lord Rosebery* (London, 1931), II, p. 608.

[23] G. W. T. Omond, *The Lord Advocates of Scotland from the Fifteenth Century to the Passing of the Reform Bill. Second Series: 1834–1880* (London, 1914), p. 31 n. 4, pp. 115–16.

[24] G. Morton, *Unionist-Nationalism* (Edinburgh, 1999), pp. 139–44.

[25] National Archives of Scotland (hereafter NAS), Lord Advocates' MSS, Memorandum by J. Moncrieff, 22 February 1855, AD 56/47/1.

Ireland and the reform of English education, the government sacrificed an important bid to abolish feudal tenure in Scotland, then in 1873 a bill to reform Scottish entail law was jettisoned for the sake of other, non-Scottish causes.[26] It is not surprising that Henry Campbell-Bannerman, who entered parliament in 1868, complained that Scottish bills were being shunted about at the convenience of the government.[27] The second Gladstone administration seemed little better. Rosebery lamented the lack of progress of the Scottish Endowments bill, which was introduced three times by the government and had the solid backing of Scottish opinion, yet was stalled by Gladstone's decision to push forward instead with Imperial and Irish questions.[28] But this was a bi-partisan problem. In 1876, a Liberal backbencher protested at stalled legislation during Disraeli's government, while in 1888, under another Tory government, a Liberal MP protested: 'Why, he asked, should the Scottish estimates be remitted to the end of the programme, coming after everything else?'[29] Between 1900 and 1909, it has been calculated, one-half of all Scottish bills were lost. Perhaps the most vehement protest came at the very end of the period, when a deputation of Liberal MPs and activists met the Prime Minister, Asquith, to explain their grievances in forthright language. They began: 'We feel we do not get sufficient time in this Imperial Parliament for the discussion of Scottish affairs'; then warming to the topic, they elaborated: 'Our complaint is not that Scottish opinion is overridden by English opinion in the United Kingdom, it is that it is too often entirely neglected.'[30]

The haphazard way in which some bills emerged onto the statute book merely underlined this sense of marginalisation. In 1888, an adroit Lord Advocate successfully managed to slip in a major commercial bill late in the evening by exploiting arcane parliamentary procedural rules. The withdrawal from the chamber of the Irish Nationalist MPs had created a hiatus in the Commons timetable, and this allowed the Scottish bill to proceed.[31]

The additional ground of complaint was that, with at best only limited time devoted to Scotland, debate was minimal, and so proper examination of bills was impossible, and finance matters were seriously under-scrutinised. No extensive parliamentary debate on the Scottish church crisis, which had begun in the mid-1830s, took place until 1842. Campbell-Bannerman

---

[26] Omond, *Lord Advocates, 1834–1880*, pp. 247–9, 271–4, 284–5.
[27] J. A. Spender, *The Life of Sir Henry Campbell-Bannerman, GCB* (London, n.d.) I, pp. 47–8.
[28] Crewe, *Lord Rosebery*, I, pp. 154–61, cf. p. 174.
[29] Omond, *Lord Advocates, 1834–1880*, pp. 311–13; H. W. Lucy, *A Diary of the Salisbury Parliament, 1886–1892* (London, 1896), p. 117.
[30] Bodleian Library, Oxford, Asquith MSS, 'Deputation of Scottish Liberal MPs to the Rt Hon. H. H. Asquith, K.C., MP', 6 May 1912, Ms Asquith 89, ff. 4–9.
[31] J. H. A. MacDonald, *Life Jottings of an Old Edinburgh Citizen* (London, 1915), pp. 446–8.

objected to the unsocial hours at which Scottish business was handled in the late 1860s, when debates were taken early in the morning.[32] Ironically, when himself Prime Minister, Campbell-Bannerman's Scottish Secretary was equally scathing about the time scheduled for Scottish business. Sinclair's major proposal, a land bill, was introduced on a Saturday afternoon, and he was wont to refer disparagingly to that slot as the 'Caledonian day'.[33] Therefore, such legislation as was enacted was often badly flawed: the 1866 Sanitary Act proved unworkable because the final appeals were to an English court which had no jurisdiction over Scotland.[34] The Housing Act of 1890 was likewise difficult to apply in Scotland.

It is true that the delay in implementing measures, of which the Scots made so much, was not unique to Scotland. Many bills in general were also dropped through pressure of business (one in four in the early 1870s), but Scottish bills did seem highly accident-prone. The case of education appears a clear illustration of this. The Disruption of 1843 made the Scottish school system, with the Church of Scotland parochial school at its core, impossible to sustain; yet effective reform was not implemented for thirty years. Between 1854 and 1856 three Scottish Education bills were not enacted, despite each being supported by a clear majority of Scottish MPs. This all seemed to emphasise that governments did not place a high priority on addressing the Scottish educational difficulty.

Preoccupied with Imperial and foreign matters, and because until the 1880s there existed no clear governmental mechanism for identifying Scottish opinion, the norm for the British administrations was to look for a broad band of agreement in Scottish civil society before tackling Scottish questions. Only when there was unmistakable evidence that something approaching a consensus had been reached in Scotland could any measure be contemplated. The constitutional expert A. V. Dicey remarked in 1867 that: 'few governments would dare to legislate for Scotland and Ireland in the face of the united opposition of the Scottish and Irish members.'[35] A decade later, Hartington made pretty much the same point, although he gave it a rather more partisan aspect. In response to mounting demands for

[32] Spender, *Sir Henry Campbell-Bannerman*, I, pp. 47–8.

[33] Lady Pentland, *The Right Honourable John Sinclair, Lord Pentland, G.C.S.I.: a Memoir* (London, 1928), pp. 88–9, 110. Cf. R. J. Finlay, *A Partnership for Good* (Edinburgh, 1999), p. 57, where it is stated that a mere six hours per parliamentary session was devoted to Scottish business.

[34] R. J. Morris, 'Victorian values in Scotland and England', in T. C. Smout (ed.), *Victorian Values* (London, 1992), pp. 41–3.

[35] Cited in C. Harvie, 'Nineteenth century Scotland: political unionism and cultural nationalism, 1843–1906', in R. G. Asch (ed.), *Three Nations: a Common History? England, Scotland, Ireland and British History, c.1600–1920* (Bochum, 1993), p. 205.

the disestablishment of the Church of Scotland, he explained the criteria which would lead to action: 'When, if ever, Scottish opinion, or even Scottish Liberal opinion, is fully formed on this subject ... the Liberal party ... will be prepared to deal with the question on its merits and without any reference to any other consideration.'[36]

Hence, the reason for the prolonged delay in legislating for Scottish education was not primarily the indifference of English ministers, but the impossibility of establishing common ground within Scotland as to reform. Denominational rivalries blocked the path, as each proposed measure in the mid-1850s infuriated at least one of the three main presbyterian churches. Only in 1872 were these problems resolved. Similarly, faced with massive rejection by Scottish opinion-formers of a Judicature bill in 1824, the government promptly withdrew it. Scottish land legislation in the 1906–10 parliament encountered difficulties in good part because of the extent of opposition within Scotland to it. A majority of Scottish Cabinet ministers opposed it, a good number of backbench Scottish MPs were unhappy, and senior Scottish Liberal peers like Rosebery and Tweedmouth mounted a vigorous resistance in the Lords.[37]

But, *per contra*, when there was unanimity of opinion in Scotland, and a pressing case for legislation, governments would act decisively. The Court of Session Act of 1868 had its progress smoothed after being jointly endorsed by the two leading Tory and Liberal lawyer-politicians, John Inglis and James Moncrieff. A decade earlier, a similar plan had been dropped when the two most senior Scottish judges disagreed before a parliamentary committee on its desirability. The Crofters Act of 1886 quickly followed both the publication of the Napier Commission's findings and the clear electoral verdict for change in the Highlands in 1885.

Concern that the introduction of a Scottish measure might have undesirable consequences in England often operated to slow down, or derail, the reform. Sinclair's land bills were impeded in part, as his biographer (and widow) remarked, by 'a timid English Smallholding Bill'. In the early 1840s, Wellington worried about a carry-over of evangelical fervour from Scotland to England if there were concessions to the former: 'When one's neighbour's house is on fire, one's own is in danger. We shall have it in England, if not extinguished in Scotland.'[38] Salisbury confessed he was reluctant to reform county government in Scotland, partly on the grounds that: 'My fear has ref-

---

[36] Quoted in T. A. Jenkins, *Gladstone, Whiggery and the Liberal Party, 1874–86* (Oxford, 1988), pp. 79–80.
[37] Pentland, *John Sinclair, Lord Pentland*, p. 90.
[38] Bodleian Library, Graham MSS (Microfilm), C. Arbuthnot to Sir J. Graham, 10 December 1839, Ms 37B.

erence to English opinion . . . [the Scottish bill's contents] will frighten English landowners . . . We shall paralyse our organisation in the counties.'[39] Hence the 1872 Scottish Education Act was radical precisely because the English act had already been passed, and qualms south of the Border had been assuaged.

Furthermore, when Scottish ministers were sufficiently determined, bills could go forward. In 1830, Peel informed the Cabinet that, in the face of the implacable resolve of the Lord Advocate, the Scottish Judicature bill would be proceeded with, even although the government had initially decided to drop it.[40] Here the threat of resignation compelled a change of mind. Where legislation was necessary, room in the legislative schedules could be found. In 1845, three major Scottish bills were piloted through parliament in one year. The most conspicuous of these was the Scottish Poor Law Act, which came only one year after the report of a Royal Commission set up because of a deep crisis in the old system.[41]

The third accusation, ignorance of Scottish peculiarities, arose from a belief that British politicians blundered when dealing with Scotland. Examples of the indifference—not to say on some occasions, plain condescension—of English politicians to Scottish matters are plentiful. The Scottish Prime Minister, Lord Aberdeen, was reminded in 1854 by a former minister of the minimal interest taken in Scotland by his Home Secretary, who was officially responsible for most Scottish business: 'You know perfectly well that Palmerston cares very little for Scotch matters . . .'.[42] Lord Lothian, Salisbury's Scottish Secretary in the late 1880s, ruefully observed that the Prime Minister 'knows nothing about Scotland or Scottish feelings, that is clear'.[43] Salisbury twice declined to visit Glasgow, because the climate was bad and the distance was too great.[44] This last point was echoed by Asquith, who complained of having to speak at 'these remote parts', specifically citing St Andrews.[45] Asquith, it should be noted, had then been MP for East Fife, the constituency contiguous to St Andrews, for over twelve years!

[39] R. H. Williams, *The Salisbury–Balfour Correspondence* (Herts, 1988), p. 284.

[40] G. W. T. Omond, *The Lord Advocates of Scotland from the Close of the Fifteenth Century to the Passing of the Reform Bill* (Edinburgh, 1883), II, pp. 297–9.

[41] Omond, *Lord Advocates, 1834–1880*, pp. 132–3, 143–4.

[42] British Library (BL), Aberdeen MSS, Panmure to Aberdeen, 23 November 1854, Add Ms 43254, ff. 232–4.

[43] Hunterston, Ayrshire, Hunter of Hunterston MSS, Lothian to R. W. C. Cochran-Patrick, 25 May 1888, Ms 1/1.

[44] Chatsworth, Devonshire MSS, Salisbury to Hartington, 9 November 1890, Ms 340/2257; BL Balfour MSS, Salisbury to A. J. Balfour, 22 September 1888, Add Ms 49688, ff. 54–7.

[45] BL Campbell-Bannerman MSS, H. H. Asquith to H. Campbell-Bannerman, 4 September 1899, Add Ms 41210, ff. 171–3.

A second aspect of ignorance was that English politicians appeared eager to avoid any unnecessary involvement in Scottish affairs when these were being aired in parliament, and where evasion was impossible, to treat any engagement as a tedious chore. The Lord Advocate voiced his dismay in 1855 at the failure of English government MPs to attend when important Scottish measures were being considered in the Commons.[46] Thirty years later, in the 1886–92 parliament, Campbell-Bannerman acted as spokesman for the opposition on Scotland. His biographer describes him as 'the natural guardian of Scottish interests and his English colleagues cheerfully placed themselves in his hands and generally retired from the scene when Scotland claimed the attention of the House'.[47]

Scottish viewpoints, however, were rarely lacking within governments: with barely any exceptions, every Cabinet between 1815 and 1914 included at least one Scot—or somebody sitting for a Scottish constituency. Even the two most quintessentially English Prime Ministers of the period had a distinct Scottish presence in their Cabinets. Wellington's 1828–30 Cabinet contained five Scots and Salisbury's 1895–1902 Cabinet had three, as well as, latterly, the Scottish Secretary. This latter tally was only one less than the Scottish Lord Rosebery's Liberal administration of 1894–5. The last Liberal governments were positively overflowing with Cabinet ministers either of Scottish origin or sitting for Scottish seats: Asquith's of 1908–14 included five such. Peel's 1841–6 government, frequently charged with failing to avert the Disruption because of ignorance of Scottish affairs, actually had four Scots in the Cabinet, somewhat above the average for the period.

In addition to the Lord Advocate, for long the political minister as well as the law officer for Scotland, junior ministers were normally given specific duties relating to Scottish matters. These ministerial appointments were most usually made either as a Scottish Lord of the Treasury, or to the Home Office, where much of the responsibility for running Scotland reposed. After 1885, of course, there was a designated Scottish Secretary, but he sat regularly in the Cabinet only from 1902.

There were also non-political factors which might have been expected to alert English politicians to Scottish sensibilities. Lord Minto, Lord John Russell's father-in-law, was described as 'a great, or as some statesmen alleged, an excessive influence' on the Premier, whose brother-in-law also happened to be his personal secretary.[48] Several ministers owned Scottish estates—Lansdowne in Perthshire, Portland in Ayrshire and Caithness, Chilston in Dumfriesshire. Many took regular Scottish holidays, mostly in

[46] NAS Lord Advocates MSS, Minute by J. Moncrieff, 22 February 1855, AD 56/47/1.
[47] Spender, *Sir Henry Campbell-Bannerman*, I, p. 110.
[48] S. Walpole, *The Life of Lord John Russell* (London, 1889), II, p. 329.

the Highlands. It was on the basis of his frequent holidays there that Peel felt competent to advise Queen Victoria on her successful Scottish tour of 1841.[49] Sir William Harcourt regularly sailed round the western seaboard of Scotland, and what he witnessed during these trips led him to take a strong anti-landlord stance during the crofters' agitation.[50] In the last forty years before the Great War, droves of politicians spent the late summer on Highland sporting estates, notably Lord Tweedmouth's shooting lodge at Guisachan, with intrigue and high political discussion filling the hours not spent destroying the local wildlife.

Additionally, care was often taken by English politicians to be fully briefed on Scottish issues before speechifying in the country. As he was about to embark on a political tour of Scotland in 1877, Hartington wrote to Rosebery: 'I shall expect you to give me a safe sentence or two on Scotch church matters.'[51] This may indeed betray ignorance, but it also suggests a willingness to take advice and counsel before expatiating.

Yet many, at the time and since, pointed to the Disruption of 1843 as translucent evidence of ignorance on the part of English politicians, who did not appreciate the nuances of presbyterianism and who were more concerned about the impact on the Church of England than they were to deal with the matter strictly on its own merits. Lord Balfour of Burleigh, the Tory Scottish Secretary sixty years after the event and a staunch member of the Church of Scotland, reflected a general Scottish standpoint when he opined that the secession could have been averted if he had been 'able to say a word to the ignorant and supine English ministers of the day'.[52]

Nevertheless, much of the crisis was located firmly within Scotland and Scottish institutions. The Non-Intrusionists' ecclesiastical framework was struck down by decisions of the Court of Session, and these verdicts were invariably confirmed in appeals to the House of Lords. Indeed, as early as 1826 the Court of Session had rejected the proposition that the Church of Scotland had any jurisdictional legitimacy beyond that conferred by parliament. Irreconcilables were to be found more within the Scottish presbyterian sects than among English politicians. The intransigence shown by Scottish Voluntaries to the pretensions of the Church of Scotland evangelicals was unwavering, and the Melbourne administration was constrained in its room to manoeuvre by the need to placate this important Whig voting interest. For

[49] C. S. Parker, *Sir Robert Peel* (London, 1891–9), I, pp. 287–8; II, pp. 537–45; cf. A. Tyrell, 'The Queen's little trip: the royal visit to Scotland in 1842', *Scottish Historical Review* 82 (2003), pp. 47–53.
[50] A. G. Gardiner, *The Life of Sir William Harcourt* (London, 1923), II, pp. 63–4; cf. I, pp. 531–4.
[51] National Library of Scotland, Rosebery MSS, Hartington to Rosebery, 2 November 1877, Ms 10075, ff. 230–1.
[52] Lady F. Balfour, *A Memoir of Lord Balfour of Burleigh, K.T.* (London, n.d.), p. 26.

the Tories, as the party whose self-proclaimed role was the maintenance of the Constitution, the concept of abandoning parliamentary sovereignty was patently unacceptable. Peel was, moreover, not ignorant of Scottish church questions — he had, after all, been Home Secretary for much of the 1820s. It is clear from his biographers' accounts that he and his inner circle of ministers devoted a great deal of time to the issue: they emphatically did not adopt a cavalier attitude.[53]

III

For much of the century, Anglo-Scottish political relations were reasonably amicable mainly because of the particular arrangements under which Scottish government was conducted. There were several elements involved here. Firstly, the central British state remained pretty much aloof from close and regular direction of Scottish administration. Unlike Ireland, there was no resident large-scale bureaucracy. It is highly significant that from 1827 until 1885, there was no minister or department with specific, designated responsibility for running Scotland. Instead there was a messy dispersal of duties between ministries. A bill of 1880, described as floating between the Home Office, the Privy Council, and the Lord Advocate's office, was held up as 'a typical example of the eddies in which Scottish parliamentary business was made to swirl'.[54]

   Moreover, there persisted in Scotland a powerful legacy of the Whig tradition, reinforced by Enlightenment principles, that good government flourished best in a local urban framework, while the state's role was regarded as valid only in exceptional circumstances. The result was a high degree of self-government within Scotland. Most parliamentary acts were optional, rather than compulsory, so local initiative determined the extent to which governmental strategies were pursued. The use of private acts permitted individual local authorities to deal with their specific problems in their own fashion, and the flow of these private acts expanded steadily as the century progressed.[55] Progressive councils, such as Glasgow, initiated a whole raft of municipal improvements, but other authorities were not obliged by Whitehall to follow suit. So, while the Central Board of Health drove forward sanitary reform in England during its lifetime (between 1848 and 1858), in Scotland it was vig-

[53] Parker, *Sir Robert Peel*, II, pp. 427–30, 486–73; III, pp. 73–150; cf. N. Gash, *Sir Robert Peel* (London, 1972), pp. 378–81.
[54] Crewe, *Lord Rosebery*, I, p. 139.
[55] See Morton, *Unionist-Nationalism*, pp. 7–10, 20–2, 37–44; L. Paterson, *The Autonomy of Modern Scotland* (Edinburgh, 1994), pp. 46–50, 54–5.

orously resisted by the medical profession, and it was not until 1892 that Scottish public health and sanitary provision were put on the same level of central control.[56]

A further aspect of the quasi-self-government that operated in Scotland was the role of the various boards which had oversight of Scottish public administration, such as those for Prisons and for Lunacy. The weightiest of these was the Poor Law Board, established in 1845, which gradually acquired the function of a central supervisor of numerous aspects of local government activity, particularly health, housing, and social welfare. Yet, compared to the English equivalent, its powers were severely restricted: any urban area with a population in excess of 10,000 could ignore the provisions of the Public Health Act with impunity. Whereas the English board had a large number of inspectors to ensure that central standards were being met, the Scottish board was acutely understaffed. The consequence was that the local urban municipal élites could disregard the views of the board, an impasse which was reinforced by the social tension between the dynamic entrepreneurial self-made councillors and the landowning individuals who were installed in charge of the boards.[57]

There was remarkably limited parliamentary scrutiny of the conduct of these boards, in stark contrast to their English equivalents, which were constantly harried by MPs. There was no direct ministerial responsibility for the Scottish boards, and, as we have seen, little time was available at Westminster for Scottish issues to be debated. Hence, between 1845 and 1870, on a mere four instances were the Scottish boards the subject of parliamentary discussion.[58]

The growing tendency to a more interventionist state from the 1870s, seeking to impose standardised and uniform delivery of service across the United Kingdom, inevitably eroded the local state which had obtained in the preceding decades. Whitehall began to apply tighter financial constraints on local government, while increasingly the solutions to the problems of a complex society were perceived to be beyond the scope of a locality. This process of London-based centralisation seems inexorably connected to the rising demand for Scottish Home Rule, which can be seen, in part at least, as a device to formalise and institutionalise arrangements which had hitherto been regarded as functioning efficiently, as well as meeting feelings of national pride. The creation of the Scottish Office in 1885, designed to

---

[56] Morton, *Unionist-Nationalism*, pp. 32–5.

[57] Ibid., pp. 30–2; Paterson, *Autonomy of Modern Scotland*, pp. 51–3.

[58] I. Levitt, *Government and Social Conditions in Scotland, 1845–1918* (Edinburgh, 1980), pp. xi–xii.

appease a sense of neglect, ironically increased the centralising tendency
which served to reduce Scottish control of Scottish affairs.

An additional ingredient was that the Scots felt mounting unhappiness at
the British government's treatment of Ireland. From mid-century, the much
more favourable treatment of Ireland compared to Scotland by the British
state became a repeated litany. Duncan MacLaren often stressed this aspect.
He noted that Scottish judges were paid less, but carried out more judicial
business, than their Irish counterparts. Scotland was underrepresented in
parliament compared to Ireland, both in terms of population and of contributions to the national revenue. Yet the Treasury persisted in spending considerably greater sums on education in Ireland (£447,000) compared to
Scotland (£130,000).[59] An additional grievance felt by the Scots was that the
Irish were perceived as being significantly less peaceable in pushing their
demands. An English Liberal remarked of the Scots that 'the quiescence of
their affairs was in strange contrast to the violently controversial character of
everything Irish.'[60]

The heightened preoccupation from around 1880 with Irish matters intensified this resentment, with the needs of three million Irish people apparently
placed ahead of five million Scots. It was increasingly felt that Scottish issues
were being relegated to accommodate the priorities bestowed on Irish legislation. As early as 1881, Rosebery complained that Scotland was 'mumbling
the dry bones of political neglect and munching the remainder biscuit of
Irish legislation'.[61] A loyal Gladstonian MP for Glasgow plucked up his
courage to tell the GOM in 1882 that after consulting his constituents, he
found that 'they are so sick of Ireland.'[62] The growing appreciation of the
serious nature of Scottish social problems from the 1880s, linked with the rise
of a social reform strand in the Scottish Liberal Party in the 1900s, sharpened
impatience at Westminster's focus on Ireland.

The swelling discontent at Scotland's treatment culminated in the demand
for Scottish Home Rule, launched in the mid-1880s. But, despite the alarm in
England, where some felt there was developing a pan-Celtic movement to
destabilise the United Kingdom and the empire, this was essentially a moderate cry: there was no interest in separation or even federalism, and no challenge to parliamentary sovereignty. Rather than a badge of nationality pure
and simple, the case was couched in terms of making Westminster more effi-

[59] J. B. Mackie, *The Life and Work of Duncan MacLaren* (Edinburgh, 1888), II, pp. 87–8, 117–20,
176–8.
[60] G. M. Trevelyan, *Sir George Otto Trevelyan: a Memoir* (London, 1932), p. 135.
[61] Crewe, *Lord Rosebery*, I, p. 142.
[62] BL W. E. Gladstone MSS, G. Anderson to W. E. Gladstone, 7 August 1882, Add Ms 44,476,
ff. 108–10.

cient by allowing Scottish business to be devolved, so that Imperial and British issues could be properly dealt with. Furthermore, interest in Home Rule for Scotland waxed and waned as the goal of self-government for Ireland drew near or receded, so conveying the impression that the Scots' commitment was essentially a reflexive response. The Scottish Home Rulers first flourished around 1886, fell away while the Tories were in office in the later 1880s, but revived when Gladstone's final ministry of 1892–4 introduced the second Irish Home Rule bill. After that measure was lost in 1894, the Scottish Home Rulers almost disappeared as a political force until the introduction of the third Irish Home Rule bill in the 1910 parliament. Now, however, the pressure for a parallel Scottish act was more intense than hitherto. Right-wing Liberals like Munro-Ferguson joined with progressives like McCallum Scott, and this may reflect a new development: the fusion of a progressive social reform agenda with a more traditional approach might be held to suggest that, politically at least, Scotland was beginning to drift away from England.

Politicians and the public in England seemed less hostile to Scots in this century compared to the previous one. However, tensions did develop as partisan allegiances diverged. The Tories, normally dominant in England after 1874, found Scotland's attachment to Liberalism frustrating, and were therefore inclined to regard Scottish issues as alien and not politically rewarding to engage with. Salisbury stated this very explicitly in 1889 in considering a contentious Scottish measure: 'We have so little to lose (or gain) in Scotland at present that if the effects were limited to that country, I should not, on a purely parliamentary sense, regard the matter as important.'[63]

Unionists saw demands for Home Rule in Scotland as a further stage in the break-up of the United Kingdom and the diminution of the doctrine of parliamentary sovereignty, and so intensified their resistance to Scottish demands. For English Liberals, too, Scottish Home Rule posed problems. If there were to be subordinate legislatures for Ireland and Scotland — and, inevitably, Wales — then clearly the same should be provided for England. But it proved beyond the wit of politicians to devise a viable scheme for English Home Rule. The most ambitious attempt was Churchill's 'heptarchy' formula, but this was never regarded as a realistic solution, and indeed the suggestion that, say, the Midlands should be regarded as being on the same footing as nations like Ireland and Scotland infuriated the Celts. So the impasse on the mechanisms of English devolution spilled over to impede Scottish self-government.

---

[63] Quoted in M. Bentley, *Lord Salisbury's World* (Cambridge, 2001), p. 55.

The rise in English national identity, which many have pointed out as a growing feature after 1880, replaced the 'Britishness' fostered in the late eighteenth and early nineteenth centuries, and sustained by Russell and Palmerston in the middle decades of the nineteenth century.[64] This added to Scotland's sense of marginalisation, the more so as a distinctive 'Scottishness' began to evolve as the century wore on. The Scottish Secretary, Balfour of Burleigh, felt compelled to protest publicly against his own Prime Minister's frequent and vehement anti-Scottish remarks. As Balfour's biographer comments, he 'took effective steps against English arrogance'.[65] A somewhat intemperate instance of growing English antipathy to the other component parts of the United Kingdom was Leo Maxse's statement in 1911 that Great Britain was 'an island in the German Ocean, governed by Scotsmen, kicked by Irishmen and plundered by Welshmen'.[66] But even here, it should be noted that the Scots come off best in this philippic against the three Celtic nations.

Nevertheless, at the moment of the greatest test of British unity, the proportion of Scots enlisting in the First World War was no different from the English and Welsh figures, and much higher than the Irish. But some of the factors behind the rise of Scottish nationalism in its more separatist mid-twentieth-century form had been raised, and the central British state's response to these demands was identified.

---

[64] See R. Collis and P. Dodd, *Englishness and Political Culture, 1880–1920* (London, 1986).
[65] Balfour, *Lord Balfour of Burleigh*, pp. 94–5, cf. pp. 92–3.
[66] Quoted in G. K. Peatling, 'Home Rule for England, English nationalism and Edwardian debates about constitutional reform', *Albion* 35 (2003), p. 75.

Index

judicial system (cont.)
  see also courts; feudalism
juries, civil, 78, 180, 253
jurisprudence, 100, 179–80, 252
  appellate jurisdiction, 179
jurists, Scots, 179

Kailyard novels, 9
Kalmar, Union of (1397–1523), 174
Kames, Henry Home, Lord, 182, 185
  Essay on British Antiquities, 180
Kellie, Earl of, 33
Kennedy, James, 202
Kent, Duke of, 161
Kerr, John, 7–8, 9, 12
Kidd, Colin, ix, 2, 5, 9, 171–87, 192
'Killing Times', 93
King, Alexander, 129, 131, 133–4
King's College, London, 231
kingship, theories of, 29
Kingsley, Charles, 246
Kinloss, Lord, 31
Kintor, David, 128–9
kirk, *see* Church of Scotland
kirk sessions, 114
Kirkwood, Sir Archy, 39
Knox, John, 7, 9, 246
Königsberg, 50
Kydd, Samuel, 249

Labour Party, 38, 249
Laing, Samuel, 248
lairds, 219–22
Lake, Gerard, Viscount (General), 191
Lanarkshire, 111
Lancastrians, 14
land law, 138
  Scottish (1906–10), 258
land reform, 247, 248, 249, 261
land tax, 112
landed classes, 117, 221–3
Landseer, Edwin, 9
Langbein, John, 77
Langford, Paul, ix, 1–2, 4, 143–69
language, dialect and accent, 162–5
Laud, William, Archbishop of Canterbury, 53
Lauder, John (advocate), 134
Lauder, Sir John, of Fountainhall, 80, 84, 86–7, 88, 89, 93, 99
Lauderdale, John Maitland, Duke of, 83, 84
Lauderdale, Lord, 164
Laudian reforms, 52, 53
law
  Borders, 49

English common, 6, 48
Irish lawyers, 48
James VI and I and the, 29
legal education, 178–9
  public and private, 139–40, 262
Scots, 6, 10, 48, 74, 78, 176, 177–80, 252–3
  Scots lawyers, 128, 177–9
  of the sea, 5, 127–41
  separate systems, 35, 127–8, 137
Law, (Andrew) Bonar, 250
Lee, William, 148–9
Leeds Constitutional Society, 200
legislatures, 10, 47–8
Leicester, Robert Dudley, Earl of, 18
Leiden, 178
Leinster, uprising (1629), 45
Leinster, Emily, Duchess of, 143–4
Lennox, Duke of, 31
Lenthall, William, Speaker, 58
Leslie, Alexander (bookseller), 206–8, 210
Levack, Brian, 78
Levellers, 74
Lewis, failed colonisation (1605), 43
Liberals, 249, 251, 258, 260, 264, 265
liberties, civil, 75–101, 123, 171–2, 184, 189
Lindsay, W. S., 248
linen trade, 111–12, 118, 122, 124, 225
literacy, 40
literature, 9, 231–46
'Little Ice Age', 109
Littlejohn, Robert, 198
local government, 113, 258–9, 262–3
Locke, John, 97
Lockhart, John Gibson, 160
Lockhart, Sir George, of Carnwath, 83
Lockhart, Sir William, 95
London, 9, 24, 45–6, 50, 55
  the Carlyles in, 231–46
  centralisation based on, 263–4
  financial crisis (1772–3), 158
  Friends of the People, 193, 194, 195
  Irish in, 155, 167
  Jews in, 155
  King's College, 231
  publishing industry, 158
  radicals in, 200–1, 208, 210
  Scots churches in, 156
  Scots migrants to, 144, 155–61, 167 (*see also* courtiers)
  Scottish Hospital, 155
  University College, 231
London Corresponding Society, 196–9, 201, 202–10
  The Moral and Political Magazine, 205, 209
Long Parliament, 63, 66, 68
Longmans, 236
Lord Advocates, Scottish-born, 249, 260
Lord Chancellors, Scottish-born, 247